GEOGRAPHY AND SOCIAL JUSTICE

Geography and Social Justice

David M. Smith

BLACKWELL
Oxford UK & Cambridge USA

First published 1994

Blackwell Publishers
108 Cowley Road
Oxford OX4 1JF
UK

238 Main Street
Cambridge, Massachusetts 02142
USA

British Library Cataloguing in Publication Data
A CIP catalogue record for this book is available from the British Library.

Library of Congress Cataloging-in-Publication Data
Smith, David Marshall, 1936–
Geography and social justice / David M. Smith
    p.   cm.
Includes bibliographical references and index.
ISBN 0–631–19025–2 (alk. paper). — ISBN 0–631–19026–0 (pbk. : alk. paper)
1. Social justice. 2. Human geography. 3. Equality. I. Title.
HM216.S53   1994
304.2—dc20   93–43835
                                                                   CIP

Copy-edited and typeset in 10 on 12 Garamond
by Grahame & Grahame Editorial, Brighton
Printed in Great Britain by T. J. Press Ltd, Padstow, Cornwall
This book is printed on acid-free paper

to Margaret, Michael, Tracey
and to the many more distant others who helped

Contents

List of Figures

List of Tables

Preface

Social justice has been an interest of mine for almost three decades. Concern over such issues as the British 'regional problem', awakened while at the University of Manchester in the mid-1960s, was sharpened by six years living in the United States at a time when the civil rights movement was broadening into a challenge to the injustice of poverty in such an otherwise affluent society. Gradual engagement with what was referred to as radical geography, during four years in Southern Illinois followed by two in Florida, turned a location theorist into one who espoused the geography of social well-being. Observation of racial discrimination in the American South was supplemented by a year's exposure to South Africa's apartheid, to consolidate a concern about structures of domination and oppression. Return to Britain in 1973 corresponded with the crystallization of a 'welfare approach' to human geography which incorporated notions of social justice.

Subsequent years have involved a variety of engagements with geographical aspects of inequality and human welfare. Reflecting the dominant mood of the times, explicit concern for social justice remained muted, for the most part. But the theme was still there, and increasingly required reassertion as social change on the world stage – east, west and south – began to resurrect some basic questions concerning the distribution of benefits and burdens under alternative economic and political arrangements.

The time has therefore come to return to social justice. But this is not so much to recapitulate an old theme as to play it out in the changing world of the last few years of the twentieth century, and in a discipline and intellectual environment quite different from when I started out. The intention is to take the basic problem of distributive justice, along with some related issues of morality, and see what can be made of this in a geographical context. In the process, something will be said about the engagement of geography with matters more commonly associated with moral philosophy than with social science. In other words, we will be concerned with normative thinking: with how we conceive of what is right or wrong, better or worse, in human affairs lived out in geographical space.

The book has been written with students in mind. That is to say, the level of exposition and choice of material reflects what I hope will provide a lucid yet challenging read for the kind of undergraduate students of geography I have encountered, over the years, on five continents. Of course, I hope it will attract a wider readership: among postgraduate students and those of my peers already concerned with social justice or who might be persuaded to re-engage the field. It is also hoped that there might be something of interest to those in other disciplines curious as to the particular perspective geography might bring to social justice. This is not a textbook, in the sense of supporting the teaching of a well-defined field of inquiry with something approaching comprehensive coverage. It is more a personal attempt to suggest the form of an engagement between geography and social justice, from which at least a heightened awareness of some important issues should emerge.

Those who deserve acknowledgement as contributing to this project are numerous. It is not that I feel extensive intellectual debts (other than to those on whose work I have drawn); indeed, this book might have been better informed by more attention to other voices, past and present. It is more that my attempt to ground the understanding of social justice in a variety of actual situations has involved the co-operation of many people in many different places, helping me to experience things as well as to facilitate the necessary visits and collaborative work on which international research depends. In the process, they have also helped me realize a collegiality that recognizes few boundaries, and which I find much more natural and congenial than the competition and commercialization currently eroding scholarship in Britain. So, to my distant colleagues and friends, my greatest thanks. Personal acknowledgements are reserved for footnotes to relevant chapters or sections.

My other thanks will be rather selective. To start at the beginning: to Guy King-Reynolds at Solihull School and K. C. Edwards at Nottingham University, for opening my eyes to geography, and to Eric Rawstron for opening my mind to the possibility of intellectual excitement in this field; to Staffordshire County Planning Department for taking only two years to divert me from a planning career; to the University of Manchester for my first academic appointment, and for encouraging me to relinquish it for America.

In the United States, to the unusual combination of faculty of diverse origins and persuasions at Southern Illinois University at Carbondale, who tolerated my emerging engagement with social and political issues with only occasional hostility; at the University of Florida, to Shannon McCune and Joshua C. Dickinson III, for the privilege of knowing and working with them. In South Africa, to Denis Fair, for encouraging my first visit and for many years of friendship from which I have learned much.

And, back in Britain, to Eric Rawstron, again, for helping me to indulge myself in my present chair until its more burdensome responsibilities caught up with me; to my most recent heads of department, Murray Gray and Philip Ogden, for support while this project came to fruition, and for tolerating (for the most part) my disdain for academic appraisal, performance assessment, research ratings, quality assurance and various other afflictions of what I still think of as academic life; to Roger Lee for reading parts of the manuscript, for some important points which I have incorporated, and for being such a sharp and supportive critic for two decades; to my other colleagues in the Geography Department at Queen Mary and Westfield College for helping to maintain a sense of cohesion and mutuality, even in these mean times; to Len Doyal for timely advice on reading; and to my students, most recently those brave enough to opt for the first offering of my course on geography and social justice, on whom most of the book was tested in draft form.

And to my family. Tracey's renaissance as a student has provided me with the opportunity to engage discourse on some important questions of social theory. Michael's philosophy books helped, as did his trouble-shooting on the Mac, along with the inspiration of his own fantastic literary prowess. Margaret was there, as always, good days and bad, not least as a reminder of what it really means to help people most in need.

David M. Smith
July 1993

Acknowledgements

The author and publisher gratefully acknowledge the following for permission to reproduce copyright material:

Figure 6.4 from George C. Galster, 'A cumulative causation model of the underclass: implications for urban economic development policy'. In George C. Galster and Edward H. Hill (eds), *The Metropolis in Black and White: place, power, and polarization*, © 1992 and reprinted with the permission of Rutgers University, Center for Urban Policy Research, New Brunswick, New Jersey: CUPR Press. Figure 5.2 from L. Doyal and I. Gough, *A Theory of Human Need* (1991), reprinted with the permission of the publisher, The Macmillan Press Ltd, Basingstoke. Figure 7.1 (a) and (b) from S. G. Solomon (ed.), *Beyond Sovietology* (1993), reprinted by permission of M. E. Sharpe, Inc, Armonk, New York. Extracts from Ivan Szelenyi, *Urban Inequality under Socialism* (1983), by permission of Oxford University Press. Extracts from John Rawls, *A Theory of Justice*, reprinted by permission of the publishers, The Belknap Press of Harvard University Press, © 1971 by the President and Fellows of Harvard College.

The publisher apologizes for any errors or omissions in the above list and would be grateful to be notified of any corrections that should be incorporated in the next edition or reprint of this book.

1

Introduction: The Return of
Social Justice

I am not worried about gaps, I do not mind people getting very rich – if
they do so by their own efforts.

John Major, *The Guardian* (2 January 1992)

Mind the gap!

Public address voice-over, Bank Underground
Station, London (contemporary)

There is much talk about gaps these days. There are gaps between the 'haves'
and 'have-nots' in our own society, and in others. There is a 'development
gap' between rich and poor nations: ever widening, or so it would seem.
There are also more technical conceptions, such as the 'income gap' which
separates people in dire need from some poverty-line earnings below which
human decency is threatened. How we respond to these situations, for
example whether or not we see those better-off as deserving their advantage,
involves considerations of social justice. But there is more to inequality than
the possibility of injustice. Gaps can be dangerous, threatening personal
safety, social order and stability. Minding the gaps may be as much a matter
of prudence as of morality.

The purpose of this book is to place social justice at the heart of human
geography. The meaning of social justice will be explored in detail in due
course; it is sufficient here to say that it concerns the distribution of society's
benefits and burdens, and how this comes about. There was much interest
in social justice in geography during the early engagement with questions of
'social relevance' a quarter of a century ago. But explicit consideration of
distributional issues subsequently became muted by the force of the structural
approaches which dominated the discipline for much of the 1970s and 1980s.
The return of social justice to the geographical agenda represents not so
much a reversion to a past paradigm as recognition that central interests of
contemporary post-structural perspectives, as well as some of the subject's
abiding concerns, cohere around considerations of morality.

Questions of social justice, morality or ethics are usually described as normative, concerned with what should be, as opposed to positive knowledge which is about what actually is. Geography (especially the physical side) shares with many related fields a strong predisposition towards positive inquiry. This reflects the conventional practice of physical science, which seeks to describe and explain the world as it is observed to be, and not to make judgements on whether this is good or bad, right or wrong.

The reasons for this emphasis have much to do with the expected and accepted role of science and of scientists in society, which includes a convention of not expressing personal values or subjective opinion – the more so if it could be construed as political. Students of society (or social scientists), including human geographers, are expected to conform; indeed a recent British Secretary of State for Education has said that geography should be concerned with facts, not opinions. Value judgements are left to politicians, priests and pundits of the mass media, and of course to the people themselves as they appraise the world and their place in it.

It is because making value or moral judgements is so much part of human life that its exclusion from the practice of science is implausible. What people believe to be right or good, in the form of ethics or codes of morality, is usually admitted as a legitimate subject of academic scrutiny: part of human existence to be described and explained by social science. But the adoption of a scientific perspective is somehow expected to suspend the faculty of moral judgement which the social scientist, as a human being, routinely and unavoidably brings to bear in other aspects of life. The recognition that scientists, including geographers, are simultaneously moral beings is an important first step in transcending the dualism between professional and personal conduct, which sets up a false expectation of detached objectivity and political neutrality when we put on our white coats or otherwise adopt scientific or scholarly identity.

Scientific and moral perspectives

The distinction between scientific and moral perspectives may be explored in an imaginary human encounter. Suppose that you and I meet, and you offer me your hand. Adopting a scientific perspective, I can observe that your hand *is*: it exists as part of your body called a hand, connected to the rest of you by your arm. If my scientific knowledge extends to biology or anatomy, I would be able to describe your hand as composed of certain chemical substances, and capable of feeling and movement by virtue of its nerves, muscles and tendons. As a medical practitioner, I might take your hand and feel your pulse, count its rate of action, and draw conclusions about your state of health. I might prescribe something to cure whatever malfunction I had been able to diagnose. And all this should be irrespective of where we are: the science should be the same, with Chinese preference for acupuncture a rare departure from 'standard' medical practice.

But there are other ways to respond to your hand. For example, I might shake it. A handshake is considered the right conduct in certain circumstances, which will vary according to the occasion, who and where you are. If you have accomplished something my handshake may signify approval in the form of congratulation; if I am male and you female, the handshake may be less obligatory; if in America it is more likely than in Britain that we will shake hands on subsequent encounters. These distinctions may be matters of behavioural convention or etiquette, but they can also convey a moral judgement on what you have done and indeed who you are. For me pointedly to refuse to shake your hand can be more than bad manners. If I take your hand in a way which might suggest affection, even sexual attraction, the gesture has a different kind of moral connotation. Whether I am considered right to behave in this way will depend on how well I know you, how visible or public the action is, whether you are married to someone else, whether we are of different genders, and so on. An act of physical contact between people is replete with moral significance. And how it is interpreted by others will depend on its context, including where it takes place.

Such differences between scientific and moral attitudes may seem straightforward. But if we examine our behaviour a little further the distinction is less clear. Suppose that I take your hand and read your palm, and then tell your fortune or advise on how to avoid some calamity. If I claim that, in doing so, I am acting scientifically, and you take this claim seriously enough to guide your future conduct, then I am guilty of deception. However, if palm-reading proceeds on the mutual understanding that it is merely innocent fun, then no harm may be done. That there can be an element of ambiguity or uncertainty in such a transaction (could there be something in fortune-telling, after all?), reflects a common-sense understanding that the boundary of what we term science is not clear-cut.

Visiting the doctor should, at first sight, generate no such ambiguity. Of course, a medical practitioner may act unethically, for example by making sexual advances to patients or telling their friends and neighbours things revealed in confidence. And he or she might be a bad doctor in a technical sense, prescribing the wrong pills or heavy-handed with the scalpel. But if we ask what is wrong with us and how to avoid such illness again, we feel entitled to a scientifically correct diagnosis and prescription for a physical (not moral) impairment.

That such an expectation is not necessarily well founded can be explained by considering possible responses to a persistent cough presented by a patient from a poor neighbourhood to a general practitioner. The doctor might simply suggest wearing warmer clothing in cold weather. Alternative advice may be to complain to the local council about the failings of the heating system in the housing block in which the patient lives. A further thought that might cross the doctor's mind (though not necessarily conveyed to the patient) could be that there is something wrong with a society that consigns some people to cold or damp accommodation while others have fine homes. There are thus alternative interpretations, or theories, concerning the incidence of coughs, and choice between them is not purely scientific. Each interpretation is true, to the extent that it identifies something implicated in people's health: how they clothe themselves, their housing conditions and the distribution of resources contributing to housing inequalities. But they differ not only as cause-and-effect explanations but also in their assignment of responsibility. While the doctor's advice to the patient may be influenced by the practicality that it is easier to put on an additional sweater than to get rehoused, for example, the implication could be that the cough is the patient's fault for not dressing sensibly rather than that of the local council or the wider society.

Choice among alternative explanations of illness can therefore involve moral judgement. More obviously, if the patient happened to be a smoker, it might be asserted that they had only themselves to blame for their cough. If this particular case is not convincing enough, then consider the explanations put forward for AIDS, which includes the suggestion that this affliction is a punishment for a particular kind of sexuality. The very definition of health and disability is closely bound up with the social construction and acceptance of what it is to be well, or to be normal.

Thus, while there are distinctions between moral and scientific perspectives, we must not view them as entirely separate. It is significant that we use the same terms of evaluation in both spheres: 'good' and 'bad' (conduct and science) and how things 'ought' to be done (treating people or conducting experiments). Moral norms are deeply implicated in scientific and critical thought; we must recognize this from the start.

Ethics, morality and social justice in geography

The explicit engagement of geography with morality and social justice dates from the latter part of the 1960s. This is not to say that before then such issues were somehow expunged from the subject, simply that their presence and significance went largely unnoticed. Any interest in philosophy tended to be expressed in concerns over epistemology, or how to know about the world, incorporated in debates on the nature and methods (or 'philosophy') of geographical inquiry. The ensuing controversies left most human geographers untroubled, however, and content with their preoccupation with landscape interpretation and regional synthesis until the adoption of quantitative methods, model-building and other trappings of location analysis or 'spatial science'. Then, under the influence of economics (including its regional science offshoot) and, to a lesser extent, of sociology, human geography came to model itself on those social sciences which had most successfully aped the physical sciences in their commitment to numerical precision, theory construction and the search for laws. Faith in value-free social science was strong enough to submerge the actual value content of the new human geography, and to subdue the voices of most sceptics.

Changes which began to take place in the discipline towards the end of the 1960s were prompted in part by a growing dissatisfaction with the spatial science approach. Substituting almost an economic determinism for the traditional preoccupation with the physical environment as controller of human affairs, the mechanistic interpretations which permeated economic and urban geography appeared increasingly inconsistent with the conduct of real people. A more behavioural approach emerged, relaxing the rigidities of *homo economicus*. But it was the eventual substitution of social relevance for scientific status as the aspiration of an increasing number of human geographers which most decisively provoked the so-called radical geography of the early 1970s. Spatial science was seen as not only dehumanizing but also diversionary, in the sense that it distracted attention from social problems and injustice.

The various twists and turns of radical geography are amply documented elsewhere (e.g. Johnston, 1991a; Peet, 1978; Cloke, Philo and Sadler, 1991). The first phase involved investigation of conditions largely ignored hitherto by human geographers, for example crime, hunger, ill-health and poverty. A geography of social well-being was soon promoted, bringing together a wide range of conditions relevant to the quality of life in a new urban or regional synthesis (Smith, 1973a; Knox, 1975). There was also a desire to influence or engage in the formulation and practice of public policy, to try to improve the world. Attention then moved on to the processes responsible for spatial disparities in people's life chances: for what was beginning to be recognized as spatial injustice.

Despite the obvious significance of social justice, published works which addressed the subject directly were rare exceptions to the descriptive or process-seeking predilections of radical geographers. The most influential treatment was by David Harvey (1972a, reprinted in Harvey, 1973; see also 1992a). He adopted the ordering of need, contribution to common good, and merit as distributive criteria, and argued that a just territorial distribution of income (broadly defined) would be such that: the needs of the people of each territory would be met; resources would be allocated so as to maximize inter-territorial multiplier effects, thus rewarding contribution to national economic good; and extra resources would be allocated to help overcome special difficulties stemming from the physical and social environment, which could be considered as cases of merit. He also proposed that, in a just distribution justly arrived at, the prospects of the least advantaged territory would be as great as possible: an echo from John Rawls's recently published *A Theory of Justice* (see chapter 3).

A year or so later came an embryonic attempt to restructure human geography around the concept of welfare (Smith, 1973b). As used in neoclassical economics, welfare concerns the overall state of a society with respect to what is produced, how and for whom, with 'where' added to introduce the space dimension. A better state of affairs with respect to any or all of the criteria of what, how, for whom and where is a welfare improvement. A further elaboration of the welfare approach contained a review of theories of social justice that might be applied to the task of judging geographical distributions as better or worse (Smith, 1977, chapter 6). Consideration of spatial or territorial aspects of justice has subsequently been extended, and continues to attract attention (e.g. Pirie, 1983; Boyne and Powell, 1991).

Geographical interest in more general perspectives on social justice soon evaporated, however. From the identification of 'hidden mechanisms' whereby distributional inequalities in the city were maintained, Harvey (1973) moved on to a Marxist interpretation grounded in historical materialism and focussed on the nature of capitalism. This perspective soon captivated an increasing number of those human geographers who no longer subscribed to spatial science or to its behavioural variant. Capital and class became the predominant categories for the elucidation of the workings of society in the geographical dimension, increasingly understood as inextricably bound up with broader economic, political and social structures.

Marxism in geography was replete with moral condemnation of capitalism and its attendant inequalities. But it was a resurgence of humanism, itself in part a critical response to the new economic determinism not far below the surface of much structuralism, which eventually generated renewed interest in what might broadly be described as the moral dimension of geographical inquiry. The 1980s saw increasing attention devoted to race and gender, and to the position of marginalized groups of 'others' disregarded in mainstream human geography. To give such people a voice in the production of their own geography was one consideration in the increasing adoption of qualitative research methods, such as semi-structured interviews, in place of formal surveys (Eyles and Smith, 1988; Lee, 1992). Power was to be transferred to the researched, instead of exclusively subjecting them to the 'gaze' of external and supposedly objective observers, who were themselves developing greater awareness of their own involvement and identity. Thus, values were becoming a more explicit element in the practice of human geography.

Values had of course been deeply implicated in the earlier radical movement (e.g. Buttimer, 1974). The question of whose interests the socially relevant applied geographers would serve highlighted the impossibility of the political neutrality widely assumed in the era of geography as spatial science. Nor could the theoretician continue to sit on the fence, as Harvey (1972b) asserted in his reference to 'counter-revolutionary' or 'status-quo' theory, which encouraged the mapping of even more evidence of 'man's inhumanity to man' rather than promoting fundamental social change.

However, geography's new preoccupation with values, or ethical and moral issues, has taken place in the context of a fundamental change in the intellectual environment. This is the emergence of what has come to be identified as postmodernism, as a challenge to the established thinking of the modern era initiated when the rationality of the eighteenth-century European 'Enlightenment' replaced the earlier world of superstition and tradition. There have been major geographical engagements with postmodernism (Harvey, 1989; Soja, 1989), and a postmodern human geography has been identified (e.g. Cloke, Philo and Sadler, 1991, chapter 6; Gregory, 1993). Important themes within postmodernism include scepticism concerning the truth claims of grand theory or mata-narratives, and an emphasis on human diversity and difference. Aspects of postmodern thinking have important implications for the way we approach morality, including social justice, as will be apparent in various parts of this book. Recent years have seen a growing geographical engagement with a range of moral issues, building up to crescendo of diverse voices in the early 1990s associated with a revitalized social and cultural geography. All we need do here is to reflect some major themes.

One important strand in this work concerns the ethics of professional practice. Just as treating the sick involves codes of medical ethics covering what is good or bad practice in a moral sense, so ethical issues inevitably arise in academic activity. Some rules of conduct are clear-cut: it is unethical to engage in plagiarism, to invent data and to falsify results. Research on politically contentious topics is sometimes accompanied by charges of unethical conduct; for example, the analysis of Jewish Israeli settlement of Palestine (discussed in chapter 9) has involved accusations of bias and the falsification of evidence (see Newman, 1991a, and other papers in *Political Geography Quarterly*, vol. 10, no. 3, 1991). Different ethical questions arise in certain kinds of survey research, especially those adopting qualitative methods; for example, whether research workers should reveal their true identity and reasons for seeking information, if this would prejudice the inquiry by making informants less likely to be forthcoming.

Ethical considerations involved in the relationship between researcher and researched dominated discussion in a book by Mitchell and Draper (1982). Subsequent debates have broadened the range of issues with which geographers have been concerned. Differential power relations are usually involved in research 'on' human 'subjects', giving the researcher(s) control of the project and the dissemination of its findings, and a claim of authoritative understanding of other people's lives which can assist their domination and oppression. Personal involvement with a group of people who may be the subject of injustice poses particular problems for the investigator imbued with the convention of scholarly detachment. Some researchers consider that they have a moral obligation to share their finding with their research subjects. Keith (1992) has raised the role of anger in writing or lecturing, in the context of the usual assumption of dispassionate academic presentation. Others have opened up the implications of male domination of the academic profession (e.g. Rose, 1993). There is also the question of intellectual property rights: who is entitled to claim the results of research, the right to publish, or any status or pecuniary advantage derived from new knowledge, are among issues raised by the increasing penetration of academic life by competitive and commercial values (see Brunn, 1989; Curry, 1991; Kirby, 1991).

An example of the explicit inclusion of a moral dimension in geographical research is provided by some interpretations of urban spatial structure. Jackson and Smith (1984, pp. 66, 77) refer to a 'moral distance' between communities and to an evolving 'moral order' to the city, as viewed by the Chicago school of urban sociology in general and the work of Robert Park in particular. Jackson (1984, pp. 174–5) describes Park as having been unusually sensitive to the variable 'moral climate' of the city's social areas, particularly those which departed furthest from the norms of bourgeois society, such as the slums, ghettos, immigrant colonies and bohemias. An underlying moral order could be discovered in parts of the city thought of by outsiders as the most socially disorganized, as exemplified by areas occupied by 'hobos' or migratory workers.

The concept of moral order has also been applied to the Victorian city in Britain. There was particular contemporary concern over parts of the city with concentrations of crime, vice and other supposed manifestations of moral degeneracy. Fear of people in other places being infected stimulated interest in the 'moral geography' of these localities, and in the design of new environments in which alternative forms of behaviour would be cultivated (Driver, 1988). The provision of subsidized housing for the 'deserving poor' was an example.

There was also a moral dimension to the way in which people used parts of the city, with a distinction between the private virtues of family life in the home and the public dangers of the streets. Moral order in the Victorian city was underpinned by its social geography, including the segregation of classes and the separation of home and work with its implicit gender division of labour (Jackson, 1989, p. 100). Who people were, and what they did where, reflected broader societal conceptions of good and bad.

The moral basis of how we attempt to explain the world has been recognized by geographers for some time. For example, Jackson and Smith (1984, pp. 200–201) stress 'the extent to which the ultimate basis for choice between rival explanations of social phenomena rests on moral criteria . . . values inhere not within the objects to be explained but within the mode of explanation itself. In this sense the very choice and implementation of one theoretical system rather than another is partly a moral decision.' In other words, those who claim a privileged status for any particular kinds of explanation are making a moral rather than scientific case, explicitly or implicitly.

The problem of explaining inner-city poverty provides an illustration. One approach would be to observe the spatial association between poverty and population characteristics, finding perhaps that members of particular racial or ethnic groups or one-parent families were concentrated in the poverty areas, which could lead to the conclusion that there is something about their way of life predisposing them to poverty. Another would be to observe the spatial mismatch between inner-city residential areas and the concentration of employment opportunities elsewhere, concluding that the problem was one of physical accessibility. A third explanation could be found in the operation of the markets for labour and housing in a capitalist economy, which tends to consign some people to unemployment and poverty and to place many of them in the inner city. As with the case of health in the previous section, there is something in each explanation. But which one we prioritize involves a moral judgement; we are allocating responsibility for inner-city poverty. The first explanation blames the victims, the second the spatial structure of the city, and the third the prevailing mode of production. Each of these will also suggest different solutions: respectively, changing personal behaviour, improving urban planning, and abolishing capitalism.

As Gregory (1978, p. 69) remarked, in discussing the relationship between science and ideology: 'science is always committed in some way, whatever its form, and the specific "means" which it makes available cannot be divorced from the specific "ends" which provide its own legitimation.' Thus, in both capitalist and socialist society, what may be considered good (social) science gains its legitimacy from its role in preserving the existing social order. The Chicago school's ecological perspective again provides an illustration. The city was viewed as an organism, in which competition for space was the natural order from which arose a specific spatial form; natural areas provided for people with different ways of life. Thus: 'Conceptualization of the city as an ecological community enabled Park to present the new metropolis as an orderly entity in which both community and freedom were realizable'

(Mellor, 1977, p. 216). The gross inequalities and the harsh conditions endured by Chicago's working poor under unrestrained capitalism could thus be conveyed as the outcome of natural forces, immune from moral approbation. (A different natural analogy was suggested in *The Jungle*, a novel by Upton Sinclair, which describes Chicago working-class life.)

Methodological as well as theoretical aspects of the conduct of geographical inquiry can have a moral dimension. For example, whether to study human attitudes by means of a formal questionnaire (which allows a limited and predetermined range of responses) or by less structured interviews (which allow respondents more freedom of expression) reflects how the researcher views the researched and chooses to treat them, as well as what is considered to be technically the best way for getting information. The claim that 'insider accounts' have greater authenticity than those of outside observers, which could encourage a more involved research strategy such as participant observation, also has a moral tone, as does the urge to empathize with the researched.

Many of the concerns of the past decade or so cohere around what is sometimes referred to as the production of knowledge. A central question raised is: what entitles, or empowers, what kind of people to describe and interpret (or 'represent') the lives of others, and with what implications for understanding the good life? Those involved in academic activity inevitably reflect something of their position in the world, spatially and structurally. What results can thus reflect the hidden or unacknowledged predilections of those dominating academic activity, who tend to be white, 'middle-class', western males. What they portray as right in a (social) scientific sense can take on a kind of moral authority which marginalizes the interpretations of others in less privileged positions. This kind of hegemonic discourse has increasingly been challenged by other voices, or those who claim to represent them.

The (re)discovery of moral concerns has thus been a major theme of human geography in recent years. A statement by the Social and Cultural Geography Study Group Committee (1991) of the Institute of British Geographers, calling for a (re)connection with 'the sorts of concerns that have occasionally appeared under the heading of moral philosophy', refers to investigations of the geography of everyday moralities, or how particular peoples in particular places hold their particular views on good or bad, right and wrong, just and unjust, and so on: codes which 'glue together their assumptions and arguments'. This is an important aspect of local culture and group identity, emphasized in a resurgence of place-specific locality studies. Locality can also provide a basis from which particular groups of people come together, find identity in common material circumstances and common political cause, and contest the 'moral ideology' of society's dominant meaning system (e.g. Eyles and Evans, 1987). The link with social justice is reflected as follows:

[I]t may be possible to discern any number of distinctively local cultures which serve as the resources for handling daily life, and which may also become oppositional and resistant to the structured inequalities blighting the lives led by many social groups of the 'wrong' class, gender, race, sexuality, age, health and so on. All manner of oppositional cultures identified with all manner of social groups, usually proceeding from some form of strong territorial base, undoubtedly do still rise up to challenge the material and ideological forces that in practice name them as 'outsiders' – as less than 'deserving' or 'valuable' members of an overall society – and treat them accordingly. What we are talking about here is indeed the contest of cultures bound up in processes of socio-economic differentiation, then, but it is also clearly the clash of moralities (of differing assumptions and arguments about worth and non-worth) which are both constituted through and constitutive of a society's socio-spatial hierarchy of 'winners' and 'losers'. (Social and Cultural Geography Study Group Committee, 1991, p. 19)

Signs of a return to more explicit consideration of social justice are to be found elsewhere (e.g. Smith, 1991, 1992a). Renewed interest in the subject is reflected in a special issue of *Urban Geography* (Laws, 1994), following a session at the 1993 annual conference of the Association of American Geographers celebrating the 20th anniversary of David Harvey's *Social Justice and the City*. Of particular significance is Harvey's own re-engagement with social justice (Harvey, 1992b, 1993). Reacting to the celebration of difference and the disdain for grand theory characteristic of much postmodern thinking, Harvey argues for the need to say something about social justice that transcends the narrow relativism of the belief that morality is entirely time and space specific, or purely a matter of local culture. More will be said of this crucial issue in chapters 2 and 3, and in the concluding chapter where we return to the possibility of universal principles grounded in people's common humanity. It is sufficient at this stage to recognize a shift of emphasis from the narrow distributional issues central to radical geography in the early 1970s to a less explicitly spatial concern with problems very much on the agenda of theorists of social justice within contemporary moral philosophy.

The changing world

Human geography, like other social sciences, responds to the wider society and its intellectual content. Just as geography as spatial science reflected some of the values and practices of an era of economic growth (which subdued distributional issues), faith in technological solutions, and reverence for computer applications, so radical geography responded to an awakening of public interest in social and environmental problems. The subsequent neo-conservative turn in western politics exemplified by the Reagan and Thatcher eras of the 1980s, with its prioritization of market solutions, tended to reduce the scope for applied research predicated on an interventionist state. In any event, the demonstrable resistance of macro-structures to urban and regional planning designed to combat uneven development focused more attention on the role of locality and individuality or human agency. The identification and interpretation of what some see as a postmodern epoch is, in its turn, challenging the conventional search for ordered regularity over space and time, in favour of disorder and incoherence as predominant characteristics of human life.

The end of the 1980s and early years of the 1990s have also seen particular changes, which provoke profound questions of social justice. The most dramatic and, to many, unexpected event was the collapse of what passed for socialism in East Europe and the former Soviet Union. This left large areas of the world with massive populations the task of creating new economic, political and social institutions, and deciding how economic rewards and positions of power would be distributed. A market-regulated economy and democratic political system was assumed, but this did not provide ready answers to some crucial issues as to how such a society is created. The privatization of state property is an obvious activity which requires clear rules, fairly adopted, if it is not simply to replace one pattern of domination by another (see chapter 7).

A further implication of the end of East European and Soviet-style socialism was that it deprived other parts of the world of an alternative to capitalism. While true communism was not necessarily an enticing or even practical proposition, there was at least the evidence of the former USSR to show that the uneven development originally expressed over such diverse lands as the Baltic republics and those of Soviet central Asia could be greatly reduced by central planning and redistribution, and that, within the cities, large volumes of adequate if not very spacious housing could be constructed in neighbourhood units complete with the basic service infrastructure. This was an attractive prospect to many Third World countries, and especially to inhabitants of poor peripheral regions and city slums. South Africa was a case in point. That dismantling apartheid should coincide with the demise of socialism has effectively deprived the liberation movement of its model for non-capitalist institutional arrangements, with fundamental consequences for redistribution in the new South Africa (as explained in chapter 8).

Of course, the inevitability of capitalism and of relatively unfettered market relations does not go unchallenged. Indeed, in the post-socialist world, if this is how it must be regarded, there is a need to examine once again some of the practical, theoretical and philosophical implications of relying largely on market forces to distribute society's product. As Harvey (1992b, p. 597) puts it:

> The collapse of centrally planned economies throughout much of the world has further boosted a market triumphalism which presumes that the rough justice administered through the market in the course of this transition is not only socially just but also deeply rational. The advantage of this solution, of course, is that there is no need for explicit theoretical, political and social argument over what is or is not socially rational just because it can be presumed that, provided the market functions properly, the outcome is nearly always just and rational. Universal claims about rationality and justice have in no way diminished. They are just as frequently asserted in justification of privatization and of market action as they ever were in support of welfare state capitalism.

Tedious though the replay of academic history is for those familiar with the critique of free-market economics and its theoretical foundations, it is necessary to return to the claims of such a system to deliver social justice. Some of the problems are revealed in the operation of a mature capitalist economy (chapter 6), as well as in societies experiencing transition (chapter 7), and are recapitulated in chapter 10.

The fact that all is not well under capitalism is (re)focusing attention on various issues related to social justice. There is a vigorous debate on the meaning of citizenship, in geography and some other disciplines. For example, Susan Smith (1989, p. 152) points out that 'markets can, and do, fail, both technically (as a distributive mechanism) and morally (as a force for social cohesion)', and that this has implications for what might be considered rights of citizenship. The political significance of such issues in Britain is underlined by the Citizen's Charter introduced by Prime Minister John Major to ensure particular levels of service performance, and the Commission on Social Justice set up at the instigation of the Labour Party leader John Smith to undertake the most thorough review of the social benefits system since the Beveridge Report which initiated the welfare state. The latter has identified a 'justice gap', between ideas of justice and the realities of injustice (IPPR, 1993), to add to the other gaps mentioned at the outset of this chapter.

Distributional issues are being highlighted by widening disparities between rich and poor the world over. This is so even in the advanced capitalist world, where economic change is generating increasing polarization: between people with relatively high pay, secure employment and generous social benefits, and others with lower-paid and less secure jobs who are more vulnerable to social deprivation. The anti-interventionist stance of Conservative governments has compounded the tightening constraints on redistribution via public expenditure imposed by sluggish economies; even Sweden's much-admired welfare state is under threat. Inequalities in income distribution widened in Britain under Margaret Thatcher (see chapter 5), and in the United States under Ronald Reagan and George Bush, yet there has been very little discussion of how this can be justified other than to invoke the sanctity of market outcomes, incentives or rewards for enterprise, and other customary elements of the prevailing political ideology.

Other significant developments include rapid advances (if this is what they are) in technology, facilitating the design and production of ever more fancy goods and services the very expense of which ensures their highly unequal availability. The growing sophistication and reach of mass media enables messages as to the nature of the good life, manifest in products or life-style consumed, to be disseminated instantly across the globe. Only a minute fraction of the world's population have any realistic prospect of emulating the mass-consuming groups of the advanced capitalist world. And as we get to know about, and to see, the plight of other peoples thousands of miles away, distance is undermined as a barrier to compassion, and to responsibility, while governments of rich countries allocate trivial proportions of their wealth to foreign aid and strengthen barriers to 'economic migrants'.

The interdependence and interconnected nature of the modern world system, articulated in particular by the international capitalist economy, has profound implications for inequality (Taylor, 1992). Consumption decisions in London or New York can have repercussions across the globe, generating work for some, redundancy for others. The richest 20 per cent of the world's population earn 83 per cent of global income; the gap between the incomes of the richest and poorest 20 per cent (controlled for inflation) grew from $1,864 in 1960 to $15,149 in 1989 (UNDP, 1992). International disparities in levels of living have become a subject for theoreticians of social justice, for so long preoccupied with distribution within nations (Barry, 1989, pp. 4–5).

With the onward march of technology and the global reach of capitalism has come a capacity to pollute the environment on a scale hitherto unimaginable. And some of the former socialist regimes so greatly prioritized economic growth that they had little regard for environmental considerations; their successors may do no better. The implication for future generations raises moral questions rather like those with respect to distant people, but in time not space (see chapter 2). This is, again, part of the question of social justice highlighted by the changing world.

Other important changes include the resurgence of nationalism in some parts of the world, including those in which colonialism and communism subdued traditional affiliations. Religion has proved a means of challenging political domination, Catholicism in Poland and (more recently) Islam in Israel being cases in point. Cults are often in the news. Old identities and their place in the world are being discarded, new ones formed.

If much is changing, much also remains the same. We still live in a world of scarcity, and of selfishness, and have not learned to do without governments, which are the three basic preconditions for the kind of conflict resolution to which theories of social justice are addressed. Conflict over scarce and contested resources can be as bitter and violent as ever, involving apparently irresolvable claims. The dispute between Jewish Israelis and Arabs over the land of Palestine is a case in point (which we will explore in chapter 9). The power of some individuals or groups to resolve conflict to their advantage, irrespective of any moral merits to the case other than might is right, can have severe consequences for those deprived of land, community or even a place to sleep (other issues examined in chapter 9). The resurrection of old conflicts, as in the former Yugoslavia, raises grave moral issues, not least of which is the question of how the outside world should respond. The 'new world order' proclaimed by some western leaders has proved, unsurprisingly, to be merely a reflection of the parochial self-interest of those with the economic and military power to implement it.

So, the time has come for a (re)engagement of geography with ethics, morality and social justice. That this is recognized in other fields can be confirmed by a cursory review of the literature. For example, Friedmann (1992, pp. vi, viii) puts the need to provide a 'morally informed framework' and 'moral justification' up-front in a text on development calling for the empowerment of deprived peoples. Sen (1987, p. 7) observes that 'the nature of modern economics has been substantially impoverished by the distance that has grown between economics and ethics', in a book designed to correct this imbalance. Etzioni (1988) has proposed a new economics focused on the moral dimension. Le Grand (1991, p. 6) refers to 'the recent revival of interest among economists, political philosophers and others in the question of distributional principles'. Even the applied field of social work has attracted a text on social justice (Jordon, 1990). Kymlicka (1990, p. 1) claims that 'the intellectual landscape in political philosophy today is quite different from what it was twenty, or even ten, years ago'; his two-volume selection from the literature on justice which has accumulated since geography's initial engagement with the field in the early 1970s runs to 1280 pages (Kymlicka, 1992).

There is some catching up to be done. That this process has begun is illustrated by a comparison between a review of Anglo-American human geography since 1945 (Johnston, 1991a) which has no index references to morality or social justice and only one to (professional) ethics, and the more extensive coverage of these and related issues in the latest edition of *The Dictionary of Human Geography* (Johnston, Gregory and Smith, 1993). The present book is an attempt much more firmly to align human geography with a movement, evident in other fields, whose time has come.

The text

Dealing with ethics and morality carries with it an obligation to be open about one's own values and motivation, insofar as these aspects of the self are understood. My return to social justice reflects a strong personal distaste for the disparities in living standards evident in the contemporary world. This applies to inequalities among peoples in both the economically advanced and underdeveloped worlds, to what I see emerging in former socialist countries, and to what I encounter almost daily travelling from a suburban home to an inner-city work-place. The grounds on which others may try to justify such inequalities are thus matters of intellectual curiosity. A personal preference for a much more equal world poses the challenge of how to argue the case as persuasively as possible.

I spare the reader the author's biographical confessions which sometimes accompany the creation of a text these days (those who feel deprived may consult Smith, 1984, 1988). All I wish to record here is that my life experience has not included dire poverty, other than to observe its impact on others. I know what it feels like to be treated unjustly, failing to get what I consider I deserve, but the matters in question were not of great consequence in comparison with what many others suffer. To be a victim of discrimination or oppression, by virtue of race for example, is again beyond my direct experience, but I have seen how awful it can be for others.

The approach adopted to the structure of the book reflects my strong belief that theory and experience of the world have to be brought together, if only in an instant of their on-going interaction through time. My perspective resembles that portrayed by Arthur and Shaw (1991, p. 10) as follows: 'Many moral philosophers today see ethical theory as a matter of working back and forth between our moral intuitions about particular cases and the general principles that account for those particular judgements or are themselves intuitively attractive, in order to weave our moral thinking into a coherent and consistent web.' That the particular cases considered here have elicited an approach by no means completely coherent and consistent reflects the stage reached in my personal process of understanding, as well as the limits to understanding itself.

I begin, in Part I, with a discussion of what should be incorporated, or at least considered, in theorizing about social justice (chapter 2). This leads to an extended review of theories of social justice (chapters 3 and 4), followed by an elaboration of my own preferred perspective to engage reality (chapter 5). My predilection for rather abstract theory may seem at odds with what some others might see as the glaringly self-evident injustices of this wicked world, as well as with dismissive postmodern attitudes to mata-narratives. But as long as such theories are part of the practice of judging the world, it is important to understand them; assessing their value is part of the project.

The case material in Part II originates very much in my own research experience. I have lived in the United States (see chapter 6) and in South Africa (chapter 8), in the sense of regarding both countries as home for a while, being from somewhere else in an historical sense but not necessarily belonging there or on the way back. I have returned frequently, the more so to the United States, mainly in connection with on-going inquiries. Visits to East Europe (and beyond) over almost two decades have enabled me to do some research there, mainly in Poland and the former Soviet Union (see chapter 7), but with much less reliance on primary sources than in the United States and constrained by my rudimentary grasp of the Russian language. Interest in Palestine is more recent, with research cultivated largely for the purpose of this book (chapter 9). Consideration of some implications for social justice of loss of community and home (chapter 9) are more speculative than the other cases presented, resting on a variety of experiences which I have been fortunate enough not to share.

Writing about parts of the world undergoing significant change carries with it the risk of the text being overtaken by events. For example, as the manuscript was going to press there was heightened political tension in Russia, escalating violence in the run-up to the first multi-racial elections in South Africa, and indications of an important break-through in resolving conflict over the land of Palestine. However, none of these events invalidate the general arguments concerning social justice in those parts of the book which deal with the cases in question. Indeed, as events continue to unfold, the pertinence (or otherwise) of the line taken here will be a useful test of how robust the arguments are. The concern is with broad principles of social justice and their application, rather than with the details of implementation.

As was indicated in the Preface, this book has been written with students in mind, but should not be considered a textbook in the sense of a tool to help teach an established body of knowledge. That the book is built on extensive original investigations underlines the false distinction between teaching and research which some blockheads are attempting to foist on British universities. In fact, I deliberately chose to write the first draft of the book while simultaneously initiating a course on the subject, testing the material on undergraduate minds which seem to have survived relatively unscathed. I leave to professional peers the task of deconstruction or whatever else a critical postmodern reading may involve, hoping that they will pass on such insights to their own students.

Honesty requires me to say something about the limitations of my own knowledge, and hence possibly of my grasp of some of the issues raised. At the end of the 1960s, writing a text on industrial location and with the benefit of formal training in economics, I had read almost everything worth reading in this field. In approaching the present text I am aware of a far greater literature, and of my lack of training (if that is what it is) in philosophy. Works on social justice can be sought in the bookshop or library under the headings not only of moral philosophy but also of political philosophy, economics, social theory and law, and some volumes would still be overlooked. I am sure to have simplified, possibly to a greater extent than specialists would consider wise, but hope to have avoided blatant error.

Citations in the text are confined to works which I have personally found useful (with a few necessary exceptions), and from which those wishing to follow matters further should benefit. I have not included strings of references to other literature, some of which might also be helpful. I have also refrained from linking this work to all relevant debates in contemporary human geography and social theory: there is simply not enough space in one volume. I use citations to attribute to others what is their due: their ideas and research findings, expressed in their own words when they say something special or when this seems to be the clearest mode of expression. Citations to particular authors may reflect the selectivity of my reading; others may have said something similar and more eloquently.

Honesty also requires me to acknowledge that one important motive for writing this book is that I enjoy writing. This is an aesthetic practice, somewhat akin to other expressions of creativity such as making music: something to play back as others may hear it. Like the musician, the writer uses stylistic devices, for example to convey complexity which may appear to elude simple verbal expression. Shula Marks (1986, p. vii) has said: 'ambiguity serves to alert the reader to the relationship between things . . . historians should be able to write in chords, for our medium distorts our intentions by its linear imperatives.' I have avoided chords, for the most part, preferring what I trust will not be too tedious a melody line, but there are a few passages in a different style which might convey something otherwise missed.

Introducing the musicality of writing here is a vehicle for raising the interdependence of science, morality and aesthetics, or of truth, justice and taste as Keith (1992, p. 559) puts it. Recognizing that words in the form of a poem can have beauty is commonplace; that the supposedly dispassionate practice of writing science, even philosophy, might have a similar element is more difficult to grasp. Yet one of the major theorists whose work is reviewed in chapter 3, Robert Nozick (1974, p. 183), describes the work of another (John Rawls), as 'lovely' and 'beautiful'. Others use the word 'elegant' to describe a certain kind of mathematical solution or theory. That which is elegant is admirable or commendable, on grounds other than, or in addition to, the truth revealed. The link between the creation of a written text, its social science, morality and aesthetics, may be more obscure in the field of geography, but is nevertheless part of our practice.

The final point concerning motivation is rather obvious. In presenting a distillation of thinking on social justice, played out on some actual situations, my hope is that this will help students of geography and others to understand what is involved in adopting this kind of moral perspective. It is not offered as an alternative to a (social) scientific perspective, as should be clear from what has already been said. But it is to complement, or supplement, the emphasis on science in an education system which tends to leave moral issues to religious instruction or to consign them to certain special fields of inquiry where they risk even greater reification than in the hands of priests. If we constantly moralize in everyday life, let us at least be more conscious of what is involved. We may even become more moral agents in the process. It would be arrogant to claim, or even hope, that the world might be a better place for this volume, but attentive readers should at least end up with a better idea of what it means to say that a situation is unjust.

Part I

Theory

Wherever something new is being created, and thus in settlement and spatial planning also, the laws revealed through theory are the sole economic guide to what *should* take place.

August Lösch, *The Economics of Location* (1954)

Effective criticism of social practices and attitudes eventually *requires* moral theory for the fundamental reason that criticism that hopes to convince must eventually step back from particular moral practices and attitudes and ask what (if anything) *justifies* them . . . Because moral theory involves the all-things-considered articulation and justification of certain ways of living over others, all sustained attempts to criticize ways of living and acting must eventually consort with moral theory.

Robert B. Louden, *Morality and Moral Theory: a reappraisal and reaffirmation* (1992)

We are accustomed, in geography, to look for some kind of theory as a guide to practice. By theory we mean an intellectual construct that enables us to make sense of the world or part of it: the way it is, or ought to be. By practice we mean doing things, undertaking projects with particular aims in view, including the possibility of understanding the world (or part of it), judging it, and changing it for the better. Thus we might look to location theory as a source of guidance as to how factories might be sited so as to maximize profits, or how settlements and other features of the space economy might be arranged so as to minimize people's coverage of distance in pursuit of necessary goods and services. This type of thinking is also deeply imbedded in urban and regional planning, with which human geography has been closely associated.

The notion that theory might provide a guide to our moral purpose and practice may be no less obvious. Faced with questions of social justice, of inequality in distribution and the process responsible, the inclination is to look to some ethical or moral theory. It is understandable that theoretical thinking appears to provide a more secure basis for judging the world, or trying to improve it, than does personal whim, intuition or observation of people's actual behaviour, especially in an intellectual climate dominated by the scientific perspective.

However, matters are by no means so straightforward when we enter the realms of ethics and morality. In spatial planning directed towards some sort of efficiency objectives, like maximizing financial gains or minimizing aggregate travel, the limits to what can be accomplished are largely if not entirely technical, related to the ability accurately to measure and model relevant attributes of the system in question and to the capacity of computers to simulate reality and to solve sets of equations. This is not to say that there is no more room for creativity or ingenuity in theory construction, simply that the elements of the system are not hard to identify and to bring into sensible relationships. But in approaching questions of social justice we encounter a different kind of constraint: on what we can know in the sense of what human reason can achieve, or, in the words of the title of one of Bernard Williams's books, to the limits of philosophy. The postmodern critique of meta-narrative has no more inviting target than theories which claim to prescribe the good life.

In Part I we explore various theoretical frameworks which may provide some kind of guide to the practice of social justice, of judging the world and seeking to improve it. In chapter 2 we consider certain elements, some if not all of which could be expected to feature in a theoretical approach to social justice. The central chapters (3 and 4) provide a substantial though by no means comprehensive review of alternative theories of social justice, divided for convenience into mainstream and reaction. Then, in chapter 5, strands of particular theoretical perspectives are developed into a more practical approach to the examination of real societies and situations, to set the scene for some aspects of the case studies in Part II.

2

Elements of Justice

Justice is a name for certain classes of moral rules, which concern the essentials of human well-being more nearly, and are therefore of more absolute obligation, than any other rules for the guidance of life.

John Stuart Mill, *Utilitarianism* (1863)

The purpose of this chapter is to introduce a number of important considerations that have a bearing on social justice. These have to be understood, at least at an elementary level, before embarking on a review of theories of social justice, as well as being significant in themselves. The concept of justice is the obvious starting point, suggesting what it means to add the prefix of 'social'. Then there is an excursion into moral philosophy, to provide what might be thought of as the deep background from which theories of social justice could be expected to emerge, as specific kinds of moral rules or principles. This leads to the notion of human rights, as distinct from wants and needs, as a possible way of giving substance to those things to which people should be entitled. Then come discussions of who is involved in distribution, that is, membership of the relevant population, where they live (the space dimension) and when (the time dimension). The chapter is rounded off by some observations on the distinction between inequality and difference, to underline the fact that all sources of human difference are not necessarily subject to the moral disapproval often elicited by observations of inequality.

Cutting across these elements of justice are some more general underlying issues, which surface in various ways in what follows and which will return in later discussions. These arise from the contested nature of justice, as a socially constructed abstraction which motivates human conduct. The central question is whether some general or universal conception of social justice is possible, or whether defence of distributional arrangements more persuasively rests on the specific predilections or functional necessities of particular societies, in particular places.

The concept of justice

Recourse to the dictionary is a common reaction on seeking a definition. In the present context it is quite helpful, revealing words which, in the English language, evoke the general concept of justice. *The Concise Oxford Dictionary* declares the adjective *just* to mean 'equitable' with respect to persons or conduct, 'fair' and 'deserved' treatment, and adds reference to 'well-grounded', 'right' and 'proper'. The same word as an adverb has connotations of exactness, getting things 'just right'. The noun *justice*, in the sense of conduct, refers to 'fairness', or the exercise of authority in maintenance of 'right'. To do justice is to treat fairly, to show due appreciation of somebody or something. To *justify* is to show the justice or rightness of something.

So, justice involves treating people right, or fairly, in a calculated way. The most obvious context is legal, criminal or *retributive* justice, with the courts expected to allocate penalties to those found guilty of crimes in an appropriate and consistent manner. That the punishment should fit the crime is a common-sense axiom of criminal justice. There is a strong implication of equality in the expectation that justice will be impartial: personal characteristics such as wealth or status should have no bearing on the finding of guilt (or innocence) or on the penalty imposed. Variations in sentences according to who, or where, people are raise suspicions of injustice.

What is referred to as *distributive* justice is analogous to retributive justice: whatever is being distributed should go to people in the right quantities. Again, such sentiments as fairness, consistency and impartiality are involved in the expectation that people in the same circumstances should be treated in the same way. A central issue in distributive justice is how to justify differential treatment, or how to identify the differences among people which are relevant to the particular attribute(s) to be distributed. This raises the distinction between *arithmetic* equality which means everyone getting exactly the same quantity of something, and *proportional* equality which means people getting something in quantities proportional to circumstances which can differ among them. These could include such criteria as need, merit and desert (see chapter 3).

That distributive justice is an issue at all is often attributed to the well-known conditions or circumstances of justice identified in David Hume's *A Treatise of Human Nature* (1739): ' 'tis only from the selfishness and confin'd generosity of man, along with the scanty provision nature has made for his wants, that justice derives its origin' (quoted in Elster, 1985, p. 231).[1] Not everyone can have everything they may claim to need (merit or deserve). The interaction of human nature with natural scarcity thus requires regulation, in the form of government, guided by some conception of morality capable of adjudicating among conflicting claims. Such would be a theory of social justice.

Justice in general is a very broad concept. To Campbell (1988, pp. 13, 19) it may take in 'all socially desirable objectives', or 'any desirable or undesirable thing or experience'. However, distributive justice is usually held to apply to limited aspects of life. For example, Griffin (1986, p. 285) confines it to 'holdings . . . material things, services, certain legal powers, money', from which their holders are easily parted. The question of what is to be distributed sometimes provokes a distinction between *economic* and *social* justice, to which other categories such as *political* justice may be added. This is argued as follows by Arthur and Shaw (1991, p. 5):

Justice in general and social justice in particular involve the distribution of benefits and burdens, but distributive justice has come to be synonymous with economic justice, that is, with the distribution of *economic* benefits and burdens. Social justice includes but is not identical to economic justice, although both are concerned in part with how to distribute things that people care about. Political powers and liberties may be distributed unjustly, yet this is not a problem of economic justice as such (unless, perhaps, the political injustice in question results from a particular economic distribution).

Tempting though it may be to try to unpack the concept of justice into sets of things with such labels as 'economic, 'political' or 'social', this would become a sterile exercise in definition, compounded by the obvious interdependence of different attributes. That distribution in the economic sphere influences distribution in the political sphere, and vice versa, seems more important than precisely what is meant by economic and political in the context of justice.

The limitations of a concept of justice as merely distributional have been recognized for some time. For example, Barry (1989, p. 355) equates social justice with distributive justice, but emphasizes its institutional basis (Barry, 1989, p. 146): 'social justice is predicated primarily of the basic structure of a society. This structure is made up of the institutions that together determine the access (or chances of access) of the members of a society to resources that are the means to the satisfaction of a wide variety of desires.' Some further implications of a narrowly distributive emphasis are explained by

---

[1] Like most of his predecessors and successors (until recently) in the field of moral philosophy, Hume uses the gender-specific form 'he', 'his', and so on. Some contemporary writers prefer she to he. The original usage is preserved in all quotations in this book; otherwise some gender-neutral form is adopted.

Young (1990a, p. 8) as follows:

> Some distributive theories of justice explicitly seek to take into account issues of justice beyond the distribution of material goods. They extend the distributive paradigm to cover such goods as self-respect, opportunity, power, and honor. Serious conceptual confusion results, however, from attempting to extend the concept of distribution beyond material goods to phenomena such as power and opportunity. The logic of distribution treats nonmaterial goods as identifiable things or bundles distributed in a static pattern among identifiable, separate individuals. The reification, individualism, and pattern orientation assumed in the distributive paradigm, moreover, often obscures issues of domination and oppression, which require a more process-oriented and relational conceptualization.

Thus, to Young, the concept of distribution should be confined to those material goods, like things, natural resources or money, which Arthur and Shaw (above) and others define as economic goods. But she sees the scope of justice in general as wider, involving a well-ordered society in which realization of the good life is not impeded by oppression and domination.

The conception of justice adopted in the present volume is similarly broad in scope. The term social justice is taken to embrace both fairness and equity in the distribution of a wide range of attributes, which need not be confined to material things. Although the primary focus is on attributes which have an immediate bearing on people's well-being or the quality of their lives, our conception of social justice goes beyond patterns of distribution, general and spatial, to incorporate attributes relevant to how these come about. While fairness is sometimes applied to procedures and justice to outcomes (Barry, 1989, p. 145), we are concerned with both. Preference for the term social justice rather than justice in general is explained not by preoccupation with the distribution of attributes which might be labelled as social, but by concern with something which happens socially, among people in a society. This is taken to incorporate the economic and political dimensions of life, insofar as they can sensibly be separated, and others which might be labelled cultural, or social in a narrow sense, but excludes retributive or criminal justice.

Thus the meaning of social justice adopted here is simultaneously distributional and relational. In an early attempt to focus human geography on the theme of welfare (Smith, 1974), the catch-phrase of 'who gets what where, and how' was adopted to highlight the central questions involved. This was a deliberate echo of Harold Laswell's definition of political science as the study of who gets what when and how, and of Paul Samuelson's definition of economics as concerning what is produced, how and for whom. The questions of who gets what where and how still seem helpful pointers to the central issues in a conception of social justice more sensitive than political scientists, economists and others (including moral philosophers) to the geographical or spatial dimension. But just as these days space is more sensibly viewed as an intrinsic feature of social (including economic and political) life rather than a separate dimension, so the distributional sphere of human welfare implicit in the notion of 'getting' is as inextricably bound up with the question of how, or the process involved. Furthermore, insofar as getting may imply a narrow, individualistic and materialistic conception of life, it must be recognized that social justice involves something more and that this could include human relationships.

These preliminary indications of the meaning of social justice should be sufficient to enable us to proceed to some related issues, concerning how people should live and treat others, what they may be entitled to, and who they are, where and when.

Ethics and morality

Moral philosophy is a necessary starting point for the elaboration of social justice, for justice is a specific aspect of the more general problem of morality, or how people should act. Social justice is concerned with how people should be treated in particular circumstances, by other people directly or within the human creation of institutions whereby behaviour is regulated. Not all actions considered to be (im)moral are necessarily (un)just; for example we do not usually think of failing in one's duty or even adultery as injustice, bad conduct though they are. But to depart from some accepted principle of justice, such as treating people the same way in the same circumstances, would also be a breach of morality and wrong.

What is good or bad, right or wrong, what people ought or ought not to do, is the subject of the branch of philosophy usually referred to as ethics but sometimes as moral theory. Ethics can be divided into two parts. The first is *meta-ethics*, which concerns the meaning of moral or ethical terms such as good and ought, and their interrelations, or what Hare (1964) described as the logical study of the language of morals. The second is *normative ethics*, which includes 'the attempt to discover some acceptable and rationally defensible view concerning what kinds of things are good (worth aiming at) and what kinds of acts are right, and why' (Hospers, 1967, p. 567). These are complex matters; what can be said here must of necessity be highly selective, glossing over many of the finer (and not so fine) points, so as to focus on those issues most relevant to social justice.

Some ambiguity surrounds the concepts of ethics and morality themselves, subject as they are to a variety of common usage. When we talk of unethical conduct it is likely to refer to some restricted context, such as medical ethics or scholarship (as mentioned in chapter 1). In everyday speech morality can refer to some broad judgement as to what is right or wrong conduct, and also to some specific aspect of life such as sexual relations ('sexual morality'). We sometimes tell stories with 'a moral', or message of some supposed profundity with respect to human behaviour and its possible consequences, being good or bad usually reaping its 'just reward'. Morality and 'moralizing' can have repressive connotations, for example where people are expected to conform to majority codes of conduct which they do not personally endorse; Christians in a Moslem country (and the reverse) or homosexuals in a dominantly heterosexual society provide cases in point.

The breadth of ethics and morality in philosophy is captured as follows by Mackie (1977, p. 9), in the opening sentences of a well-known text:

> A moral or ethical statement may assert that some particular action is right or wrong; or that actions of a certain kind are so; it may offer a distinction between good and bad characters or dispositions; or it may propound some broad principle from which many more detailed judgements of these sorts might be inferred – for example, that we ought always to aim at the greatest general happiness, or try to minimize the total suffering of all sentient beings, or devote ourselves wholly to the service of God, or that it is right and proper for everyone to look after himself.

Such statements express what Mackie refers to as first-order ethical judgements, belonging to the realm of the normative, as opposed to second-order statements which concern what goes on when someone makes a first-order statement, that is, the thinking, reasoning, terms and meanings involved, or the meta-ethical referred to above. If we accept the argument of Mackie (1977, p. 105) and others that 'no substantive moral conclusions or serious constraints on moral views can be derived from the meanings of moral terms or the logic of moral discourse', this leaves the broad first-order statements of moral values as possible starting points for theories which might inform thinking about social justice.

But before following this route, a taste of some of the difficulty arising from moral terms may be helpful. Take the word 'good'. We can describe something as good if it performs a useful function well, for example a good knife cuts well. We can describe a person as good if they perform a certain role well. A common example is taken from sport: that someone is a good batsman or batswoman can be argued from their batting average, and demonstrated conclusively if a particular average is taken to separate the good from the rest. But whether they are a good man or woman is a different question: one involving moral rather than technical judgement. That Mike Gatting is (or was) a good batsman is hard to dispute, but whether he is a good man depends on how we judge his leading a cricket team to South Africa under apartheid. A further complication is raised when we recall that 'good' can be an aesthetic as well as a technical and moral judgement. A cricketer like David Gower may bat with special style, even elegance, characteristics to be applauded (literally) for their own sake, as long as some runs are scored in the process. What is good in human conduct has a moral dimension, for example acting with virtue, honour or even justice, which can be distinguished from other commendable traits. But recognition of this meaning of good does not necessarily lead us to the discovery of what is good conduct in general, or what it is to be just in particular.

Consider also what is meant by 'ought'. It should not be hard to distinguish between a moral sense of what ought to be done and one with no immediate moral content. If someone tells me that I ought to be at the airport an hour before my flight time in order to be sure of my reservation, then this simply identifies one act which is necessary for the performance of another. Taking the trip need have no morally commendable purpose: I am merely doing my job as a visiting lecturer. However, I should keep my (implicit) promise of arriving in time. If I was on a mission of mercy or a hired assassin on the way to work, whether I catch the flight might be considered more obviously good or bad from a moral point of view. The statement that I ought to give money to charity seems to have clear moral content, in that this may be a good thing to do rather than merely prudent. But even this case is not straightforward: there could be a prudential element to the rich giving to charity, if this helped to keep the poor content with the status quo. And it is not obvious that giving to others makes charity morally commendable; feeling good may be reward enough. Furthermore, to say to the poor that they should give to charity carries no conviction if they cannot afford to do so: for 'ought' to carry the strength of moral *obligation*, as something that *must* be done, requires the necessary wherewithal or ability (the dictum of ought implies can). There is the further complication that morality is not the only or most personally compelling basis for what people ought to do: for example, who is to say that it is better for me to give to charity than to buy Christmas presents for my family?

These and other considerations have lead most contemporary philosophers to seek guidance beyond the realm of moral terms. Some go further, and doubt the usefulness of morality and moral theory itself. For example, Williams (1985, pp. 174, 196) says of morality that 'we would be better off without it . . . There are many philosophical mistakes woven into morality', involving 'deep rooted and still powerful misconceptions of life'. Williams prefers a process of 'reflection' to ethical theory, which he sees as attempting to reduce everything to one pattern (Williams, 1985, p. 198):

A respect for freedom and social justice and a critique of oppressive and deceitful institutions may be no easier to achieve than they have been in the past, and may well be harder, but we need not suppose that we have no ideas to give them a basis. We should not concede to abstract ethical theory its claim to provide the only intellectual surroundings for such ideas.

It is also claimed that there are no objective values, the position of *moral scepticism*, or *subjectivism*, is taken to the extreme of asserting that moral judgements are merely expressions of a person's own feelings or attitudes.

However, others take contrary positions. For example, Louden (1992) strongly reasserts the need for moral theory, as a guide to explanation, conceptual exploration and criticism, as well as to feed our imagination and curiosity. And Brown (1986, p. 134) states that 'Political philosophy needs moral objectivity. Without it we would have nothing to say to those tough characters ... who want to run society their way', and resurrects the view that 'political philosophy must rest on an objective theory of the good'. That apparently diametrically opposed positions should be held among philosophers is a reflection of, among other things, disagreement about what is meant by ethical or moral theory. Skimming the surface of the debate helps to reveal something of the scope and limitations of moral philosophy as a guide to social justice.

The kind of thing philosophers have in mind when they talk about important or even ultimate moral values (or Mackie's first-order ethical judgements, mentioned above) include duty, right, virtue and justice itself. These are things that matter very much, and may also relate to commendable character traits. We might be tempted to add other things, such as happiness, liberty, welfare, equity, efficiency, security, creativity, community, compassion and so on. While their status as moral values is debatable, they do share the common property that they are indisputably good for human life, things we would chose to have rather than not. However, they can come into conflict (e.g. equity with efficiency, freedom with security), so it would be helpful to have a way of adjudicating between them, elaborating how they contribute to the good life. This would be a moral theory.

There is a long tradition in moral philosophy claiming that some ultimate theory of the good is to be discovered as part of the fabric of the world: the position of *moral objectivity*. This is not a matter of the physical discovery of some tablets of stone or holy grail, convenient though this would be if everyone could accept their authenticity. And it is not something that can be accomplished by empirical observation in the conventional scientific mode of inquiry. Nor is it sufficient to pronounce the words of God, in the teleological tradition that dominated moral thought for so long, as the authority of the divine is unlikely to convince infidels or atheists. It is more a case of human reason and some special intuition arriving at objective, transcendental values. The careful and sustained study of human nature, after the fashion of Aristotle for example, might find the point of human life, from which what is good will be made clear. This is the kind of project Brown (1986, p. 138) has in mind when he asserts: 'We have, then, an objective ground for a theory of the human good. It is our human nature.'

One outcome of such deliberations could be to conclude that what is good is simply what is good for each of us as individuals. At its extreme, this becomes *egoistic hedonism*, or the single-minded pursuit of personal pleasure. But even if a world populated by philosophers arrived at this position by a process of pure reason, they would soon find by experience reasons to reject it. We have sound, selfish motives to be concerned for others, the more so as we recognize our mutual interdependence in the community and the world at large: it is a matter of practical necessity. In the process, we may learn to value others for their own sake, even without moral exhortation.

The sense of objective most commonly adopted in contemporary moral philosophy involves intersubjective agreement as the basis for accepting moral values. Habermas (1990) proposes what he terms *discourse ethics*, postulating: 'Only those norms may claim to be valid that could meet with the consent of all affected in their role as participants in practical discourse' (p. 197). In other words, if everyone concerned engages freely and equally in a co-operative search for moral truth, nothing coercing anyone except the force of argument, then this procedure validates the outcome. The geographical context could be a community, nation or the entire world. To claim universal validity requires that moral principles do not merely reflect what Habermas refers to as 'the intuitions of a particular culture or epoch'.

What is involved is not therefore the exercise of a special mental facility providing privileged access to moral truth, but something which appeals to considered convictions as to what would be right or wrong in certain situations (Barry, 1989, p. 260). People communicate with one another, codes of morality emerging as they learn to live together. Hence the view that morality is made, or invented, rather than discovered, arrived at as part of living in society rather than distilled from knowledge of some supra-natural realm. That we should seek what might be regarded as post-facto rationalization in the form of divine law or some such is understandable: this kind of objective validity would, to some people, give moral values special authority.

The rejection of divine law, coupled with the practical difficulty of discourse among equals generating universal moral truth, raises the role of philosophers themselves in a world of human diversity. McCarthy (1990, pp. vii–viii) makes the following observations:

> To suppose that all the questions of the good life dealt with under the rubric of classical ethics – questions of happiness and virtue, character and ethos, community and tradition – could be answered once and for all, and by philosophers, is no longer plausible. Matters of individual

and group self-understanding and self-realization, rooted as they are in particular life histories and traditions, do not admit of general theory; and prudential deliberation on the good life, moving as it does within the horizons of particular lifeworlds and forms of life, does not yield universal prescriptions.

And to Mackie (1977, p. 48): 'the radical diversity of the goals that men actually pursue and find satisfying makes it implausible to construe such pursuits as resulting from an imperfect grasp of a unitary true good.' Such argument leads thinking about morality away from the possibility of grand theory or universal principles, to the position of *ethical relativism*. Moral values are regarded as more than mere personal preferences, but are restricted in their validity to specific groups or cultures. What is right for their members is not necessarily right for others. Quoting Mackie (1977, p. 36) again:

> The argument for relativity has as its premise the well-known vari-
> ation in moral codes from one society to another and from one
> period to another, and also the difference in moral beliefs between
> different groups and classes within a complex community. Such vari-
> ation is in itself merely a truth of descriptive morality, a fact of
> anthropology ... Disagreement about moral codes seems to reflect
> people's adherence to and participation in different ways of life.

This leads to the central question identified at the beginning of the chapter. Either we accept spatial and temporal specificity of conceptions of morality or the good life, or we find ways of adjudicating between them. In the absence of universals, the latter course runs the risk of cultural imperialism, imposing our own supposedly superior standards on others holding more 'primitive' beliefs. But the former position would require us to accept human sacrifice or cutting off the hands of those convicted of stealing in some societies, for example, on the grounds that it works for them: the rains do come regularly and the rate of theft is remarkably low. And others would have to accept our bizarre practices, such as bestowing status and authority on some men (not women) by virtue of the chance of birth to those ennobled by some ancient and perhaps befuddled monarch, on the grounds that it works for us, helping to maintain a social hierarchy and keeping the lower orders in their place.

A way out of this dilemma is to recognize that certain features of a way of life, expressed as a moral code, may have a *functional* justification within a particular society, but that this does not necessarily warrant their approval from a moral point of view. To give moral approval to harsh punishment depends to some extent on the kind of social order it helps to maintain. Furthermore, while the survival of a society may be held by its members to depend on such practices as human sacrifice, this could be shown scientifically not to be true: it actually has no bearing on when the rains come. It could even be argued that practices objectively required for the survival of some societies at some times, like cannibalism or drowning baby girls, are so objectionable as not to justify continuing social reproduction. The moral values asserting equal individual worth, and that people should be regarded and treated as ends in themselves and not means to the ends of others, could be deployed in support of this position. There must, surely, be some external, possibly universal, transhistoric, standards to which local and time-specific social practices can be called to account.

Such arguments help to reveal the continuing tensions between the observed fact of moral relativism and the urge to transcend the here and now in pursuit of universal moral values or an all-embracing moral theory. A possible approach to compromise is to recognize that there are ideas with very wide appeal to people's moral sensibilities (like equal individual worth), itself a fact, even if they are not unambiguously ordered within some grand theory of the good. There is point to the argument of Louden (1992) that 'anti-theorists' like Bernard Williams ask too much of moral theory, which they see as defective to the extent that (among other faults) it lacks universals, means of comparing moral values, and rational ways of resolving any moral disagreement or conflict. Louden (p. 140) conceives of moral theory less ambitiously, as 'any sustained attempt to give an account of how moral agents ought to live and act', and argues that this should (among other things): be empirically informed; be non-reductionist, recognizing a plurality of values rather than deriving them from a single standard; recognize that not all conflicts in morality can be resolved; and be a guide to people's practical deliberations. Among other advantages claimed for this conception over more rigid, formalized theories, is that it is more in keeping with what Louden (p. 89) describes as 'the particular perceptions of individual moral agents and the local practices of moral communities'. The geographer weary of abstraction should warm to such a view.

It remains to give such a perspective a little more substance, by briefly considering some of the implications. A starting point with clear links to social justice is an assertion made by Griffin (1986, p. 61) that a moral theory grants some form of equal respect to people, and justifies trade-off of one person's good against another's by appeal to a certain range of human values. In other words, the task is to justify favouring one person over another, or treating equals differently. The moral principles or judgements which make such a theory specific are commonly expected to be: (1) *prescriptive*, in the sense of specifying what is good and/or ought to be done; (2) *universalizable*, so that the same applies to other relevant similar actions, and impartially to everyone in the same circumstances; and (3) based on considerations of human *well-being* or ill-being.

The first of these positions suggests that moral considerations should be imperative, overriding all other considerations, and all-pervasive in the conduct of human life. It requires only slight relaxation to see morality as not necessarily overriding all other considerations in prescribing human action nor pervading everything including the most trivial acts, but as something very important: much more than one of many points of view but rather, 'something to which all points of view must answer' (Louden, 1992, p. 62).

The second criterion, that of universalization, is usually held to be beyond dispute, indeed a hallmark of moral reason. It reflects the so-called golden rule of Christianity ('do to others as you would have them do to you'), and Kant's categorical imperative of 'so act that you could wish the maxim of your actions to become a universal law of human conduct' (Hospers, 1967, p. 508). This is the essence of equal respect. Universalization can take different forms, such as: looking at the world from the place of others but with one's own values, mental and physical qualities, social status and resources; putting oneself in the place of others but with one's own values alone; or putting oneself in others' minds as well as shoes and looking at things from their point of view. The discourse ethics proposed by Habermas (1990, see above) is a particular approach to universalization, as is the social contract in John Rawls's approach to justice (see chapter 3).

However, some see universalization and impartiality as dangerous, and even impossible in the real world of differences among peoples. As Young (1990a, pp. 104, 106) asserts:

> It is impossible to adopt an unsituated moral point of view, and if point of view is situated, then it cannot be universal, it cannot stand apart from and understand all points of view . . . A 'moral point of view' arises not from lonely self-legislating reason, but from the concrete encounter with others, who demand that their needs, desires, and perspectives be recognized.

Powerful though universalizability and impartiality may be as criteria for moral judgements, they must be sensitive to actual, relevant differences in situations, in peoples and their circumstances, that justify differential treatment. Hence the call in some quarters for contextual moral theory, in which 'morality must be situated concretely, that is, for particular actors in a particular society' (Tronto, 1987, pp. 657–8). There must be room in moral theory for people to find defensible solutions to the real issues in their lives, but such an approach must be sensitive to the dangers of 'anything goes' implicit in narrow subjectivism and relativism. Hare (1978, p. 132) provides a fitting conclusion from mainstream moral philosophy: 'that ethical reasoning *can* provide us with a way of conducting political argument about justice and rights rationally and with hope of agreement; that such rational arguments have to rest on an understanding of the concepts being used, *and* of the facts of our actual situation.'

This leaves the third consideration raised above, that of human well-being or ill-being. There is a long tradition, extending back to classical Greece, of philosophical contemplation of some broad conception of the good life. The state of *eudaimonia* in the work of Plato and Aristotle, usually translated as human 'happiness' or 'flourishing', suggests a general sense of well-being, or 'the shape of one's whole life' (Williams, 1985, p. 34). While expressing scepticism as to the applicability of the concept of well-being to particular actions, Williams (1972, pp. 88–9) states that: 'if one's approval of such more general things as policies, institutions, dispositions, sorts of motives, etc., is to count as moral approval, then one must suppose that these policies, institutions, etc., minister in some way to the achievement of some kind of human well-being.' The importance of giving substance to the notion of well-being brings us back to human nature: to what it means to be human, and to live well.

It is at this point that broader issues of morality focus directly on social justice, which is centrally concerned with the distribution of sources of human well-being. Practical consideration of this issue is reserved for chapter 5. Here we pursue a related and extremely influential strand of morality: that of rights.

Rights

To say that people have a right is to require them to be treated in a certain way, to get something to which they are entitled or at least to raise this expectation. There is a clear link with the moral principle of equal concern: 'If we are to treat people as equals, we must protect them in their possession of certain rights and liberties' Kymlicka (1990, p. 50) reminds us, adding that the question of which rights and liberties has been the concern of most of the political philosophy written in the past twenty years. Attempting to specify what people are, or should be, entitled to is also a possible approach to the question of what we mean by well-being, for rights must contribute to human well-being if they are as highly valued, and struggled for, as is apparent in many parts of the world.

Rights are special, and are different from what are usually referred to as *wants* and *needs*. We make distinctions in everyday discourse. We typically say of our wants that they should be 'met' and not, perhaps, 'frustrated': wants are expressions of purely personal desires, often of quite a frivolous nature. Of needs we are more likely to say that they should be 'satisfied', a term which carries some quantitative implication like 'fulfilled' (fully filled); what is required should not be 'denied'. To assert a need is to appeal to some external standard, however implicitly, which may legitimate something that would otherwise merely be a want. Thus, when we talk about someone 'needing' a heart transplant, the reference is likely to be to a clinical judgement made external to the patient in question. There is also a consequential judgement involved: that this particular need for a surgical procedure should be satisfied, in order to improve or save life, although this falls short of an imperative for there may be competing demands on the surgeon's time. We may try to elevate mere wants into needs in order to strengthen their validity, though when I say that I 'need' a beer those listening know that this is merely a want (unless I am perhaps dying of thirst) and will feel no moral pressure to buy me the drink.

Of course, if I had already bought someone else a drink, I might feel entitled to have one bought for me in return. This is the kind of thing we mean by a right: an obligation embedded in some social or institutional context where expectation has moral force. There is a morality to the reciprocity of 'buying your round', taking your turn, returning something borrowed, or telling the truth. In everyday speech, rights should be 'guaranteed' or 'respected', not 'violated', words which express the force with which we assert a right as opposed to a want or need. And it is not simply a reflection of the nature of the relationship involved, such as the expectation of something in return, but also of the importance of the kind of things which we are inclined to enunciate as rights, such as protection from arbitrary arrest, freedom of speech, and life itself.

Rights in general have certain common features (Waldron, 1984, pp. 14–15). Rights are characterized by their *strength* as particularly important interests, by their *urgency* in the sense of priority over other interests (e.g. over needs and wants), and by their *peremptory* nature in that they may exclude certain actions such as preventing people from voting or torturing them, for people have a right to vote and not to be tortured. Rights which relate to what people should have are sometimes termed *positive*, those which say what should not happen to them are *negative*. A distinction is sometimes made between rights as *derivative*, held and respected insofar as they promote some ultimate good (in the way property rights are thought by some to promote welfare maximization), and as *foundational* or derived from our humanity (Brown, 1986, pp. 102–3).

Rights are sometimes regarded as purely individual, and hence individualistic or emphasizing individual interests. However, we do talk of the rights of particular groups in society, such as racial or ethnic minorities, women and political dissidents, if it is felt that they are being denied something to which they are entitled. In any event, rights can never be entirely individual, because they imply an *obligation* or *duty* on others. This is most obvious in the case of rights with a peremptory character; the requirement not to treat people in a particular way, frequently upheld by the law, is often stronger than the requirement to do something positive to or for them.

There are divergent views as to the property of rights, in a literal as well as figurative sense. Take Hart (1984, p. 83) for example:

> Rights are typically conceived of as *possessed* or *owned by* or *belonging to* individuals, and these expressions reflect the conception of moral rules as not only prescribing conduct but as forming a kind of moral property of individuals to which they are as individuals entitled; only when rules are conceived in this way can we speak of *rights* and *wrongs* as well as right and wrong actions.

This proprietorial conception, from a paper originally published in 1955, has largely been superseded by a more relational concept of rights, of the kind suggested by Young (1990a, p. 25):

> Rights are not fruitfully conceived as possessions. Rights are relationships, not things; they are institutionally defined rules specifying what people can do in relation to one another. Rights refer to doing more than having, to social relationships that enable or constrain action.

Young also points to a growing body of feminist-inspired moral theory which challenges the conventional 'ethic of rights' with its emphasis on impartiality and impersonality, on the grounds that this 'corresponds poorly to the social relations typical of family and personal life, whose moral orientation requires not detachment from but engagement in and sympathy with the particular parties in a situation' (p. 96). This raises another dimension of the relational character of rights, and of social justice (as we shall see in chapter 4).

Discussion of rights is frequently associated with situations of conflict, which further emphasizes their social context. 'Questions about rights generally arise when it is proposed that the interests of one or more individuals should be traded off for the sake of others' or in the name of some allegedly more important moral or political ideal' (Waldron, 1984, p. 19). They thus directly address one of the basic ingredients of a moral theory, as specified by Griffin (above). The desire of people to move around as they please, to walk the hills and dales, is constrained by the rights of private property owners. The rights of people to play loud music at home is constrained by the right of neighbours to be protected from noise.

The extent to which rights might be regarded as protecting people from the power of the state is expressed in a well-known analogy: 'Rights are best understood as trumps over some background justification for political decisions that states a goal for the community as a whole' (Dworkin, 1984, p. 153). Thus the local council may think that the community would benefit from a new road, but I can invoke a right not to have it go through my garden without an appeal being heard. But rights can also express entitlements from the state: for example, the right not only to a full and fair hearing of my case, but also to the legal services required to make it as effectively as possible.

An important distinction can be made between *legal* and *moral* rights. Legal rights are the more secure, because they can be asserted or defended in the courts. Obvious examples are the right to vote if on the electoral role, to be paid for one's labour according to a contract agreed with an employer, and to the security of one's premises from trespass. Moral rights may appeal to some general principle, such as giving people a say in affairs that concern them, but without legal guarantees. To be consulted about matters affecting family members, such as a delinquent child or infirm parent, is of this kind, as is the right students might seek to contribute to the design of their courses. Struggles are frequently engaged to make moral rights legal, the vote for black South Africans being an obvious case.

Legal and moral rights may be further subdivided. *Liberty-oriented* rights, sometimes referred to as civil and political rights, concern people's freedom of action and participation in political, community and national life, such as the franchise and rights of assembly. *Security-oriented* rights (or *claim* rights) refer more to economic and social requirements to protect people's physical and material status, such as unemployment and social security benefits. As liberty-oriented rights often simply protect individual freedom they tend to be more readily enshrined in laws than security-oriented rights, which require more government involvement and expenditure. The relative emphasis on liberty or security in the struggle for rights depends very much on the specific situation of actual societies. Capitalist societies tend to prioritize individual liberty and property rights, while socialist societies place more emphasis on collective entitlements from the state. Basic civil liberties are more of an issue in South Africa than in Britain, where social security is a major concern.

These points indicate that, in practice, rights are in some respects relative. Even more obvious are the cases of some peoples, such as Australian aboriginals, whose conception of themselves as part of nature rather than as human individuals generates particular rights to land not shared by others. However, some rights may be held to be universal in that they apply to all people everywhere and at all times, as well as inalienable in that they can neither be given nor taken away, and of overriding importance so that they take precedence over all other considerations (Campbell, 1988, p. 41).

Moral rights which are supposed to be universal are often referred to as *human rights*. 'Human rights are possessed by everybody in the world because they are human. People are equally entitled to them regardless of their gender, race, colour, language, national origin, age, class or religious or political creed' (Selby, 1987, p. 8). The emphasis on equality is an important feature of human rights, which appeal not to the maxim of treating people the same in the same circumstances and differently if the circumstances differ in a morally relevant way, but to strict impartiality in the sense that it does not matter who, when and where people are. The rights themselves can have different strength, however. Selby (p. 8) goes on:

> Some human rights are more important or *basic* than others. The right to life is the most basic of all for without it all other rights are in jeopardy ... Among other *basic human rights* are the right to be recognised as a person before the law, the right to equal protection in law and freedom from arbitrary arrest and detention. Basic human rights provide the foundation upon which the enjoyment of other human rights depends. They are also rights which cannot be restricted or taken away without affront to human dignity and which any society has a fundamental duty to protect at all times.

The particular rights referred to here, though widely espoused, are not necessarily universally accepted. They are certainly not universally respected in practice: the relativity of actual rights, like moral codes, is a matter of common observation – hence the contemporary preoccupation with affronts to human rights in certain parts of the world. Nor is it universally agreed that the idea that our common humanity, our equal capacity for pleasure and pain and so on, necessarily justifies any rights as *natural* attributes of humankind, whether or not they might be applied equally. Human beings differ from other species by virtue of their capacity to reason (for example, about rights), but they could reason that they have no greater rights than other natural creatures. (Whether animals might have rights, such as not to be killed for human entertainment or sustenance, is a matter which we shall not explore, other than to observe that, like humans, they are in fact treated differently from place to place.)

Some thinkers associated with postmodern attitudes see any definition of human nature as 'dangerous, because it threatens to devalue or exclude some acceptable individual desires, cultural characteristics, or ways of life' (Young, 1990a, p. 36); that is, it denies important elements of human difference. Furthermore, to MacDonald (1984, p. 36), 'no natural characteristic constitutes a *reason* for the assertion that all human beings are of equal worth'. And the moral sceptic points out: 'To say that someone has a right, of whatever sort, is to speak either of or within a legal or moral system: our rejection of objective values carries with it the denial that there are any self-subsistent rights' (Mackie, 1977, p. 173). However, the idea of a range of universal rights, equally attributed to all by virtue of common humanity, has strong appeal, even without invoking the proposition of natural human rights.

Whether derived from our nature or our reason (arguably part of our nature, hence the problem), it is hard to see any human rights as absolute, or inalienable, in practice. 'A right is absolute when it cannot be overridden in any circumstances, so that it can never be justifiably infringed and it must be fulfilled without any exceptions' (Gerwith, 1984, p. 93). The right to life, arguably the highest, makes the point: the death penalty is still used in many countries, and most are still prepared to send men and women to wars in which some will certainly die. The circumstances in which the right to life is not considered absolute are exceptions, justified by reference to some higher good such as the survival of a society or the saving of more lives than are lost, though a comparative body count is far from convincing as a moral justification for military action. Deliberately to sacrifice one's own life for others carries particular virtue. Without pursuing these matters further, it is evident, again, that in practice even the more basic human rights are no more than strong moral claims, that may yield to what some consider to be higher moral imperatives.

That human rights are not in practice absolute does not necessarily undermine their egalitarian character. The *objects* of the rights may be hierarchically ordered, for example the protection of life may come before the protection of property, but the *subjects* of the rights (all life-holders, or property-owners) should be treated the same. The egalitarian content of human rights has very important implications for social justice. Belief in the equal moral *worth* of human beings provides an argument for prioritizing the fact of being human over other possible distributive criteria, at least with respect to some of what is distributed. Thus, 'since we do believe in equal value of human well-being and freedom, we should also believe in the prima-facie equality of men's right to well-being or freedom' (Vlastos, 1984, p. 58). Paraphrasing Vlastos further, Waldron (1984, pp. 19–20) suggests:

> [R]ights have priority over other considerations like utility and desert because they reflect the conditions under which it becomes possible for an agent to recognize and act on considerations like utility and desert. It is plausible to suppose that freedom of thought and self-expression and the satisfaction of elementary needs are conditions of this sort . . . we must leave intact at least those interests that are central to each person's capacity to recognize and understand reason and moral argument.

The implications of requiring everyone to have those kinds of needs satisfied, which must extend well beyond bare subsistence, are profound indeed (we return to them in chapter 5).

A further attraction of the concept of rights is that it requires specificity. In claiming or denying a right, it is important to know exactly what someone is or is not entitled to. A statement of rights is a common means of a society or its leaders being precise about aspirations, if not necessarily intent. For example, the *Declaration of Rights of Men and Citizens* enacted by the First French Republic in 1791 asserted: 'Men are born and remain free and equal in rights . . . these rights are liberty, property, security, and resistance to oppression.' The first ten Amendments to the Constitution of the United States (the *Bill of Rights*) specifies certain freedoms people should not be denied, for example freedom of worship and speech, and other rights including to bear arms, not to be subject to unreasonable searches and seizures, and how people should be treated if accused of a crime. The Supreme Court has the task of interpreting the Constitution in cases where people consider their rights to have been infringed. Britain is an exception (although in another age the Magna Carta did promise that no man [sic] would be denied justice); hence some calls for a bill of rights.

At the international scale, the United Nations adopted the *Universal Declaration of Human Rights* in 1948, as what was supposed to be a common standard of achievement for all peoples and all nations. It includes both liberty-oriented and security-oriented rights. While carrying the moral authority implicit in its origin, the *Declaration* was not legally enforceable; indeed, Griffin (1986, p. 389) describes it as so profligate as not to be a precedent of much interest. In 1966 the United Nations produced the *Covenant on Civil and Political Rights* and the *Covenant on Economic, Social and Cultural Rights*, which are legally binding on those nations which formally ratified them. Under the civil and political heading, everyone has the right to: life (sentence of death may be imposed only for the most serious of crimes); liberty and security of person; freedom of thought, conscience and religion; equal treatment in the courts; to be presumed innocent until proved guilty; peaceful assembly, freedom of association and to take part in public affairs. No one shall be subject to: torture, slavery, forced labour or arbitrary interference with privacy, family, home or correspondence. Economic, social and cultural rights for everyone are to: the enjoyment of just and favourable working conditions; form trade unions; an adequate standard of living; the enjoyment of the highest attainable standard of physical and mental health; education; and to take part in cultural life and enjoy the benefits of scientific progress.

An important geographical question is whether people can be said to have a right to, literally, a place in the world. That they are is seldom made explicit, yet Walzer (1983, p. 43) reminds us that, in his classic *The Elements of Law*, Thomas Hobbes recognized the right to a place to live among things necessary for life. This is sometimes extended into an argument for the right to private property, in the form of land ownership required to guarantee security of a place to live as a legal right. John Locke proposed a natural law of property, revived by Robert Nozick in one of the theoretical perspectives reviewed in chapter 3. However, a right to own land differs from other commonly enunciated rights, in that it concerns appropriation of the scarce material world, and can impinge on the rights of others to meet such vital needs as food and shelter. At the extreme, private ownership of land, by restricting access, can deprive others of a place to live, even of the right to life. Thus land rights, manifest in private ownership or other forms of tenure, are of paramount importance to the link between geography and social justice.

We will return to this issue in the context of 'basic needs' in chapter 5, and in case studies of claims to land, territory and place in chapters 8 and 9. It is sufficient here to conclude with a further assertion of the extent to which the issues of rights and justice are interrelated (Peffer, 1990, p. 366):

> [H]uman rights can be seen to be intimately connected with social justice. Human rights and principles of social justice are similar in that they both: (1) are concerned with fundamental human needs or interests (as opposed to, say, 'mere desires'); (2) issue in coercible obligations (i.e. obligations that the state or, in some cases, other individuals can legitimately force us to meet); (3) provide a basis for justifying our actions and, in some cases, invoking the protection or aid of others; and (4) provide grounds for justifying or criticizing social institutions, programs, or policies.

Membership

A crucial question with respect to rights, and to social justice in general, is that of who is included, or excluded. Universal human rights apply to everyone by definition, at least in principle, but most of the rights that matter most to people depend on the governments of nation-states, and within them often on local governments. Furthermore, it is at the level of the national aggregate that questions of distributive justice are still most frequently raised.

Michael Walzer is widely credited with giving the question of membership the prominence it deserves in social justice. He claims (Walzer, 1983, pp. 31, 63):

> The primary good that we distribute is membership in some human community. And what we do with regard to membership structures all our other distributive choices: it determines with whom we make these choices, from whom we require obedience and collect taxes, to whom we allocate goods and services.

The theory of distributive justice begins, then, with an account of membership rights. It must vindicate at one and the same time the (limited) right of closure, without which there could be no communities at all, and the political exclusiveness of the existing communities. For it is only as members somewhere that men and women can hope to share in all the other social goods – security, wealth, honor, office, and power – that communal life makes possible.

The question of membership is deeply geographical, often defined simply by *where* people are. We will consider some general issues in this section, then merge the discussion with a more explicit exploration of the role of geographical space (following an earlier exposition in Smith, 1990a).

The term *nation* is usually applied to a population group, or a people, with certain unifying characteristics. A *state* is a particular political unit, or jurisdiction with territorial delimitation, possessing sovereignty within its boundaries as recognized by others. The concept of the *nation-state* expresses identity between a people and their sovereign geographical space. The modern conception of the nation-state emerged from European monarchies in late feudal times and became codified as nationalist doctrine only at about the time of the French Revolution. And it was not simply a case of each national group wanting its own territory in some proprietorial sense. There was a growing recognition that the kind of aspirations people were developing (as expressed, for example, in the declarations of rights accompanying the American and French Revolutions) required new relationships between government and the people: new institutional forms.

In the early years of the modern nation-state, the legal rights associated with citizenship were rather restricted. They were largely confined to the protection of persons and property from more obvious threats, from constraints on free trade and productive enterprise, and to rudimentary equality under the law. Not even the franchise was universal, in Britain until early this century, for example. But the power of organized labour, assisted by practical philanthropy, steadily increased the range of economic and social rights to which citizens were legally entitled, the right to form trade unions and to receive unemployment benefits being cases in point. Finally, the institution of welfare states in Britain and elsewhere after the Second World War greatly extended the benefits associated with citizenship of particular countries.

There is much contemporary interest in the concept of *citizenship*. Taylor-Gooby (1991, p. 94) points to arguments for 'an expansion in the bundle of rights to which individuals are entitled by virtue of membership in the state, whether to defend individual liberties . . . to advance the interests of less powerful groups . . . or to serve as a basis for equal freedom in civil society'. Citizenship has also been used as a means of political critique 'through which to explore systematic discrepancies between the obligations required of, and the rights extended to, members of a nation-state' (S. Smith, 1989, p. 148), pointing to enduring variations in the availability of rights or opportunities to exercise them.

Membership as inclusion or exclusion takes two forms: bestowing (or withholding) citizenship, and actually making available (or otherwise) what are supposed to be universal rights at the level of the nation-state. The protection of liberty-oriented rights and, even more so, the provision of benefits associated with economic and social security rights, involve costs. The state may therefore have reason to restrict citizenship, if only because the provision of rights bears ultimately on those who pay taxes. Indeed, a principle of justice is often invoked linking both contribution and benefit to citizenship.

One obvious example of the citizenship decision is with respect to immigrants from other countries. They may be denied formal citizenship and the full rights associated with it for some time after initial entry, for example in the United States where 'naturalization' is required. Such a process is a kind of rite of passage, like gaining membership of a club by demonstrating one's worth (in a moral sense) according to whatever values the nation or group espouses. Political refugees are generally made welcome, especially if fleeing from regimes the receiving country considers objectionable; those simply seeking a better life in a material sense may be judged less deserving, with the term 'economic migrant' having moral as well as descriptive content. Another example is the migrant worker, who may labour for years in a foreign country without full citizenship and associated rights. The common descriptions of 'host' country and 'guest' worker imply a relationship different from membership of the same national community, with different obligations and responsibilities.

Internal exclusion can take a variety of forms. At the extreme it can involve regarding some people as not completely human (Kuper, 1974, pp. 11–14), thus legitimating the denial of full human rights; the treatment of Jews in Nazi Germany and blacks at times in South Africa are cases in point. Many nation-states incorporate 'minorities', distinct from the dominant population in some way that is held to justify different and often unequal treatment. The sources of minority identity are principally racial, ethnic or religious, but they can also relate to role in the social relations of production, for example slaves or serfs who do not enjoy the same formal rights as the rest of the population. Other relevant considerations may be property ownership, which was once a qualification for the franchise in Britain, and gender which restricted the franchise in Britain within living memory and can still limit the access of women to some walks of life. Those deprived of equal rights may actually be majorities in some societies, or virtually so, whether 'natives' under colonial regimes, blacks in apartheid South Africa or women in many parts of the world.

While the means whereby some kinds of people are denied full rights may be informal and indeed illegal, the manipulation of citizenship is a not uncommon device. For example, in South Africa under apartheid, people not classified as 'white' were for long denied the vote even though they had South African citizenship; some had their citizenship and political rights transferred to new states created partly for this purpose (the former 'homelands' or 'Bantustans'). The state of Israel offers citizenship to any Jew from anywhere by virtue of the 'right of return' to what is claimed to be their historic homeland, but denies some rights to large numbers of Arabs living within the Israeli national territory. Further aspects of both these cases will be explored in later chapters of this book; these brief references are merely to provide further instances of the control of membership, and to link the issue to the crucial ingredient of geographical space.

Space

Geographical space is deeply implicated in social exclusion. Social interaction usually implies physical propinquity (modern means of communicating over long distances notwithstanding), and to separate people spatially can be an effective means of exclusion as well as control. The prison, asylum and leper colony are examples of total spatial exclusion of people seen to threaten society in some ways which justify curtailment of rights, while the ghetto within which Jews were once confined in some European cities could be almost as rigid a form of containment, leading ultimately to annihilation (see chapter 9).

Racial segregation in urban residential space is often associated with at least partial social exclusion. Thus, most public housing projects in American cities and some (usually inferior) council blocks in British cities are occupied exclusively by blacks. Groups distinguished by ethnicity or religion may also be subject to a not entirely voluntary form of spatial segregation. Of course, the spatial sorting of groups within a nation-state or its cities may to some extent reflect an unproblematic diversity of a population expressing their differences by making choices among alternative living environments. However, the assertion of a healthy pluralism can be used to mask cleavage and conflict, serving an ideological role in conveying a false sense of community and harmony and implying that particular institutional arrangements somehow resolve conflict in a manner which prevents the domination of some people by others.

Three further aspects of geographical space which impinge on social justice may be introduced briefly here; they will reappear, in various guises, in other parts of the book. The first is the extent to which moral beliefs, and within them principles of social justice, may arise within particular geographical settings or localities. This has already been touched on in chapter 1, and is part of the broader question of relativism raised earlier in this chapter. The Social and Cultural Geography Study Group Committee (1991, p. 16) cite Kant's emphasis on 'the common-sense moral assumptions that all of us routinely make in our everyday lives in order to establish what should be done, who should be trusted, where we should go, and so on', which is closely bound up with local culture. They see the possibility of such talk leading to deeper principles concerned with freedom and justice, providing a basis for inquiring into the preconditions of grander moral systems.

There is also Hegel's notion of ethical life, or *Sittlichkeit*: 'a concretely determined ethical existence that was expressed in the local folkways, a form of life that made practical sense to the people living in it', as Williams (1985, p. 104) describes it. However, he is worried about 'how local the view of these folkways can properly remain, and whether they can be criticized, ranked, or transcended'. Localized, common-sense systems of morality may embody a functionally necessary, or at least tried and trusted, set of beliefs which enable a local population to conduct their daily lives, but whether they might, of themselves, lead to something grander can hardly be divorced from their content. Local community codes of morality can incorporate repressive attitudes, for example towards women and people perceived as dangerously different, which we would hardly wish to universalize and which we may feel good reason to condemn. This aspect of relativism will reappear in chapter 4, in the discussion of communitarianism.

The second issue is that of the role of distance in moral responsibility. As Mackie (1977, p. 79) points out, we may well say that 'if someone is writhing in agony before your eyes, or starving on your doorstep, this is in itself, quite apart from your feelings, a reason for you to do something about it if you can . . . There may well be dispute about how near, in some sense, others must be to me for their needs to count as a reason for me to do something about them, and how strong a reason it will be.' Tronto (1987, p. 660) draws attention to the eighteenth-century Scottish writer Francis Hutcheson's analogy between the strength of our closest and furthest emotional ties and the ties of gravity. Human compassion as well as the ability to help may be subject to the distance-decay effect beloved of geography as spatial science.

But Africa's starving millions and other distant people in need are now brought to our homes on the television screen almost daily, to motivate concern and reaction, even without invoking universal responsibility. However, facing limits to what anyone can do, it is understandable to put those close to us, in any sense, first, and hard to deem this immoral or unjust. The sentiment of special responsibility for our loved ones had a long history before the contemporary emphasis on the 'ethic of care' advocated by some feminists (see chapter 4). Tension between universality and impartiality on the one hand, and the reality of spatially mediated human contact and attachment on the other, is an important link between geography and contemporary moral philosophy (see for example Friedman, 1991), to which we will return.

The third issue is that of the spatial scale of analysis for the discussion of social justice. There is a long tradition among philosophers, at least since Plato, of assuming the state (or, now, the nation-state) to be the appropriate unit for discussions of distributive justice. As Barry (1989, p. 5) reminds us, within this historical context the issue of international (re)distribution is of fairly recent origin; it is only in the past two hundred years that the process of uneven development has opened up such enormous disparities at the international scale. And it is within a similar time frame that the plight of the poor in our own (European) cities has become a moral issue rather than being accepted as part of some natural order. The question of the appropriate level of territorial (dis)aggregation is a familiar problem in geographical analysis, the usual answer to which is that it depends on the research problem. With respect to social justice with a territorial dimension, however, the scale adopted will to a large extent define the problem itself, for the degree of inequality observed will be very much a function of scale. Demonstrating this is reserved for chapter 5; it is sufficient here to recognize this further aspect of how deeply geographical space is implicated in social justice.

Time

Consideration of time will be brief here, and elsewhere in this volume; the challenge of space is task enough. The time dimension is not easy to handle in morality and social justice. The central problem is that of what responsibility, if any, present people have to those at other times. The usual context is the future, but past generations may also have a claim on our attention.

Looking to the past, we may have a moral obligation to repay debts in the most general sense. We owe the dead at least respect, and occasional honour as we remember those who did great things or were close to us in lineage. Homage and remembrance require resources: time and some money which could be devoted to those here and now. Monuments are erected and graveyards tended, often as sacred places associated with religious rites. To defile or destroy what some people hold sacred is objectionable, perhaps even unjust to both the living and the dead in the sense that they are deprived of something to which they are entitled. Places are the repository of much that is valued from the past; the significance of their loss is explored in chapter 9.

There are some more obvious ways in which the past may place obligations on the present. For example, the system of hereditary titles granted to the so-called nobility in Britain, along with a seat in the House of Lords, is patently undemocratic, but its abolition does raise the question of whether this would deprive present families of some legitimate benefit earned (presumably) by an ancestor. If property and perhaps intelligence can be inherited why not a title, or even a throne? This is part of the broader moral question of whether past good fortune or luck should be allowed to influence present life chances.

The other side of this coin is the possible claim of some group(s) of people in the present to be compensated in recognition of how badly those who went before them were treated. This is the issue of *reparation*, or compensation for past injustice and how this affects people in the present (see Waldron, 1992). The usual argument is for some form of 'positive discrimination' or 'affirmative action', to make up for previous negative discrimination experienced in particular by racial or ethnic minorities. Such action is not hard to justify, but becomes more difficult if it is asserted that membership of a formerly deprived group should have priority over superior competence in filling jobs, especially if the outcome has a bearing on the well-being of others. A related issue is the possible return of property expropriated under colonialism (e.g. in South Africa) or socialism (e.g. in East Europe), matters to be taken up in chapters 7 and 8.

Who gets what where at present is very obviously related to the past. Young (1990a, p. 29) makes a particularly telling point:

> Evaluating patterns of distribution is often an important starting point for questions about justice. For many issues of social justice, however, what is important is not the particular pattern of distribution at a particular moment, but rather the reproduction of a regular distributive pattern over time.

Young may not have had a spatial distribution in mind, but the stability or otherwise of spatial patterns of inequality over time may give us special leverage in looking at particular situations (as will be shown in chapter 6).

What of the future? What do we owe future generations? At least survival, it might be argued. This could imply not eating the seed corn, selling the family silver, or fouling the equivalent of the nest, and certainly not blowing everything up in a nuclear holocaust. A thorough, universal commitment to equality could imply ensuring future generations at least the same level of living as we enjoy, with serious implications for what we are entitled to do with the earth and its resources, and to the atmospheric and aquatic environment. (The relationship between environmentalism or the green movement and social justice is not considered further in this book.) Of course, if we take an optimistic view of our capacity for technological progress we may feel able to bequeath future generations a better life than ours, just as we are better-off in many respects than our ancestors. This sense of inequality over time is consistent with human progress, and hard to quarrel with from a moral standpoint.

A special difficulty with the future is that we do not know how long it will be, and whether we should allow for the possibility of an infinitely distant responsibility for others in time (and possibly in space, if we open morality up to beings on other planets). Here we certainly reach the limits of what we can know, and perhaps what we can reason about with any sort of practical implication. Perhaps the only conclusion is that our present actions do have a bearing on how long the human future will be, and that if we value humankind we should make its life as long as possible.

Inequality and difference

It remains to say something about the crucial distinction between inequality and difference. Inequality can be thought of as a particular kind of difference between people, about which moral questions arise. Social justice is concerned with this sort of difference: injustice is differential treatment in circumstances when, and where, there are no morally relevant differences between the individuals or groups concerned. Similarly, it is unjust to treat people the same if there are morally relevant differences between them.

However, the distinction between inequality and other kinds of differences is not quite as straightforward as might appear at first sight. This can be demonstrated by the following somewhat ambiguous comments of Friedrich Engels writing to Karl Marx in 1875 (as translated in Buzlyakov, 1973, p. 108):

> Between one country and another, one province and another and even one locality and another there will always exist a *certain* inequality in the conditions of life, which it will be possible to reduce to a minimum but never entirely remove. Alpine dwellers will always have different conditions of life from those of people living on plains.

There is an implication here that differences in physical environment will induce differences in how people live, manifest perhaps in what people produce and are able to eat, and whether they construct their dwellings from wood or stone. This is an obvious enough proposition for the geographer brought up on the relics of environmental determinism. But whether such differences qualify as inequality is another matter. They would, if the quality of people's diets or housing were inferior in the alps compared with the plains. But this is not what Engels seems to have in mind. He is referring to different ways of life, perhaps with different habits and customs as well as attitudes to food and housing: differences in culture to which it is hard to take moral exception. We are not referring to local moral codes which all but dedicated relativists might feel able to compare against some external standards, for example if people in the alps practised infanticide and those on the plains showed an unusual reverence for human life. We have in mind less weighty but nevertheless non-trivial differences in everyday human practice, like their material artifacts, their music, their courting rituals or sporting pursuits.

But, even in the realm of culture, the distinction between inequality and mere difference, between the moral and non-moral, is not made with complete certainty. Cultural superiority exists, as a human attitude, and this has moral content. We may dislike the music of others, thinking ours better: an aesthetic judgement, but one that can have moral undertones such as associating jazz or punk rock with bad behaviour and people. And we may even judge their courting rituals as immoral, if they do things to one another which we would not. As Jackson (1989) and others recognize, culture is an arena of conflicting values, in which people compete for the power to prescribe what is right, even normal. And this takes place at the interface of aesthetics and morality.

A society's dominant culture may be contested by those who prefer to behave differently, or who have no choice. They may not be able to afford access: Walzer (1983, p. 105) reminds us of Lee Rainwater's axiom that money buys membership in industrial society, in the sense of being able to participate in the prevailing norms of rampant material consumption. Those who are unable to conform, or choose to hold other norms, or in some way seem to threaten the prevailing order and its value system, may be marginalized from the mainstream and even physically contained or excluded.

Anthropologists have identified various forms of exclusion of particular people at particular times, as part of the ritual of small agrarian or hunter-gatherer societies (e.g. at puberty, coming of age or bereavement), as well as of individuals whose appearance or behaviour fails to fit some prescribed norm. This also applies to the treatment of some of those identified or labelled as deviants or dangerously different in more 'advanced' societies today. As Sibley (1988, p. 410) has remarked: 'there are many recent instances of collective action against groups who appear to threaten the perceived spatial and social homogeneity of localities, whether the threat comes from ethnicity, sexual orientation, disability or life-style.' He sees this process as similar to the purification and cleansing rituals of more 'primitive' societies.

This can be illustrated by the case of the AIDS 'epidemic' thought to be associated with homosexuality, one early response to which was to suggest that those afflicted be confined to separate living areas so as not to infect others; spatial exclusion would also reinforce a view of heterosexuality as the norm, in response to the prevailing 'moral panic'.

This kind of practice may be self-reinforcing: 'once initiated, the many "mainstream" fears and prejudices regarding certain "outsider" groups often feed into concrete social practices through which distinctions between these "mainstream" and "outsider" peoples are *reproduced* and even rendered more acute' (Philo, 1989, p. 259). There is a specific, socially constructed conception of normal and acceptable conduct, conformity to which assists its reproduction. The mentally ill are special victims of spatial exclusion (Taylor, 1989), and particularly unwelcome when 'released into the community' as the jargon of contemporary social policy describes it. Some people with unusual physical characteristics may be subjected to similar exclusion, in an environment not built with their different needs in mind, in a society which defines them as 'disabled' or even abnormal.

The point of all this is to emphasize the moral dimension to aspects of differentiation which do not fall within the usual ambit of distributive (in)justice and its underlying concern with (in)equality. It is also to reassert some elements of the earlier discussions of membership, and the impartiality with which people are supposed to be treated once they are included. There is a strand in contemporary thought associated with postmodernism which celebrates human variability; dominant cultures are accused of suppressing or denying difference. For example, the conventional conception of community represents an urge to see people in unity with one another, to value and enforce homogeneity, which often operates to exclude or oppress those experienced as different 'others' (Young, 1990a, pp. 227–9, 234; see chapter 4). Such differences need not have strong or indeed any overt moral content, but tend to assume it in the process of separation from the mainstream, and hence become relevant differences insofar as the actual distribution of society's benefits and burdens is concerned. The treatment of people defined as disabled (physically or mentally) provides important insights into a society's construction of normality, and its response to those deemed different.

As we now proceed into the rather abstract realm of theories of social justice, we will require further reminders of the need for sensitivity to difference, as part of any thorough concern about inequality.

3

Theories of Social Justice:
(i) Mainstream

Through contact with other societies, people come to realize that social arrangements are not a natural phenomenon but a human creation. And what was made by human beings can be changed by human beings. This realization sets the stage for the emergence of theories of social justice. For a theory of social justice is a theory about the kind of social arrangements that can be defended.

In Plato's time as in ours, the central issue in any theory of social justice is the defensibility of unequal relations between people.

Brian Barry, *Theories of Justice* (1989)

The point has now been reached for a review of alternative theories of social justice. The purpose is to identify the main features of the most influential current perspectives, that is, those which attract affiliation and intellectual interest today. To describe them as alternatives is not quite correct, as there are common features at least to some of them. But each of the perspectives considered makes its appeal to a different source of authority, to different higher-order values. Each theory therefore has something to say about what matters most in life, as well as addressing the specific issue of social justice which itself may be what matters most.

The task of comparative theoretical analysis is described as follows, in the introduction to a collection of readings on economic (we would say social) justice (Arthur and Shaw, 1991, p. 1):

The problem of economic justice can be expressed with remarkable simplicity: On what basis should economic goods and services be distributed? Answers to this question, however, are as numerous as those to any important philosophical issue. Some (libertarians) believe that the operation of a free market guarantees justice. Others (utilitarians) hold that the needs or interests of people should be of primary concern. Still others look to how much is deserved, as measured by

Theories of Social Justice: (i) Mainstream   53

labor time, effort, or contribution, as the basis for distribution. Equal distribution, since it seems to reflect the common humanity shared by all, is also viewed by many to be the core of economic justice. The philosophical problem is to decide which among these and other positions is in fact superior, and to give reasons for one's conclusions that will convince others.

This chapter and the one that follows seek to identify the more persuasive or less convincing features of different perspectives. The possibility that there may be a superior position will be reserved for chapter 5. In the meantime, we should bear in mind the warning of another reviewer: 'There has been an explosion of interest in the traditional aim of finding the one true theory of justice, but the result of this explosion has been to make that traditional aim wholly implausible' (Kymlicka, 1990, p. 4).

How, then, to structure the discussion? Various possible classifications of theories could be adopted. For example, a distinction can be made between *teleological* theories, which prescribe what is right in pursuit of some ultimate goal, and *deontological* theories, which rest on convictions as to the rightness of acts in themselves (Campbell, 1988, p. 46). Barry (1989, p. 374) reduces the task of justifying inequality, on the assumption that it is 'the product of human convention and not underwritten by any deep natural or metaphysical inequality between human beings', to two general approaches: one based on constraining self-interest for mutual advantage, the other on what would be acceptable from the standpoint of impartiality. However, we need something easier to impose on the range of perspectives of interest, and follow closely but not exactly the categories adopted by Kymlicka (1990). Readers faced with some unfamiliar '-isms', adding to those which already clutter the geographical lexicon, should understand that the terms of common usage adopted here are merely convenient shorthands for the sets of ideas within which there can be considerable diversity.

Some caveats must be stated at the outset. What follows here and in chapter 4 is not comprehensive with respect to the range of perspectives covered. For example, we omit the work of game theorists, to which Brian Barry devotes such considerable attention despite finding them more sophisticated technically than philosophically (Barry, 1989, p. 139). Nor can each of those selected be done full justice; summaries of a few pages inevitably involve simplification, as well as concentration on a few crucial texts. The length constraint of this book is the only justification for what might otherwise be considered unreasonable and possibly hazardous brevity. We try to capture the essence of each approach, leaving further reading to fill in some detail: this can include more thorough reviews of alternative perspectives (Brown, 1986; Campbell, 1988; Kymlicka, 1990) and also broad collections of selected readings (Arthur and Shaw, 1991; Kymlicka, 1992;

or for more classical content Solomon and Murphey, 1990; Combee and Norton, 1991). We try to keep the geography in view, if not always up-front, but to be spatial is not a major preoccupation of this review.

The division into two chapters, dealing respectively with what might be considered mainstream approaches (this chapter) and reactions to them (chapter 4), should not be regarded as a rigid or even particularly significant distinction. Similarities between them may be as important as the differences.

Egalitarianism

The obvious starting point is the possibility that the principle of equal distribution, along with the specification of such institutions as will ensure this outcome, is all we need by way of a theory of social justice. Some support for this position has already been provided, in the discussion of human rights in the previous chapter. To be required to justify *in*equality carries strong implications that equal treatment is what we are entitled to expect, as the natural point of departure before relevant differences among people are allowed to assert differential claims. It should also be borne in mind that the rich and otherwise powerful members of society, with most to lose from egalitarianism, often have the greatest capacity to publicize their view and to try to persuade others, especially in these days of expensive mass media; it would not therefore be surprising if arguments for an equal or more equal distribution were muted in everyday discourse. The egalitarian case may thus deserve more attention than it gets.

That the terms equality and equity are easily conflated and confused reflects a long-standing link between justice and equality, expressed vividly in the context of rights (Vlastos, 1984, p. 41):

> The close connection between justice and equality is manifest in both history and language. The great historical struggles for social justice have centred about some demand for equal rights: the struggle against slavery, political absolutism, economic exploitation, the disfranchisement of the lower and middle classes and the disfranchisement of women, colonialism, racial oppression.

Equality is taken for granted in some spheres of life, in most parts of the world, as of right. However, the broader case for equality can be made most powerfully not by reference to rights but by recognizing the difficulty of finding moral justification for unequal treatment.

The accident of birth, to whom, when and where has a major bearing on individual life chances, yet there can surely be no moral ground for such an outcome: a matter of chance, over which people have no control. The inheritance of wealth or social status (like a title) is not entirely indefensible as a social practice, and hard to take away if enshrined as a legal right, but it does not follow that the individuals concerned deserve their advantage. The same could be said of natural aptitudes such as physical strength, dexterity or intelligence, which, again, can be viewed as the results of some natural lottery. It could also be argued that advantages derived from early socialization, such as learning to value education in a home full of books, carries no greater moral approval than those derived from biology. Thus, occupational differences arising from a combination of natural aptitudes, a good education and a supportive home life would not justify any inequality in remuneration: the doctor deserves no more than the unskilled labourer.

There is an important geographical point to all this. The advantages some people get from being born somewhere with bountiful natural resources or an advanced social and economic environment, with first-rate schools, hospitals and so on and plenty of well-paid jobs available, are difficult if not impossible to justify morally. It could be argued that the local infrastructure has been built up by the efforts of people in the past, in part to benefit the present generation, and that this is something to which they are therefore entitled. But how did local advantage arise in the first place? If in the natural resource base, then this is surely morally irrelevant, purely a matter of luck unless the possibility of a land of milk and honey bestowed on God's chosen and deserving people carries conviction. They could have worked harder than others blessed with the same resources, but from whence did their superior capacity or inclination for work come if not from morally irrelevant natural or socially acquired attributes? And even if local advantage can be justified by some moral argument, are the fortunate right to keep other people out (e.g. controlling immigration) so as not to lose their benefits to the equalizing force of free population movement?

A possible response to the problem of inequality of fortune is illustrated by the argument of Rakowski (1991) that no one should have fewer resources or opportunities than anyone else, when such discrepancies are the result of ineluctable chance events beyond the control of individuals. People ought therefore to start life with an equally valuable bundle of resources, including not only material goods but also physical and mental capacities. Furthermore, justice requires redistribution to maintain this equality over time. However, there are also some obvious difficulties. One is the purely practical problem of equalizing and maintaining the equality of morally irrelevant conditions from which advantages arise, or of compensating people for the attributes they lack and for which muscle or brain transplants are not feasible (or ethical). Social policy directed towards equal opportunities is the usual response, for example ensuring education or training without reference to social or geographical origin, though such aspirations are frequently subverted in practice by the tendency of those initially and fortuitously advantaged to ensure institutions capable of perpetuating their privilege.

Another problem is that it is by no means obvious what equality actually means in some practical contexts. This is sometimes explained with reference to the distinction between resources and welfare (e.g. Arneson, 1989), or between inputs and outputs (or outcomes). To equalize *inputs* means, for example, spending the same on education, whoever and wherever people may be, so as to ensure equal opportunities to be educated and to enjoy the benefits to be derived therefrom. But this may not ensure equal *outputs*, in the sense of the same educational attainment on the part of each individual, or school, because other things will be involved such as the intelligence or motivation children bring to school and the kind of homes they return to. To try to ensure equality of outputs, or pupils' capabilities, will usually require unequal inputs. If the final *outcomes* can be thought of as the jobs obtained after school, or their levels of pay, or the ultimate happiness of those concerned, this may not be distributed in the same way as the outputs. Two schools may graduate children with identical attainment levels, but the local labour markets may offer different employment opportunities the equalization of which could require locally differentiated expenditure on economic regeneration, for example. Thus, alternative approaches can appeal to the same general idea of treating people equally, with possibly conflicting results.

A further difficulty with strict egalitarianism, and the one with most weight in the scales of social justice, is that it is possible to find morally defensible ground on which to treat people uneqally. This was implied in the previous paragraph: to achieve equality in a certain respect may require inequality in another. Thus: 'It is as unjust to treat unequals equally as it is to treat equals unequally. The problem is to decide what differences are relevant' (Ginsberg, 1965, p. 66), as we recognized in the previous chapter. Here we introduce the grounds usually accepted as relevant differences; they will feature in subsequent discussion of various theoretical perspectives.

A false start helps to explain that things are not straightforward. People's ability, effort and contribution to society might each be invoked as just ground for favourable treatment, but as Arthur and Shaw (1991, pp. 133–5) point out, the first two of these criteria soon take us back to the morally irrelevant, in that ability to do certain kinds of work, hard and well, may simply reflect natural aptitude or environment. Furthermore, the more able can be lazy and therefore judged less deserving. As to effort, it is hard to think how my effort composing these paragraphs could be compared with that expended by a surgeon saving a life, a social worker sorting out a child abuse case, or a window cleaner braving bitter weather. And, appealing though it can appear, contribution is replete with similar difficulty: someone can write a profound novel or build a sturdy wall, but who can say which is the greatest contribution to society without refining the concept further?

Vlastos (1984, p. 44) introduces familiar, more convincing criteria in the maxims of: to each according to worth, need, merit and work, to which he adds to each according to the agreements people have made. *Worth* demands equal treatment if we accept the equal worth of all people simply as human beings, but to be more 'worthy' than others in some sense could be held to justify receiving more of something, if only respect. *Need* could also raise egalitarian expectations if people are held to share common needs by virtue of their common humanity (a matter to which we will return in chapter 5), but need also provides grounds for unequal treatment, according to unequal need: more health care for the sick, more educational expenditure on the ignorant, more police in high-crime neighbourhoods, expressed in spatially differentiated levels of resource allocation, are familiar examples. *Merit* implies some other qualities on which people can be graded, with respect to the performance of some role with special skill or dedication, overcoming unusual difficulties, beyond the call of duty and so on, justifying additional remuneration sometimes referred to as merit payments. *Work* is unequally paid according to what people do and how well they do it ('the rate for the job'), although whether people really get what they deserve from their labour is a matter of some controversy (as will be shown in chapter 4). *Agreements* people have made, and according to which they could be treated unequally, would include various forms of legal or social contracts among individuals and groups, although the question of (in)equality in bargaining power will arise in any attempt to deem the outcome of ostensibly free agreement as just.

All these claims to unequal treatment are underpinned by the broader concept of *desert*. Indeed, the notion of people getting what they deserve, in some sense, is deeply implicated in both theories of social justice and people's common-sense understanding of distributional issues (Miller, 1991, 1992).

Another way of looking at departures from equality is to ask about their purpose, or functional value to others or to society at large. In an earlier discussion (Smith, 1977, pp. 137–40), it was suggested that *survival* and *efficiency* are objectives which could transcend the egalitarian claims of equity, with survival having the strongest imperative. In early societies the hunters on whose prowess the tribe depended for food might have had a special claim, as did those thought to be able to ward off evil spirits. Certain roles performed in contemporary society, for example by monarchs, generals, scientists, priests and (however implausibly) politicians, may have special claims recognized on the grounds of contribution to society's on-going reproduction if not to survival in a physical sense. Efficiency, or getting the most out of limited resources, can justify incentives, which may simply be reflected in people's pay (e.g. piece rates), but which may also comprise other benefits designed to attract people to fill demanding roles (e.g. various privileges of the bureaucratic elite under socialism). The essence of claims grounded in either survival or efficiency is that unequal treatment is justified by contribution to the common good. Indeed, perhaps the most powerful moral ground for inequality is that everyone gains from it: a proposition to which we will return.

We may now move on to other theoretical perspectives, in which the possibility, or certainty, of unequal treatment is defended. But before proceeding it should be recognized that they may still contain elements of egalitarianism. Indeed, Kymlicka (1990, p. 4) follows Ronald Dworkin in claiming that every plausible theory has the same ultimate value, which is equality. By this is not meant strict equality in the sense of an equal distribution of some bundle of goods or even resources and opportunities. It is more a case of theories of social justice all doing what egalitarianism requires of governments: that they treat each person (citizen) with equal consideration, concern and respect. It is putting substance to this requirement, specifying what is so good that it should be distributed equally, that differentiates theories of social justice. As Kymlicka (1990, pp. 43–4) puts it:

> In deciding which particular form of equal treatment best captures the idea of treating people as equals, we do not want a logician, who is versed in the art of logical deduction. We want someone who has an understanding of what it is about humans that deserves respect and concern, and of what kind of activities best manifest that respect and concern.

That each matters equally, at least in these ways, resonates with the tradition of human rights and impartiality, without assailing contemporary calls to give due regard to difference. This sense of equality provides a bench-mark against which to evaluate any theory of social justice, along with considerations of the likely degree of inequality in a more specific sense, such as distributional outcomes, that the theory in question would countenance.

Utilitarianism

Bernard Williams (1985, p. 92) has described utilitarianism as 'the most ambitious of extant ethical theories'. Its origins are to be found in the work of the eighteenth-century philosopher and social reformer Jeremy Bentham and his nineteenth-century successor John Stuart Mill (see Mill, 1863). Utilitarianism was a radical doctrine when introduced: a challenge to the prevailing beliefs in divine will, aristocratic authority and superstition as the principle guides to how people should act. It still has its followers, and is deeply implicated in some contemporary understandings of economic affairs.

Utilitarianism goes well beyond the issue of social justice, to incorporate a full moral theory or scheme for living and judging life. Succinctly defined, utilitarianism is 'the theory that the only sound, fundamental basis for normative (or moral) appraisal is the promotion of human welfare' (Lyon, 1984, pp. 110–11). Other terms may be substituted for welfare, and take on special meaning in some versions of utilitarianism: the most common are pleasure, happiness, utility and well-being. Thus, 'the utilitarian appeals to the sentiment of generalized benevolence, and speaks to others who feel this sentiment too and for whom it is the over-riding feeling' (Smart, 1978, p. 106). This is quite a challenge, in a far from benevolent world.

Utilitarianism finds application in broad arenas of human life as well as guiding individual conduct. These include political and economic institutions and public policies, as well as entire social structures. A distinction is made between *act utilitarianism*, which concerns the direct link between an individual action and the good it generates, and *rule utilitarianism*, which concerns the rules or institutions people devise and which mediate between action and their welfare consequences. Someone with a utilitarian disposition may act to promote immediate welfare by helping an old person cross the street, for example, or they may behave according to such rules as reciprocity or market exchange to produce the best eventual welfare outcome.

Preoccupation with a well state of humankind as the ultimate good, towards which all activities should be directed, makes utilitarianism a teleological as opposed to deontological theory (as explained above). Another way of putting it is that utilitarianism is *consequentialist*, with acts judged by their good or bad consequences; they are instrumental or means in the promotion or otherwise of human welfare or well-being.

Utilitarianism reflects the moral principle of equal concern in requiring *impartiality*, giving the same weight to each person's welfare and asking each to consider everyone else equally with themselves in deciding what to do. As we shall see, utilitarianism has a strong egalitarian streak, in both its formulation and expected outcomes.

A further important property is the exhortation to *maximize*. This is not to seek the greatest good of the greatest number, as Bentham once put it, for it is impossible simultaneously to maximize these two things. It is to achieve or promote as much aggregate or total good as possible, subject to some constraint such as personal budget or society's available resources.

In classical utilitarianism what was to be maximized was pleasure, or the absence of pain. These are properties which all people would wish to have, and in as great a quantity as possible. But the hedonistic implications of the single-minded pursuit of individual or even collective pleasure are not universally appealing. And it has even less appeal when Nozick (1974, pp. 42–5) and others point out that pleasure might be maximized by being hooked up to a machine designed for this purpose; real possibilities include drugs providing states of euphoria, and children of the affluent society continually engaged in a computer game while parents provide the life-support system.[1] Pleasure is clearly not all that matters in life. The concept of happiness, as an individual state, is less loaded with hedonism, and this term is usually preferred to pleasure. Another possibility is to think of all valuable experiences, within which some would include the aesthetic and creative.

More contemporary versions of utilitarianism are closely related to neo-classical economics and its welfare theory. The focus here is on individual (consumer) preferences, the satisfaction of which yields *utility*. People act so as to get as much utility as possible from their limited resources, within the general structure of market exchange. While this notion is often confined to commodities acquired by spending money, it is in principle capable of generalization to all things from which people derive satisfaction, positive or negative, even interpersonal relations (as attempted in Isard et al., 1969; see also Smith, 1973b, pp. 57–8). The aggregate of individual utility is *welfare*, which is what society is supposed to maximize.

Horrendous problems accompany the concept of utility, recognized in modern texts on welfare economics (e.g. Johansson, 1991) and examined in a geographical context by Smith (1977, chapter 3). The most obvious is the unreality of the behaviour postulated: real human beings simply do not engage in precise calculations of how to maximize their satisfaction through an intricate set of trade-off possibilities. One of the reasons is that, while the cost of many things people value can be compared via the common measuring rod of money, this is not necessarily the same as the satisfaction people get from their consumption, which may yield a surplus well above the cost (e.g. if they get a bargain). The difficulty of actually measuring utility is compounded when moving beyond market transactions: that all things from which we derive satisfaction are somehow commensurable, capable of expression in some common unit, is clearly implausible, for real-life experience is made up of diverse, irreducible elements. Other problems arise with the interpersonal comparisons of utility required to aggregate individual experience into collective welfare, which need not detain us here (the literature of welfare theory provides extensive coverage).

There are also problems inherent in the concept of preferences. The idea of satisfying those preferences that yield greatest individual utility runs into difficulty with certain special relationships, such as those with people closest

---

[1] I am grateful to Michael Smith for this idea.

to us or to whom we otherwise have an obligation. For example, we may get more satisfaction from spending money on our family or on further high living than from paying off our credit card debt. Some people may have strong preferences for things which harm them, addictive substances for example, and it is hard to allow their indulgence the full weight demanded by individual equality: indeed, we may want to deny them any weight at all. Recognizing everyone's preferences and giving them equal weight could also require concessions to people who hate blacks, enjoy inflicting pain, or have other evil inclinations, though racists are easily dealt with by showing that their preference for treating certain other people in an inferior way conflicts with the impartiality required of utilitarianism.

These kinds of difficulties may be addressed by confining the concept of preferences to those deemed 'rational' or 'legitimate', and excluding those considered narrowly selfish or simply bad, although this risks prioritizing a particular way of life. This leads to the notion of external preferences, for what others should have or do (like not consuming narcotics or like having a good education), as opposed to internal preferences relating to our own lives. Closely related is the generation of externalities (external effects), whereby satisfying one's own preferences can have an impact on the (dis)satisfaction of others, 'passive smoking' being an obvious example. Externalities are a specifically geographical problem, as they often arise simply from the proximity of people with conflicting preferences.

Utilitarianism has some difficulty with the question of membership, raised in the previous chapter. One possible answer as to who is to count is everyone affected by the act, policy or whatever. To the classical utilitarian all are to count and no one more or less than anyone else. This implies everyone everywhere, including the future: 'The consequences of his actions stretch indefinitely into the future, and the happiness to be maximized is that of all sentient beings, whatever their position in space and time ... Distance in time is no more pertinent to utilitarian considerations than is distance in space' (Smart, 1978, pp. 112–13). This is a geographical point, with some profound implications, as Brown (1986, p. 28) explains:

> [T]he utilitarian cannot treat societies in isolation, for he cannot ignore the contribution one society could make to the welfare of another. Thus, according to some utilitarians, our society (any rich society) should organize so as to maximize its foreign-aid programme – for it is amongst the world's poor that the greatest increase in utility can be made for a given amount of resources.

World-wide repercussions and their extension into an infinite future undermine the practical plausibility of a utilitarian calculus. But recognition that utilitarianism has implications for the international redistribution of wealth provides a convenient lead into the broader question of distributive justice. There is an initial problem of some magnitude to encounter: 'The concept of justice as a *fundamental* ethical concept is really quite foreign to utilitarianism' (Smart, 1978, p. 106); all that matters is maximization. That this can conflict with egalitarian outcomes is obvious: the sum total of well-being can be increased by any act, policy or institution which increases the well-being of some people somewhere more than any associated losses to others elsewhere. Thus, one person's life might be sacrificed to provide organs to save the lives of more than one other without assailing the principle of equal concern (each life still counts for one). Similarly, we in a rich country are justified in taking resources from a poor country, as long as their losses are less than our gains in a calculation which gives the same weight to their interests as to ours. Such outcomes are hardly appealing to our intuitions about what is right or just.

However, all is not lost, in the sense of finding a more attractive conception of justice within utilitarianism. The maximization of some abstract good is a dubious moral imperative, if we hold that moral obligations are to actual people (Kymlicka, 1990, p. 34), so it might be better to appeal to something about people's actual experience, something empirical. This is what Hare (1978, p. 126) describes as 'that good old prop of egalitarian policies, diminishing marginal utility, within the range that matters, of money and of nearly all goods'. The concept of diminishing marginal utility is common-place in economic theory. It simply asserts the general observation that as we have more of something, each additional unit gives us less satisfaction or utility than the previous unit. Thus to the thirsty person the first drink may be bliss, the second very satisfying, the third merely pleasant, and so on, until the last one hardly satisfies at all (indeed, its impact may be negative, if 'one too many'). Similarly, a drink will give greater satisfaction to a person dying of thirst than to someone who has just imbibed as much as they wish.

The egalitarian redistributive implications were recognized by Pigou (1920, p. 89) in his early classic on welfare economics: 'It is evident that any transfer of income from a relatively rich man to a relatively poor man of similar temperament, since it enables more intense wants to be satisfied at the expense of less intense wants, must increase the aggregate sum of satisfaction.' Transferring wealth from rich to poor countries is an obvious analogy. But it is important to recognize that the reference here is to the means towards human happiness or well-being, not to the end state itself. Money, like drinking, is subject to diminishing returns in the form of satisfaction, but this is not true of happiness or well-being, which we always wish to increase and of which we can never have too much. Maximization of the end state in aggregate requires equality in distribution under conditions of decreasing marginal utility, for the aggregate can always be increased as

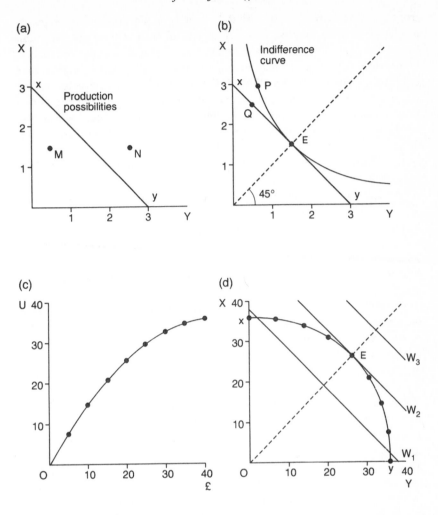

Figure 3.1   The egalitarian implications of decreasing marginal utility.

long as it is possible to redistribute means (like money) from those with less intense wants (the rich) to others with more intense wants (the poor). This is the real revelation of utilitarianism.

The implications can be illustrated in some simple graphic presentations. In figure 3.1a the axes X and Y represent two goods which a consumer can combine in various quantities. The units could be number of items, or the utility to be derived from their consumption. The straight line joining points x and y represents those combinations which exhaust the money available, and is the consumer's budget constraint defining the 'production possibilities frontier'. A utilitarian will not wish to have any combination of the two goods inside the frontier, such as point M, as this offers less than the maximum possible utility, nor can he or she aspire to any point above the line, such as N, because there is not enough money for this. But there will be indifference to all combinations along the line, as they all represent the same maximum. If the axes are now taken to represent two people, or the inhabitants of two places, a similar conclusion can be drawn: there will be equal satisfaction with any combination on the line. The utilitarian is not concerned about distribution; either X or Y could get all, or nothing.

Now, introduce the condition of decreasing marginal utility. The 'indifference curve' or 'welfare contour' in figure 3.1b represents combinations of X and Y giving the same total satisfaction or welfare under this condition. The curve is a curve, and convex to the origin of the graph, because at high levels of consumption of one good (e.g. of X at point P) the more of this we would be prepared to give up for some more of the other good. Or, substituting people or places: the more the one has, the more we would shift to the other to satisfy more intense wants. With the indifference curve exactly symmetrical, to treat X and Y the same, the only combination on the production possibilities frontier x to y satisfying the preferences reflected in the curve is point E: equality (i.e. a point on the diagonal line at 45 degrees to the axes, representing all equal distributions). All other points on the curve, such as P, are beyond the resource constraint. All other points on the line, such as Q, would generate less welfare than on the indifference curve.

The same outcome can be shown in a different way. In figure 3.1c the curve represents the decreasing increments of satisfaction (U) arising from successive expenditure of the same additional increments of money (£) on some good: that is, decreasing marginal utility. In figure 3.1d the various possible combinations of two goods with the utility generating characteristics shown in figure 3.1c are plotted. This can also be read as distribution among two places, X and Y. (That each of the specific combinations identified by a dot in figure 3.1d corresponds with the relevant quantities on the curve in figure 3.1c can easily be verified.) Now, add a family of indifference 'curves' W, representing successively higher levels of total utility or welfare (1, 2, 3); the fact that they are straight lines reflects the utilitarian claim that the distribution of the end state does not matter. Again, the combination satisfying the condition of maximization within the resource constraint is equality (E).

The egalitarian implications of utilitarianism are well recognized. For example, 'With just the assumption of diminishing marginal utility we can derive the conclusion that utility is most likely to be maximized if income is divided equally' (Barry, 1989, p. 176). And Smart (1978, p. 116) claims that in practice, 'the general tendency of utilitarianism may well be towards an egalitarian form of society'. Why, then, does this finding not rate more prominence in debates on social justice?

One answer is that an egalitarian morality or theory of justice is uncomfortable in inegalitarian societies, like those of the advanced capitalist world in which the doctrine of utilitarianism was devised and elaborated. But there is another reason, not unrelated to the first but more technical. This is that those strands of utilitarianism which were incorporated into neoclassical economics became submerged in an abstract formalism which did its best to eliminate the value judgements thought to impinge on distributive issues. This theory gave prominence to other features of a competitive, market economy: the free play of supply and demand was supposed to ensure the most efficient allocation of limited resources to the production of the combination of goods most highly valued by society, derived (somewhat mysteriously) by aggregating individual preferences. In addition to preferences for goods, society was held to have undefined distributional preferences, the satisfaction of which would involve the optimum distribution of the preferred unspecified bundle of goods. This is the formal state of welfare maximization. No further individual utility or collective welfare can be derived from producing anything different in any different way and for anyone else.

Once this state of equilibrium is established, the only change to be approved of (or 'welfare improvement') would have to conform to the famous *Pareto criterion*, whereby in the realm of distribution aggregate utility is allowed to increase as long as no one is made worse off as a consequence. Among other perverse outcomes, this would allow the rich to become richer as long as the poor were made no poorer. In other words, the maximizing stance of classical utilitarianism was preserved, but its egalitarian content yielded to a (re)distributional principle which tended to support the status quo in an unequal society. That the neoclassical welfare edifice rested on some highly unrealistic assumptions, as well as being undermined by the various problems associated with a utility calculus outlined above, was demonstrated decades ago by Graaff (1957) among others (see also Smith, 1977, in a geographical context). What is of particular concern, in the context of social justice, is the moral basis of a doctrine which appears to prioritize what people already have, and their right to retain and indeed increase it, even in the face of the dire need of others. It is to one possible explanation, and justification, that we now turn.

Libertarianism

What we mean here by libertarianism is sometimes prefixed by the adjective right, to distinguish it from the 'left-libertarianism' of some anarchists and socialists who stress the value of freedom. However, we shall not consider anarchism here, simply 'right-libertarianism', henceforth without the prefix lest right be construed from a moral point of view. It should nevertheless be recognized that some extreme libertarians of the right share with some on the left the view that the state can be dispensed with, though different conceptions of freedom are involved in the conclusion that people are best left ungoverned.

As the name implies, libertarianism prioritizes the value of individual *liberty*. Often taken to be synonymous with freedom, liberty invokes the ability to do what one wishes with minimal or no constraint. Thus, 'The individual . . . is to have a definite sphere of unfettered activity (or inactivity) where for anyone to interfere, and this includes the state, is to commit a wrong' (Brown, 1986, p. 87). This sphere typically involves personal private property. That such an arrangement claims an elevated social purpose is explained as follows by Hayek (1944, p. 78):

> [T]he system of private property is the most important guarantee of freedom, not only for those who own property, but scarcely less for those who do not. It is only because the control of the means of production is divided among many people acting independently that nobody has complete power over us, that we as individuals can decide what to do with ourselves.

Such a situation is usually associated with a capitalist or free-market economy, with very little state involvement.

Libertarians tend to view the free market as inherently just. Some, like Hayek (1944), stress the minimization of tyranny. Others argue the case on utilitarian grounds (e.g. Friedman, 1962): that the efficiency of such a system maximizes aggregate welfare. Both these perspectives are consequentialist, viewing the market as instrumental in achieving some greater good. However, we will examine a version of libertarianism which is grounded in certain rights all people are supposed to have, equally, recognition of which is held to be a fundamental moral value.

The best-known exponent of this form of libertarianism is Robert Nozick, whose *Anarchy, State, and Utopia* (1974) is one of the contemporary classics of political philosophy (for a fuller examination, see Wolff, 1991). Nozick (1974, p. ix) begins with the assertion: 'Individuals have rights, and there are things no person or group may do to them (without violating their rights). So strong and far-reaching are these rights that they raise the question of what, if anything, the state and its officials may do.' These rights concern the private ownership of resources and the freedom of owners to exchange, benefit from or dispose of what they own how they wish.

Nozick begins by examining anarchy, and concludes that people would agree that some form of state would be preferable but that it would be minimal. State activity would merely be to protect people from force, theft and fraud, to enforce contracts, and so on. It would not include the power to coerce some people to come to the aid of others, or to prevent people from doing themselves harm. This is not to be a 'nanny state', merely a 'night-watchman'.

Nozick then sets out an *entitlement theory* of justice. (The term entitlement theory is sometimes preferred to libertarianism.) People are entitled to what are described as their *holdings*, subject to the manner in which they acquired them originally or to the means by which they were transferred from other people. Thus (p. 151):

> If the world were wholly just, the following inductive definition would exhaustively cover the subject of justice in holdings:
>
> 1. A person who acquires a holding in accordance with the principle of justice in acquisition is entitled to that holding.
> 2. A person who acquires a holding in accordance with the principle of justice in transfer, from someone else entitled to the holding, is entitled to the holding.
> 3. No one is entitled to a holding except by (repeated) application of 1 and 2.
>
> The complete principle of distributive justice would say simply that a distribution is just if everyone is entitled to the holdings they possess under the distribution.

Any distribution is just, no matter how unequal it may be, as long as it arises from another just distribution (no matter how unequal that may have been) by legitimate means.

In addition to the principles of just original acquisition and transfer, a third principle is required: that of rectification of injustice in holdings, whereby past injustices with respect to how people came by their holdings are corrected.

The role of the state would be confined to the maintenance of the system required to facilitate the protection of property rights and the application of the principles involved in ensuring the justice of holdings, past and present. This would be the only rationale for exacting taxes. 'Taxation of earnings from labor is on a par with forced labor' (p. 169), so there is no case for the state using this means of financing welfare services, for example. People who might be in need of something other than their own holdings, or what they could obtain from their use or exchange, would have to rely on gifts or the voluntary charity of others. No amount of suffering on the part of some people is great enough to justify the involuntary transfer of holdings from those who are better-off, such is the strength of people's rights to their own holdings. In Nozick's term, they act as 'side constraints', to be observed absolutely not merely for the most part.

A geographical reading of Nozick's theory would stress the entitlement of territorially-defined groups of people to the resources of the land that they occupy, providing they came by it justly. Taxation for redistribution among regions or neighbourhoods of a city would not be allowed. Citizens of nation-states would be encouraged to view their resource base as theirs by right, with aid to people in poor countries an entirely voluntary matter without moral obligation.

How far Nozick's conception of a just society departs from more familiar notions of distributive justice is emphasized by the following elaboration (pp. 149–50):

> There is no *central* distribution, no person or group entitled to control all the resources, jointly deciding how they are to be doled out. What each person gets, he gets from others who give to him in exchange for something, or as a gift. In a free society, diverse persons control different resources, and new holdings arise out of the voluntary exchange and actions of persons. There is no more a distributing or distribution of shares than there is a distributing of mates in a society in which persons choose whom they shall marry. The total result is the product of many individual decisions which the different individuals involved are entitled to make.

This closely resembles the conventional textbook rationale for the imaginary free market of multitudinous autonomous individuals pursuing their own self-interest on the basis of the resources they happen to own. The emphasis on choice has a similar resonance with free-market rhetoric. Nozick (p. 160) actually enunciates the maxim of: 'From each as they choose, to each as they are chosen', to encapsulate the entitlement conception as competitor with other theories with different maxims of the same 'from and to' form.

In explaining the superiority of his theory, Nozick distinguishes three principles of justice, which he refers to as historical, end-state and patterned. His entitlement theory is *historical*, depending on how the present distribution came about, that is, from an earlier just distribution by means of a just process. The *end-state* principle is concerned with how things are distributed according to some structural consideration(s), such as maximizing the sum total of utility. The *patterned* principle involves distribution according to some such dimension(s) as need, merit or contribution to society. The historical principle is to be preferred because the 'past circumstances and actions of people can create differential entitlements or different deserts to things' (p. 155). Interfering with this history on the basis of a utilitarian conception or some supposed alternative criteria of desert is to perpetrate an injustice.

There are a number of strands to Nozick's underlying moral case for his entitlement theory, brief examination of which can expose something of their strength and weakness. First, and perhaps most implausible (given the degree of inequality which the theory would sanction), is an egalitarian argument, grounded in the Kantian conception of treating people equally as ends in themselves, not merely means, that is, they have inherent moral status. Thus, some people 'may not be sacrificed or used for the achieving of other ends without their consent' (p. 31), and this includes taking some of their money (by taxation) to aid others worse-off as this violates the rights of the better-off to the holdings to which they are entitled.

If this argument seems rather reified, Nozick offers a more intuitive defence of people's rights to sole benefit from their entitlements, unless they choose otherwise. He cites the now famous case of a star basket-ball player (Wilt Chamberlain), who would surely be entitled to an agreed share of the price of admission to watch him perform, on the grounds that the spectators would be freely parting with their money and he would be freely realizing the benefits of his natural talent. This appeal of intuition can be placed on a possibly firmer footing by invoking the principle of *self-ownership*. This extends the concept of ownership of material resources to the natural endowments of skill, strength, intelligence, and so on. Whereas it is often held that such outcomes of the chance of birth carry no moral weight as claims on the distribution of other benefits (see discussion of egalitarianism above), Nozick's view is that people are entitled to (have the right to) rewards derived from the exercise of such talents in just the same way as they may use and benefit from other holdings. And those born disabled, for example, bear the consequences. Referring back to his three alternative principles, Nozick (p. 172) claims: 'End-state and most patterned principles of distributive justice institute (partial) ownership by others of people and their actions and labor. These principles involve a shift from the classical liberals' notion of self-ownership to a notion of (partial) property rights in *other* people.' Thus, the disabled person seeking help from the sports star asserts the right to something, literally, of the other.

The concept of self-ownership, as elaborated by Nozick, has been subjected to thorough critique (e.g. Cohen, 1986a, 1986b), the details of which need not concern us here. It may be sufficient to refer to the argument of Okin (1989a) that, taken to its logical conclusion, the concept would require women, as producers of babies literally by their own labour, to have the right to dispose of their offspring as they choose. If we concede that men also have a part in this process of production, then parents would have property rights over their children, which contradicts the initial principle of self-ownership.

More practical difficulties face the ownership of non-personal attributes, such as land and other natural resources. If the present distribution is just, people's holdings must have been acquired by just means, but how far back should this be traced? Legal titles may have been transferred by legal means from one owner to another, but how was the property in question originally taken into private ownership? It could have been acquired by mutual agreement, even purchase, which would be just if we disregard the possibility of an unequal power relation between buyer and seller. But it could have been acquired illegitimately, by deception, fraud or force, in which case the principle of rectification would have to be invoked and the property returned to its original holders. It may have been acquired long ago, from people who had no conception of private ownership, perhaps holding land in common; restitution in such a case raises particular problems. That these kinds of issues are not merely theoretical is illustrated by actual, contemporary questions of entitlement to land in circumstances of earlier expropriation (as we shall see in the case of South Africa and Israel in chapters 8 and 9).

The original appropriation of the external, natural world seems rather a case of 'finders keepers' (Elster, 1992, p. 230). But Nozick attempted to address the problem by appealing to elements of John Locke's defence of the enclosure of the common lands in seventeenth-century England. Locke's basic principle was that everyone has an exclusive right to their own person and their own labour, including that portion of what God originally gave to all in common with which they have mixed their labour (Mackie, 1977, p. 175). However, private appropriation of something could be justified only where there is enough of it, and as good, left in common for the use of others. Thus, drinking from a stream is permitted, because there is plenty of the same left for others. Damming the stream and diverting it to irrigate our land to the exclusion of the use of others would not be justified. But there is a proviso, which strengthens the claims of those inclined to appropriate: that others may not actually lose from the process. An example would be if my irrigated land provided all the previous stream users with employment from which they derived at least as much income as before. The obverse, as Nozick (p. 178) put it, is: 'A process normally giving rise to a permanent bequeathable property right in a previously unowned thing will not do so if the position of others no longer at liberty to use the thing is thereby worsened.'

This sentence reads rather like the Pareto criterion explained above, in the section on utilitarianism, which justifies a change in distribution if some are thereby made better-off but none worse-off. How such a determination can be made is by no means straightforward. For example, those whose incomes are no less than before they came to work on my land may actually consider themselves worse-off than they were when on their own plots and in control of their own destinies. Not only does this approach suggest the kind of utility calculus which Nozick explicitly rejects, but it also risks undermining respect for people as ends: if diverting the stream has made my neighbours my employees, then they could be regarded as means to my economic ends. At the very least, their liberty has been constrained. Nozick's libertarianism is ultimately grounded in rights, not in liberty as such. The right of some to own property, once realized, clearly affects the liberty of others, whose freedom of action is thereby limited. So it is on the specific conception of rights that the moral justification for his entitlement theory must stand, or fall. This is a right of total control over oneself, personal attributes and property, as long as this does not interfere with the rights of others to do likewise. The negative emphasis must also be recognized, not only that people are constrained from interfering with others using their property as they wish, but also the denial of rights even to bare sustenance unless provided by people's own holdings (in the absence of charity).

It is the specific and narrow conception of rights that worries the many critics of Nozick's work. For example, Brown (1986, pp. 102–10) emphasizes the foundational (or deontological) status of these rights: they are good in themselves, rather than derivative (or teleological) in pursuit of some higher good. Nozick's side-constraints impose absolute limits on people's actions. Taken to its logical conclusion, this conception of rights could require us to respect the right of others to act in a manner which might cause a catastrophe, even inadvertently, as might be the case if the dam I had built across a stream burst and enveloped the village below. But as soon as we concede an overriding right to avert a catastrophe we introduce a consequentialist argument, about just how much suffering must be endured before property rights are constrained. As Singer (1991, p. 209) points out, Nozick refrains from stating whether his constraints may be violated to avoid a catastrophe; if he conceded the point, he would have to show how 'this thin end of the utilitarian wedge can be accommodated while resistance to other utilitarian considerations is maintained'.

Nozick's rights are highly individualistic, and based on a conception of human nature which is hard to accept. As Cohen (1991, p. 219) remarks: 'The people in his state of nature are intelligible only as well socialized products of a market society.' They can hardly be real people, living in real communities, depending on others, feeling compassion. Otherwise, the Wilt Chamberlain case could carry no conviction: not to tax a millionaire in order to help people in dire poverty simply does not appeal to the intuitive sense of fairness which must be part of any plausible theory of social justice.

Singer (1991, p. 201) underlines the obvious point that, if we reject the idea of independent individuals and start with people living together in a community, it is not obvious that rights should be restricted to those against interference with the freedom of others. Criticizing Nozick's appropriation of Kantian equality, he points out that Kant recognized that we have an obligation to help others. 'It can, indeed, well be argued that rational beings have rights of recipience precisely *because* they are ends in themselves, and that to refuse a starving person the food he needs to survive is to fail to treat him with the respect due to a being that is an end in itself' (Singer, 1991, p. 202). As he reminds us, the right to life is widely seen as a right of recipience, as well as a right against interference.

There is also the possibility that private ownership of resources may not be the form of 'holding' most likely to promote human freedom (Sterba, 1986, p. 25). It is not obvious why the right to exclude others is a superior conception of freedom to the right not to be excluded from the benefit of common resources. Collective or state ownership might actually enhance people's freedom, unless this is conceived very narrowly in terms of individual proprietorial rights.

For these and other reasons, the reaction of most contemporary moral and political philosophers is dismissive of Nozick's project. To Brown (1986, p. 110), his defence of libertarianism is ill-conceived, the individual rights with which he begins being given no real justification. Further (p. 99), 'Nozick's theory is essentially Utopian in the worst sense of that term: it has no practical relevance. Like the Garden of Eden before the Fall it can offer no insight into the problems of what we are to do here and now, since we are left ignorant of what principles are to inform our choices. The theory has application nowhere.' And to Elster (1992, p. 230), it has no implications for public policy. Even those who recognize a powerful moral defence of private property in Nozick's work tend to find his night-watchmen state too minimal a response to the regulatory and welfare needs generated by contemporary capitalism.

A final point is that libertarianism should not be confused with neo-conservatism, although both may be encompassed by the term 'new right'. Neo-conservatism, of the kind espoused during the Thatcher reign in Britain and the Reagan–Bush era in the United States, incorporates libertarianism in support of the (relatively) free market and in the rhetoric of reducing state interference in economic affairs. However, this creed is far from libertarian with respect to people's personal conduct, seeing itself as custodian of certain 'traditional' values and strongly disapproving of some 'non-conforming' life-styles. Thus the freedom of such people as hippies, travellers, atheists, homosexuals and even drug addicts would pose no problems for libertarians, providing that they respected other people's liberty and property, but they become targets for a form of authoritarian moralizing at the hands of neo-conservatives. Neo-conservatives may indeed enhance the state apparatus of social control, and in the process exclude some different others from full membership (part of the process of differentiation referred to at the end of chapter 2). Libertarians include everyone in principle, for everyone owns at least themselves. However, they are prepared to accept depths of depravity and deprivation which neo-conservatives would not permit, and which most others would judge as wicked or grossly unjust.

Contractarianism

The approach usually described as contractarianism (or contractualism) is concerned with the kind of agreement, or contract, people might reach in order to satisfy some conception of justice. A situation is postulated, usually a simplified abstraction of social reality, and a process of deduction derives the likely consequences in the form of some rule(s) of distribution or institutional arrangements. The conditions under which people are assumed to operate may reflect aspects of their actual character, such as a degree of selfishness, different natural advantages and bargaining power. They can also include moral values taken to be important in guiding the outcome. For example, the situation may involve acceptance of some version of the principle of universalization, such as everyone putting themselves in the place of others and seeing things from their point of view.

A simple example can ease us into this way of theorizing about social justice. The problem posed is how to cut up a cake on a school tea-table. On the assumption that the cake is small in relation to aggregate appetites (scarcity), that all pupils would like to get as large a slice as possible and will seek to achieve this (act selfishly), and that they will be prepared to accept some form of regulation (or government) instead of simply fighting over the cake, one possible solution is to give the job of cutter-up to a teacher taking tea elsewhere and with no personal interest in the outcome, who could be expected to give equal consideration to the interests of all pupils. Distribution is assigned to an impartial observer or arbiter, who could be expected to cut up the cake into equal slices – except perhaps if there was general acceptance that prefects deserved larger shares. Another solution would be to have a pupil cut up the cake, but insist that he or she has the last slice, which will be the smallest if the others act selfishly. The general principle in this case would be for the distribution to be sanctioned by whoever was likely to be worst-off, by virtue of last choice. While the outcome could be as equal as cake-cutting skill permits, this need not necessarily be so: the cutter might recognize the right of prefects to choose first and to expect a larger slice than others, and that it is prudent to make provision for this element of unequal entitlement. The point is to arrive at a distributional arrangement that all involved consider just.

Work in the social contract tradition has a long history, and considerable variety. The focus here will be on John Rawls's *A Theory of Justice* (1971), one of the most influential contributions of modern times. Robert Nozick (1974, p. 183), whose own theory summarized above was in part a critical response to Rawls, describes the latter's book as 'a powerful, deep, subtle, wide-ranging, systematic work in political and moral philosophy which has not seen its like since the writing of John Stuart Mill, if then ... Political philosophers now must either work within Rawls' theory or explain why not.' Bernard Williams (1985, pp. 77–8) describes Rawls's theory as 'the richest and most complex contractual account of ethics yet advanced'. While attracting extensive critical review, Rawls's book remains a source of inspiration and fruitful development today, not only within mainstream moral philosophy (e.g. Barry, 1989) but also in Marxism (Peffer, 1990: see chapter 4). The discussion here will be confined to the main elements of Rawls's theory and of the reaction to it; more complete examinations are provided elsewhere (e.g. Brown, 1986; Kymlicka, 1990; Kukathas and Pettit, 1990; see also the symposium in *Ethics*, 99, 1989; also the response to his critics in Rawls, 1993).

A few comments on the context of Rawls's work will set the scene. At the time he wrote his book, Rawls saw the field caught between the two extremes of utilitarianism on the one hand and intuitionism, with its plurality of first principles which might guide social justice, on the other. He sought an alternative to utilitarianism, and to any theory which subordinated the notion of right to that of good (i.e. the consequentialist position that what is right is so because of its contribution to some ultimate good such as utility). In short, he wished to establish social justice as right, independent of any conception of the good. He also sought a comprehensive theory which could structure different intuitions as to first principles or foundational values in social justice, resolving conflicts between equality, liberty, efficiency and so on by establishing priorities among them.

The circumstances in which a theory of social justice has to operate comprise two kinds of conditions. The first are the objective circumstances which make human co-operation possible and necessary (Rawls, 1971, pp. 126–7):

[M]any individuals coexist together at the same time on a definite geographical territory. These individuals are roughly similar in physical and mental powers; or at any rate, their capacities are comparable in that no one among them can dominate the rest ... Natural and other resources are not so abundant that schemes of cooperation become superfluous, nor are conditions so harsh that fruitful ventures must inevitably break down.

The second are the subjective circumstances of the people involved (p. 127):

> [W]hile the parties have roughly similar needs and interests, or needs and interests in various ways complementary, so that mutually advantageous cooperation among them is possible, they nevertheless have their own plans of life. These plans, or conceptions of the good, lead them to have different ends and purposes, and to make conflicting claims on the natural and social resources available.

The circumstances thus described, with some further elaboration, provide a setting in which people have to find some solution to the problem of resolving conflict over scarce resources, as self-interested individuals seeking to pursue their own versions of the good life.

As we have seen, the utilitarian solution is to require everyone to act so as to maximize utility or welfare, while the libertarian allows people to do as they wish with whatever they come to own legitimately as long as others can do the same. Rawls comes up with a quite different formulation of social justice, as something right in itself and not merely dependent on its good consequences, that is, a deontological as opposed to teleological theory. There are things which people find useful in pursuing their life plans, and justice is concerned with their distribution, arrived at by the structure of society and its institutions. The objective is not to maximize some ultimate, intrinsic good, but to distribute fairly. This 'justice as fairness' is ultimately the right thing to do. Rawls (p. 303) states his *general conception* of justice as follows:

> All social primary goods – liberty and opportunity, income and wealth, and the bases of self-respect – are to be distributed equally unless an unequal distribution of any or all of these goods is to the advantage of the least favoured.

This is knows as the *maximin* principle, because it requires the maximization of the conditions of those at the minimum. Not least among its attractions is an appeal to those common human intuitions which tend towards egalitarianism but recognize that some inequality may be justified, especially if society's poorest members are thereby made better-off. Thus, when assessing the justice of a society's structure and institutions, there is one simple and sufficient test: 'Does this set of institutions operate in such a way that the worst-off group – those who do least well out of them – could not do any better under any alternative set of arrangements?' (Barry, 1989, p. 216). If the worst-off could be made better-off by some alternative, even with greater inequality, then this would be more socially just. 'Injustice, then, is simply inequalities that are not to the benefit of all' (Rawls, 1971, p. 62). A natural duty of justice arises from respect for the 'equality between human beings as moral persons' (p. 19).

Equality is clearly seen as an initial expectation, departures from which are the subject of evaluation on the grounds of social justice. Further, the circumstances in which justifiable inequalities will arise involve co-operation among the parties, or social groups, so that any advantages going to one will assist the other. Initially, no one would have less than is possible in an equal division of social primary goods; 'when the fruitfulness of social cooperation allows for a general improvement, then the existing inequalities are to work to the benefit of those whose position has improved least, taking equal division as the benchmark' (p. 102).

The question of who are the worst-off would be answered by a specific income or social group, thought of as fairly broad segments of society. Rawls does not raise the possibility that they could be defined geographically, for example as the people of the worst-off region or city neighbourhood, but there seems no objection in principle. However, there is the complication that making those in the worst-off place as well-off as possible could conflict with the same objective with respect to the worst-off population group. And with different spatial scales, from local to international, similar problems can arise (for discussion of the international case see Barry, 1989, pp. 183–9; Peffer, 1990, pp. 404–12). There is also the fact that, whereas people may not be free to move out of their social class, if they are free to move from a poor area to a rich one and thereby improve their lot in life this may render a strategy of assisting the poor area redundant. Making the position of the least advantaged neighbourhood or region as favourable as possible thus gains validity as geographical mobility is reduced (Smith, 1977, p. 143).

Rawls's general conception requires further elaboration, with respect to the criteria relevant to deciding how well-off people are. To take income is an obvious possibility, but this is only one of the social primary goods to be distributed. People with the lowest incomes may not be worst-off in other respects. And it is possible that incomes of the poorest could be raised by inequalities with respect to other social primary goods; for example, by restricting their liberty so as to force them to work harder or to do things which would undermine their self-respect. Some refinement is therefore needed, which Rawls (1971, pp. 302–3) provides in the following principles and priorities:

First Principle
Each person is to have an equal right to the most extensive total system of equal basic liberties compatible with a similar system of liberties for all.

Second Principle
Social and economic inequalities are to be arranged so that they are both:
(a) to the greatest benefit of the least advantaged, consistent with the just savings principle [to ensure the position of future generations], and
(b) attached to offices and positions open to all under conditions of fair equality of opportunity.

First Priority Rule (The Priority of Liberty)
The principles of justice are to be ranked in lexical order and therefore liberty can be restricted only for the sake of liberty . . .

Second Priority Rule (The Priority of Justice over Efficiency and Welfare)
The second principle of justice is lexically prior to the principle of efficiency and to that of maximizing the sum of advantages; and fair opportunity [(a)] is prior to the difference principle [(b)].

This is how Rawls resolves possible conflict between basic values, the term lexical priority meaning that a prior principle must be fully complied with before a lower one is considered; in other words, one cannot be traded off for another. The three ordered priorities, by the names usually ascribed to them, are the *maximum equal liberty principle*, the *equal opportunity principle*, and the *difference principle*. Thus liberty comes before opportunity, which comes before the constraint on inequality, and only then may such other familiar considerations as efficiency or utilitarian welfare come into play.

Rawls arrived at this formulation as a result of a social contract, to which people are supposed to agree in certain specific circumstances. These constitute the *original position*, or state of nature, in which people are required to consider the social arrangements to which they would subscribe. Thus (p. 12):

Among the essential features of this situation is that no one knows his place in society, his class position or social status, nor does any one know his fortune in the distribution of natural assets and abilities, his intelligence, strength, and the like. I shall even assume that the parties do not know their conceptions of the good or their special psychological propensities. The principles of justice are chosen behind a veil of ignorance. This ensures that no one is advantaged or disadvantaged in the choice of principles by the outcome of natural chance or the contingency of social circumstances. Since all are similarly situated and no one is able to design principles to favour his particular conditions, the principles of justice are the result of a fair agreement or bargain. For given the circumstances of the original position, the symmetry of everyone's relations to each other, this initial situation is fair between individuals as moral persons, that is, as rational beings with their own ends and capable, I shall assume, of a sense of justice.

This original position is purely hypothetical, set up to facilitate thinking about social justice. Rawls's deduction is that, in this situation, individual self-interest would lead people to prioritize liberty, opportunity, and constraints on inequality reflected in the principle of the worst-off being as well-off as possible, in this order. Faced with the unknown possibility of being a member of the worst-off group (or a resident of the worst-off locality), they might well want perfect equality among groups (or localities), for this would mean that they were bound to be as well-off as possible. But if some inequality could make everyone better-off, this would be even better, even if they ended up the worst-off. The difference principle thus preserves the equal moral worth of members of a society, while not requiring equal outcomes.

The liberties with which Rawls is concerned are the kind of rights which would be expected to be distributed equally on the basis of citizenship of a liberal democracy: the right to vote and stand for office, freedom of speech and assembly, liberty of conscience and freedom of thought, freedom of the person and the right to personal property, freedom from arbitrary arrest, and so on (Rawls, 1971, p. 61). If not already assured, these would have the first priority. Equal opportunity is also familiar, though Rawls challenges the prevailing view that accepts unequal rewards for different occupational roles open on the basis of equal opportunity, by requiring them to benefit everyone. While liberty and opportunity come lexically prior to the constraint on inequality in Rawls's theory, it is the difference principle which has attracted most attention: it is this feature that departs most evidently from the way liberal democracy works in practice.

Some of the implications of the difference principle can be explored in the kind of diagrams used in the section on utilitarianism. In figure 3.2a, the line xy represents combinations of one or all social primary goods, as they could be distributed between X and Y, which can stand for groups such as social classes or the inhabitants of two different places (regions or neighbourhoods of a city). The point E, where the 45-degree diagonal intersects the resource frontier, represents an equal distribution. Any move from E as the initial position, to A or B for example, makes either X or Y worse-off than before, so the difference principle would require a return to E as this position is the only one which makes the worst-off (whether X or Y) as well-off as possible. So, without introducing any further considerations, equality must be the just solution. (It should be noted, in passing, that Nozick's libertarianism tells us nothing whatsoever about what would be just in this situation: anything goes, as long as it conforms to the criterion of holdings legitimately arrived at).

But suppose that more goods can be made available, so positions beyond

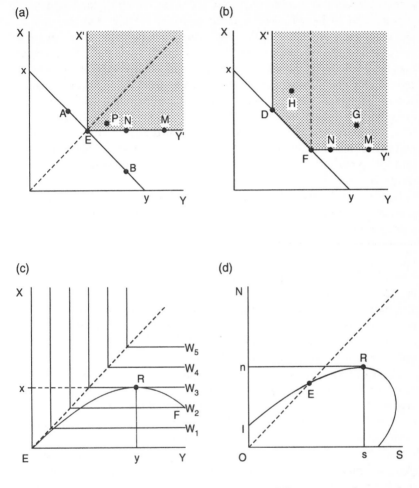

Figure 3.2   Aspects of the application of John Rawls's difference principle in simple situations.

(Source: (a) and (b) based on Smith, 1977, p. 152, figure 6.3 b and c; (c) based on Rawls, 1971, p. 76, figure 6; (d) based on Smith, 1977, p. 142, figure 6.2b).

the line xy to the right become feasible. Anywhere within the shaded area bounded by the lines X'EY' has the property that neither X nor Y would be worse-off than before (the lines of the L-shaped figure thus formed are simply constraints imposed by the original position E). Any move into this area would be a Pareto improvement (see above), as one or both parties would be better-off while neither would be worse-off. This would apply to point M and N where Y gains but not X, as well as to P where both gain but only slightly. However, whereas M would be much preferable to P in a utilitarian calculus in which X and Y count for the same, for the massive gain to Y at M would generate more aggregate welfare than the sum of the small gains for both at P, Rawls's maximin criterion would make P more socially just because here the level of the worst-off X is higher than at M. Indeed, the maximin principle is indifferent as to points N and M, for the increased inequality moving from N to M does nothing to benefit X: society gains nothing from the better-off becoming even better-off (see Johansson, 1991, pp. 32–3). Social justice requires whatever point within the shaded area makes the worst-off (X or Y) as well-off as possible. As Barry (1989, p. 227) explains it: 'The difference principle picks out the most egalitarian of all the Pareto-optimal arrangements satisfying the requirement that everyone should gain from inequality.'

In figure 3.2b, the original position F is set at something other than equality: Y is better off than X. This is the actual situation of real societies, arrived at by what is not necessarily a just process. As before, neither of the points M and N make X better-off, so would not commend themselves on the basis of the maximin principle. Anywhere in the shaded area above the lines X'DFY', such as G, could make the worst-off better-off, and this even includes such points as H where the worst-off has now become Y but where Y is better-off than X in the original position F (of which D would be Ys equivalent). Note that anywhere in the shaded area to the left of the dotted line vertical from F is better than the original F by the maximin criterion, but not by the Pareto criterion as Y has become worse-off than before.

The difficulty arriving at the single unique point of social justice in these diagrams arises from a failure to build in the interdependence of the two parties. By this we mean the fact that how much of the social primary goods is available for distribution depends on how much each party produces, within a co-operative framework which also influences how the total is shared. Natural assets and abilities, which Rawls sees as similar but not identical, may enable one party to produce more than the other, but the difference principle requires the total to be distributed equally unless inequality works to the advantage of the worst-off. This is illustrated in figure 3.2c, following Rawls, where E is the original position of equality. The curve ERF represents, in Rawls's terms, the contribution to X's expectations made by the greater expectations of Y. As we move up along the curve from E, inequality increases, but this is justified as Y's gains also generate (lesser) gains for X. The L-shaped indifference curves or welfare contours indicate increasing levels of social welfare away from the origin of the graph, after the fashion of conventional neoclassical analysis, their shape (as in figure 3.2a and b) being explained by the fact that society is indifferent to how well-off the best-off is as long as the worst-off is as well-off as possible. The worst-off X does as well as possible where the curve reaches the highest welfare contour, W_3 at point R. Here X gets x and Y gets y. This is the unique maximin position. It is not, as in utilitarianism, a matter of 'shuffling about a fixed stock of goods', as Rawls (1971, p. 77) puts it, but identifying that single distribution which makes the worst-off as well-off as possible.

Another version of this analysis may be explored, following an earlier attempt to work through the difference principle in a spatial context (Smith, 1977, p. 142). In figure 3.2d we take N and S to be two regions North and South. We introduce a resource frontier concave to the origin, of similar form to the curve in the conventional analysis (e.g. figure 3.1d), but of somewhat different shape: part of it slopes up to the right, to show that the position of N improves as S improves, and vice versa. This could be because additional investment in one region stimulates further production of social primary goods, and also promotes growth in the other as a result of trade or an inter-regional multiplier effect. In other words, in the left-hand part of the diagram, incentives for N to produce more have spill-over benefits for S, which is what Rawls has in mind with respect to inequalities making all better-off. Starting off from an initial point of inequality I, reflecting unequal resource endowment, N remains better-off until E (equality) is reached. Thereafter the advantage shifts to S, and a situation of the kind depicted in figure 3.2c takes over. The position R is the eventual socially just outcome, for here the position of the worst-off (N) is as high as possible. Any departure from this point in the direction of lesser inequality (to the left) or even greater inequality (to the right) makes N worse-off. The distribution n and s is socially just; anything other than this, including equality, is unjust by the maximin criterion.

This graphic analysis highlights contrasts between what the maximin criterion would sanction compared with a utilitarian conception, which permits some losses for the worst-off if the gains by the better-off are sufficient to increase total utility or welfare. It also underlines the interdependence of the position of parties under Rawls, and the rationality of the worst-off conceding to others some of the fruits of efforts from which all benefit. However, the difference principle and the original position from which it is derived are by no means uncontentious, and it is to the main lines of critique that we now turn.

Critics of Rawls challenge the idea of the original position, the conditions imposed, and the particular conception of justice which people are supposed to have chosen. The idea of an original position can be defended, as long as it is taken to be an intellectual abstraction to facilitate the derivation of principles of justice and not an historical state of nature or possible contemporary reality. However, there is the serious practical objection that in the real world the present initial position virtually everywhere is not one of equality, something to which we return in chapter 5. Clark (1985, p. 152) criticizes Rawls's failure to provide real geographical context: 'the original position is a very moral place. It is characterized by equality of position, material assets and individual rights.' The priorities supposedly arrived at from this position are understandable, but it is possible to think of situations where people might put basic survival needs before liberty: the right to vote or stand for office may be less important than food to someone starving. As Bloom (1975, p. 252) put it: 'The problems he addresses are those of civil liberties in nations that are already free and the distribution of wealth in those that are already prosperous.' In short, insofar as Rawls's theory is dependent on his original position, it is (geographically) relative, and Utopian to the extent that there is no indication of how real societies may reach this position.

The conditions assumed in the original position have also led to the criticism that Rawls implicitly favoured a liberal, individualistic conception of justice. Furthermore, he saw a liberal, democratic and market-regulated society as most likely to provide it. His people prioritize individual liberty, are motivated by self-interest in a stratified society rather than oriented towards community, and the nature of the social primary goods specified implies a particular life-style that has no special claims to superiority over others. As Brown (1986, p. 71) puts it: 'the original position, the characteristics of the people therein and the objects of choice specified combine to make the principles chosen liberal principles.' Rawls's intuition tells him that some form of liberal, welfare-state democracy under capitalism will be fair, and his principles tend to substantiate such a position.

Rawls concedes that he has, in effect, an intuitive sense of justice, which the original position reflects and which it generates as the difference principle. 'A conception of justice cannot be deduced from self-evident premises or conditions on principles; instead, its justification is a matter of the mutual support of many considerations, of everything fitting together into one coherent view' (Rawls, 1971, p. 21). He is engaged in a process of *reflective equilibrium*, whereby intuition or considered convictions about justice in real situations interacts with more abstract deliberations until they somehow cohere (p. 48). In other words: 'His principles of justice are mutually supported by reflecting on the intuitions we appeal to in everyday practices, and by reflecting on the nature of justice from an impartial perspective that is detached from our everyday position' (Kymlicka, 1990, 70). It is Rawls's personal intuition built into this process to which various commentators take exception. Rawls's own response has been, in effect, to reassert faith in liberal democratic institutions, that is, to convey his notion of justice as a political rather than metaphysical project (in the words of the title of a paper: Rawls, 1985).

Rawls (1985, 1993) sees a particular kind of society as capable of an 'overlapping consensus' of philosophical, religious and moral doctrines sustaining his particular conception of justice. He believes that this would enable us at least to conceive of how social unity and stability could be achieved, in a society marked by deep divisions between opposing and incommensurable conceptions of the good. The obvious problem, as Peffer (1990, p. 303) puts it, is that, 'even if such an overlapping consensus could be achieved under the conditions he outlines, there is not the slightest reason to believe that there is any presently existing society (or will be any society for the foreseeable future) in which all these conditions are met; i.e., in which all members of society – or even all major groups within society – accept all of the values that Rawls claims are part of 'our' democratic political culture.' As far as the present is concerned, even in what we take to be liberal democracies, Peffer's brutal realism is a simple empirical fact.

This leaves the question of whether people in the original position would actually arrive at Rawls's difference principle. Barry (1989, pp. 214, 411) points to the vast literature on the subject, and to the fact that no other aspect of his theory has met with such uniform hostility. It would be tedious to list all the objections and counter-examples; a selection must suffice. One claim is that people in Rawls's original position are unduly cautious; if more inclined to take risks they might not be so concerned with the state of those worst-off, hoping to be among the well-off in a highly unequal society. They might approve of a pool of cheap, exploited labour, if they thought their chances of being in it small and the prospect of taking advantage of it great. People in the original position might be prepared to agree only minimum subsistence for the worst-off, so as to discourage unproductive 'free riders' and to make more available to the 'hard toilers' (Sterba, 1986, p. 8). In any event, it is difficult to see how the highest possible level of living for the worst-off group in society is to be established in practice, if above bare subsistence, except by some political consensus in which the well-off may exert disproportionately strong, self-interested influence.

Some commentators claim that Rawls's procedure is not actually contractarian. There is no bargaining and calculation of a strategy to resolve known conflicts of interest, as in the usual game-theory formulations; it is more the case of what an ideal observer might arrive at, viewing society from the original position (Brown, 1986, pp. 64–5). Some critics have developed their own influential perspectives, following different versions of a social contract. For example, *mutual advantage* contractarianism works out the implications of differences in the bargaining power of people propelled by their own self-interest, constrained only by whatever advantages there may be in co-operation. This is exemplified by the work of David Gauthier (1986). People have no inherent moral status or duties to the disadvantaged, merely power to bring to a bargain. As Kymlicka (1990, pp. 131–2) sees this approach, mutual advantage may be the best we can hope for in a world without natural duties or objective moral values, but this provides not an alternative account of justice but an alternative to justice itself. We shall follow this uninviting path no further, simply recommending Barry (1989, Part III) for a fuller exploration of its relationship with the more familiar conception of justice as impartiality.

A more fruitful if by no means unproblematic alternative to Rawls's contractarianism has been provided by Ronald Dworkin (1981), who holds that what happens should be sensitive to people's ambitions. He makes their resources equal at the outset, while permitting them choices concerning their life plans – between productive activity and idleness, for example. People are supposed to accept the consequences of these choices, manifest in inequality, and not expect to be subsidized by others. But they would subscribe to insurance, at a level determined behind a veil of ignorance, against the unknown possibility of natural disadvantage such as physical handicap. A weakness attributed to Rawls's theory is that people are not rewarded for effort unless this benefits the worst-off, but are nevertheless able to gain from certain morally irrelevant natural advantage such as talent if this benefits the worst-off (e.g. Fried, 1983, pp. 45–6). Thus, 'the difference principle is both an over-reaction and also an insufficient reaction to the problem of undeserved inequalities. It is insufficient in not providing any compensation for natural disadvantage; and it is over-reaction in precluding inequalities that reflect different choices, rather than different circumstances' (Kymlicka, 1990, p. 85). The difficulty is arriving at some just balance between the outcomes of choice and circumstance.

The treatment of natural advantage or disadvantage leads us to a final and crucial element in Rawls's theory. This is a justification for the difference principle and its maximin criterion which operates independent of the device of the social contract, to which Barry (1989) has drawn particular attention. Rawls makes a distinction between natural assets and environmental effects such as social and geographical background, and identifies equal opportunities with the elimination of all factors except genetic endowment (Barry, 1989, p. 222). Natural advantage enables some people to be more productive than others, and to gain occupational positions carrying material advantage, but the consequent inequality can be justified only insofar as the disadvantaged also benefit. It may well be asked, as Kymlicka (1990, pp. 71–2) does, why Rawls confines his initial equality to social primary goods, rather than also including such 'natural primary goods' as health, intelligence, vigour, imagination and other natural talents which may be affected by social institutions if not actually distributed by them. This is the point that Barry (1989, p. 225) follows to its logical conclusion:

(1) the (liberal) ideal of equal opportunity is that all environmental differences that affect occupational achievement should be eliminated;
(2) this will entail that all remaining differences are of genetic origin; but
(3) if (as is assumed) the case for eliminating environmental differences is that they are morally arbitrary, all we should be doing is making

occupational achievement rest on genetic factors which are (in exactly the same sense) morally arbitrary; therefore (4), since what is morally arbitrary should not affect what people get, differences in occupational achievement should not affect income.

Rawls is clearly saying that '*everything* about the sources of occupational achievement is contingent and morally arbitrary ... there is no case at the most basic level of justification for anything except equality in the distribution of primary goods' (Barry, 1989, pp. 225–6). Rawls thus has a *prima facie* case for the justice of equality, without the device of the social contract. The difference principle could be regarded as a pragmatic concession to the reality that unequal incomes and so on can work to the advantage of all and especially of the worst-off. This second-best solution in the form of the difference principle should not, however, obscure the strength of the egalitarian content of Rawls's theory.

4

Theories of Social Justice:
(ii) Reaction

[I]t is a welcome aspect of contemporary theories of justice that in general they do strive to formulate ways of thinking which may enable us to stand outside our own inherited notions of the good society and help us to think creatively and purposefully about how we might move towards a better, perhaps a more just, form of social life.

Tom Campbell, *Justice* (1988)

The theories reviewed in chapter 3 originated within the liberal tradition of what we think of as western democratic societies, which tends to prioritize individual liberty while making gestures towards equality as a moral ideal. Impartiality is the hallmark of the application of reason to the problem of social justice in the abstract. In practice, this kind of theory confronts, and is embedded within, the institutions of modern capitalist society, characterized by highly unequal property relations and life chances which seek legitimation within the discourse of justice itself. This chapter reviews approaches which are in various ways critical of the liberal tradition, and of certain aspects of modern thinking. They also have different light to shed on central concerns of the previous chapter, in particular the case for equality and the tension between relativism and universality in social justice.

Marxism

Marxists tend not to have much respect for the institutions of liberal democracy. They may even hold the very idea of social justice in contempt. Morality itself may be viewed with suspicion and hostility, as a manifestation of an ideology or false consciousness which keeps people in their place as compliant members of an exploitive economic system and oppressive social order.

However, there is more to Marxism than these caricatures might imply.

Marxists have always been concerned with social justice, however obliquely, and there has been a surge of interest in the link between Marxism and morality in recent years (e.g. Buchanan, 1982; Lukes, 1985; Nielson, 1984, 1988; Peffer, 1990). Among other outcomes has been the realization that Marxism and liberalism may not be poles apart on some important issues. Once again, the treatment here must be highly selective. It will gloss over many points of debate among Marxists as to what the great man actually said, or intended to say, or might have said with the benefit of hindsight or access to the subsequent development of moral philosophy. The material covered here has been chosen to explore aspects of Marxism which address moral issues significant to social justice. We will conclude with a piece of work which finds common ground between a Marxist morality and the theory of social justice propounded by John Rawls.

Before proceeding, it is necessary to recognize certain basic features of Marxism, and of the historical materialism with which Marx is so strongly associated. A society comprises a particular *mode of production*, which consists of the *forces of production* (the physical or technical capacity to produce goods and services) in the form of the means of production and labour, and the *relations of production*, which concern how the productive forces are brought together in a social sense. The social relations of production comprise the base or economic (sub)structure which determines the superstructure of legal and political institutions. However, there can also be influences in the other direction: the superstructure can affect the relations of production (e.g. by laws which consolidate private ownership of the means of production), just as the level of development of the productive forces can be influenced by the relations of production (e.g. capitalist social relations may promote technical innovation and economic growth more effectively than socialism).

There is an historical sequence of modes of production, from early primitive communist societies governed by reciprocity, through slavery and feudalism, to capitalism, with socialism and eventually full communism supposed to complete the process. Under slavery the relations of production allow some people to own others, while under feudalism some (landowners) have special claims over the labour of others (e.g. serfs). With the advent of capitalism workers are free to sell their labour as they wish, but private ownership of the means of production sets up conflict over the value of what is produced. The change from one mode of production to the next arises from tensions or contradictions between the social relations of production and the level of development of the productive forces. Thus, for example, taking advantage of the technological progress associated with the Industrial Revolution required more flexibility in the use of labour than was permitted under feudalism. The struggle between mutually antagonistic class interests plays a crucial role in social transformation, culminating in the eventual overthrow of capitalism and its replacement by socialism.

This perspective on the structure of society and the course of history is positive, in the sense of claiming to be explanatory of the world. It is subject to the analytical test of whether it actually makes sense of society and of social change, and to the empirical test of whether what is proposed actually takes place, including the prediction of the final demise of capitalism, which has thus far proved to be false. But it is mainly the normative content of Marxism which concerns social justice. At the most general level is an assertion of the moral superiority of socialism (and eventually communism) over capitalism, and that the transformation of one into the other is desirable as well as (supposedly) inevitable from a scientific point of view. More specifically, there are certain features of any class-divided society, like slavery, feudalism and capitalism, to which moral exception is taken. Of particular concern are alienation and exploitation, and their association with the capitalist mode of production – explication of which was Karl Marx's primary concern.

We will examine briefly the concept of *alienation* first. Marxists argue that wage labour alienates people from their most important capacity, because it turns the worker's ability to labour into a mere commodity at the disposal of someone else. Furthermore, work under capitalism is often mindless and without any intrinsic satisfaction. People are alienated when their essential human capacities are thwarted, when they are prevented from realizing their potentialities, from fulfilling themselves as human beings. The creative process of work, of producing things, is crucial to human fulfilment or happiness, and this is frustrated by the wage-labour relationship. Alienated labour is not free in the sense of being self-determined by the worker, nor is it conducive to the establishment of genuine human community or self-realization.

This conception of alienation is sometimes described as *perfectionist*, claiming that certain ways of life constitute human excellence or perfection and are therefore to be promoted. Socialization of the means of production would be a way of achieving the freedom to work without alienation, for self-realization in harmony with others, rather than being used for the ends of some others (the employers). The perfectionist interpretation harks back to Aristotle and his concept of human flourishing.

As Elster (1985, p. 219) puts it: 'the ideal of self-actualization for Marx had an absolute, transhistoric character ... There can be little doubt that Marx throughout his life adhered to a quasi-Aristotelian ideal of the good life for man.' Communism would promote a society in which all (including women) could become fully human, fully realizing their potential as all-round creative beings.

Important as the concept of alienation is, and unpleasant as the actual experience may be, it cannot of itself provide satisfactory grounding for a theory of social justice. Nor can the condemnation of capitalism and the superiority of socialism or communism be argued entirely or even convincingly on alienation. Points against the concept itself include the fact that alienation is an individualistic experience, and that prioritizing satisfaction from work involves a rather narrow conception of the good life. Furthermore, to work as alienated labour may not be the worst thing in life; it may be better than poverty or starvation if these are the actual alternatives. And alienation in the sense of dull, repetitive work is by no means confined to capitalism: wage labour under socialism may be just as dehumanizing (as vividly described by Haraszti, 1977). So it is the other aspect of wage-labour relations – exploitation – that Marxists tend to emphasize in the critique of capitalism.

Like alienation, the concept of *exploitation* is by no means unproblematic, having provoked voluminous and on-going technical debates in Marxism and beyond. It is also far from straightforward as a concept with moral import, as we shall see. The notion of exploitation is closely connected with the labour theory of value associated with Marx and certain classical economists such as David Ricardo, which sees human labour expended as the ultimate source of all value. The value of anything made by people should reflect the quantity of labour necessary to produce it, including the means of production used up in the process (the product of past labour). However, the power vested in private ownership of the means of production enables those capitalists and landowners in this privileged position to appropriate some of the value of what is produced by those they employ (i.e. 'surplus value'), in the form of profit, interest or rent. Exploitation can exist in any class society (e.g. the slave-owner exploits the slave, the feudal landowner the peasant), but the primary concern in Marxism is with capitalist exploitation.

The point here is not to explore the validity of the labour theory of value, or the distributional implications of the extraction of surplus value, but to consider the morality of exploitation. That this is subject to different interpretations is itself revealing of some fundamental issues which arise in linking Marxism to social justice. We will by-pass the question of whether Marx himself was consistent in what he actually wrote (see for example the exchange in Geras, 1985, 1992, and McCarney, 1992), and concentrate on the general argument. The starting point is the relativist position often attributed to Marx, and to Marxism in general, that moral-ity and social justice are internal matters to specific societies or modes of production. This is enunciated by Friedrich Engels (1878, p. 666) as follows:

We therefore reject every attempt to impose on us any moral dogma whatsoever as an eternal, ultimate and forever immutable ethical law on the pretext that the moral world, too, has its permanent principles which stand above history and the differences between nations. We maintain on the contrary that all moral theories have been hitherto the product, in the last analysis, of the economic conditions of society obtaining at the time.

Thus, 'Marx thinks that capitalist exchange is just according to the relevant conception of justice [under capitalism] and that capitalist appropriation of surplus-value falls outside the field of reference of that conception altogether' (McCarney, 1992, p. 33). It is this narrow, legalistic view of justice, along with the supposed scientific status of historical materialism, which has encouraged the interpretation that Marx was not interested in morality except as an aspect of ideology or beliefs which function to make the oppressed classes accept their position.

However, while Marx does not actually describe surplus appropriation as unjust, he does refer to it in such terms as theft, embezzlement and robbery, which amounts to the same thing: to the invocation of transhistoric, non-relative normative standards. The way capitalists purchase labour-power under the wage contract may be just under bourgeois norms, in that they cover the value of labour-power as determined in the market place, but this level of surface appearances obscures what happens when labour is put to use, for it is able to produce something of greater value than what the workers in question are paid, and this surplus accrues to the capitalist. So, what appears to be equal exchange of money for work actually enables the capitalist to get something for nothing, the product of unpaid labour.

Now we come to what is perhaps the most interesting step in the argument over the morality or justice of the capitalist wage relation. This is that, if exploitation is said to involve capitalist expropriation of what actually belongs to someone else (i.e. is really theft), this implies some right or entitlement on the part of labour to the value of what it has produced. If this is not the same argument as is associated with the self-ownership thesis of Robert Nozick's libertarianism (see chapter 3), it comes perilously close. An economist similarly devoted to individual liberty as Nozick makes the point: 'Even the severest internal critics of capitalism have implicitly accepted payment in accordance with product as ethically fair' (Friedman, 1962, p. 167). He reads into the Marxian concept of exploitation the assumption that labour is entitled to the surplus value by virtue of the capitalist ethic of to each according to what they produce. Marx (1875, p. 387; emphasis in original) explains equal right as follows:

The right of the producer is *proportional* to the labour they supply; the equality consists in the fact that measurement is made with an *equal standard*, labour.

But one man is superior to another physically or mentally and so supplies more labour in the same time, or can labour for a longer time; and labour, to serve as a measure, must be defined by its duration or intensity, otherwise it ceases to be a standard of measurement. This *equal* right is an unequal right for unequal labour. It recognizes no class differences, because everyone is only a worker like everyone else; but it tacitly recognizes unequal individual endowment and thus productive capacity as natural privileges. *It is, therefore, a right of inequality.*

Marx is clearly asserting a right to the product of (morally arbitrary) natural attributes. Again, we can allow Milton Friedman (1962, p. 166) to make the point: 'The man who is hard working and thrifty is to be regarded as 'deserving'; yet these qualities owe much to the genes he was fortunate (or unfortunate?) enough to inherit.' Of course, Marx recognized this conception of equal right or payment by product as 'bourgeois right', which would eventually disappear under communism, but, as we shall see below, this takes us onto a broader level of social justice.

Shortcomings of the concept of exploitation are not confined to the inegalitarian and individualistic implications of payment according to product. Other problems include the difficulty of deciding who has actually produced what in a complex modern economy. There is also the fact that some of those worst-off under capitalism are not necessarily themselves the victims of exploitation; they may be unemployed, or wageless women working as housewives. And some who are exploited in the technical sense may enjoy high rewards and enviable life-styles which nothing could persuade them to swap for communism. A form of exploitation may even exist under socialism, according to some interpretations, with the state as brutal an expropriator as any capitalist. These and other complications have prompted some refinement and reformulation of the concept of exploitation (summarized in Kymlicka, 1990, pp. 169–83). While some Marxists still adhere to a classical version of exploitation as a canon of the critique of capitalism, others are now more inclined to see exploitation as an aspect of unfair advantage within broader distributional arrangements which include uneven access to resources in general and to the means of production in particular. This is a deeper injustice, of which exploitation is but one manifestation.

In place of bourgeois right, as reward according to labour contribution, Marx advocated distribution according to need. The obvious example is that a worker with a family needs more than a single person. He explains that rights cannot be higher than what is consistent with the prevailing economic structure and its level of cultural development. Thus the bourgeois right to be recompensed in accordance with contribution to what is produced will persist in the first phase of the society which replaces capitalism. Then (Marx, [Elster, 1985, p. 388]):

In a higher phase of communist society, after the enslaving subordination of the individual to the division of labour . . . has vanished; after labour has become not only a means of life but life's prime want; after the productive forces have also increased with the all-round development of the individual, and all the springs of cooperative wealth flow more abundantly – only then can the narrow horizon of bourgeois right be crossed in its entirety and society inscribe on its banner: From each according to his ability, to each according to his needs!

The fact that full communism was supposed to eliminate Hume's conditions of justice, by replacing material scarcity with abundance, and human selfishness by harmony, is another reason why Marx was not explicitly concerned with distributive justice. Creation of the ideal society, without even the need for a state, was sufficient in itself.

What Marx had actually proposed, however implicitly, was a conception of justice containing ordered principles. This is explained by Elster (1985, p. 230) as follows:

Marx had a *hierarchical theory of justice*, by which the contributional principle provides a second-best criterion when the need principle is not yet historically ripe for application. Capitalist exploitation is doubly unjust, since it obeys neither principle. The 'equal right' of the first stage of communism, is also unjust, but less so, since only the needs principle is violated.

Geras (1992, pp. 57–8) explains Marx's 'moral hierarchy' in slightly different terms, to stress its transhistoric character:

[C]ommunism will be morally superior to the historically transitional formation in which the labour-contribution principle prevails; which, for its part, will be similarly superior to all modes of production whose standards and practices have been exploitative. The judgement covers virtually all of recorded history, and some more yet to come (if it is actually to come).

Thus (Geras, 1992, p. 39):

Marx's work, whatever else it may be, and his disclaimers to the contrary notwithstanding, is an indictment of capitalist society in the light of transhistorical principles of justice (among other moral values); an indictment, that is to say, in the light of non-relativist normative standards, pertaining to the social distribution of benefits and disbenefits, resources and burdens.

However, the ultimate triumph of communism is not the end of the matter. Such a society has not yet come about, and if something like it did emerge from the collapse of capitalism it is by no means certain that Hume's conditions of justice would be eliminated. And if shortage and selfishness still prevailed, specific principles of distributive justice would be required. To have everyone contributing to the general availability of goods and services according to their ability, including personal advantages arising from natural attributes, is a fairly straightforward proposition (disregarding the issue of incentives), but the actual implementation of distribution according to need is much more difficult.

If a society were capable of producing no more than the basic necessities of life for its population, distribution according to need would be a simple egalitarian project. But even if it fell short of producing abundance, something better than bare subsistence would be a reasonable expectation of a communist society, especially if competing with the (uneven) affluence of capitalism for the moral approval of moderately selfish people. One response is to recognize the similarity, or identity, of people's needs, as human beings, and to distribute whatever there is equally so as to equalize people's material living standards, hopefully at a high level. But this assumes that everyone does have much the same need, even in conditions of moderate affluence. Recalling the concept of alienation, the needs principle could be interpreted as ensuring equality of self-actualization: 'If the highest value is self-realization ... it should be realized for each and every individual to the highest extent compatible with its realization to the same extent for everyone else' (Elster, 1985, p. 232). But there can be different individual routes to self-actualization, some of which may require more resources than others, unless the state is to decide for people.

This brings us back to familiar difficulties in comparing individual levels of satisfaction in a utilitarian calculus. For example, one person's self-actualization (akin to maximizing satisfaction) may require simple needs, another's the indulgence of expensive tastes. To try to confine consideration to 'reasonable' needs merely displaces the question to another level. Scarcity and self-interest make conflict inevitable, and there have to be means of resolution. Other issues include the extent to which the needs principle requires needs to be met which arise from informed but unfortunate choices (for example, to smoke), and people to be compensated for such natural disadvantages as extreme physical handicap (e.g. does it imply a right to the replacement of a defective limb?).

These and other difficulties with the concept of need have been debated extensively in the liberal literature on social justice (and we will have to return to them in chapter 5). But they appear not to have greatly troubled Marxists. Thus Kymlicka (1990, p. 186) concludes that 'the needs principle does not compete with liberal theories of equality, for it is simply at a less-developed stage of formulation'. This conclusion raises the possibility that an essentially liberal formulation might advance the cause of social justice built on Marxian foundations.

Such a project has been explored by Ronald Peffer (1990). His objective is to develop a moral and social theory which is informed by the spirit of Marx's radical humanism and egalitarianism, is based on empirical theses central to the Marxist political perspective and in particular on his analysis of capitalism, and is consistent with the basic normative position of the superiority of socialism. As a society characterized by abundance and unselfishness, without a state or any coercion, is unrealistic, the conditions of justice are bound to prevail. Therefore, 'Marx (and Marxists) need theories of social justice and/or human rights insofar as they are concerned to claim that socialism – as opposed to fully-fledged communism – is morally preferable to capitalism, and that the government of a socialist society has legitimate political authority to which the political obligations of its citizens correspond' (Peffer, 1990, p. 10). They must therefore 'face up to all of the problems found in traditional social and political philosophy' (p. 13).

An examination of the writings of Marx leads Peffer to the conclusion that, while he does not have a fully developed theory of morality, he does have a normative moral perspective. This is based on the three primary values of freedom (as self-determination), human community, and self-realization. Marx holds an implicit theory of right action or obligation that recommends the promotion of certain 'nonmoral goods' (as Peffer describes them, i.e. things that are desirable but from which people do not derive moral credit). So (p. 5):

> [H]e demands not simply the maximization of the primary nonmoral goods of freedom, human community, and self-realization but a radically egalitarian distribution of these goods (or at least the good of freedom). Further, he takes the nonconsequentialist notion of human dignity rather than pleasure, happiness, or human perfection as the ultimate court of appeal in moral reasoning.

Peffer (p. 46) construes this as a deontological position. Although the concepts of alienation and exploitation are central to Marx's moral perspective, they can be analysed in terms of the other 'more basic' values of freedom, community and self-realization (p. 35). Marx's notion of equal freedom is elaborated as follows (pp. 317–18):

> [H]e is committed to an equal distribution of freedom or, more specifically, to a maximum system of equal freedom, both positive and negative. Marx's concept of positive freedom . . . includes a right to equal participation in social decision-making processes and a right

to equal access to the means of self-realization, where the latter is best construed as an equal opportunity to attain social positions and offices and a genuinely equal opportunity to acquire social primary goods.

The negative rights concern the familiar constraints on undue interference. It is this commitment to social and economic freedom which leads directly to questions of distributive justice and human rights. Specifically, there is a need for a theory relating to the distribution of the benefits and burdens of social co-operation.

An examination of the work of John Rawls leads Peffer (pp. 364–5) to the view that 'his theory is essentially correct and that under the impact of egalitarian consistency and even a minimal set of Marxist empirical assumptions, it will justify the Marxist's basic normative political positions'. Similarities between the views of Marx and Rawls include the fact that they both are: concerned with evaluating basic social structures, aware of the importance of social institutions, aware that in all societies up to now an individual's life prospects are almost totally shaped by a natural and social lottery, contend that social structures and conditions should be subject to conscious control, are committed to the notion of human dignity and individual worth, and are egalitarian but reject the possibility of strict equality. Differences between Marx and Rawls are said to be based almost entirely on empirical rather than evaluative considerations. Further examination of Rawls's theory and various objections from a more egalitarian or Marxist perspective lead to a reformulation of Rawls's basic position, as set out in chapter 3 (Peffer, 1990, p. 14):

(1) Everyone's basic security and subsistence rights are to be met: that is, everyone's physical integrity is to be respected and everyone is to be guaranteed a minimum level of material well-being including basic needs, i.e., those needs that must be met in order to remain a normal functioning human being.

(2) There is to be a maximum system of equal basic liberties, including freedom of speech and assembly, liberty of conscience and freedom of thought, freedom of the person along with the right to hold (personal) property, and freedom from arbitrary arrest and seizure as defined by the concept of the rule of law.

(3) There is to be (a) equal opportunity to attain social positions and offices, and (b) an equal right to participate in all social decision-making processes within institutions of which one is part.

(4) Social and economic inequalities are to be justified if and only if they benefit the least advantaged, consistent with the just savings principle, but are not to exceed levels that will seriously undermine the equal worth of liberty or the good of self-respect.

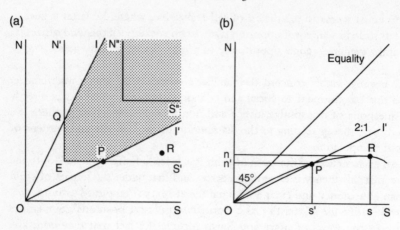

Figure 4.1   Some implications of Rodney Peffer's modification of John Rawls's theory of justice.

Comparison with Rawls's original principles indicate that Peffer has somewhat altered the priorities, and strengthened the egalitarian content. Security and subsistence rights (1) have been given priority over basic liberties (2), and over any other principle of social justice (p. 419). The Rawlsian difference principle is preserved (4), but the permissible degree of inequality is to be constrained by considerations of equal human worth.

Figure 4.1 illustrates implications of Peffer's modification of Rawls's theory. To introduce a geographical context we will follow the two-region case used in the previous chapter (figure 3.2). In figure 4.1a the L-shaped line N′ to S′ represents the minimum level of material well-being required by Peffer's condition (1). The lines extending from the origin of the graph (O) to point I and I′ are inequality constraints required by condition (4), here representing the arbitrary ratios of 2:1 with respect to what goes to the North and South and vice versa. The shaded area defined by these two constraints (conditions 1 and 4) indicates permissible distributions. From Q to E to P the operative constraint is the minimum standard; from I to Q and I′ to P it is the maximum permitted degree of inequality.

Figure 4.1a helps to reveal some difficulties encountered when Rawls is modified in the way Peffer proposes. First with respect to the minimum standard: what is the relationship between this (the L-shaped N′ to S′) and the Rawlsian maximin or indifference curve where the worst-off is as well-off as possible (also L-shaped, as in figure 3.2)? At the position E, which would represent Rawls's original state of equality, the minimum standard and Rawls maximin must coincide. Any minimum standard less than N′ S′ makes the worst-off less well-off than they would be in the Rawls position. Anything better is not feasible without more production. And if more production could make a higher L-curve feasible, for example at $N''S''$, then again Peffer's minimum standard and the Rawls's maximin must coincide. The minimum standard cannot be higher than this new L-curve, and for it to be lower makes the worst-off worse-off than they could be, which is hardly the purpose of a minimum standard. Thus, it is difficult to see what the imposition of a minimum standard adds to the original Rawls formulation. Rawls (1971, p. 285) himself refers to a social minimum in the context of his difference principle, but the relationship between the two appears to be strategical, in the sense that one might be used to effect the other.

Turning to Peffer's constraint on the degree of inequality, there are two ways in which this might operate (Peffer, 1990, p. 395). One is to include the social bases of self-respect among the goods to be maximized for the least advantaged, which would simply make Rawls's difference principle more comprehensively egalitarian. The other is to suggest that self-respect can be negatively affected by inequalities in wealth and income, and to constrain this. Such a proposal disallows certain positions which Rawls would permit if the difference principle is confined to wealth and income. These are in the angles of the lines N' and I and S' and I'. Positions such as R would make the worst-off region N better-off than at some positions within the shaded area, such as P. It would also make S better-off. But R is not permitted by Peffer, as inequality here is too great.

The implications of both situations can be explained more easily in Rawls's own graphics (figure 4.1b, which is simply a different version of 4.1a). Following the argument in figure 3.2c, progress up the curve from O to P, with increasing inequality (i.e. departure from the diagonal at 45 degrees), benefits the worst-off N, but Peffer stops at point P with the distribution n' and s' because to go further assails the 2:1 inequality constraint. Rawls would continue to point R, with the distribution n and s, where n is above the minimum standard at n'. This maximin, at n, makes N as well-off as possible. And no higher minimum standard is feasible. At R both regions are better of than at P. Making both worse-off with respect to wealth and income seems a high price to pay so as not to 'seriously undermine the equal worth of liberty or the good of self-respect', which is the objective of Peffer's inequality constraint.

The conclusion is that Peffer's reformulation of Rawls's theory, though intuitively attractive, lacks complete conviction. This should enhance the appeal of Rawls's original theory to Marxists, who are similarly concerned with people's basic needs (Campbell, 1988, p. 196). Further consideration has to be given to the relationship between some basic minimum and how inequality is constrained, and with respect to what kind of goods. This is taken up in chapter 5.

While the convergence of liberal and Marxist perspectives on social justice might be a fitting conclusion, there is a further possibility to consider. In a review of Peffer's book, Nielson (1991) takes a sceptical swipe at the very idea that Marxist critical theory needs a theory of morality or justice, despite having himself contributed substantially to such endeavours (Nielson, 1984, 1988). Constructing and examining such theories is not without interest, but he doubts their value in assessing issues of social policy or even deciding between capitalism and socialism. In reaching the 'wide reflective equilibrium' involved in interaction between considered moral convictions and the actual state of the world, as advocated by both Rawls and Peffer, Nielson prefers to appeal to what he terms 'moral truisms' rather than to theories of social justice and morality (Nielson, 1991, p. 25):

> All we need is truisms such as it is a bad thing to suffer unnecessarily, to be malnourished, to live in abject poverty, to be starving and the like. A society which causes or even allows such misery where it can be prevented without bringing in its train still greater misery is quite plainly an evil society. We do not need to back up such moral judgements with a fancy moral theory or even an unfancy moral theory. We only need a rather rudimentary moral sensibility or what Engels once called a sense of human decency.

If most Marxist empirical theses are tenable, Nielson claims that, given some moral truisms, the Marxist's basic normative political positions concerning the superiority of socialism follow, without what he describes as, 'entangling ourselves in the complexities, ambiguities and extensive contestedness of moral theory'. However, this still leaves the question of what actually happens under socialism, which we will explore in chapter 7.

Communitarianism

One of the basic values stressed in Peffer's recovery of Marx's moral theory is community. A life of communal harmony is supposed to be achieved by the transformation of capitalism into socialism and eventually communism, with the elimination of the conflict intrinsic to a class-divided society. Individualism and class affiliation will yield to a collectivist identity, sometimes described as 'new communist man' (and, presumably, woman), motivated to contribute production to society according to their ability and to take from communal assets only in accordance with their need. Such is the idealism that socialism has thus far been unable to achieve in practice.

But there is another strand of thought that prioritizes community. Communitarianism points out that communities already exist, in the form of groups of people with common social practices and shared understandings which make up their distinctive culture or ways of life. Such a conception stands between the two extremes of individual self-determination involving the pursuit of one's own conception of the good life, and perfectionism which advocates some transhistoric prescription. Communitarians thus reject individualistic notions of the self, along with the idea of a neutral state indifferent to alternative views as to the good life, characteristic of liberalism. They also reject any ideal mode of life promoted by the state, as under socialism. They prefer to see the common good manifest in existing community ways of life.

Writers who fall under the heading of communitarians, or who have some affinity with this doctrine, present a variety of views, not all of which are directly relevant to social justice. We will look at some of these very briefly, then concentrate on two particularly influential works which provide quite different perspectives on community as well as powerful critiques of some central themes in established thinking on social justice.

To some communitarians, a genuine community does not need principles of social justice. Even if Hume's circumstances of moderate scarcity and self-interest prevail at the level of nation-states, requiring rules to guide distributional arrangements, this may not apply to other situations in which conflict over resources is not strong enough for justice to become the primary virtue. The family represents the extreme case, with a way of life characterized by mutual selfless generosity in which there is no place for the notion of fair shares. Sandel (1982, p. 31) sees a range of intermediate cases, characterized in varying degrees by the circumstances of justice: 'These would include, at various points along the spectrum, tribes, neighbourhoods, cities, towns, universities, trade unions, national liberation movements and various nationalisms, and a wide variety of ethnic, religious, cultural, and linguistic communities with more or less clearly-defined common identities and shared purposes.' Justice comes into play only as a remedial virtue, when the benevolence, solidarity and fraternity (or sorority) of the community has not proved sufficient to resolve some distributional issue.

Communitarians are hostile to the emphasis on individual autonomy in liberal formulations of justice. They reject the idea of atomistic human beings, self-sufficient, somehow free-floating outside a society: 'A conception in which the self, shorn of all its contingently-given attributes, assumes a kind of supra-empirical status, essentially unencumbered, bounded in advance and given prior to its ends, a purely subjective agency' (Sandel, 1982, p. 94). Theories emphasizing the isolated individual detached from a social setting perpetuate a myth, a misrepresentation of real life. Rather, individuals should be seen as situated or embedded in society, in communities, and dependent on them. There are clear echoes of popular perspectives in contemporary social and cultural geography here.

The tension between individual autonomy and community in the contemporary world is well captured by Walzer (1990). He emphasizes the role of four kinds of mobility – geographical, social, marital and political – in unsettling people, often literally. 'We are more often alone than people once were, being without neighbors we can count on, relatives who live nearby or with whom we are close, or comrades at work or in the movement' (p. 13). Associations and affiliations nevertheless survive: 'people are born into very important sorts of groups, born with identities, male or female, for example, working class, Catholic or Jewish, black, democrat, and so on. Many of their subsequent associations (like their subsequent careers) merely express these underlying identities, which, again, are not so much chosen as enacted' (p. 15). A central feature of liberal society is that people are free to leave as well as to form associations. Thus, association and community are always at risk: 'The boundaries of the group are not policed; people come and go, or they just fade into the distance.'

Group membership is an important theme of Michael Walzer's *Spheres of Justice* (1983), to which reference was made in chapter 2. That his concern is broader is signalled by the subtitle: *A defence of pluralism and equality*. This book has exerted considerable influence in the decade since its publication; one reviewer of theories of social justice describes it as 'the best starting point for research in this area' (Miller, 1991, p. 391). At the outset, Walzer identifies the aim of equality as a society free from domination, a practice always mediated by some set of social goods. He rejects high philosophical abstraction in favour of an approach which he describes as 'radically particularist', and not greatly distanced from the world in which he lives. This has its source, he thinks, 'less in a universalist conception of persons than in a pluralistic conception of goods . . . Men and women do indeed have rights beyond life and liberty, but these do not follow from our common humanity; they follow from shared conceptions of social goods; they are local and particular in character' (p. xv). His approach is thus relativist, with an obvious appeal to the geographical notion of local specificity.

Principles of justice are, to Walzer, a human construction and pluralistic in form. There is no single, universal set of primary or basic social goods. They take on meaning in relation to those people for whom they are good, and this gives rise to reasons concerning how and to whom they ought to be distributed. 'All distributions are just or unjust relative to the social meanings of the goods at stake . . . Social meanings are historical in character; and so distributions, and just and unjust distributions, change over time' (p. 9). And where meanings are distinct, distributions must be autonomous, so every such social good or set of goods constitutes a separate distributive *sphere* within which only certain criteria and arrangements are appropriate.

Walzer's theory of goods is linked to the central theme of domination by the category of *dominant goods*. A good is dominant 'if the individuals who have it, because they have it, can command a wide range of other goods' (p. 10). An obvious example is capital, which in capitalist society is readily converted into prestige and power. Technical knowledge can play the same part in a technocracy. Monopolistic control of a dominant good creates a ruling class, whose members occupy the top of the distributional system.

Recognition of the distinctive meaning of different goods leads to the concept of *complex equality*. The conventional or 'simple' concept of equality involves the equal distribution of the single good of money, of a range of goods, or in more abstract formulations an imaginary collective good. Complex equality is explained thus: 'Equality is a complex relation of persons, mediated by the goods we make, share and divide amongst ourselves; it is not an identity of possessions. It requires, then, a diversity of distributive criteria that mirrors the diversity of social goods' (p. 18). This is supposed to ensure independence between different autonomous spheres of justice, which could otherwise compound a particular pattern of inequality.

The link with domination and the concept of dominant goods is expressed in the following principle, which comprises the core of Walzer's theory (p. 20):

No social good x should be distributed to men and women who possess some other good y merely because they possess y without regard to the meaning of x.

To exemplify: health care (x), the meaning of which is to prevent or cure illness, should not be distributed to people merely because they have money (y). Similarly, education should be distributed independently of income, wealth and health. The implication is that a strong correlation between the distribution patterns in these and other spheres would raise suspicions of injustice. Although Walzer does not make the point himself, patterns in this context can be interpreted in a geographical sense.

The idea of distributive justice presupposes a bounded world within which distribution takes place. This can be the nation-state, or a smaller community. As was recognized earlier (chapter 2), Walzer sees membership of some human community as the primary good that we distribute to one another. Who we are, and where, defines the context for the resolution of distributional issues in relation to such criteria as need:

one of our needs is community itself: culture, religion, and politics. It is only under the aegis of these three that all the other things we need become *socially recognized needs*. (p. 65)

Every political community must attend to the needs of its members as they collectively understand them, distributing goods in proportion to need, and recognizing the underlying equality of membership. These general principles are intended to apply to any community in which the members are each other's equals (p. 84).

Walzer elaborates these broad theoretical foundations. He refers to the tyranny of market power manifest in the ownership of commodities, distorting distribution in other spheres. Money can provide access to political office and to further power: office, like money itself, is a dominant good. Educational advantage can be of the same kind, and its provision should be detached from the cause-and-effect chain compounding inequality through domination. Thus, 'schools, teachers and ideas constitute a new set of social goods, conceived independently of other goods, and requiring, in turn, an independent set of distributive processes' (p. 198). Given the conspicuous failure of his own (American) society to uphold the principle of complex equality (a matter we shall explore in chapter 6), it is hardly surprising that Walzer concludes that the dominance of capital outside the market makes capitalism unjust, preferring a decentralized, democratic socialism with a strong welfare state (pp. 315, 318).

Walzer's conception of justice emphasizes what he describes as its parts: different social goods and their spheres of distribution. His account of its whole, relative, character is as follows (p. 312):

> Justice is relative to social meanings. Indeed, the relativity of justice follows from the classic non-relative definition, giving each person his due, as much as it does from my own proposal, distributing goods for 'internal' reasons. These are formal definitions that require, as I have tried to show, historical completion. We cannot say what is due to this person or that one until we know how these people relate to one another through the things they make and distribute. There cannot be a just society until there is a society; and the adjective *just* doesn't determine, it only modifies, the substantive life of the societies it describes. There are an infinite number of possible lives, shaped by an infinite number of possible cultures, religions, political arrangements, geographical conditions, and so on. A given society is just if its substantive life is lived in a certain way – that is, in a way faithful to the shared understandings of its members.

Walzer (p. 314) concludes: 'There are no external or universal principles that can replace it. Every substantive account of distributive justice is a local account.' Appealing though this may be to the geographical mind, sensitive to local differentiation, Walzer is open to familiar criticism of moral relativism. He claims that, 'in matters of morality, argument simply is the appeal to common meanings' (p. 29). But this implies a local consensus, whereas the reality may be one of differences resolved in favour of those with the most power to influence the debate or the design of institutions and distributional arrangements. The outcome could easily be conservative, as in Walzer's own American society where 'shared meanings' may not be shared with or mean much to some marginalized groups. And, of course, people are capable of sharing meanings others elsewhere reasonably find objectionable. Meanings are an arena for conflict, but when Walzer (pp. 313–14) recognizes this he appears to see the challenge to unshared meanings originating within the society in question rather than externally. Reviewing Walzer's book, J. Cohen (1986, p. 468) doubts whether there is a clear boundary between what is 'inside' and what is 'outside', between community norms and critical standards, between common-sense morality and philosophical ethics. Campbell (1988, pp. 203–4) is similarly critical of the communitarian tendency to accept the consensus ideas of our own political setting.

While such views identify a flaw in Walzer's relativist conception of morality, which bears on how particular societies will arrive at distribution in specific spheres, it does not necessarily undermine the entire concept of complex equality. The general idea that advantage in one sphere of life should not lead to advantage in another sphere retains at least its plausibility as a universal, non-relativist principle of social justice, applicable in a wide range of actual situations (some of which will be suggested in case studies in Part II).

In *Justice and the Politics of Difference*, Iris Marion Young (1990a) shares Micheal Walzer's preoccupation with domination, but with a radically different perspective on community. Whereas Walzer displays definite communitarian sentiments, within a broader theory of social justice, Young adopts a distinctly anti-communitarian stance. She is also critical of what she sees as a preoccupation with distribution in conventional perspectives on justice (as we saw in chapter 2). Her point of departure is that, 'instead of focusing on distribution, a concept of justice should begin with the concepts of domination and oppression' (p. 3). This is elaborated as follows (p. 25):

The distributive paradigm implicitly assumes that social judgements are about what persons have, how much they have, and how that amount compares with what other persons have. This focus on possession tends to preclude thinking about what people are doing, according to what institutional rules, how their doings and havings are structured by institutionalized relations that constitute their positions, and how the combined effect of their doings has recursive effects on their lives.

Preoccupation with the distributive paradigm of justice functions ideologically. For example, in welfare capitalist societies it distracts attention from interest-group politics, the organization of production, decision-making structures and status differentiation, hence reinforcing their depoliticization. The structures behind distribution patterns thus go unchallenged.

Young also objects to universal theories of justice, which fail to recognize particular institutional situations. To be useful in assessing justice and injustice in practice, theories must have reference to the actual social context: this much is shared with communitarianism. Universal theories conflate moral reflection with scientific knowledge as seeing, observing and trying to figure out how something works, whereas: 'Rational reflection on justice begins in a hearing, in heeding a call, rather than asserting and mastering a state of affairs, however ideal' (p. 5).

Young adopts what she describes as *critical theory*. By this she means situated analysis and argument: 'a normative reflection that is historically and socially contextualized' – further echoes from communitarianism. 'Critical theory reflects as illusory the effort to construct a universal normative system insulated from a particular society' (p. 5). We must begin with the given circumstances from which an interest in justice arises. Young's analysis is situated, for the most part, in the contemporary United States, in which political movements representing various minority groups see deep institutional injustices but find little affinity with contemporary theories of justice.

Another, related point of Young's critique of conventional perspectives on justice concerns impartiality, which requires all moral situations to be treated according to the same rules. She sees this as inconsistent with the fact that (in)justice arises in actual situations. Furthermore, impartiality can lead to another major problem: that of denying the differences among people which are relevant to how they are treated (see chapter 2). It expresses 'a logic of identity which seeks to reduce difference to unity' (p. 97).

As well as being 'situated', a conception of justice should be 'enabling', concerned not only with distribution but also with 'the institutional conditions necessary for the development and exercise of individual capacities and collective communication and cooperation' (p. 39). Young's central concern is with how social institutions subject some people to domination and oppression. By *domination* she means 'structural or systematic phenomena which exclude people from participating in determining their actions or the conditions of their actions' (p. 31). The concept of *oppression* refers to 'structural phenomena that immobilize or diminish a group' (p. 42). Oppression constrains self-development; domination constrains self-determination. By group Young means a collective of persons differentiated by cultural forms, practices or way of life, examples being men and women, age groups, and racial, ethnic and religious groups. A group is not the same as a community, as we shall see.

Young recognizes five 'faces of oppression'. The first is *exploitation*, which can especially affect members of racial minorities and also women in the home. The second is *marginalization*, which concerns the exclusion of people from useful participation in social life in the form of labour; again, racial groups may be the particular victims, but others such as the aged and single mothers can also suffer. The third is *powerlessness*, whereby people do not participate regularly, or even ever, in making the decisions that affect their lives and actions. These three forms of oppression all refer to power relations arising out of the social division of labour: who works for whom, or does not work at all, and how the content of work defines one institutional position relative to another – the privilege of the professions, for example.

The fourth face of oppression is *cultural imperialism*, which involves the universalization of a dominant group's experience and culture and its establishment as the norm. This is sometimes attributed to the attitude Europeans bring to their interaction with people of a different culture, seeing them and making them out as inferior 'others'. The fifth is *violence*, a form of injustice which the distributive paradigm seems ill equipped to capture. Obvious examples are violence against women in the home, racial minorities, ethnic or religious groups such as Jews, and people beaten up for what others regard as peculiar sexual orientation.

Culture is deeply implicated in the process of oppression. To Young, American society exemplifies this: 'Group oppressions are enacted in this society not primarily in official laws and policies but in informal, often unnoticed and unreflective speech, bodily reactions to others, conventional practices of everyday interaction and evaluation, aesthetic judgements, and the jokes, images, and stereotypes pervading the mass media' (p. 148). Unintended actions of this kind should be judged unjust. It requires little imagination to draw aspects of other societies into such an interpretation.

In his recent return to the theme of social justice, David Harvey makes much of Young's formulation, which he describes as one of the best recent statements. He uses the five faces of oppression as the basis for propositions about social justice and the institutional arrangements it requires. He adds a sixth principle, in recognition of the ecological implications of what we do for people in the future and for other inhabitants of the globe. This is: 'that just planning and policy practices will clearly recognize that the necessary ecological consequences of all social projects have impacts on future generations as well as upon distant peoples and take steps to ensure a reasonable mitigation of negative impacts' (Harvey, 1992b, p. 600).

The kind of arrangements which Young sees as combatting injustice manifest as domination and oppression are consistent with her emphasis on structures and institutions, while not entirely neglecting distribution. She defines justice (p. 91) as:

the institutionalized conditions that make it possible for all to learn and use satisfying skills in socially recognized settings, to participate in decision-making, and to express their feelings, experience, and perspective on social life in contexts where others can listen.

This requires certain distributional outcomes, like the satisfaction of people's basic needs, but her egalitarianism is broader. Referring to social equality as a goal of social justice, she says (p. 173):

Equality refers not primarily to the distribution of social goods, though distributions are certainly entailed by social equality. It refers primarily to the full participation and inclusion of everyone in a society's major institutions, and the socially supported substantive opportunity for all to develop and exercise their capacities and realize their choices.

In considering non-oppressive social arrangements, Young is clear about what they cannot be. This is community, in the usually understood sense of people in a particular locale, sharing as specific heritage, a common self-identification, a common culture and set of norms. This is the ideal often invoked in daily life, as well as in academic accounts such as that of Michael Walzer. But this 'privileges unity over difference, immediacy over mediation, sympathy over recognition of the limits of one's understanding of others from their point of view' (1990b, p. 300). Such a conception is based on a particular notion of identity associated with communitarianism, which Young (1990a, p. 229) claims 'represents an urge to see people in unity with one another in a shared whole'. Calling on experience in the United States today, she points out that membership of such a community can set up 'an oppositional differentiation from other groups, who are feared or at best devalued' (1990b, p. 311).

Young's objections to community rest partly on a postmodern critique of identity, which emphasizes the difference among people, but she regrets that this can lead to a complete absence of relationships and shared attributes, to 'absolute otherness'. The conventional conception of community, which emphasizes common understanding, goes to the other extreme of denying difference between subjects. This can have oppressive consequences: 'The desire for community relies on the same desire for social wholeness and identification that underlies racism and ethnic chauvinism on the one hand and political sectarianism on the other' (1990b, p. 302). The process of denying difference is also connected to impartiality in moral reason, with its emphasis on treating people the same in similar situations, without giving adequate attention to whether people or their circumstances are actually the same.

Another objection to the conventional conception of community is that it prioritizes face-to-face relations among people. Young sees this as overlooking the fact that interaction is actually mediated over time and space. This point concerns especially the geographical reality of contemporary life, which transcends the dated ideal of the localized community (1990b, 314):

Even societies confined to a limited territory with few institutions and a small population devise means of their members communicating with one another over distances, means of maintaining their social relationship even though they are not face to face. Societies occupy wider and wider territorial fields and increasingly differentiate their activities in space, time, and function, a movement that, of course, accelerates and takes on qualitatively specific form in modern industrial societies.

Young's prescription for a just society is similarly spatial. She sees the city as facilitating the formation of groups which can somehow overcome the limitations of atomistic individualism on the one hand and the forced homogeneity of community on the other. The aim would be social differentiation without exclusion, and the expression of varied life-styles. Cities involve the being together of strangers; finding affinity with some should not lead people to deny a place to others. The essence of life is to be open to unassimilated others. Social justice involves 'equality among groups who recognize and affirm one another in their specificity' (1990a, p. 248). Social policy should be 'group-conscious', recognizing that social justice requires special treatment of specific groups. The necessary structure would involve regional government, with mechanisms for representing the interests of its diverse neighbourhoods and towns.

Young's conception of social justice manifest in group formation within an appropriate spatial structure, while appealing to the geographical imagination, is essentially Utopian. It is not clear how this is to be achieved, against the existing forces of domination and oppression. And the notion of groups is not clearly differentiated from the conventional community. There are repeated references to the currently excluded groups, to women, blacks, latinos, poor working-class people, gay men and lesbians, but, there can be multiple and perhaps conflicting identities (Harvey, 1992b, p. 600; Minnesota Geography Readings Group, 1992, p. 592). Nevertheless, Young has provided a powerful critique of some of the conventional content of theories of social justice, and of the conceptions of morality and rationality on which they rest. Like the work of Michael Walzer, with which she shares a concern with the historically and geographically situated nature of social justice, Young has moved the field significantly from abstraction to reality.

Feminism

Feminism asserts that *gender* has been and continues to be an organizing principle in social life. Any attempt to make sense of the world as if it were ungendered is to risk a fundamentally flawed analysis (Hanson, 1992, p. 570). A feminist questions the gender arrangement of society, and works to change it in a way that would give women more power and in which gender would cease to be an important consideration in the distribution of life chances. Feminists are particularly concerned with the different and unequal experiences of women, including the fact that women are treated unjustly by virtue of their gender. There is also a proposition that women think about things like social justice in ways significantly different from the male or masculine point of view. Like the other -isms reviewed, feminism covers a variety of perspectives; indeed, some contemporary writers prefer the plural form of 'feminisms'.[1] Discussion here is confined to work with a particular relevance to social justice and its underlying morality.

For a long time it was held that women were, in some way, naturally inferior to men. While this position now seems to have largely yielded to the notion of an equal humankind in the discourse of moral philosophy, social reality has yet to catch up. And there is also a claim that conceptions of humankind itself are often modelled on male norms.

The subordination of women may be as old as human history, but it is to the rise of capitalism that its particular contemporary form is usually attributed. Thus (Oakley, 1974, p. 156):

> Industrial capitalism is the economic and social system in which the present alienation and oppression of women as housewives has arisen. But other forces also act to maintain the home-centredness of women's identity. A set of myths about women's place in society provides the rationale for the ideology of gender roles in which femininity and domesticity are equated.

It should, however, be noted that socialism as actually practised (in East Europe and the former Soviet Union) by no means liberated women from such roles. In fact, they were more likely to add full-time employment to domestic labour, the burden of this dual role often being reinforced by male chauvinism. The opportunity for women to advance in some spheres of work may have been easier than under capitalism, but they seldom attained positions of supreme power or authority.

It was *discrimination* between males and females in access to economic, political and social benefits and positions of advantage in contemporary capitalist society which first attracted the attention of feminists. Discrimination is sometimes defined as the arbitrary or irrational adoption of gender, race or some other irrelevant characteristic in distribution, but what was observed appeared to be more deliberate. Discrimination against women was a non-arbitrary and perfectly rational way of men retaining their position of domination. The analogy with racial discrimination is very close: like males, white people felt superior to others (blacks, or all those defined pejoratively

---

[1] Thanks to Gillian Rose for helpful comments on this section in draft.

as 'non-white'), and acted accordingly. To be female and black is to be doubly disadvantaged.

The societal response to gender discrimination, when finally recognized as a problem, was to pass 'gender-neutral' laws against discriminatory practices, in the liberal tradition of equal opportunities. This was analagous to outlawing racial discrimination. That the actual results have been limited in both spheres is a matter of the everyday experience. MacKinnon (1987, p. 32), says that sex equality law 'has been so utterly ineffective in getting women what we need and are socially prevented from having on the basis of a condition of birth: a chance at productive lives of reasonable physical security, self-expression, individuation, and minimal respect and dignity.'

Laws against discrimination have been based on what MacKinnon terms the *difference approach*, which involves an obsession with sex difference as the ground for the differential and unequal treatment of women. The prescription which follows is to allow women equal access to what men have, just like giving blacks access to what whites have. The problem with the conventional approach of equal opportunities is that women are simply being admitted to a world of institutions and positions largely defined by men in their own interests. The guiding point of view is in fact *masculinist*. An obvious example is the normal, almost natural expectation that people in employment will work full-time and regular hours. This clearly conflicts with family responsibility for children, and other dependants such as the elderly, unless someone other than the employed (usually a wife) can perform these caring roles. It is most unlikely that a group of mothers would have designed the nine-to-five working day. Women are constrained, by their (assumed) gender role as carers, from full and equal participation in the patriarchal society built on male interests and values which may still include some sense of natural superiority.

Such arrangements are not only masculinist but *sexist*, perpetuating differentiated gender roles and the dichotomous identities on which they rest. 'The term "sexist" characterizes cultural and economic structures which create and enforce the elaborate and rigid patterns of sex-marking and sex-announcing which divide the species, along sex lines, into dominators and subordinates. Individual acts and practices are sexist which reinforce and support those structures' (Frye, 1983, p. 38).

In place of the difference approach, MacKinnon advocates a *dominance approach*, which recognizes and challenges male domination. Its goal 'is not to make legal categories trace and trap the way things are. It is not to make rules that fit reality. It is critical of reality' (1987, p. 40). The prescription is to give women equal power in social life. This involves the power to define institutions and roles, not merely the freedom to fill those defined by men. This is essentially a political project, a necessary precondition to the actual realization that the moral equality of all people, of which so much is made in the discourse of social justice, applies equally to men and women.

Whether viewed from the perspective of difference or domination, the examination of gender inequality and injustice in mainstream literature is usually confined to the public realm of economic, political and social life. This is understandable insofar as social justice, as conventionally conceived, is concerned with broad social structures and institutional arrangements. The private realm of the family is usually regarded as beyond justice, as in some communitarian accounts (see above), or family life may simply be assumed to be just without further scrutiny. However, what happens in the family can be highly relevant to social justice. One reason is that the family may reinforce restrictive gender roles, implicit in the ideology that the woman's place is in the home. The family might thus be a locus of struggle against domination, in general and in its specific version of unreasonably demanding and perhaps violent husbands or male partners. Most violence against women in contemporary Britain is in the home, not on the streets.

Furthermore, as the place of primary socialization, the home is where children learn about human relations, including its internal division of labour and its structure of authority. It is also here that they may learn a sense of justice, observing and participating in a process of sharing things (equally or otherwise), of being cared for, and of caring for others. Thus, feminists are critical of the failure of major theorists of social justice to bring the family into their deliberations, as relevant to people's concept of justice as well as a possible locus for injustice.

The concept of community is also subject to a feminist critique. Young (1990b) points to the tension which feminists have found in the experience of community: they expected their groups to fulfil a desire for community against the alienation and individualism of capitalist patriarchal society, but this sometimes helps to reproduce group homogeneity which risks denying the significance of difference among women with respect to race, class and so on. She also claims that many feminists have retained a communitarian vision of the ideal society, even believing that women are better able than men to realize this because their culture is less individualistic and competitive than that of men, more oriented towards care and mutuality (Young, 1990b, pp. 300–1). Her alternative vision of the unoppressive society, outlined in the previous section, involves a critique of this idealization of community.

Similar sentiments are expressed by Marilyn Friedman (1989), who finds communitarians a perilous ally for feminist theory. The original or 'found' community of place, with its focus on family, neighbourhood, school, church and so on, can be highly oppressive towards women. She contrasts this with the 'chosen' or created community, including friendships, which would facilitate critical reflection on the accepted moral legitimacy of local community values. Friedman (p. 316) claims that 'urban communities of choice can provide the resources for women to surmount the moral particularity of family and place which define their moral starting point'.

The question of how people actually think and feel about morality and social justice brings us to what is perhaps the most challenging position emanating from feminism: that there may be a distinctive point of view held by women, significantly different from that of the men who dominate the profession of moral philosophy. Moral philosophy is not an exclusively male preserve, and it is probably no more strongly male than physics, mathematics and engineering, for example. But it is significant that, until the appearance of Iris Marion Young in the previous section, all the 'major thinkers' whose theories have been explored in this book were male, as were almost all the other authors cited. If the male point of view on social justice is but one partial and gender-specific view, then we (and humankind) may be in deep trouble.

Carol Gilligan (1982) is generally credited with having first proposed that there could be gender differences in moral thinking. She reported the findings of a research project in developmental psychology, showing that, whereas almost all the male respondents subscribed to a conventional conception of justice (of the kind reflected in mainstream theories), most of the women focused on what she described as the *ethic of care*. Gilligan (1982, p. 19) explains this as follows:

> In this conception, the moral problem arises from conflicting responsibilities rather than from competing rights and requires for its resolution a mode of thinking that is contextual and narrative rather than formal and abstract. This conception of morality as concerned with the activity of care centers moral development around the understanding of responsibility and relationships, just as the conception of morality as fairness ties moral development to the understanding of rights and rules.

She further elaborates (Gilligan, 1987, p. 20):

> Theoretically, the distinction between justice and care cuts across the familiar division between thinking and feeling, egoism and altruism, theoretical and practical reasoning ... The moral injunctions, not to act unfairly towards others, and not to turn away from someone in need, capture these different concerns.

The case of abortion can be used to illustrate this distinction. A common interpretation is of conflicting rights between mother and foetus. The sanctity of human life may be invoked, and the status of the foetus as a person debated, with the issue of termination resolved in law by time since conception. In competing discourses, the 'pro-life' and 'pro-choice' lobbies deliberately confront each other at the level of what are portrayed as ultimate moral values, in the justice tradition. In contrast, the ethic of care would focus on the connection between foetus and mother: on whether this particular relationship would be better extended or ended. The stress is on mutual interdependence, rather than on separate rights. But Gilligan recognizes that the justice and care perspectives are not strict alternatives, but different dimensions of the situation. For example, the decision to terminate the relationship cannot be divorced from its likely quality, as experienced in two lives which will to an extent be separate. The circumstances of particular abortions require attention to the actual context in making moral judgements guided by general principles.

Gilligan's work suggests a number of differences between the two distinct (possibly masculine and feminine) moral perspectives, summarized as follows by Kymlicka (1990, p. 265):

1. Moral capacities: learning moral principles (justice) versus developing moral dispositions (care);
2. Moral reasoning: solving problems by seeking principles that have universal applicability (justice) versus seeking responses that are appropriate to the particular case (care);
3. Moral concepts: attending to rights and fairness (justice) versus attending to responsibilities and relationships (care).

Other characterizations portray the male point of view as rational, impartial and dispassionate, that of the female intuitive, emotional and particularistic. The ethic of care challenges the essentially masculine perspective, following modern scientific reason, of the knowing subject as 'a gazer, an observer who stands above, outside of, the object of knowledge' (Young, 1990a, p. 125). (Perhaps nothing more eloquently captures the stereotypical male philosopher as D. H. Lawrence's description of Bertrand Russell as 'all disembodied mind').

There is controversy over whether the Gilligan's ethic of care really represents a gender difference in moral thinking (Tronto, 1987, pp. 644–6). While Gilligan sought to extend the moral domain to incorporate care, her empirical distinction in people's responses has been widely interpreted as evidence of gender differentiation. This carries a risk of reaffirming gender stereotypes, in particular some accepted views of white femininity, to the neglect of the differences among women emphasized in contemporary feminism, and of similarities between women and men. Reviewing the literature, Miller (1992, p. 581) concludes: 'the consensus among those who have examined men's and women's views of justice experimentally is that differences in abstract conceptions of justice are not substantial, but that there are some differences in *"justice behaviour"*.'

The possibility of gender differences raises the strategic problem that any point of view associated with women could be judged inferior: as a mere diversion from the (male) norm or at best a corrective to the conventional wisdom. There is also the question of whether the ethic of care, if distinctive of women, is psychological or social in origin. And, if social, does female subordination prevent them from reaching a proper sense of justice as the pinnacle of intellectual attainment, or is the ethic of care actually something superior which is generated by the experience of caring, of which men are largely deprived?

These kinds of issues lead Tronto (1987, pp. 656–8) to suggest that the ethic of care should be understood within the context of moral theory, rather than as a given fact of gender differentiation. Otherwise, she says, it can be dismissed as 'a parochial concern of some misguided women'. She advocates an alternative to the conventional moral point of view characterized by universalizability, impartiality and concern with what is right: a contextual moral theory. In this, morality must be 'situated concretely', for 'particular actors in a particular society'. Contextual moral theory stresses moral character, sensitivities and imagination, and an understanding of the balance between caring for self and for others.

As an alternative to the abstract, uninvolved formalism of conventional moral theory, the ethic of care encounters some problems. One is the simple geographical reality, recognized in chapter 2, that we may care most for those close to us, or charity begins at home. How far should our boundaries of care extend; how wide should we spin the web of relationships through which we exercise care? Posing these questions, Tronto (1987, pp. 657–60) points out that prioritizing our own restricted network can be conservative, perhaps generating unreflective preferences from which can grow 'hatreds of difference' of the sort Young condemns, and which is a weakness of relativism in general.

It is not, therefore, surprising to find attempts to establish a position between narrowly-confined and unrestricted caring. Transcending the former requires recognition of a more than parochial responsibility which might in some specific context be global. Avoiding the latter, it is necessary to preserve some personal autonomy and discrimination, otherwise we stop and care for everyone in need, every beggar or homeless person we encounter on the way home from work, or place everything else in our lives (including our families) secondary to caring for world-wide others. As Young (1990a, p. 105) remarks: 'Moral reason certainly does require reflection, an ability to take some distance from one's immediate impulses, intuitions, desires, and interests in order to consider their relation to the demands of others.' Furthermore, the capacity to pursue certain of our projects, like making a modest living and being somewhat satisfied with life, may be a precondition for effectively caring, in the practical sense of being able to do things for others. Perhaps the really virtuous can transcend all constraints, but who in reality are they?

If the ethic of care is more than a prescription for private personal conduct, if it is really concerned with social justice in the public sphere, it must say something about social structures and institutions. It is not obvious what they should be, except caring in themselves and supportive of those in caring roles. Perhaps the nature of capitalism, as a selfish, individualistic and competitive system, constrains care as something broader than a personal ethic, or confines it to institutions added on rather than intrinsic to this form of society. Perhaps confidence in the state as benevolent carer under welfare-state measures or socialism is misplaced, and allows too little room for the personal ethic. In any event, care and justice cannot helpfully be regarded as independent, mutually exclusive realms of either individual or social life.

Building bridges between the ethic of care and the conventional justice perspective has generated some re-evaluation of mainstream theory, including that of John Rawls. He is criticized by some feminists for following the Kantian tradition of prioritizing reason over feelings (Okin, 1989b), and taken to task for recognizing the importance of the family in the development of a sense of justice but failing to apply the rigour of his general theory to justice within the family. However, as Kearns (1983, p. 38) concedes, Rawls does try to integrate into his conception of justice idealized familial values of mutual concern (not always realized in practice); she cites the following (Rawls, 1971, p. 105): 'Members of a family commonly do not wish to gain unless they can do so in ways that further the interests of the rest. Now wanting to act on the difference principle had precisely this consequence.'

Okin (1989b, pp. 247–8) goes a step further, in claiming that Rawls's principles of justice are founded not on mutual disinterest and detachment but on empathy, and concern and care for others, and on an awareness of their differences. She adds the important proviso that his construction of the original position eliminates biases that might result from particular attachments to others, as well as from particular characteristics of the self: 'Surely impartiality in this sense is a reasonable requirement to make of a theory of justice.' Rawls (1971, p. 476) himself said: 'the sense of justice is continuous with the love of mankind.'

Further integration of the different voices can be expected. As Bair (1987, p. 56) concludes: 'the best moral theory has to be a cooperative product of women and men, has to harmonize justice and care. The morality it theorizes about is after all for all persons, for men and women, and will need their combined insights.' The particular insight of the ethic of care, largely missing from conventional justice perspectives, captures something of the reality of human interdependence, not just as a fact but as a feeling. A fitting conclusion is provided by a familiar historical reference which evokes these sentiments (though not with today's gender neutrality):

No man is an *Iland*, intire of it selfe; every man is a peece of the *Continent*, a part of the maine; if *Clod* bee washed away by the *Sea*, Europe is the lesse, as well as if a *Promontorie* were, as well as if a Mannor of thy *friends* or of *thine owne* were; any mans *death* diminishes me, because I am involved in *Mankinde*. (John Donne, *Devotions* – Meditation XVII, 1624)

5

Returning to Equality: Justice as Equalization

Society is produced by the wants, Government by the wickedness, and a state of just and happy equality by the improvement and reason of man.

Percy Bysshe Shelley, *An Address to the Irish People* (1812)

Our review of theories of social justice, while possibly exhausting, was by no means exhaustive. However, it should have been sufficient to lay the groundwork for the next, and final, step before exploring the application of social justice to some actual situations. This chapter provides a bridge between theory and practice. It is in some respects a flimsy structure, covering rather briefly a number of important topics which have attracted considerable interest in the literature of a variety of disciplines, from the abstractions of moral philosophy, through theoretical and applied economics, to the real-world preoccupations of development planning. And we have to skip lightly over some relevant but well-trodden geographical ground in order to cover what may be less familiar. However, what we are able to say should be sufficient for the purpose in mind.

We begin with a particular perspective on social justice: a synthesis of selected strands in certain of the theories reviewed in the previous two chapters. This proposes that situations in the real world should be judged according to their tendency towards equalization. No claim is made that this is a complete and definitive alternative theory, merely that it is an intuitively attractive and morally defensible starting point from which to engage reality. This process itself may lead to the strengthening or modification of the equalization perspective, as something possibly of universal application.

Moving from theory to practice then requires us to be more specific about some things which have thus far remained rather vague. We explore the idea of a minimum standard of living, and the related question of whether there are any universal 'basic' human needs, and if so, what they might be. This leads to consideration of how human needs are satisfied in generating human well-being. There is a brief technical discussion of the measurement of outcomes, with particular reference to the degree of inequality manifest in actual situations and the trends that may be observed. Finally, we return to geography, emphasizing the spatiality and territoriality of various aspects of social justice in reality.

Social justice as equalization

The various theories of social justice reviewed in the previous chapters all have their distinctive features, including what are in some cases incompatible basic values. For example, it is impossible to reconcile the libertarian or entitlement theorist's prioritization of rights in property with a theory which calls for the maximization of some conception of the good life, or ones which prioritize equality of outcomes or justice itself. Faced with this, it is tempting to follow the line encouraged by the contemporary postmodern turn, and withdraw from the realm of grand theory into a form of evaluative ethical relativism. We simply choose our favourite theory according to our own moral judgements.

But there is another approach, which involves faith in at least the possibility of universal principles of social justice. This is to seek common ground among alternative perspectives, and see what might be made of it. As was indicated in the initial discussion of egalitarianism in chapter 3, every theory may be viewed as having the same ultimate value: that of equality in some respect. Kymlicka (1990, pp. 4–5) prefaces his review of the major competing theories with the proposition that they all share the same 'egalitarian plateau' (as Ronald Dworkin has put it), that is, each attempts to define the social, economic and political conditions under which members of a community or society will be treated as equals. And Amartya Sen (1992, p. 3) comments: 'the major ethical theories of social arrangements all share an endorsement of equality in terms of *some* focal variable, even though the variables that are selected are frequently very different between one theory and another.'

But to make any progress we will have to narrow down the conceptions of equality with which we are concerned. We will include neither the libertarian conception of equality manifest in equal freedom to benefit from one's holdings, nor the claim of equal individual weight in some utilitarian maximizing calculus. These conceptions permit degrees of inequality which assail powerful intuitive notions of what is consistent with accepting the equal moral worth of individuals, though we remind ourselves in passing that utilitarianism has greater egalitarian import than is often supposed.

Nor can we be satisfied with a preoccupation with difference almost to the exclusion of human similarity (a not entirely helpful postmodern fetish), which can allow inequalities in through the back door, in the guise of responses to differences of dubious moral relevance. And the otherwise appealing ethic of care needs more egalitarian content than it seems to possess, if it is not to degenerate into a parochial and localized concern for people who happen to be closest to those best able to care. Michael Walzer's idea of spheres of justice also requires careful attention to the risks of relativism, though his notion of dominant goods is a powerful constraint on inequalities in different spheres compounding one another.

What we have in mind initially is to narrow down the concern of (in)equality to some good or set of goods which has to do with people being well in the most general sense. At this stage the unspecified collective good or bundle of goods beloved of economists will suffice. For the time being we will side-step the distinction between equality of resources (inputs) and of welfare (outputs), which greatly and properly complicates the application of egalitarian policies. Having established a basic theoretical position, these and other complexities can be tackled later in this chapter.

A review of alternative perspectives on social justice almost twenty years ago led me to advocate the axiom of *the more equal the better* (Smith, 1977, pp. 152–7). Two decades on, and informed by a further review of a burgeoning field, I find myself in the same position. Indeed, I believe that this position can now be argued with greater conviction. Very simply, the perspective proposed is this: *that social justice is manifest in reductions in inequality: in a process of returning to equality*.

Three important points must be made before this principle is elaborated and defended. The first is that it is grounded in the here and now: in the reality of a world of actual, existing inequality, not in some abstract state of nature or clean slate onto which we can etch perfectly just social arrangements. The second point is that this perspective is dynamic, concerned with change, with the movement from one state of affairs to another, which can be in stages and might never be completed. The third point is that the objective of reducing inequality, of moving towards equality, need not require a commitment to the achievement of perfect equality, soon or ever. Perfect equality may be held out as an ideal, to which we may aspire in the abstract, but in the real world of moderate scarcity, selfishness and actual inequality it is practically impossible, and not necessarily right.

At the time of its original proposition, the principle of the more equal the better gained strength from the abiding tradition of egalitarianism. For example, Ginsberg (1965, p. 73), recognizing the diversity of grounds on which inequality might be justified, suggested that 'judged by any of these criteria the wide differences in wealth now accepted are disproportionate and that there is, therefore, a strong case for reducing inequalities, even if there is no agreement as to what would constitute proportional equality'. Particular support was found in Sen (1973), who proposed a well-known graphic portrayal of inequality – the Lorenz curve – as a possible measure of the level of welfare (p. 61):

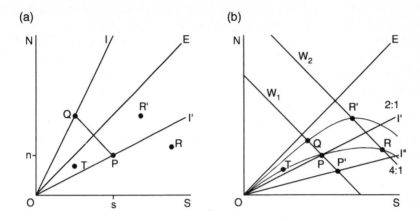

Figure 5.1   Some implications of social justice as equalization.
(Source: (a) based on Smith, 1977, p. 152, figure 6.3d).

The fact that one distribution has a higher Lorenz curve than another can be taken as a *prima facie* case that it is a better distribution from a welfare point of view . . . While the Lorenz ranking is not in itself compelling, the onus of demonstration may well be thought to lie on the person wishing to reject this ranking on other grounds.

A distribution with a higher Lorenz curve, or a lower Gini coefficient as a measure of the degree of inequality represented by the curve (see later in this chapter), would be 'Lorenz-superior', as Sen (p. 64) put it. While the terminology is that of welfare economics, and while the devices in question are not without their technical problems, translation into social justice is straightforward: *the more equal, the more just* – or provide a convincing argument to the contrary.

Now that the principle has been established, it can be subjected to some critical scrutiny in simple graphic presentations of the kind used in previous chapters. In figure 5.1 the axes can be taken to represent two regions, North and South, although individuals or socio-economic groups can readily be substituted (even males or females, blacks and whites, for those seeking a gender or racial perspective). The distributional issue concerns some collective good, though the dominant good of income or wealth can be substituted for greater reality as long as the limitations of such a unidimensional view are born in mind. In figure 5.1a the existing distribution is point P, the regional shares being indicated by n and s. The North has an advantage of 2:1. This ratio is the prevailing degree of inequality, marked by the lines from P to I′ and Q to I (the latter being the equivalent of PI′ if the positions of the two regions were reversed). Justice as moving towards equality (the diagonal line from the origin of the graph out to E) requires a position within IQOPI'.

Presented in this way, the analysis is very similar to that for Peffer's constraint on the degree of inequality, explored in figure 4.1. The only difference is that, now, the constraint on further inequality is established by the existing degree of inequality, not by some level beyond which human dignity is thought to pay too much. However, the equalization principle is subject to the same powerful objection as in Peffer's case. It disallows positions, such as R, which make both regions better-off but at the price of greater inequality. There is a further objection that was not raised in the discussion of Peffer's case: that the rule of the more equal the better would permit positions (such as T) in which both regions are worse-off than before.

The difficulty in maintaining the 'Lorenz' constraint in these situations was recognized in the original presentation (Smith, 1977, p. 156). Here reference was made to Sen (1973, p. 58) again, who saw Pigou's earlier resolution of the conflict between quantity and distribution as follows: 'while a really big decrease in the inequality of the distribution of incomes could perhaps be approved even if it was accompanied by a small reduction in the value of national product, few increments in its value could be approved at the expense of increased inequalities.' Thus, the possibility of some pay-off relationship was recognized. The question then becomes one of how much the Lorenz constraint might be violated to prevent outcomes which are otherwise extremely unattractive, which is consistent with the non-compelling nature of the constraint as Sen saw it. Peffer (1990, p. 391) also recognizes the problem.

Further clarification can be obtained by integrating Rawlsian graphics with the situation depicted in figure 5.1a. In figure 5.1b we show the Rawlsian co-operation curve from O (the original position of equality) to P (our existing position) and on to R (the maximin) where the worst-off region N is as well-off as possible. R violates the inequality constraint I'. Both T and P can be read as sequential positions adopted in reaching R. To Rawls there would be no question of going back to T (to reduce inequality) from our current position P, but he would insist that we went on from P to R: the increase in inequality here benefits the worst-off. The only permissible move along the curve towards greater equality would be upwards to the left towards R, from the right-hand extremity of the graph, indicating retreat from a position where inequality had become so great as to generate losses for the worst-off.

This analysis undermines the imposition of an inequality constraint, unless we are prepared to say that reducing inequality is important enough to justify losses to the poor, and perhaps to everyone else. But, how do we actually know what position really makes the worst-off as well-off as possible? How do we know whether society really has gone far enough along the Rawlsian path, or even too far? What is more, in the context of the present graphic analysis, how do we even know whether the path identified as OTPR is really the one from which the worst-off stand to benefit most?

Suppose that the relevant trajectory was in fact the higher one shown in figure 5.1b, culminating in the higher maximin of R'. This would then justify the imposition of the inequality constraint I' (based on existing position P), and enable the equalization move from P to Q, or from R to R', to be justified without violating Rawls. Note that we have placed P and Q on the same production frontier or welfare contour W_1, and R and R' on W_2, so that the aggregate well-being is the same as at P and R respectively: it has merely been redistributed. Or suppose the actual existing situation has been P' (with an inequality ratio of 4:1 indicated by I''): this would have made the equalizing move P' to P justified. But it is not sufficient simply to manipulate lines and curves in a diagram to sustain the case for justice as equalization. Reference must be made to the empirical plausibility of situations in which equalization will necessarily benefit the worst-off.

It is tempting to pose the question in the context of the worst-off people in the world (for example, in central Africa's starvation belt), and ask whether they are really as well-off as they can possibly be, given the world's present aggregate wealth. But instead we will seek an answer closer to home. As these paragraphs are being written (March, 1993), unemployment in Britain has reached 3 million (over 10 per cent of the 'working' population), and the number unemployed for more than a year exceeds 1 million. For many residents in parts of British cities and towns affected by plant closures, the prospect of a job in the foreseeable future is probably somewhere between evens and zero. In Poplar in East London, close to where I work and under the shadow of the insolvent Canary Wharf skyscraper monument to the Thatcher enterprise culture, unemployment is almost one in four. Merseyside and the Scottish highlands have qualified for the highest level of European Community development aid. A new programme for 'community care' for society's most vulnerable (including the mentally ill and aged) is being introduced, funded by hard-pressed local authorities already sacking staff and closing facilities. Homelessness has become visible on London's streets. And so on. That the worst-off people and places in Britain today are as well-off as possible is implausible.

Is even greater inequality likely to improve the lot of Britain's worst-off? The answer is, almost certainly, no. Inequality increased during the 1980s (for some evidence, see later in this chapter), and it is very hard to associate this with a Rawlsian improvement. Returning to figure 5.1b, the real world of contemporary Britain is probable represented by something like P, or even P', with the relevant Rawlsian path the one leading to R'. All this is, of course, somewhat speculative. But it makes much more intuitive sense than to assert that the actual present position is a Rawlsian maximin, or that further erosion of the welfare state so as to avoid increasing taxes on the rich is somehow to the advantage of the worst-off.

What may have happened here, and in much of the rest of the world, is something like this. From a position close to equality lost in the mists of time, some people were able to gain advantage associated with acquisition of property, including natural resources. That they may well have done this unjustly, requiring Nozick's restitution, is beside the point for the moment. A dominant group emerged, identified by their property holdings, and possibly also by other characteristics such as ethnicity, gender and geographical location. Their economic power translated into the political power to subordinate and exploit other groups, thereby exacerbating inequality and further reproducing relations of domination and oppression. As more refinements of life became available, the well-off needed even more of what has become the dominant good of wealth to acquire them, ratcheting up the degree of inequality still further. The oppressed may eventually have been able to force concessions from the dominant class, hence reducing inequality somewhat. But the crucial question is whether inequality in distribution, originally or subsequently, was ever required to pass the test of Rawls's difference principle. If not (which is surely the case), then society may simply have embarked on a trajectory destined to reproduce inequality, possibly increasing for a time, possibly decreasing, but without any reference to whether the worst-off were thereby advantaged. That the outcome, today, makes the worst-off worse-off than they might have been with historical reference to the Rawls principle, comprises a strong argument for justice as equalization.

Inequality today, in capitalist, market-dominated economies, is grounded in an historical process of unequal acquisition of property. The existing distribution is a function of past distributions which, if unjust by whatever criteria, simply perpetuate injustice. And the present projects injustice into the future. Hence the calls sometimes made for a once-and-for-all-time radical redistribution of wealth and property ownership, to eliminate entrenched hierarchies (e.g. Kymlicka, 1990, p. 86). Even Robert Nozick (1974, p. 231), looking back into history, concedes this possibility, as at one point he appears to endorse Rawls's position:

> [A]ssuming (1) that victims of injustice generally do worse than they otherwise would and (2) that those from the least well-off group in the society have the highest probability of being the (descendants of) victims of the most serious injustice who are owed compensation by those who benefitted from the injustices . . . then a *rough* rule of thumb for rectifying injustices might seem to be the following: organize society so as to maximize the position of whatever group ends up least well-off in the society . . . past injustices might be so great as to make

necessary in the short run a more extensive state in order to rectify them.

Arguing for justice as equalization will inevitably face opposition from the vested interests who gain from inequality, and who have been able to marshal so much reverence for market outcomes and their association with social justice. Neoclassical economics has performed a powerful ideological role, in the hands of those whose primary purpose seems to have been to deflect criticism of distributional inequalities. As was mentioned in chapter 3, the egalitarian implications of the marginal utility of income have not figured prominently in the adoption of elements of utilitarianism. Yet, as Sen (1992, pp. 24, 95–6) points out, as far back as 1920 this provided the basis for Hugh Dalton's 'principle of transfer' whereby a shift of income from rich to poor would be a distributive improvement, with an equal distribution maximizing social welfare.

Similarly, the rectification principle is far less frequently cited than those aspects of Nozick's entitlement theory which lend support to existing distributional inequalities. Yet as Barry (1989, p. 218) puts it, 'From Locke to Nozick there is a long and disreputable tradition of using a fairy story about the way in which acquisition might have occured as the basis for a defence of the status quo.' Barry's own analysis pushes Rawls's theory to the limits of its egalitarianism (see chapter 3), as expressed in the following modification of the difference principle (Barry, 1989, p. 292):

[I]f we ask what we are saying about an action or an institution when we say it is unjust, the general answer is, I suggest, this. We are claiming that it cannot be defended publicly – that the principles of distribution it instantiates could reasonably be rejected by those who do badly under it.

Barry (1989, pp. 232–3) sees some merit in the argument that, as all inequalities are morally arbitrary, it is the worst-off who should determine how great such inequalities should be. He cites in this connection Steven Strasnick's concept of the dictatorship of the worst-off, and points out that, in an article subsequent to his book, Rawls himself explicitly introduced the idea of the worst-off having a veto on any move away from equality (see also Rawls, 1993, p. 282). The original exploration of social justice in spatial systems by David Harvey (1972a, p. 97), influenced by Rawls, implied a similar arrangement in suggesting that making the worst-off region as well-off as possible might require the least fortunate always to have the final say (Smith, 1977, p. 146).

It might therefore be pertinent to ask, rhetorically, whether existing degrees of inequality in countries like Great Britain and the United States, and the institutions responsible for them, would be defended by those who do worst under them: by the worst-off groups in society, or by the inhabitants of the worst-off region or district of a city. Perhaps this should be put to the test of public opinion, with the franchise confined to the worst-off. Of course, some would find this too severe a test of institutions and their outcome: not uninvolved enough according to Griffin (1986, p. 183). Perhaps it is too far from the principle of equal concern, and the proposition that social arrangements have to be credible to all participants in the system (Sen, 1992, p. 17). But there does seem at least a pragmatic case for giving the worst-off a special voice, if short of a veto. If equalization is taken to be the first priority of social justice, it may require some restriction of the kind of freedom usually upheld in liberal democracies.

In any event, the principle of the more equal the better seems the best operational version of social justice to hand. It is in tune with an intuitive sense that inequality has gone too far, in most parts of the world if not necessarily everywhere, at least for those who suffer most from it. The explicit incorporation of Rawls's difference principle can act as a constraint on equalization itself going too far. Social justice as equalization is, potentially, a universal principle with which reality can be engaged. All we need add at this stage, lest it not be taken for granted, is that the principle should apply in all relevant circumstances. That is, justice as equalization should apply wherever and whenever inequality is an issue, whether geographically, among socio-economic groups, by ethnicity, race or gender. And the greater the inequality, the more urgent the application of the principle.

Minimum standards

The next step is to take a more practical look at how social justice as equalization might be advanced. One possibility involves the adoption of some minimum standard of living designed to raise the position of the worst-off. This could be funded by redistribution from the better-off, and adjusted upwards over time as economic growth permits so as further to reduce the degree of inequality.

The idea of a minimum standard is familiar in both theory and practice. It is basic to the welfare state with its guaranteed levels of social security, and to socialism with its basic provision of services via collective consumption. It is an obvious response to unmet need, the reservations of libertarians notwithstanding, without any commitment to perfect equality other than of the minimum provision. Sometimes portrayed as a safety-net or padded floor, it has particular appeal in fairly well-off capitalist societies with democratic institutions. It is a practical expression of the 'split personality' which James Mead thought every citizen should develop: acting selfishly in the market place and altruistically at the ballot box (cited in Barry, 1989, pp. 394–5). It is also very much in line with the actual beliefs and practices of professional decision-makers at the local level, at least as identified in the United States by Elster (1992, p. 238):

> To maximize total welfare seems inhuman, to maximize minimum welfare seems inefficient. The common-sense conception of justice is somewhere in between these conceptions. One should maximize total welfare, subject to a fixed floor constraint on individual welfare.

Rawls (1971, pp. 276–7, 284–6) recognized the role of a 'social minimum' in the context of implementation of his difference principle. A fairly high guaranteed minimum is derived by Dworkin (1981), in his social contract, which has people starting off with equal resources and subscribing to insurance against handicap, lack of talent or natural disadvantage (mentioned in chapter 3): an attempt to reconcile the conflict in Rawls's theory between accepting the moral arbitrariness of natural endowment and allowing people to benefit from these same endowments as they pursue their own life plans. The minimum standard arises from people's willing sacrifice of part of their own likely benefits if naturally well-endowed and choosing advantageous life plans, for security against the possibility of being naturally ill-endowed, without simply requiring those who pursue well-rewarded lives to subsidize those who freely choose idleness whether talented or otherwise. In short, it appeals to self-interest rather than altruism.

Fried (1983) provides a justification for a minimum standard which explicitly rejects the egalitarianism underpinning both Rawls and Dworkin's approach. He denies that handicaps or differences in talents are morally arbitrary in any sense that would provide a basis for redistribution. As free, moral persons in the Kantian sense, we are entitled to our talents as part of what we are (the self-ownership argument adopted by Nozick; see chapter 3). But, unlike conventional libertarians, Fried (1983, pp. 51–2) finds a simple intuitive basis for a duty to share (and to care): as others share with us our moral worth, they also have lives which they are seeking to live:

> To be indifferent to the misery of others is to devalue our own moral worth. We must therefore care for others. This care is what I contend is the moral basis for our duty to share, for the duty in society and therefore in states to institute systems of redistribution ... That concern seems to me to carry with it no implications that if we do not have equality we should be embarrassed. It carries with it, unlike the term fair shares, no implication about equality at all. For it is the need itself, the misery itself, which makes the claim upon us for our sympathetic concern as fellow human beings.

The entitlement to a minimum standard can also be invoked in the context of rights. As Griffin (1986, p. 311) puts it, 'human rights protect a certain kind of value. In the case of this right, what is protected is the value attached to our carrying out an autonomously chosen life-plan. The minimum is defined as the necessary material provision for our being able to do so.'

Fried (p. 52) provides a particular answer to the practical questions of how and in what terms a minimum standard is to be determined:

> A person has a claim on his fellows to a standard package of basic or essential goods – housing, education, health care, food; i.e. the social (or decent) minimum – if by reasonable efforts he cannot earn enough to procure this minimum for himself.

He speculates that in a state with well-established democratic institutions and with certain levels of essential goods and services achieved (implicitly, something like the United States), there will be a substantial needy 'underclass' amounting to perhaps one-fifth of the total population. The social minimum with which they should be provided would be established by what is enjoyed by a particular reference group, which he identifies as unionized unskilled workers. This is a specific version of the notion that the minimum should represent what most people already have (Griffin, 1986, p. 44). The clear implication is that minimum standards must be relative to life in a particular society, and of course to what can be afforded. It should increase as the average increases (Rawls, 1971, p. 285).

There is, however, a sting in Fried's tale. What the poor should get is: 'those things necessary to sustain life and the human capacities, to discover opportunities and to participate in the life of the community', and not income as such (Fried, 1983, p. 59). This is to ensure that they have the means to avoid hunger, cold and ill health; if they would rather spend money on drink than food, there is no claim on others to subsidize such free preferences. There is, of course, a long-established social-policy practice to the contrary, making benefits available in cash rather than (or as well as) in kind. However, money can be avoided by direct provision of such things as shelter, health care and food (e.g. America's food stamps). But not to have the freedom to make any spending choices at all is hardly consistent with participation in the life of a community where rampant consumption is the norm, at least among the fortunate four-fifths. Hence the predominant form of the minimum involves an income supplement, available to all as something on which people can count whether more or less than required for basic needs, in the universalist spirit which inspired the original welfare state.

While there may be no egalitarian implications to a minimum standard, it does appear to be based on some assumption about the equal moral worth of individuals and their capacity to pursue their life projects. But more practically, any minimum standard which is worth implementing would surely narrow the gap between the worst-off and the rest. How high the standard is set, and with what qualifications or strength of entitlement, is a matter of practical politics. The higher the minimum standard, the more progress there will be towards equality.

There is a final, geographical point of some significance. The further the minimum standard is extended, for example beyond the local-authority, or the national boundaries which usually protect the well-off from supporting the poor elsewhere, the more egalitarian the implications. To introduce the time dimension tightens the screws even further. Rawls (1971, pp. 282–93) recognized that saving for future generations has implications for what present people can have. And as Sterba (1986, p. 15) explains: 'the provision of that minimum not only in our own society but also to distant peoples and future generations as well would put severe limits on the permissible inequalities of wealth and income that could obtain in any society.' (It could even require something like the socialization of the means of production, he asserts). Thus, if we take seriously the equal moral worth of all people everywhere, provision of a minimum standard, given present limitations on the world's resources, has severe egalitarian implications.

From needs to well-being

The idea of a minimum standard leads to the question of what is usually referred to as *basic needs*. Indeed, some of the issues involved have already been anticipated in the previous section. It might even be argued that they are actually the same thing, in the sense that certain needs are basic for instrumental reasons, as the minimum required to live a certain kind of life. It could also be that people should be entitled to have such needs met as of right; Peffer (1990, p. 14, quoted in chapter 4) uses the term rights as well as minimum level and basic needs in his first principle of justice. However, it seems useful to maintain a distinction, so as to examine the concept of basic needs in its own terms. This also relieves basic needs of the safety-net implication with which minimum standards are often associated, and allows for the possibility that a set of needs deemed basic might be above the minimal level defined by survival, human decency or some other perhaps ungenerous criterion. Whether basic needs can be translated into human rights will remain an open question.

If we can identify a set of basic needs arising purely from what it is to be human, and therefore independent of place (and possibly also of time), then their equal provision could build some substance onto a universal approach to social justice with egalitarian content but short of strict equality. And, if pushed high enough, a level of basic need, like the minimum standard, could be used to promote equalization. But surely, the diversity of humankind and of real societies and their cultures poses the problem of relativism, just as in Fried's account of the minimum standard. The argument to be explored here is that it is in fact possible to talk about basic human needs at a universal level, with enough specificity to be useful if not necessarily in great detail as to their exact nature and quantities. We will approach the issue from different disciplinary perspectives, to see how they converge on universal needs for human well-being.

The resolution of practical problems does not figure prominently in moral philosophy, preoccupied as it is with prior questions of meaning. Such is the case with human needs and well-being. The lengthy exploration of these concepts by Griffin (1986) stresses that needs, unlike desires, have to do with one thing being a necessary condition for another. Some needs arise simply from the ends we have chosen (such as a pen, so as to write), but some are basic in the following sense (pp. 41–2):

> [T]hey are needs we all have just by being human ... We usually speak of basic needs as if they were not only basic but absolute: humans need food and rest and health – not *for* anything; they just do ... they are what we need to survive, to be heathy, to avoid harm, to function properly ... *Well-being* ... *is the level to which basic needs are met.*

Basic needs have a 'quite special moral importance', setting up obligations or claims on others. In this sense they are like rights. The link with minimum standards in this account is that basic needs 'involve a norm falling below which brings malfunction, harm, or ailment'.

Getting closer to what well-being actually involves can be assisted by consideration of what a good life comprises for humanity in general, in the spirit of the perfectionism sometimes associated with Aristotle's notion of *eudaimonia* or human flourishing. Griffin (1986, pp. 67–8) comes up with the following values: accomplishment, the components of human existence (autonomy, the basic capacities which enable action, minimum material goods, freedom from pain, and liberty), understanding, enjoyment, and deep personal relations. Brown (1986) also adopts an approach grounded in human nature (a form of ethical naturalism), with a similar list of *basic human goods* (p. 159):

1. The means of subsistence; adequate food, clothing, shelter and so on.
2. Pleasure; I take it that the persistence of hedonism through the centuries has some significance. Human beings do indeed value

pleasure for its own sake, so that it can be described as an irreducible aspect of the truly good life.

3. Work, rest and play; these constitute the basic activities that human beings must engage in if their lives are to be well-balanced, if they are to develop as human beings.

4. Social relationships (having, for example, friends, lovers and perhaps even rivals): these constitute the proper social context for the pursuit of the basic good activities, and reflect the fact that we have social, and not just private, needs.

Well-being or the good life is what successfully combines these basic goods. This systemization is accomplished through what Brown (1986, pp. 138, 162) claims to be an objective theory of the good for man (and presumably woman), derived from the practice of science and the process of living.

Brown (p. 167) goes on to draw the following (re)distributional implication:

If a social structure systematically denies to some the possibility of enjoying some or all of the basic goods then it is to be improved upon, if possible. An improvement would be a system which provides more people with basic goods even at the cost of denying others inessential goods (inessential, that is, to a basically good life).

This principle could be restated in terms of the relative marginal utilities of basic and inessential goods. However, Brown prefers to portray it as a revision of the familiar Pareto criterion, proposing that some people can be made worse-off to improve the lot of others, depending on the kind of goods involved. In other words, some people's luxuries can be sacrificed for other people's essentials.

We now turn to a contribution from economics: not from the abstractions of welfare theory, which tries to avoid value judgements by using the unspecified concept of utility, but from the work of one of the few exponents of this 'dismal science' to place ethical considerations in the centre of his work. Amartya Sen (1992) recognizes the diversity of humankind and the plurality of considerations relevant to the good life, or the 'spaces' (in his non-geographical sense) in which questions of (in)equality can arise. Like Michael Walzer, he sees divergencies in the characteristics of inequality with respect to different spaces (i.e. spheres or variables) as consistent with human heterogeneity. He avoids couching his argument in terms of basic needs, because of their invocation of specific commodities. His perspective on the way in which goods are converted into well-being places primacy on the notion of human *capabilities*. This is summarized as follows (Sen, 1992, p. 129; emphasis in original):

The particular approach to equality that I have explored involves judging individual advantage by *the freedom to achieve*, incorporating (but going beyond) *actual achievement*. In many contexts, particularly in the assessment of individual well-being, these conditions can, I have argued, be fruitfully seen in terms of *the capability to function*, incorporating (but going beyond) the actual functionings that a person can achieve. The 'capability approach' builds on a general concern with freedoms to achieve (including the capabilities to function).

Thus primary goods or resources are the means through which people have the capabilities to function in ways that promote their well-being. For example, food maintains peoples' physical capacity for work, which is a function necessary to obtain money, which in turn helps achievement with respect to goods, services and experiences valuable to well-being.

The relativism implicit in Sen's stress on human diversity surfaces, along with a specific sense of basics, in the particular context of the extreme poverty of developing economies. Here there may be a relatively small number of centrally important functionings (and the corresponding basic capabilities), for example 'the ability to be well-nourished and well-sheltered, the capability of escaping avoidable morbidity and premature mortality, and so forth' (p. 45). There is some congruence with what others would include under the heading of basic needs. In other contexts, Sen claims, the list may have to be much longer and more diverse. Poverty is defined as 'the failure of basic capabilities to reach certain minimally acceptable levels' (p. 109), which involve inadequacy (of income, for example) not just lowness. Deprivation is relative insofar as commodities are concerned, but to see poverty in capability terms is a universal. He concludes (p. 116; emphasis in original):

> The absolute-relative correspondence relates to the variable commodity requirement for the *same* functioning (e.g. a much larger need for commodities in rich countries to achieve the *same* functionings, such as taking part in the life of the community, or – to go back to Adam Smith's example – appearing in public without shame). While the minimally acceptable capabilities to function may *also* vary from society to society, the variable commodity requirement for the *same* capabilities does not, in itself, require that we take a basically 'relativist' approach to poverty, provided we see poverty as capability failure.

We move on to a perspective from development planning. John Friedmann (1992) has elaborated 'alternative' development strategies which emphasize the political *empowerment* of the poor. Making a particular point of the morality of development, he echoes some philosophical positions which we have already encountered, using the three foundations of human rights, citizenship and human flourishing in claiming that 'every person is entitled both to adequate material conditions of life and to be a politically active subject in his or her own community' (p. 10). He is not asserting anything approaching the dictatorship of the worst-off, merely the right of deprived populations to challenge the elites whose views on development usually prevail.

The basic-needs perspective was part of an approach to development planning which emerged in the 1970s, with an emphasis on redistribution as essential accompaniment to the economic growth which had hitherto dominated mainstream thinking. The World Bank and the International Labour Office became committed to this strategy, the latter producing a minimum definition of basic needs to include the following (Friedmann, 1992, pp. 59–60):

1. Minimum requirements of a family for private consumption (food, shelter, clothing, etc.);
2. Essential services of collective consumption provided by and for the community at large (safe drinking water, sanitation, electricity, public transport, and health and education facilities);
3. The participation of the people in making the decisions that affect them;
4. The satisfaction of an absolute level of basic needs within a broader framework of basic human rights; and
5. Employment as both a means and an end in a basic-needs strategy.

However, such aspirations clashed with the interests of the Third World elites, who were more concerned with growth than redistribution, which greatly restricted the basic-needs approach in practice.

Friedmann's pragmatic planning perspective leads him in a distinctly relativist direction when it comes to the actual implementation of a basic-needs strategy. Poor countries are unable to afford what might be considered basic needs in those that are rich. There are also the simple environmental considerations which make winter heating more important in some parts of the world than others, for example, along with variations in people's tastes and preferences. Friedmann (p. 63) also insists that a basic-needs approach reflecting 'relative urgencies and scarcities' should be applied at the sub-national scale, by regions, towns and villages. A datum such as the number of calories per day needed for a healthy and active life has to be translated into a specific programme, which requires a territorially differentiated approach. Thus the spatial aspect of development, to which Friedmann has always been so sensitive, does encourage relativism at the level of what must actually be done. But he nevertheless espouses a universal general conception of poverty as *disempowerment*. This can be read as a political expression of Sen's capability failure.

We could follow the tension between relativism and universality further, through other texts. For example, Young (1990a, p. 91) refers explicitly to modern industrial societies when she says that justice requires 'a societal commitment to meeting the basic needs of all persons whether or not they contribute to the social product ... If persons suffer material deprivation of basic needs for food, shelter, health care, and so on, then they cannot pursue lives of satisfying work, social participation, and expression.' It is not clear why such a general formulation cannot be universal; presumably it is the resource constraint again. Walzer's relativism is tempered by the concessions that 'there are some goods that are needed absolutely' (1983, p. 65), and 'security is provided because all citizens need it' (p. 67).

However, we will round off the discussion with one further reference: to Len Doyal and Ian Gough's *A Theory of Human Need* (1991), which combines insights from philosophy and political science. They begin by taking the relativists head on. They allude to a wide agreement in modern thought that universal and objective human needs do not exist or cannot be formulated coherently. Orthodox economics prioritizes personal preferences, the 'new right' laud individual self-determination, Marxists stress the historical and social specificity of need, the opponents of cultural imperialism assert that needs are group-specific, 'radical democrats' see needs as discursive, while phenomenologists say needs are socially constructed. Doyal and Gough counter this consensus by arguing that all these positions implicitly presuppose what they purport to reject (some elements of their case have already appeared in earlier chapters of this volume). Preference or want satisfaction requires some normative judgements if its content is to be specified and measured. Acceptance of a minimum safety-net on the part of the new right implies some notion of objective need. Human need and other transhistoric values are central to the Marxist critique of capitalism. Assertions of cultural autonomy and respect for group standards cannot exclude the possibility of external critique. Similar arguments undermine narrow versions of the social construction position, although it has to be recognized that ultimately the notion of human need, like morality itself, is a human construct.

Doyal and Gough's position reflects the naturalism of some others whose work has been cited. Human nature sets natural boundaries on human needs (p. 37): 'Our mammalian constitution shapes our needs for such things as food and warmth in order to survive and maintain health. Our cognitive aptitudes and the bases of our emotionality in childhood shape many other needs – for supportive and close relations with others, for example.' Against the various forms of relativism, they argue that all people share one obvious need: *to avoid serious harm*. This goes beyond the evidently harmful failure to survive in a physical sense, to incorporate impaired social participation or pursuit of objectives deemed valuable by the individual in a specific social milieu, which can vary with culture, place and so on. What they say about need is objective, 'in that its theoretical and empirical specification is independent of individual preference', and universal, 'in that its conception of serious harm is the same for everyone' (p. 49).

This universal goal generates two basic needs. One is for the *physical health* to continue living and able to function effectively. The other is for the *personal autonomy* or ability necessary to make informed choices about what should be done and how to go about doing it in a given societal context. These basic needs in turn require the satisfaction of certain *intermediate needs*, for adequate nutritional food and water, protective housing, and so on (see figure 5.2). That all people share these needs is hard to contradict.

In addressing the issue of distribution, Doyal and Gough propose the following expansion of Rawls's difference principle (p. 132): 'inequalities will be tolerated to the extent that they benefit the least well off through leading to the provision of those goods and services necessary for the optimization of basic need-satisfaction.' This makes what it means for the worst-off to be as well-off as possible more specific. The optimization of need satisfaction will also be a necessary condition for the achievement of those rights and liberties prioritized in Rawls's first principle (see chapter 3). The similarity with Peffer (1990) is evident (see chapter 4).

Doyal and Gough's approach is made all the more useful by the attention given to the practical application of their theory. They show how the extent to which needs are satisfied can be measured by appropriate indicators, not only within but also between cultures. For example (p. 219), they propose that satisfaction of the need for adequate housing could be measured by proportion of people homeless, proportion in structures that do not protect against normal weather, proportion lacking safe sanitation facilities, and proportion living above a specified ratio of persons per room. Comparisons can then be made, without denying people the freedom to express individual or cultural preferences in the construction, appearance, layout and adornment of their homes. Thus, many of the actual goods and services required to satisfy needs are culturally variable. Basic needs are always universal, Doyal and Gough (p. 155) assert, but their 'satisfiers' are often relative. They compare this distinction with Sen's analysis of poverty, which is absolute with respect to capabilities but relative with respect to the commodities required to alleviate it.

Doyal and Gough's theory is summarized in figure 5.2. They set out their universal goals under the headings of participation and liberation (the latter echoing Friedmann's empowerment). These require an 'optimum' level of basic need-satisfaction, in its turn dependent on the minimum necessary satisfaction of intermediate needs. At the bottom of figure 5.2 are various societal preconditions for need-satisfaction, which relate to the structure

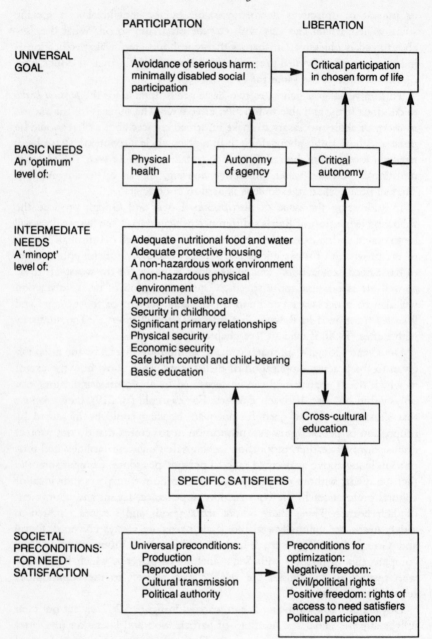

Figure 5.2   Outline of a theory of human need.
(Source: Doyal and Gough, 1991, p. 170, figure 8.2).

of the economy as well as its culture and politics. Cross-cultural education is identified as a means of encouraging mutual understanding. Critical autonomy involves the capacity to examine and question forms of life, including one's own, that of the society in which one lives, and those of others.

Further details of how levels of need-satisfaction can be measured and compared must be left to Doyal and Gough's book, except for a few matters to be dealt with later in this chapter. It is sufficient simply to draw attention to their full list of suggested indicators (p. 190), and to some bold attempts at numerical comparisons between different parts of the world (their chapter 12). It is their general conclusion that matters most in the present context: 'Relativists are wrong: objective welfare *can* be compared and evaluated over space and over time' (p. 269).

This is broadly the conclusion arrived at by the others whose perspectives have been outlined here. And it would be remarkable if it was otherwise, for this would mean that there was no way of saying that life is better here than there, now than then. People are in fact making such judgements much of the time, in deciding how to live and improve their lives, and it would be odd if moral philosophers, economists, planners and the like really considered them misguided. However, we must note that the case for universal needs has been made in rather general terms. It might be wise to acknowledge the point made by Griffin (1986, p. 44) that, while there is a rationale for fixing a line between basic and non-basic needs, this could change as society changes. This is consistent with human progress, but to preserve some universal conception will be necessary if progress itself is to be identified. As Rivlin (1971, p. 144) put it, in the early years of social indicators, 'to do better, we must have a way of distinguishing better from worse'.

We must also recognize the limits to universalism. It is important to bear in mind that, in assessing progress towards the realization of well-being and its equalization in actual societies, the culturally and historically specific means must be taken into account. And this involves sensitivity to local conditions, not the unexamined imposition of external values. Otherwise, we could become cultural imperialists. There is a delicate balance to be struck between defensible universals and particular means towards need-satisfaction, which acknowledges and respects the authenticity of preferences arising from human difference.

Producing well-being

A particular feature of Doyal and Gough's approach to human need, shared by those of Brown, Friedmann and Sen outlined above, is its attention to the structure of society. By this we mean the organization of production, exchange and consumption, and the social relations, institutional arrangements and cultural practices through which this is realized. The importance of social structure and institutions is recognized in most contemporary accounts of social justice, but its specifics are often submerged by abstraction. Raising the role of the structure of society here helps to move the discussion on from redistributional strategies to the way in which needs are actually satisfied (or otherwise), as contributions to human well-being unequally experienced by people over time and space.

The briefest sketch will be sufficient. Figure 5.3 represents the fundamental features of how any society functions. At the core is the process of material production whereby human labour and the means of production in the form of instruments (capital equipment) and resources (natural or created) come together. As was recognized in the discussion of Marxism in chapter 4, different modes of production are characterized by the level of development of the productive forces (or the technical capacity to produce) and the social relations through which people participate as individuals and classes (e.g. as workers, capitalists and landowners under capitalism). First call on the productive output is reproduction of the means of production which have been used (e.g. allowance for depreciation of capital assets and non-renewable resources), of labour (day-by-day, generation-by-generation), and of the institutions regulating the process. These will be 'basic' requirements in the sense of functional necessity for society's on-going reproduction, like the most basic of individual needs; anything less, and society will be in decline.

Surplus production beyond that needed for the simple reproduction of society at its present level of living or well-being can be deployed in investment in new means of production and in ways of enhancing labour productivity (e.g. more expenditure on education or health care). How much actually goes towards improved living standards for the mass of the people, as opposed to sustaining further accumulation of capital or luxury consumption on the part of an elite, will depend on the mode of production and on how actual societies operate with respect to the distribution of the surplus. Some conception of basic individual need may be influential in this process, from which the final state of well-being will arise. In a diagram similar to figure 5.3, Doyal and Gough (1991, p. 232, figure 11.1) take luxury goods out of production before need-satisfiers contribute to the consumption of households (see Smith, 1979, p. 38, figure 2.2 for another possible model).

The resolution of (re)distributional issues will be closely related to the institutions subsumed under the general heading of the *social formation*. This includes the state apparatus at the national and local scale, the laws (upholding various forms of rights, for example), and the specific cultural practices, beliefs and ideology which help to bind a society together and to make sense of the process of living. It is within this arena that a society will form, reproduce or modify whatever moral values and sense of social justice

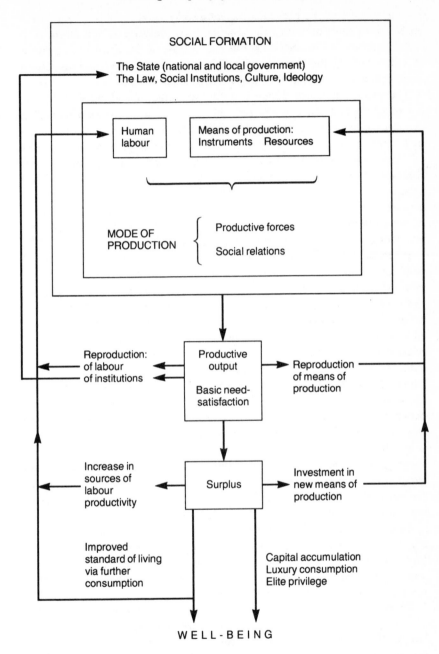

Figure 5.3   Outline of the process of social development.
(Source: based on Smith, 1987, p. 34, figure 2.3).

prevail, specific to the particular society insofar as they will be part of what enables it to function within the conditions of scarcity and selfishness. And it will be here that those seeking universals will assert them, informed by what they know of life elsewhere, as part of the process of critical discourse about society which will include challenges to prevailing norms.

The extent to which people's needs are satisfied and their well-being enhanced depends on how this structure operates, in particular places. That the actual outcomes are expressed in various degrees and patterns of inequality is a matter of common observation. Geographically uneven endowments of resources and technical capacities combine with the prevailing social relations of production to generate such outcomes, with the state, political process and other elements of the social formation ameliorating or perhaps exacerbating the inequalities manifest in the economic sphere. The capacity of some group(s) to dominate and oppress others may be part of the process generating and perpetuating this form of structural inequality.

It remains to say a little about more technical aspects of the process of need-satisfaction, and the link with human well-being. This allows us to resurrect the distinction between resources and welfare set aside at the beginning of the chapter (though not far beneath the surface in the discussion of basic needs), in the context of means and ends. Again, the framework of Doyal and Gough (1991) is helpful, highlighting the sequential cause-and-effect relationship between satisfiers, intermediate and basic needs.

Of course, similar ideas have been around for some time. In research stimulated by the United Nations engagement with development issues, Drewnowski (1974, summarized in Smith, 1977, pp. 35–9) made a distinction between a population's *state of welfare* and its *level of living*, proposing that the former depended on the latter. He defined welfare (the term well-being would be preferable in the present context) in terms of people's somatic status (physical development), educational status (mental development) and social status (social integration and participation). This is close to some of the conceptions of basic need outlined in the previous section. Level of living involves nutrition, clothing, shelter, health, education, leisure, security, social environment and physical environment: these could be referred to as intermediate needs. Just as people's *stock* of pecuniary wealth is maintained (or otherwise) by *flows* of income, so their state of welfare or well-being arises from their level of living. Such notions provided a basis for a general economic model of human need-satisfaction.

There are horrendous difficulties involved in the construction of such a model, the possibility of which featured in the literature of the 1970s (e.g. Smith, 1973a, pp. 73–7; 1977, chapter 7). Central to these problems is the fact that the cause-and-effect relationships (or production functions) involved are poorly understood. For example, it is far from clear how a nation's physical or mental status can best be enhanced by a given level of additional expenditure on health or educational services. Defining the outcomes, in terms of physical and mental status, will be a subject of contention, for example whether health is best measured by mortality rates or by the ability of the living to function effectively. Then it will not be clear whether health (however defined) is best improved by spending more on health services (and within them on hospitals, doctors or nurses, reactive or preventive care), or by improving people's housing, safety at work or vulnerability to unemployment, all of which have a bearing on their physical status.

At the root of this problem is the fact that human need-satisfaction, in the broad sense of how well-being is determined, is not perfectly analogous to the conventional process of production in economics, modelled on manufacturing. How to produce the most shirts or washing machines from a given investment is a fairly simple exercise in optimal resource allocation, involving well understood technology. The question of how to get the most out of expenditure on social services is far more complicated, not least because the output is less clearly defined than that of a factory. In limited spheres of activity there is evidence that certain practices are more cost-effective than others. But there is no objective or scientific means of demonstrating how best to improve a nation's health, nor that the government can improve the lives of the governed more by favouring health, education or crime protection in the next round of public spending. And it is doubtful whether the contemporary cult of performance assessment, whereby services providers are judged by numerical indicators of attainment, will make decisions on resource allocation much more convincing. It may merely focus attention on what can most easily be measured. What it means to improve people's bodies, minds and lives will remain matters of contention, for such uncertainty and ambiguity is part of what it means to be human.

It is, nevertheless, possible to arrive at some broad empirical generalizations as to the relationship between some human needs and the resources required to satisfy them. An example is provided in figure 5.4a, where the length of life people can expect in most of the world's nations is plotted against GDP per capita (adjusted for purchasing power parity). The clear impression is of successive increases in GDP generating decreasing increments of life expectation, insofar as there is a direct cause-and-effect link between the two conditions. This form of relationship is frequently encountered in other spheres, and is a version of the condition of decreasing marginal returns which was introduced in the discussion of utilitarianism in chapter 3.

This relationship is generalized in figure 5.4b, as a need-satisfaction curve (see Smith, 1977, p. 37 for an earlier version). At lower levels of satisfiers or resource inputs, more output or need-satisfaction can be generated than

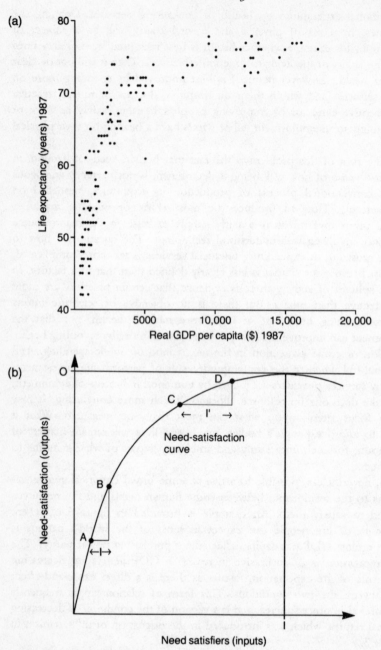

Figure 5.4   The relationship between inputs and outputs (need satisfiers and need-satisfaction), (a) specific (by nations) and (b) general.
(Source of data: UNDP, 1990).

at higher levels: compare the inputs required (I) to move up from point A to B with C to D (I'). There is thus an efficiency case (supported by utilitarianism) to shift resources to positions down the curve, where more needs are satisfied for the same expenditure. At level O, no further improvements in need-satisfaction are technically possible, a position which might be represented by the minimum residual infant mortality or illiteracy, for example, that no further increase of spending on health care or education can affect.

Whether the curve then becomes a plateau at the optimal level of inputs (as in figure 8.1 in Doyal and Gough, 1991, p. 163) is an empirical question. So is the possibility of an eventual turn down of the curve, with too much input (e.g. too much gastronomic indulgence making people ill, too many cars on the road causing accidents), or, more generally, further increases in society's wealth having adverse effects on well-being. What is certain is that, if such a position is reached, the resources involved should go to some other people, somewhere else.

Measuring inequality and equalization

We now have to address more directly the empirical identification of inequality and trends towards (or, perhaps, away from) equalization. This book is about morality rather than measurement, but if we are to bring our perspective to bear on real-world problems the question of measurement cannot be avoided. Indeed, it is a matter of ethics as well as of scientific practice to measure as well as possible.

First, a few words about the measurement of well-being itself. Interest in national levels of life quality, development or well-being began to attract serious attention in the 1960s. Academics, politicians and some popular writers came to question the prevailing preoccupation with material prosperity and economic growth as the be-all and end-all of life, raising issues concerning the social and environmental costs. The adequacy of such pecuniary measures of national prosperity and progress as gross national product (GNP) or per capita income was challenged. Calls for more social content to systems of national accounting generated what became known as the social indicators movement, which gathered strength in the United States and soon influenced western European thinking. The US Department of Health, Education and Welfare (1969, p. 97) provided a frequently cited definition of a *social indicator*, as

a statistic of direct normative interest which facilitated concise, comprehensive and balanced judgement about conditions of major aspects of a society. It is in all cases a direct measure of welfare and is subject to the interpretation that, if it changes in the 'right' direction, while other things remain equal, things have gotten [sic] better, or people are 'better off'.

The breadth of possible conditions amenable to social indicators was clearly expected to be considerable.

The first impetus for the compilation of sets of national indicators came from the United Nations. Concern about international disparities in what was usually termed development, accompanied by recognition that money is not all that matters, stimulated the search for measures to augment GNP. The prevailing methodology was to subject large sets of data to multivariate statistical analysis, so as to derive a single index which would incorporate as much information as possible from the range of conditions originally selected. Comparisons among nations would then be made (see Smith, 1977, chapter 8; 1979, chapter 2 for further discussion; also Doyal and Gough, 1991, chapter 8). The extent to which such exercises could effectively withstand charges of cultural imperialism depended on how far (almost literally) those responsible could distance themselves from the (usually) Anglo-American or Eurocentric predispositions which can easily colour what are claimed to be universal conceptions of development or well-being.

Studies of inequality within single nations are relieved of some of the problems of international comparison. For example, numerical data for different parts of one country are more likely to have been compiled using the same definitions and with similar degrees of accuracy than in the case for different countries. There may also be more of a consensus on the ingredients of the good life than among nations of contrasting cultural traditions.

Attractive though this general approach proved to be, as a means of measuring something as broad in scope as well-being, it has some obvious difficulties. Many individual indicators are highly correlated with one another, and although composite indicators can overcome problems of data overlaps and redundancy, the statistical techniques required are incomprehensible to most politicians and ordinary people (and to not a few academics), which tends to obscure the meaning of the results. Added to this is the questionable accuracy of data on many conditions compiled in countries lacking reliable methods of counting and compilation, along with the possible instability of definitions from one country to another as well as over time. Thus subsequent refinements of the United Nations development index eventually yielded to the need for greater simplicity and less data.

One device which has featured prominently in the literature is the *Physical Quality of Life Index* (PQLI) (Morris, 1979). This is the average of just three indicators, representing infant mortality, life expectation and basic literacy. More recently the United Nations Development Programme (UNDP, 1990) has introduced a *Human Development Index* (HDI) of similar simplicity. It combines life expectancy at birth and the adult literacy rate with gross domestic product per head adjusted for purchasing power parity (two of the three were plotted in figure 5.4a). But, like all other such attempts to compare the life of nations on some quantitative scale, the HDI has come in for criticism. For example, the introduction of additional considerations can produce conflicting results: in 1990 the United States ranked seventh, but ninth if the index is adjusted to take into account inequality in income distribution, and tenth if adjusted for gender inequality (Naser, 1992).

The fact that even the simplest attempts at comparisons involving multiple criteria fail to yield unambiguous answers to the question of where life is best, better or worse lead to arguments for one single indicator. Income or gross product (per capita) is obviously very important, as indicative of access to direct sources of individual need-satisfaction and of society's capacity to provide public services. Such measures are also good predictors of many other aspects of life. But it is commonly observed that as national wealth increases the people's well-being does not improve in the same proportion, as was suggested above in the discussion of figure 5.4. Life expectancy is sometimes proposed as an alternative, but long lives can be miserable just as short ones may greatly satisfy those who know no other. The identification of geographical patterns of inequality must therefore come to terms with the conceptual and practical problems inherent in the use of multiple criteria. Much can be learned from a limited and carefully selected group of indicators, as will be shown in chapter 6.

Measuring the extent or degree of inequality is necessary if the facts of equalization (or its reverse) are to be established. There is a huge literature (for example, Sen, 1992, pp. 93–4 lists almost one hundred references on the measurement and evaluation of inequality). Discussion here will be confined to those methods which are both frequently used and fairly robust in their requirements of data which are not always either perfectly valid measures of the conditions of interest or reliable in the sense of perfect accuracy.

Regional inequality in the United Kingdom can be used as an illustration (for other explorations of measurement problems in the same context, see Smith, 1979, pp. 122–35; 1987, pp. 13–21; also Green, 1988). The problem is to determine whether there was equalization during the 1980s. The variable to be used is GDP per capita, and the spatial frame of reference is the eleven standard regions of the UK usually adopted for official statistical purposes (table 5.1). The reference dates are 1981 and 1990.

The simplest measure of inequality is the *range* of the observations, from highest to lowest, but this is obviously no use as the actual values in 1990 are much higher than in 1981. This problem is overcome by the *ratio of maximum to minimum* values, which shows an increase in inequality over the decade, but this ignores values other than the extremes. An alternative which measures the spread in the data, and also takes into account the fact that pecuniary (and

Table 5.1 Changing regional inequality in Gross Domestic Product (GDP) in the United Kingdom during the 1980s

| | GDP per capita (£) | | per cent of UK | |
Region	1981	1990	1981	1990
North	3439	7233	93.9	88.2
Yorkshire and Humberside	3381	7562	92.3	92.2
East Midlands	3555	8054	97.0	98.2
East Anglia	3539	8408	96.6	102.5
South East	4271	9703	116.6	118.3
South West	3420	7779	93.4	94.9
West Midlands	3329	7611	90.9	92.8
North West	3640	7421	94.5	90.5
Wales	3071	6960	83.8	84.9
Scotland	3542	7592	96.7	92.6
Northern Ireland	2882	6181	78.7	75.4
United Kingdom	3663	8201	100.0	100.0
Range	1389	3522		
Ratio of maximum to minimum	1.48	1.57		
Mean (m)	3461	7682		
Standard deviation (s)	350	885		
Coefficient of variation (100 x s/m)	10.11	11.52		
Mean percentage deviation			9.07	10.10

Source of data: *Regional Trends*, 27. London: HMSO, 1992.

other) measures may increase over time simply with inflation (or progress), is the *coefficient of variation*, or the standard deviation divided by the mean. This, like the ratio of extreme values, can be used to compare different conditions as it is independent of the actual units of measurement adopted.

Another way of standardizing sets of data for different conditions and at different times is to convert them into standard scores, with the mean set at zero and the standard deviation at unity. An alternative is to use index numbers, such as proportions of the national average; inequality can then be measured by the *mean percentage deviation*, or the average departure of regional percentages from the national figure of 100. The results in table

Table 5.2 Changing distribution of income and wealth in the United Kingdom during the 1980s, by different measures

Measure	Year(s) of data		
	1981	1988–9	1990
Gross weekly earnings (males)			
(a) highest decile as per cent of median	168		181
(b) lowest decile as per cent of median	64		68
difference (a–b)	102		113
Gross weekly earnings (females)			
(a) highest decile as per cent of median	172		179
(b) lowest decile as per cent of median	68		63
difference (a–b)	104		116
Household incomes			
(a) per cent going to top fifth	36.0	40.0	
(b) per cent going to bottom fifth	7.8	7.9	
difference (a–b)	28.2	32.1	
Real median income (£ per week)			
(a) top fifth	298	402	
(b) bottom fifth	94	100	
ratio (b/a)	3.17	4.02	
Marketable wealth plus pension rights			
(a) per cent owned by top tenth	34		37
(b) per cent owned by bottom half	21		16
difference (a–b)	13		21

Source: Social Trends, 21, 22, 23. London: HMSO, 1991, 1992, 1993.

5.1 confirm the move towards greater regional inequality identified by the other measures.

The general strategy of using multiple measures to establish at least the direction of a trend is further illustrated in table 5.2. Here the issue is whether the distribution of income and wealth in the United Kingdom as a whole became more or less unequal during the 1980s. Various fairly simple ways of identifying distributional inequality adopted in the annual Social Trends all point in the same direction: to inequality having increased (see the widening differences between what goes to the groups who fare best and worst). As at the regional scale, these observations raise the question of whether social justice in the UK regressed during the 1980s: by the criterion of justice as equalization, it did.

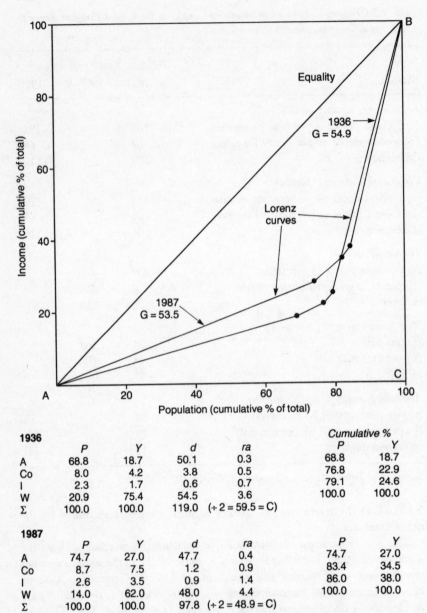

1936					Cumulative %	
	P	Y	d	ra	P	Y
A	68.8	18.7	50.1	0.3	68.8	18.7
Co	8.0	4.2	3.8	0.5	76.8	22.9
I	2.3	1.7	0.6	0.7	79.1	24.6
W	20.9	75.4	54.5	3.6	100.0	100.0
Σ	100.0	100.0	119.0	(÷ 2 = 59.5 = C)		

1987						
	P	Y	d	ra	P	Y
A	74.7	27.0	47.7	0.4	74.7	27.0
Co	8.7	7.5	1.2	0.9	83.4	34.5
I	2.6	3.5	0.9	1.4	86.0	38.0
W	14.0	62.0	48.0	4.4	100.0	100.0
Σ	100.0	100.0	97.8	(÷ 2 = 48.9 = C)		

Figure 5.5   Measuring inequality in income distribution by population group in South Africa. Abbreviations: A – Africans, Co – Coloureds, I – Indians, W –Whites; P – population, Y – income; d – difference between P and Y, ra – ratio of advantage Y/P, C – coefficient of concentration, G – Gini coefficient.

(Source of data: Smith, 1990, p. 7, table 1.3, supplemented from various publications of the South African Institute of Race Relations).

Table 5.3 Calculation of index of concentration (C) at different levels of territorial aggregation

	P	Y	I*	|Y–Y*|	P	Y	Y*	|Y–Y*|
City A (rich)	20	45	10	35				
City A (all)					100	50	50	0
City A (poor)	80	5	40	35				
City B (rich)	40	40	20	20				
City B (all)					100	50	50	0
City B (poor)	60	10	30	20				
Totals	200	100	100	110	200	100	100	0

$$C = \tfrac{1}{2} \Sigma |Y–Y*| = 55 \qquad C = \tfrac{1}{2} \Sigma |Y–Y*| = 0$$

Source: Smith (1977, p. 136), table 6.2. The symbols $\Sigma |Y–Y*|$ indicate summation irrespective of the sign of Y–Y*. P – population, Y – income.

Let us now consider the device introduced in the initial discussion of the principle of justice as equalization: the Lorenz curve and its related measure the Gini coefficient. The context is a society with more dramatic inequalities than the UK: South Africa (the subject of a case study in chapter 8). We ask whether inequality in income distribution, among the four race groups officially recognized until the abolition of apartheid legislation, has decreased over the past half century. The techniques to be applied require data in the form of percentage distributions. Figure 5.5 includes data on income and population by race groups for 1936 and 1987, along with some necessary calculations.

The *Lorenz curve* is drawn as follows. First, the observations (race groups) are placed in order of their *ratio of advantage*, which is simply percentage of income divided by percentage of population. The larger the ratio, the more the group has of income compared with their share of population. Then the cumulative percentages (as listed) are plotted against one another on a graph, with the results shown. Perfect equality would produce a 'curve' along the diagonal from A to B. The degree of inequality is indicated by the extent of departure of the Lorenz curve from this line.

The *Gini coefficient* is the proportion of the triangular area ABC between the line of equality and the Lorenz curve. The more severe the curve, the greater the degree of inequality, and the higher the coefficient on its scale from 0 to 100. The actual results show that G = 54.9 in 1936 and 53.5 in 1987. Bearing in mind the likelihood of considerable inaccuracy in both population counts and estimates of people's incomes in South Africa, the difference between these figures is hardly decisive in confirming a trend towards racial equality. The percentage figures show that the Africans have substantially increased their share of income at the expense of the Whites, but that this has been accompanied by changes in share of population in the same direction, thus reducing the element of redistribution.

Figure 5.5 shows another calculation which can be performed on the same data. The *coefficient of concentration* is calculated by summing the differences between percentage of income and population for each group, ignoring the sign (plus or minus), and halving the result, which gives a measure of inequality on a scale from 0 to 100. This produces a clearer indication of decreasing inequality, from C = 59.5 in 1936 to C = 48.9 in 1987. The fact that this measure and the Gini coefficient provide somewhat different results emphasizes the importance of the method adopted, and the wisdom of using alternatives if possible.

Finally, we must recognize the geographical problem of aggregation in the measurement of inequality. All measures of inequality are sensitive to scale, for the simple reason that a fine level of disaggregation will reveal extreme values (high or low) which will be hidden at courser spatial scales. Table 5.3 provides an imaginary illustration. Two cities, A and B, have identical populations, and both are divided into a rich and a poor neighbourhood. The figures on the left show the distribution of population and income, from which a concentration coefficient of 55 is calculated. But suppose we took the two cities as undifferentiated wholes. The figures on the right show that the two cities each have half their total combined population and half their income, so the degree of inequality (C) is zero.

That the finding of equalization, or otherwise, can be scale-dependent is a sobering observation. This is one of the issues to be explored in practice in chapter 6.

Returning to geography

These last observations bring us back to the spatiality of social justice. While questions of space, distance, place and territory have surfaced as the need arose in the earlier discussions, it is necessary to conclude our general deliberations with a reassertion of the geography of it all. We do not require much detail, as some of the issues were introduced in chapter 2 and many others are well covered in literature generated by the discipline's earlier engagement with distributional aspects of justice (Smith, 1977). And, as with some other topics, workers in other disciplines are now more familiar with the benefits of a geographical perspective than they used to be.

The first, obvious point is to recognize the abiding significance of the local (regional or national) resource base in the unequal capacity to satisfy people's needs. Added to this is transformational efficiency as a spatial variable. Different territorially defined groups will encounter varying degrees of difficulty, requiring varying levels of inputs, in achieving the same amount of progress or attaining the same eventual goal of need-satisfaction or well-being. For example, if the two positions depicted by A and B and C and D in figure 5.4b refer to different localities, then the differential resource requirements are clearly portrayed. And, not for the first time, there are redistributive implications: the same resources devoted to need-satisfaction in places with relatively low levels will achieve more than in places with high levels. This is an important part of the case for justice as spatial equalization.

The next point is that there is an influential body of literature, both theoretical and empirical, to suggest that regional equalization of living standards may be a predictable if not entirely natural tendency in real societies (for a review, see Lipshitz, 1992). Under capitalism the free mobility of capital, labour and so on seeking the highest returns is supposed to bring about a convergence of regional incomes, following an initial period in early stages of economic development when inequality increases. This is the famous 'inverted U' hypothesis, whereby the degree of inequality among regions (and groups) by nations is plotted against their per capita income, with a result resembling the letter U upside down. Under socialism convergence is supposed to take place through central planning specifically directed at the goal of equalization.

What actually happens is a bit more complicated. At the international scale the gaps are obviously widening, as the advanced industrial world deals itself ever loftier material standards while in some other parts of the world starvation is rampant. And we do not need fancy development indicators to show this. The problem of responsibility to, and for, distant peoples is a challenge for moral philosophers of a conventional orientation, and also for those espousing the ethic of care, to which we will return in chapter 10.

The role of space in unequal distribution at a more local scale was one of the major revelations of geography's initial engagement with social justice. Simple extensions of industrial location analysis helped to model the unequal distribution of the benefits (and burdens, or disutilities) generated by various kinds of public and private facilities (Smith 1977, chapter 5; 1981a, chapter 14). The distance–decay effect is central to this process. One of the most persuasive concepts from this era is that of the 'hidden mechanisms' of (re)distribution identified by Harvey (1973, chapter 3), and recently rediscovered by Young (1990a, p. 245) in her exploration of the contemporary city as a place where justice and difference are mediated. As she says (pp. 241, 248): 'Inequalities of distribution can be read on the face of buildings, neighbourhoods, and towns . . . the full extent of oppression and domination they involve can be understood only by considering culture and decision-making structures as they affect city geography, activities and distributions.'

What is locally available to people is, of course, an outcome of broader processes of uneven development, as a social product the elucidation of which is a major contemporary concern of our discipline. Differences from place to place in resources in the most general sense, obvious to geographers for ages, are now increasingly recognized in mainstream accounts of social justice.

For example, Barry (1989) sees local differences in the quality of schools as an important aspect of environmental differentiation analogous to the (morally irrelevant) natural endowment of individuals. Doyal and Gough (1991) are also sensitive to such matters. And Le Grand (1991, p. 108) takes up the issue of access with commendable geographical clarity: 'Poor families, or those who for some other reason are 'locked into' a location that is poorly endowed with facilities, could well be viewed as suffering inequitable differences in access.' It may have taken a long time for such revelations to penetrate the often spaceless world of economics, but the coincidence with the return of social justice to geography is a happy one. And it is not only under capitalism that urban inequality poses challenges to social justice (see chapter 6): the same is true of the (former) socialist cities of East Europe, as we shall see in chapter 7.

Another theme the time of which has clearly come is that of locality as a resource. Political jurisdictions have the responsibility to distribute a variety of services, and some goods, and they have their own operational conceptions of justice which Elster (1992) explores. But it is not simply a matter of the practices of local government. The idea that local networks of friendship, kinship and mutual support form part of what people draw on in their struggle to satisfy their needs is central to some current debates in cultural and social geography, as was observed in chapter 1. That there can be geographical inequality in the voluntary sector has been pointed out by Wolch (1989, p. 215): 'some local jurisdictions have far greater voluntary resources upon which they are able to draw for service augmentation, public sector substitution, and political action.' There is also a link with political empowerment, which Young (1990a) among others recognizes. Groups marginalized if not totally excluded from effective participation in national decision-making may find more scope locally, ultimately perhaps to project their power more broadly. Or perhaps not. The power of local economic and political elites to maintain their control can be considerable, as we shall see in chapter 6.

These questions lead to the central importance of territory, and of place, in people's lives. Whether humankind has some territorial imperative like certain other species, as Ardrey (1971) supposed, is debatable. But what is certain is that people need a place, a place to occupy, a place to live. Unlike some other needs, this does not arise from any functional necessity, though having a place does help to meet certain ends. Human beings have no choice but to occupy a space, a place: they just do (as Griffin, 1986, said about other basic needs). This truism has some profound implications for social justice. And the nature of this place, its position on the opportunity surfaces generated by the human creation of human geographies, has a vital bearing on the quality of people's lives.

John Friedmann (1992) has some pertinent observations in this context, as part of his politics of alternative development. With his mind on the world's poor, he identifies a number of bases of social power, as the principle means available to a household in the production of its life and livelihood. These are defensible life space, along with surplus time, knowledge and skills, appropriate information, social organization, social networks, instruments of work and livelihood, and financial resources. Defensible space (a notion first developed by Oscar Neuman in his book of that title) is defined by Friedmann (1992, pp. 67–8) as follows:

> The territorial base of the household economy, defensible life space includes the physical space in which household members cook, eat, sleep, and secure their personal possessions. In a wider sense, it extends beyond the space called 'home' to the immediate neighborhood where socializing and other life-supporting activities take place, chiefly in the context of the moral economy of nonmarket relations. Gaining a secure and permanent foothold in a friendly and supportive urban neighborhood is the most highly prized social power of all, and households are prepared to make almost any kind of sacrifice to obtain it.

For those of us who are able to take this kind of place for granted, the last sentence is a potent reminder that there are vast numbers of people who cannot. He goes on to stress the importance of territoriality (p. 133):

> Territory is coincident with life space, and most people seek to exercise a degree of autonomous control over these spaces.
>
> Territoriality exists at all scales, from the smallest to the largest, and we are simultaneously citizens of several territorial communities at different scales: our loyalties are always divided.
>
> Territoriality is one of the most important sources of human bonding: it creates commonweal, linking present to the past as a fund of common memories (history) and to the future as common destiny.

Territoriality nurtures an ethic of care and concern for our fellow citizens and for the environment we share with them.

We have encountered some of these sentiments already, and a few problems which they raise, but these words are nevertheless a powerful invocation of what place means to people.

Given all this, to deprive people of their territory, their community or their home, would seem at first sight to be a heinous act of injustice. It would be like taking away any other source of basic need-satisfaction, on which people depend absolutely. Hence the devotion of a chapter (9) in this book to the issue, to the question of how such acts might be justified, and the cost to those who thereby lose. But this experience is not simply deprivation: there is a literal necessity to be re-placed. People who have lost their place, for one reason and another, must be provided with or find another. There is no question about it. People need it. They just do.

Part II

Case Studies

'Just' and 'unjust' are central terms that can be applied to societies as a whole, and in principle, at least, they can be applied to societies concretely and realistically conceived.

> Bernard Williams, *Ethics and the Limits of Philosophy* (1985)

[W]e see all around us in our societies huge inequalities in political power, in social standing, and in the command over economic resources. The degree of inequality on each of these dimensions is different in different societies, and so is the extent to which a high position on one is associated with a high position on the others. South Africa is not easily confused with Scandinavia.

> Brian Barry, *Theories of Justice* (1989)

The task of Part II of this book is to see how the concept of social justice might be applied in practice. The intention is to present some case studies, in which various perspectives introduced in Part I can be used to explore the justice (or otherwise) of particular situations in different parts of the world. While the approaches reviewed in previous chapters have not always had a clear geographical focus, their application in the chapters which follow has a more obvious but by no means exclusively spatial or territorial emphasis. This is not only to reassert the spatiality of social justice, stressed at various points in Part I, but also to show that some notions from theories of social justice which were not necessarily developed with space in mind can help to illuminate geographical issues concerning distribution and the structures responsible for inequality. The approach is deliberately eclectic at times, allowing the more helpful theoretical perspectives to emerge in their confrontation with reality.

Something of the rationale and experience guiding choice of the cases was explained in chapter 1. Their specific purpose may be introduced briefly here. In chapter 6 we focus on the United States city, to explore the issue of justice as equalization developed in chapter 5. The particular question of racial equalization will be examined, with evidence drawn from selected southern cities. In chapter 7 we move from capitalism to socialism, looking at the kind of inequalities which emerged in certain East European cities up to the end of the 1980s. We consider how the reality of these cities might be reconciled with the egalitarian expectations of socialism, and comment briefly on how things are changing under post-socialist regimes. Chapter 8 takes the case of South Africa, posing the question of reparation as compensation for past injustice along with the scope for redistribution after apartheid, and asking what claims to social justice the new society might be able to make. In chapter 9 we take a number of cases of territorial or place deprivation, and try to show what it means for people to lose the most obviously geographical right they might claim: to somewhere in which to live communally with others, and to call home.

The predominant style of exposition should be familiar to a geographical readership, but each chapter has an epilogue in a different voice underlining some points already made and evoking some other dimensions of the situation.

Before proceeding it is necessary to stress that coverage of the chosen topics is highly selective. The intention is not to summarize the voluminous literature on inequality in the American city or the land issue in South Africa, for example – far from it. The focus will be on social justice from the outset, with provision of the minimal background required to contextualize the problem under review. Selected references will direct the reader to more comprehensive treatments. But, in addition to revealing the intrinsic interest of an approach grounded in social justice, it is hoped to demonstrate that such a focus has the capacity to take us to the heart of the case in question, explaining what makes it so important in the changing world.

A brief concluding chapter (10) consolidates some of the most important themes to emerge from the cases: the implausibility that markets can generate social justice, the superiority of some kind of egalitarianism, the possibility that this provides the basis for a universal perspective on social justice, and a final reassertion of the importance of social justice to geography.

6

Inequality in the United States City

We hold these truths to be self-evident, that all men are created equal, that they are endowed by their Creator with certain inalienable rights, that among these are life, liberty and the pursuit of happiness.

United States of America, *Declaration of Independence* (1776)

We seek not just freedom but opportunity – not just legal equity but human ability – not just equality as a right but equality as a fact and as a result.

President Lyndon Johnson, speech at Howard University (1965)

If I grow up, I'd like to be a bus driver.

Lafeyette Rivers (Chicago ten-year-old), quoted in
Alex Kotlowitz, *There Are No Children Here* (1991)

One of the most poignant recent accounts of life in urban America describes the experiences of two boys in a Chicago public housing project called Henry Horner Homes. Participant observation enabled Kotlowitz (1991) to portray the day-to-day struggle to survive in an environment of poverty, unemployment, decaying housing, crime, drugs, gang warfare and endemic violence. As the boys' mother put it, 'there are no children here. They've seen too much to be children.' Life was itself uncertain enough that one of the boys responded to the question of what he wanted to be when he grew up in terms of *if*, rather than when. The equal right to life, liberty and the pursuit of happiness is far from secure for some people in some places in the United States today, three decades after the civil-rights movement and more than two centuries after the elevated assertions of the *Declaration of Independence.*

The United States of America epitomizes freedom to many people elsewhere. They still clamour to enter as immigrants, following the millions who preceding them as the new nation was forged by refugees from the dire poverty, religious persecution, brutal pogroms or stultifying tradition which constrained the liberty of so many Europeans in the nineteenth and early twentieth centuries. The 'founding fathers' of the United States insisted on a written constitution which soon incorporated a bill of rights, the better to make the entitlements of citizenship clear. Thus a wide range of freedoms are guaranteed by law, as was pointed out in chapter 2. However, what is omitted is significant: the nation owes no one a living. People are expected to support themselves and their families, for the most part, with the state nearer a Nozick-style night-watchman guarding individual liberty than a nanny holding a comfortable social security safety-net.

Those who succeed in this fiercely-competitive society realize the arche-type American dream. This is usually defined not so much in terms of abstract ideals such as liberty, more with respect to the material comforts of a nice house with all 'mod-cons', on an attractive plot, in a safe and secure neighbourhood, good schools for the children, supportive commu-nity, church and so on. A better life than before, and better still to come. But there is a price, paid by those who for one reason or another fail to realize the dream, and find that life in what Michael Harrington (1962) originally described as 'the other America' can be harsh and unforgiving. Their places are the rural backwaters far from the expanding metropolitan areas and by-passed by the inter-state highways, the declining industrial towns or mining settlements, and the inner-city pits of deprivation like Chicago's Henry Horner Homes, where one in three children live in poverty, well over half have only a single parent, and reaching adulthood educated and without a criminal record is a singular achievement.

We concentrate attention in this chapter on a group of people who are disproportionately represented among the inner-city poor, and whose ancestors did not, for the most part, choose to come to America in the first place. These are the thirty million blacks, or African-Americans,[1] who make up roughly one in eight of the population of the United States today. We will see how far recent decades have revealed an improvement in social justice, by our criterion of equalization, indicated by narrowing (or otherwise) the gap between the black and white populations. The relative experience of African-Americans, especially since the civil rights movement of the 1950s and early 1960s, illuminates the crucial issue often described as racial (in)justice in America, and also provides insight into the broader structure of this society and its capacity to live up to the ideals celebrated in the nation's sacred texts and so much admired elsewhere. The geographical

---

[1] The term 'black', which replaced 'negro' in the 1970s, has been superseded by 'African-American' in much academic writing. Some use African-American primarily to denote ethnicity, reserving black for the Bureau of the Census racial definition. While such changes may indicate significant shifts in identities and perceptions, and not merely in what might be considered 'politically correct' usage, they do not have much bearing on the central issues of this chapter. Black and African-American are used interchangeably here, or follow the preferred usage in work under discussion.

context within which equalization will be explored is the city. But first, some brief observations on the question of scale will help to set the scene.

The question of scale

In chapter 5 it was pointed out that choice of geographical scale is crucial to the identification of the degree of inequality, and of any tendency towards equalization. Scale is also important to the human experience of inequality and injustice, for the reference group(s) relevant to how people perceive their lives in comparison with others is to some extent a function of information, mediated by distance. Thus, for African-Americans, the national numerical picture of progress (if this is actually the case) is likely to be less significant than what has happened in their own neighbourhood, and how this compares with other parts of the town or city which they encounter in their daily lives.

National aggregate figures are nevertheless a useful starting point. Table 6.1 lists the ratios of advantage of the white population over the blacks on selected economic and social conditions, for census years from 1960 to 1990. Median family income shows a narrowing of the gap from 1960 to 1970, but a subsequent rise in the ratio and virtually no change during the 1980s. The proportion of families living under the officially defined poverty level reveals a somewhat different trend, with the gap being reduced successively since 1970. Life expectation shows a similar trend, but figures for infant mortality indicate increasing racial inequality after a fall in the 1960s. The education measures both show the two race groups getting closer.

There are some mildly encouraging indications in these figures, especially with respect to education, which is the key to access to the better employment opportunities on which depend increased income and all that goes with it. However, the pace at which the gap has been narrowing gives cause for concern. For example, if the rate of reduction from 2.61 to 1.77 over thirty years for the proportion of people with four or more years of college continues, it will take the same period again for the difference between the races to be eliminated. The rate of convergence of proportion living in poverty since 1970 is such as to require a further century and a half to complete. For family income, the reduction from 1960 to 1990, if projected into the future, would take 240 years for the ratio of whites to blacks to converge on unity. And for infant mortality, of course, the immediate problem is to prevent further widening of the gap.

Revealing though these kinds of data are, with respect to the very limited progress towards equalization in recent decades, we require a scale of

Table 6.1 Ratios of advantage of white over black population in the United States, on selected economic and social indicators, 1960–90

Indicator	1960	1970	1980	1990
Median family income	1.81	1.63	1.73	1.72
Percentage of persons below poverty level	3.09	3.38	3.19	2.98
Life expectation	1.11	1.12	1.09	1.08
Infant mortality	1.93	1.83	1.96	2.16
Percentage of children completing high school	1.65	1.33	1.10	1.10
Percentage of persons over 25 with 4 or more years at college	2.61	2.57	2.09	1.77

Source: Statistical Abstract of the United States, 1992, supplemented from earlier editions. Note that the latest available income data refer to 1989.

analysis which gets closer to people's actual lives, and to the dynamics of change which have an impact on them. The finer (or more local) the scale, the more spatially separated and concentrated the black population becomes; the more inequality is revealed, and the less convincing the convergence trend. For example, a study of the ten south-eastern states from 1960 to 1980 at the county level shows that, although for median family income and median school years completed the ratio of highest to lowest counties was reduced, the gap widened for infant mortality and proportion of housing lacking complete plumbing (Smith, 1987, pp. 51–2). The crucial distinction at this scale is between affluent city suburbs, with their largely white populations, and rural counties with high proportions of blacks, as Bederman and Hartshorne (1984) have demonstrated in the state of Georgia.

The geographical selectivity of economic development in the so-called Sunbelt South has been examined by Lyson (1989). He portrays a region 'checkered with places that are best characterized by their slow growth, declining industries, and static or falling living standards ... It is composed of people and places that have been and remain mired in the economic backwaters of the country' (p. 2). This corresponds largely with the 'black belt' in which African-Americans are concentrated, between the Piedmont uplands and the Atlantic coast, along the Gulf coast and the banks of the Mississippi, into the mountains of Appalachia and the remote areas of the Ozarks. Those living here are at an increasing disadvantage in competing for highly mobile capital, which looks much more favourably towards the regional metropolitan centres with their more highly skilled and educated populations. Lyson (1989, pp. 45, 71) concludes:

[R]egardless of the measure of economic well-being, one cannot escape the conclusion that the rural and black-belt labor market areas [LMAs] of the South have remained relatively poorer and more underdeveloped *vis-à-vis* their more urban counterparts ... More distressing, perhaps, is the fact that in many instances there appears to be a growing divergence between the relatively affluent urban LMAs in the South and the economically distressed rural and black belt LMAs ... The gaps in human capital and general social welfare between the rural and black belt LMAs and the large and mid-size urban places that seemed to close somewhat during the federally sponsored War on Poverty, now seem likely to grow wider again.

So, convergence may be evident at a national scale, but within the South it may be more a case of increasing inequality among local communities, with race a relevant consideration.

It was within this region, the old cotton-belt South, that the black population was largely confined during the era of slavery. Emancipation was followed by some migration to northern cities, in search of work as well as a less racially repressive social environment. Thus by 1990 the south-eastern quadrant of the United States (comprising the seventeen states of the South Atlantic, East South Central and West South Central census divisions) accounted for 15.8 million African-Americans, almost exactly half the nation's total. Their share of the region's population was 18.5 per cent, compared with 12.1 per cent nationally. A substantial rural black population remains in the South, in contrast to the rest of the country, but migration in recent decades has shifted the balance very much in favour of the cities.

If there are clear and continuing inequalities in living standards between the black rural population and white urban residents, those between the inner-city poor and the affluent suburbanites are even more marked. There is a well-established generalization that divides the American city into deprived black ghetto surrounded by better-off and largely white suburbs, with the African-American poor sometimes augmented by Hispanics and other ethnic minorities usually of recent immigrant origin. The spatial association between race and various economic and social indicators was analyzed and mapped in detail in various studies undertaken during the era of radical geography in the latter part of the 1960s and the 1970s, reflecting a heightened societal awareness of the problem of racial injustice (e.g. Smith, 1973, chapters 4, 9; 1979, pp. 179–94).

This kind of research was not merely of academic interest. Some city governments set up their own monitoring programmes, incorporating sets of social indicators, to guide resource allocation policy. Of particular significance is the small town of Shaw, Mississippi, where a group of black residents used information on the difference in service provision between the strictly

segregated black and white neighbourhoods at the end of the 1960s to bring
a court action. The issue at stake was whether such discrimination breached
the 14th Amendment to the Constitution, which guarantees all American
citizens 'equal protection of the law'. The eventual verdict agreed that such
unequal treatment was a denial of equal protection, and in this sense an unjust
infringement of legal rights (Smith, 1979, pp. 46–8).

The spatial correspondence between poor economic and social conditions
and the black population took on a particularly threatening aspect in civil
disturbances or riots in a number of American cities in the latter part of
the 1960s. The most serious was in the Watts district of Los Angeles, a
location where the lowest levels of income, the highest population densities,
the highest school drop-out rates and the highest rates of crime coincided
with a high concentration of poorly-housed blacks (Smith, 1987, p. 24).
About a hundred people died, twice as many as in riots in the same city a
quarter of a century later when a jury declined to convict white policemen of
severely beating a black suspect, fortuitously recorded in its horrific detail on
cine-film and replayed repeatedly thereafter on national television. (It took
a second trial on the grounds of infringing the victim's civil rights to secure
conviction of two of the assailants.)

The urban uprisings, followed by the murders of the Rev. Martin Luther
King Jr and Robert Kennedy, prompted Presidential commissions of investigation into the causes of civil disorders and violence in America in general
and its cities in particular. Unsurprisingly, the racialization and localization
of poverty were found to be deeply implicated. The fundamental justice of
American society became a more potent political issue than at any time since
the abolition of slavery. A quarter of a century later, it is pertinent to ask what
progress has been made in the direction of a just society in which race has no
bearing on people's life chances.

The rationale behind choice of the city as the scale for our investigation
is implicit in what has already been said. All that need be added is that it is
within the metropolis that the post-war decades of economic growth have
created opportunities for the upward economic and social advancement
of African-Americans, and for their outward movement insofar as the
traditional spatial constraints of segregated ghetto residence have been
relaxed. And it is as mayors of major cities that blacks have been
able to attain formal political power, still largely denied them at the
state and national level. If justice is manifest in racial equalization,
then it is within the cities that the outcome should be evident, both
in numerical data and in the experience of living more equal lives.

The spatial frame of reference within the city is the local neighbourhood,
as identified by the 'tracts' used by the Bureau of the Census for statistical
purposes. These tracts are designed to be relatively homogeneous with
respect to the economic and social characteristics of their populations.

The fact that many tracts remain largely occupied by either blacks or whites enables comparisons to be made between those parts of the city with a predominance of one group and the other. While this is not as precise as interpersonal comparisons, it does enable some broad judgements to be made as to the process of racial equalization with a spatial dimension.

We explore trends in the city of Atlanta, Georgia, in some detail, reconstructing the pattern of race–space inequality as it has changed from 1960 to 1990. Something of the process behind this is suggested, including the politics of a city renowned for its commitment to growth and in the hands of black mayors for two decades. Evidence from some other cities is then examined briefly, to check the consistency of what has been observed in Atlanta. The chapter is concluded by returning to the broader national context, within which the Atlanta experience can be related to the enduring American paradox of injustice with a racial dimension.

Inequality in Atlanta, Georgia

Atlanta occupies a position of great strategic and symbolic importance in the struggle of African-Americans for social justice. Here is the birthplace and tomb of the Rev. Martin Luther King Jr, his Ebenezer Baptist Church, which played such a prominent part in the early civil-rights movement, and the Centre for Nonviolent Social Change which bears King's name. Atlanta was the first major southern city to elect a black mayor, Maynard Jackson (in 1973), who currently (1993) holds the office again following the high-profile black politician Andrew Young (President Carter's Ambassador to the United Nations). It is also the city of Lester Maddox, who built a successful campaign for state Governor on the notoriety achieved by refusing blacks entry to his restaurant at the end of the era of segregation. And the Ku Klux Klan have not entirely disappeared.

The post-war years have seen Atlanta transformed from a regional service centre to national and international prominence. To such familiar local corporations as Coca Cola, Georgia Power and Southern Bell have been added national company headquarters and a series of architectural extravaganzas in the form of major hotels competing for lucrative conventions as well as the business and vacation traveller. Roughly one gigantic new edifice a year is added to the already dramatic sky-line, the more startling at night as their upper stories joust with one another in a tournament of lights. There is a commuter monorail service, adding to freeways perpetually under reconstruction to accommodate ever widening traffic flows. And now the 1996 Olympic Games provides further opportunities for the civic boosterism and prestige projects at which the city excels.

The city of Atlanta had a population of just under 400,000 at the time of the 1990 census. Two-thirds were black. The population had fallen from 425,000 in 1980 and 495,000 in 1970 when the proportion of blacks was 57 per cent. In 1960, at the beginning of the period of our investigation, the city had 488,000 residents, only 38 per cent of whom were black. The falling numbers are explained to a large extent by the clearance of densely-populated inner-city residential areas, while the changing racial composition is the outcome of black population growth accompanied by the large-scale movement of whites to new suburbs beyond the city limits.

The city of Atlanta as a political jurisdiction accounts for only about 14 per cent of the total population of over 2.8 million in the wider metropolitan area. In those parts outside the city, whites predominate to the extent of accounting for about four-fifths of the population. As befits its standing as mega growth centre of the 'new South', metropolitan Atlanta expanded its number of residents by almost one-third during the 1980s, outstripping the 27 per cent growth of the 1970s as its suburbs and office parks extended ever further into the surrounding counties of rural Georgia. Atlanta Metropolitan Statistical Area ranked twelfth in the nation by population size in 1990.

Atlanta was the subject of one of the early geographical studies identifying the spatial association of levels of living and racial composition of the population. Using census tract data for 1970, Bederman (1974) showed that the areas of lowest 'quality of life', based on a range of economic and social indicators, corresponded quite closely with those in which the black population exceeded 60 per cent. However, the association with race was by no means clear-cut: both the predominantly black and predominantly white tracts revealed a considerable range of life quality. While most white areas were well-to-do if not extremely affluent, there were some with low levels of living. And while most black tracts were poor, a few could compete with well-to-do white tracts.

Bederman's study had, in fact, caught the city in the early stages of breakdown of the traditional dichotomy of poor black inner city and better-off white suburbia. Atlanta had a small black middle class going back at least three generations, and its own (segregated) institutions including colleges of national distinction. During the 1950s and 1960s considerable black residential expansion out of the inner-city ghetto had taken place, mainly in a westerly direction. This had enabled blacks with the resources to acquire decent housing in neighbourhoods which rapidly turned over from white to black occupancy. Black suburbanization gathered strength during the 1970s and continued into the 1980s, as the locus of search swung to the south-west and south of the city centre. Further outward pressure was created by the urban renewal programmes of the 1950s and 1960s, which displaced large numbers of inner-city black residents (see below). As the pressure on white neighbourhoods mounted, they moved out, usually to the northern suburbs, their flight further stimulated by the increasingly black complexion of the city schools.

The outcome of this process of racial residential re-sorting at the metropolitan scale is illustrated in figure 6.1. This maps the proportion of population black, by 167 census tracts (or combinations thereof necessary for comparison with earlier years). The distinction between the predominantly black southern part of the metropolis and the largely white northern part is striking. The degree of residential segregation by race is indicated roughly by the fact that 54.4 per cent of the census tracts contained over 90 per cent blacks or over 90 per cent whites in 1990, compared with 66.4 per cent in 1980 and 75.5 in 1970. This suggests a reduction in segregation. However, suburbanization of the black population has involved spatial spill-over and continuing racial transition, rather than stable integration in the sense of creating racially mixed neighbourhoods (Clark, 1988).

Figure 6.2 shows the pattern of median family income for 1989. The concentration of lowest-income tracts in the inner city is clear. Tracts in the second-lowest category are mainly to the south of the inner city, largely confined to the city limits. The two highest income categories are confined entirely to the northern half of the metropolitan area. The relatively high degree of association between income and black proportion composition of the population evident when comparing figures 6.1 and 6.2, is confirmed by a correlation coefficient of $-.703$.

With this background, we may move on to the central question of changes in the patterns of inequality over time, or whether there has been a trend towards race–space equalization. The findings presented here are part of the outcome of an on-going research project,[2] earlier results of which, along with further background, are set down elsewhere (Smith 1981b, 1985a, 1985b, 1987, chapter 4). Whereas the earlier research, covering the period 1960 to 1980, involved a range of economic and social indicators, the analysis here is confined to the crucial ingredient of income. Median family income is a close predictor of tract variations on other indicators; for example in 1980 median family income had a correlation coefficient of .927 with median value of

[2] The research reported here and in the next two sections would not have been possible without the long-standing collaboration of Sanford Bederman, at Georgia State University. Peter Muller made the facilities of the Geography Department at the University of Miami available as a research base in recent years; Tom Boswell helped with access to 1990 census data. Financial support has been provided by the Economic and Social Research Council. Most of the work involved in compiling comparable sets of data for Atlanta and the three Florida cities from 1960 to 1980 was undertaken by Stephen Pile as research fellow. Various officers of city governments made time and data available. None of those involved bear any responsibility for the interpretations offered in this chapter.

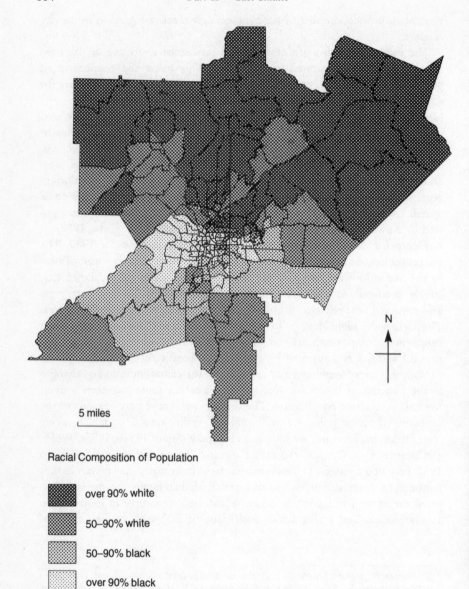

N

5 miles

Racial Composition of Population

over 90% white

50–90% white

50–90% black

over 90% black

Figure 6.1   Racial composition of census tract populations in metropolitan Atlanta, Georgia, 1990. For definition of the metropolitan area, see note to table 6.2.
(Source of data: *Census of Population and Housing*, 1990, summary tape file 3A, preliminary results).

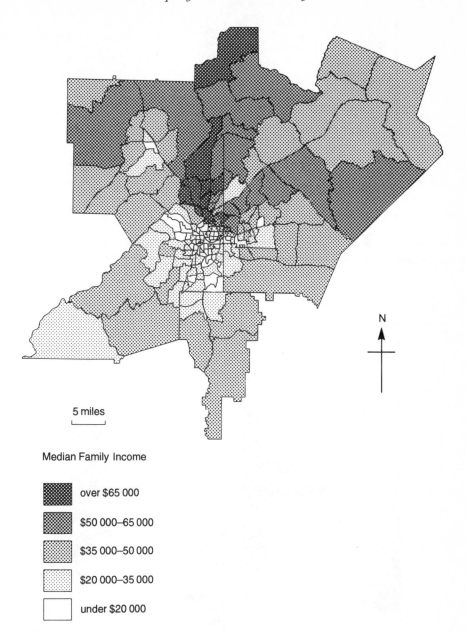

5 miles

Median Family Income

over $65 000

$50 000–65 000

$35 000–50 000

$20 000–35 000

under $20 000

Figure 6.2   Median family income by census tract in metropolitan Atlanta, 1989.
(Source of data: *Census of Population and Housing,* 1990, summary tape file 3A, preliminary results).

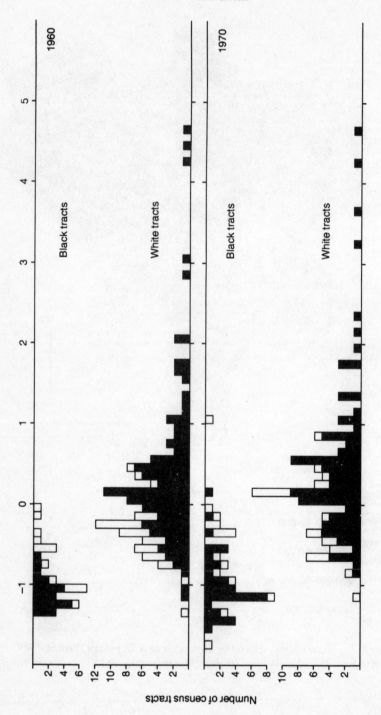

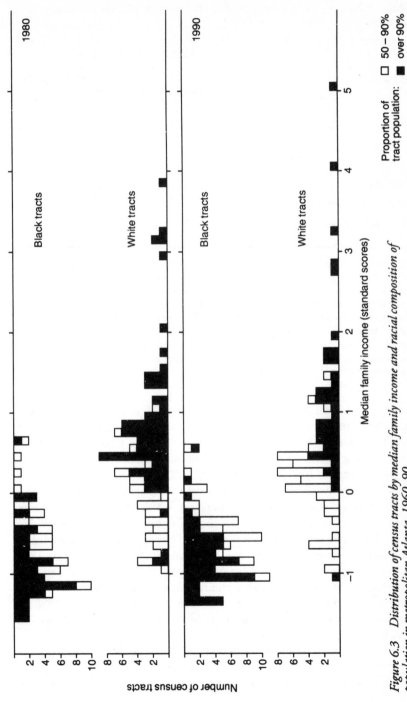

Figure 6.3 Distribution of census tracts by median family income and racial composition of population in metropolitan Atlanta, 1960–90.
(Source of data: *Census of Population and Housing*, 1990, summary tape file 3A, preliminary results).

Table 6.2 Median family income ($) by census tracts in Atlanta metropolitan area, 1960–90

Tracts		1960	1970	1980	1990
All tracts:	mean	6,023	9,907	17,877	35,216
	maximum	18,548	29,793	54,081	150,001
	minimum	2,261	2,273	2,907	4,999
	ratio max:min	8.2	13.1	18.6	30.0
	coefficient of variation	45.2	43.1	53.0	65.0
White tracts:	mean (w)	7,121	12,001	25,928	62,423
Black tracts:	mean (b)	2,973	5,709	9,667	17,024
White ratio of advantage (w/b)		2.40	2.10	2.68	3.67
White tracts: coefficient of variation		38.9	35.1	33.0	40.9
Black tracts: coefficient of variation		16.7	29.2	48.0	52.8

Source of data: *Census of Population and Housing* (data for 1990 from preliminary returns). For the purposes of this case study, Atlanta metropolitan area is the Standard Metropolitan Statistical Area as defined in 1980 (comprising the counties of Cobb, Fulton, Fayette, DeKalb and Gwinnett). The tracts comprise 167 census tracts or combinations thereof required to compile data on the same areal units for the four census dates. White tracts are those with over 90 per cent of their population white, black tracts have over 90 per cent black.

owner-occupied housing units, –.769 with proportion of housing units with more than one person per room, and .814 with proportion of population over 25 graduating from high school. Income is thus a dominant good, in Michael Walzer's sense, its unequal distribution generating similar inequalities in other spheres of life.

Table 6.2 provides the basic numerical information required to assess trends towards equalization (or otherwise) within metropolitan Atlanta. First, the mean, maximum and minimum figures are listed for all 167 tracts. The ratio of maximum to minimum provides a crude measure of the degree of inequality, which has increased steadily from 1960 to 1990. By this measure, Atlanta has become a markedly more unequal city. The coefficient of variation confirms a steady rise in inequality since 1970, after a slight fall in the 1960s. The increases from 1970 to 1980 and to 1990 are large enough confidently to assert that the Atlanta metropolis has become more unequal.

The crucial question of the relative status of the black and white population can be answered with reference to the ratio between the mean values for tracts with over 90 per cent whites and over 90 per cent blacks. The figures show a decrease from 1960 to 1970, indicating a move towards equalization. But thereafter the gap widens, the more so in the 1980s. Since 1970, race–space inequality has evidently increased substantially.

The final two rows of figures in table 6.2 compare trends among the predominantly white and predominantly black tracts, by the 90 per cent criterion. The differences are revealing. While there have not been marked or orderly changes in the degree of inequality among white tracts, as measured by the coefficient of variation, this is not the case for the black tracts. The tracts with over 90 per cent blacks have become steadily more unequal, especially during the 1970s, although the 1980s show a distinct slackening off of this trend.

What has been happening in metropolitan Atlanta over the period under investigation can be further clarified in figure 6.3. This plots the predominantly white and predominantly black tracts respectively, for each of the four years, with median family income transformed into standard scores (where mean is zero, standard deviation unity) so as to make data for all years strictly comparable. Tracts with over 90 per cent one race or the other are emphasized by solid shading; the rest of the tracts are added to complete the picture.

In 1960 the distribution of predominantly black tracts was tightly bunched around or just below the –1.0 mark. This corresponded with the bottom end of the distribution of white tracts, which tailed out to the very rich north-side neighbourhoods. By 1970 the black tracts had spread out quite considerably, with the poorest relatively worse-off than in 1960 but the better-off now reaching the middle of the distribution of white tracts. Further spreading of the black tracts was evident by 1980, with the continuation of suburbanization of the emerging middle class. However, the visual impression of the distribution of black tracts in 1990 is of little if any further spread, as suggested by the coefficient of variation in table 6.2. By now, the tendency of the bulk of the predominantly white tracts to maintain their numerical distance from the predominantly black tracts, suggested in 1980, can be clearly detected. In fact, taking the over 90 per cent tracts alone, only two of the black tracts in this category overlap with any of the corresponding white tracts (with the exception of the poorest of the white tracts, which covers an atypical area occupied largely by poor young migrants to the city). Thus, the predominantly black and predominantly white parts of metropolitan Atlanta remain as divided as in previous decades, insofar as family income is concerned. And this despite encouraging pointers towards black advancement. For race to cease to be relevant to family income, that is, for racial equalization truly to have taken place, the two distributions depicted in figure 6.3 (top and bottom) would be mirror images. This remains far from being the case.

As to the actual conduct of people's lives, racial separation largely remains.

A British reporter visiting the city found 'an unspoken code of social apartheid' (BBC News, 27 August 1993), thirty years after Martin Luther King's famous speech articulating the aspirations of his people: 'I have a dream...'

The political economy of disequalization in Atlanta

Understanding the process of disequalization in Atlanta requires reference to both the local context and external events. Attention here will be confined largely to local considerations, leaving the broader national forces bearing on the status of African-Americans to the penultimate section of this chapter. The immediate focus will be on city politics and some of the consequences with respect to economic development, deeply implicated in unequal access to the benefits of life in a rapidly growing and changing metropolis.

Atlanta politics has been the subject of sustained and detailed scrutiny. Atlanta was the unidentified 'regional city' featured in a seminal study of community power by Floyd Hunter (1953). He identified an interlocking and tightly cohesive network of individuals and institutions, within which the local business elite ran city government largely in their own interests. This was by no means an unusual arrangement in the American city; in Atlanta it had two particular consequences which had an important bearing on the experience of the African-American population.

The first was that breaking out of the confines of the inner-city ghetto was made easier than in many similarly segregated cities. As pressure for black residential expansion built up, informal agreements involving city government, black community leaders and the real-estate business facilitated black acquisition of housing within a wedge extending westwards from the city centre (Hartshorne et al., 1976, pp. 46–50; Smith, 1981b, pp. 10–14). Once established, this enclave swung southwards, with the eventual consequences illustrated in figure 6.1. There was vigorous white opposition, but city government recognized that failure to accommodate the aspirations of at least the well-to-do black population could undermine the image of a city portrayed by mayor William Hartsfield as 'too busy to hate'. Furthermore, the time was clearly coming when blacks would constitute a majority of the city's electorate. Thus, relatively progressive attitudes on race (by the prevailing standards of the South) were viewed as helpful to social stability and economic growth. While elected positions and city government offices remained in white hands, the black middle class gained some access to local government at a time of rigid exclusion in most other cities.

The other major achievement of the established power structure was to ensure the continuing viability of the central business district, the decline of which has been a feature of many other American cities. An important element in this strategy was the elimination of large areas of poor, mainly black housing around the city centre, under the guise of urban renewal or slum clearance, and facilitated by freeway construction and other public works projects. This had the effect of making the central business district (CBD) secure for the massive capital investments in the office, hotel and entertainment complexes which subsequently transformed the city centre. Such was the impact of urban renewal that about one in seven of the city's population were displaced during the decade 1956 to 1966 (Stone, 1976, p. 227). The city failed to rehouse the vast majority: only 5000 public housing units were built during 1957–67, while 21,000 dwellings were demolished in the central part of the city (Hartshorne et al., 1976, p. 44).

So, while the emerging black middle class was taking advantage of suburbanization, along with access to increasing business and professional opportunities, many of the inner-city poor were forced out of their neigh-bourhoods into the next zone of deteriorating property. And most of the whites prospered, with the growing economy, the main exceptions being those of low or modest means who bore the brunt of racial residential transition, which left the rich north-side neighbourhoods untouched. The urban renewal era in Atlanta has been described in detail by Clarence Stone (1976), in an elaboration of the concept of 'system bias' which captures the capacity of city government single-mindedly to pursue narrow, sectional interests with little concern for those, literally, in the way. This analysis, like the 'institutional imbalance' still found by Hunter (1980) a quarter of a century after his original study, provided a potent challenge to the more conventional pluralistic interpretation of American city politics.

Atlanta entered the 1970s with a residual concentration of poverty around the city centre, albeit displaced a few blocks by urban renewal and related projects. Bederman and Adams (1974) found the spatial incidence of pov-erty closely associated with the distribution of the black population. High correlations were also observed with families having a female head, low number of years of school completed, and employment in service-related jobs (usually lowly paid). In these respects, Atlanta's syndrome of inner-city black poverty conformed closely to what was encountered across much of metropolitan America.

The 1970s was an important decade in Atlanta's political development. In 1973 Maynard Jackson became the first black mayor of a major southern city. This abrupt shift of formal political power created immediate expec-tations of benefits for the poor (largely black) people and neighbourhoods which the city had hitherto neglected – except as obstacles to the physical renewal necessary for economic progress. As Eisinger (1980, p. 74) put it, 'the triumph of black power was seen as having displaced a ruling class, dramatically divorcing economic influence from political power'. That the reality turned out to be more of the same, in the sense of the prevailing form of government and its major beneficiaries, is in part a reflection of the relative weakness of city authorities in the United States, which constrains local redistributional possibilities. But it also reflected the manner in which the coalition of interests which had prevailed for the previous quarter of a century had been able to re-form under black leadership.

This process has been described in detail in a second major work by Clarence Stone (1989; for a brief account, see Stone, 1990). The central concept around which he builds his interpretation is that of the urban political 'regime', or the informal arrangements that surround and complement the formal workings of government authority. The capacity for action, in particular with respect to major development projects, depends on the nature of the regime: 'What makes governance in Atlanta effective is not the formal machinery of government, but rather the informal partnership between city hall and the downtown business elite. This informal partnership and the way it operates constitutes the city's regime; it is the means through which major policy decisions are made' (Stone, 1989, p. 3). It is more than an informal grouping like a neighbourhood organization, however, for it has access to institutional resources and is empowering in the sense of enabling its supporters to co-operate in realising their projects. The concrete expression of the regime is a governing coalition who come together repeatedly to make important decisions.

Race is central to the process Stone terms 'structuring', whereby events occur in a structured context and help to reshape structure through the interplay of change and continuity as regimes form and re-form. (There are echoes of the concept of structuration developed by Anthony Giddens (1984) here.) The shape of the regime, including the incorporation of blacks, was far from inevitable, but rather came about through the action of human agents, like mayor Hartsfield in the early days, making conscious political choices. The regime was also required to respond to events which challenged its capacity for self-perpetuation.

The latter part of the 1960s and early 1970s generated instability in Atlanta politics. Discontent within inner-city black neighbourhoods affected by urban renewal grew, as Stone (1976) recounts, and the programme was stopped. The new generation of black opposition was not drawn into the city's informal structure of governance, however, and the traditional coalition seemed to be unravelling. This was the context within which Jackson was able to gain election.

At first the white business elite felt itself marginalized. Affirmative action diverted city construction contracts and other business to black firms, and city jobs from the police to the planning department were opened up to blacks (Eisinger, 1980). However, the need to attract and hold investment capital, and to maintain downtown property values, still bound together city government and business, and as the mayor discovered the limitations of his

power to effect redistributive change he was pulled back towards accommodation with business, albeit more tenuous than in the earlier coalition.

Under Jackson's successor, Andrew Young, electoral and economic power
were quickly reunited. The neighbourhood movements which had formed
to fight urban renewal remained political outsiders, having failed to build
more than ad hoc alliances over largely local issues. As Stone (1989,
p. 132) explains: 'Divisions of race and class are formidable, especially
when amplified by geographic fragmentation and particularly if collective
action is based on solitary appeals.' It is significant that the most conspicuous
success in recent years, insofar as urban social movements in Atlanta are
concerned, was the frustration of a grandiose project to build a four-lane
'parkway' through predominantly well-to-do white neighbourhoods to the
Carter Presidential Museum and Library.

Thus, the only major difference between the black mayoralties and the
original coalition was that blacks gained formal political power, which
could be traded with the white elite for some economic benefits. But
such benefits as construction jobs did not necessarily spread far into the
black community. Furthermore, the number of employment opportunities
created by affirmative action in the public sector was quite small, and at
a cost to whites of modest means in the labour force rather than to the
white elite (Eisinger, 1980, pp. 166, 195). As Stone (1989, p. 147) puts it:
'The network of insiders has enlarged, but it is still small, leaving out most
of Atlanta, black and white.' What he describes as investor prerogative still
prevails. Or, in the words of some earlier commentators (Hartshorne et al.,
1976, p. 55), land speculation is a way of life in Atlanta, in a state where until
1989 there were no comprehensive land-use planning laws.

Stone's interpretation of city politics in Atlanta over recent decades
does not claim simply that business commands outcomes. It is more a
question of positioning itself to shape policy, within a network of civic
contacts. Elite power is not absolute but constrained, and this is not so
much by the (strictly limited) countervailing power of outsiders as by the
maintenance needs of the governing coalition itself. This cohesion requires
give-and-take, and above all the incentive to co-operate implicit in the
axiom of 'go along to get along'. He stresses not only the resources at
the disposal of business to promote its shared purpose, but also closure to
wider community concerns and the inability of outsider groups to mount
a challenge to the regime. The burden to break in is placed on any
challenging group. And nothing necessarily obliges the regime to respond:
'Opposition is inconsequential unless it can be organized on a mass basis and
transformed into an alternative capacity to govern' (Stone, 1989, p. 228).

Stone is aware of the issue of social justice, and treats it explicitly,
saying: 'Instead of promoting redistribution towards equality, such a system
perpetuates inequality' (p. 241). The case of Atlanta effectively illustrates how

the resources and ingenuity of those who own and control capital can meet and accommodate challenge to their power, in the form of a majority black electorate, with only a temporary disturbance and partial restructuring of their means of domination.

However, understanding the process of regime politics has to be augmented by some broader considerations, more comprehensively to address the pattern of disequalization which we have observed. The economic context must be recognized, including the national recession of the early 1970s which severely constrained construction activity at the time of affirmative action in city hall, after the building boom of the 1960s. The subsequent economic upturn was followed by the sluggish 1980s. However, both manufacturing and service activity in Atlanta appear to have performed better than at the national scale, as reflected in the continuing rapid population growth of the metropolis (Fleischmann, 1991, p. 99). The conspicuous failure of the 1980s to realize the relative advancement of the African-American population which would have been manifest in a trend towards equalization must be understood against a background of a by no means unfavourable economic situation.

This possible paradox leads to recognition that the exclusionary nature of Atlanta's political regime intersects with what appears to be increasing socio-economic polarization. At the heart of this process is class alliance and cleavage, interpenetrating and to some extent eroding the old dichotomy of race. Commenting on the Jackson mayoralty, Burman (1979, pp. 447–9) points out that the new black elite were in many ways the image of the white power structure: 'Their attitude, like that of their white counterparts, has been characterized by a hard-headed pragmatism which is aimed solely and explicitly at the extension of the benefits of the American system to themselves rather than to posing any fundamental challenge to that system.' The policies they pursued were largely sectional, 'aimed primarily at advancing their own status rather than that of the black community as a whole'; Jackson 'has been unable to meet the demands for change made on him by the poor black community'. The advance of the black middle class had left the rest of the black population probably worse-off in relation to the whole of American society than it had been ten years earlier.

Various subsequent examinations of Atlanta's on-going saga reach broadly similar conclusions. For example, Clark (1988, pp. 117–18) asserts: 'Atlanta's development policies include few equity-promoting or representation-expanding features that might counter the interests of economically powerful groups . . . Atlanta continues to be dominated by a coalition of city officials, corporate leaders, and middle-class black leaders who concur on the community-wide benefits of downtown revitalization.' She also points out that, as in most southern cities, organized labour is weak and does not operate as a constraint on business interests. Reed (1987, p. 204) describes Atlanta as 'perhaps the archetype of the hegemony of development elites in local politics', and suggests that, throughout the period of the so-called Atlanta miracle, the costs of progress have been concentrated 'repeatedly on the city's quiescent black citizenry'. And Fleischmann (1991) points out that, while two-thirds of seats on the City Council are held by blacks, almost all members are professionals with strong ties to the business community. This does not encourage the politics of redistribution; indeed, 'there is a danger of Atlanta becoming a bifurcated city of the college-educated and an "urban underclass", with few residents in between' (p. 98).

Thus, substantial numbers of African-Americans still inhabit areas of poor housing and environmental quality, with their socio-economic status improved little if at all since the era which preceded black power. And, as was shown in the previous section, the 1980s have revealed limitations even to the extent to which a black middle class, at the neighbourhood scale, is achieving the levels of income comparable even with the lower end of the white distribution. Whatever else may be revealed, as Atlanta gears up to the 1996 Olympic Games in an ecstatic display of self-promotional civic chauvinism, it is unlikely to be an advance of social justice as racial equalization.

Some other cities

An obvious question arising from the study of a single city is how far this typifies the experience of metropolitan America as a whole. That there are some unique features to Atlanta's story is obvious, but it is also clear that neither this nor any other city can isolate itself from powerful national forces bearing on such an issue as racial (dis)equalization. There is a substantial literature which permits some comparison with other major cities (e.g. Browning, Marshall and Tabb, 1990; Eisinger, 1980; Savitch and Thomas, 1991; Stone and Sanders, 1987). However, rather than attempting to summarize studies conducted often from differing perspectives, and usually without explicit attention to social justice, we will present findings from three other cities which can be compared directly with those from Atlanta.

The three cities have been chosen deliberately for comparative purposes. They share Atlanta's south-eastern regional location (they are in Florida), and hence some of its historical and cultural setting. They all have a substantial African-American population. But they each have particular characteristics which differentiate them from Atlanta, and from one another. Space available here permits only the most sketchy background, and very limited results of on-going research (for more details, see Smith and Pile, 1993).

The city of Jacksonville, Florida, had a population of 635,000 in 1990, a quarter of them black. Unlike Atlanta, this city covers the vast majority of its metropolitan area, which housed 907,000 people in 1990. While Jacksonville has expanded steadily over the past two decades, from 504,000 people in 1970 and 541,000 in 1980, it was only during the 1980s that it began to aspire to the same pace of economic growth as Atlanta has enjoyed since the 1950s. And while Atlanta's political regime was open to blacks at a relatively early date, their experience in Jacksonville has been more one of strict subordination. Jacksonville has a past marked by inept and at times corrupt city government, as well as what one newspaper has described as 'a sordid history of race relations that has never really been resolved' (*St Petersburg Times*, 8 October 1989). While the situation improved somewhat during the 1980s, the prospects for African-American advancement have been less favourable than in Atlanta.

The city of Tampa forms part of another Florida metropolitan area, the rest of which is made up of the city of St Petersburg. Like Jacksonville, a quarter of its population is black (280,000 in 1990), but here there is a second 'minority' population, of diverse origin but subsumed under the official census category of Hispanics, who account for 15 per cent of the city's inhabitants. The question raised is how far the presence of the Hispanic population may have had a bearing on the fortunes of the African-Americans. Although some of the Hispanics are poor, in aggregate they are better-off than the blacks, and comparable with the white population in certain respects. Like Jacksonville, Tampa has not enjoyed the prosperity of Atlanta in recent decades, though the landscape of both Florida cities bear the imprint of scaled-down versions of Atlanta's downtown redevelopment and slum clearance.

The city of Miami resembles Tampa in that it has an Hispanic population. But here the scale is much greater, Miami having become the centre of what has been described as the Cuban diaspora with large-scale immigration from the rigours of the Castro regime. In 1990 the population of Dade County, virtually coincidental with the Miami metropolis, was 1,937,000, of whom almost half were classified as Hispanics. A total of 564,000 were from Cuba, and there were almost 30,000 classified as black Hispanics. The number of non-Hispanic blacks was 370,000, a little less than 20 per cent of the metropolitan total. However, the diversity of the Miami population, including possibly 100,000 Haitian blacks, and the likelihood of substantial undercounting due to illegal immigrants eluding the census takers, makes the category of 'black' or 'African-American' somewhat problematic. However, the possible impact of the economic and political empowerment of Cuban emigres on the status of blacks in Miami has attracted considerable interest in an extensive literature (Boswell, 1991).

Confining attention again to median family income, the first point of comparison is the degree of spatial association between this variable and the racial composition of the population. Table 6.3 lists correlation coefficients

Table 6.3 Correlation between median family income ($) and proportion of population black (%) by census tracts in Atlanta and three Florida cities, 1960–90

City area	1960	1970	1980	1990
Atlanta city	–.573	–.559	–.669	–.737
Atlanta metropolitan	–.540	–.589	–.703	–.703
Jacksonville city (lesser)	–.769	–.777	–.808	
Jacksonville city (greater)		–.652	–.663	–.656
Tampa city (lesser)	–.539	–.600	–.613	
Tampa city (greater)		–.618	–.629	–.659
Miami metropolitan	–.477	–.489	–.519	–.441

Source: calculated from *Census of Population and Housing*. Jacksonville (lesser) refers to the city before the incorporation of some surrounding areas, to become greater Jacksonville; lesser and greater Tampa refer to the city before and after boundary extensions. Gaps indicate data not supplied.

for the city of Atlanta as well as the metropolitan area, for two definitions of the cities of Jacksonville and Tampa (explained in the footnote to the table), and for Miami as defined by the metropolitan statistical area. The remarkable thing about these figures is their consistency over the years, and among the cities. The only exception to the generally strong (negative) association between level of income and proportion of tract population black is in Miami, where the somewhat lower correlations are explained by low incomes among immigrant (mainly white Hispanic) families, and possibly among the retirees who figure prominently in Miami's population. Otherwise, the only difference of note is the somewhat stronger association between race and income in 1990 in Atlanta compared with Jacksonville and Tampa.

Turning to the question of equalization, table 6.4 lists summary data on trends in the three Florida cities, in a form which is directly comparable with the findings in metropolitan Atlanta in table 6.2. The coefficients of variation for all tracts irrespective of their racial complexion reveal disequalization, most marked in Miami, least in Jacksonville. But in none of the three cities, at any time, is the degree of inequality as high as in Atlanta. Among the tracts with over 90 per cent of population black, increasing inequality is again consistently revealed, least marked in Jacksonville but with little difference between the other three cities. The ratio of advantage of predominantly white over predominantly black tracts shows the most marked disequalization in Tampa, almost as great as in Atlanta, with a steady if less pronounced increase in Miami. Jacksonville is out of line, with no appreciable change except for within the old city limits from 1970 to 1980.

Table 6.4 Summary indicators of trends in inequality in median family income by census tracts in three Florida cities, 1960–90

City area	1960	1970	1980	1990
(a) Coefficient of variation for all tracts				
Jacksonville city (lesser)	35.2	35.0	44.8	
Jacksonville city (greater)		35.4	37.7	40.9
Tampa city (lesser)	33.6	37.4	43.4	
Tampa city (greater)		33.8	38.9	51.4
Miami metropolitan	28.8	34.8	40.2	55.6
(b) Coefficient of variation for black tracts				
Jacksonville city (lesser)	18.4	18.9	25.7	
Jacksonville city (greater)		31.7	38.2	42.4
Tampa city (lesser)	–	25.5	41.4	
Tampa city (greater)		25.7	38.3	49.4
Miami metropolitan	13.1	21.6	28.4	39.7
(c) Ratio of advantage white:black tracts				
Jacksonville city (lesser)	1.98	1.91	2.63	
Jacksonville city (greater)		1.98	2.05	1.95
Tampa city (lesser)	–	2.13	2.51	
Tampa city (greater)		1.93	2.28	3.31
Miami metropolitan	1.77	1.88	2.04	2.50

Source: calculated from *Census of Population and Housing*. (–) indicates no tracts in this category at that date.

Some of the differences between the cities are explicable in terms of local conditions. For example, what particularly differentiates metropolitan Atlanta from the other cities is its higher overall median family income, even more evident with respect to its predominantly white tracts (where the 1990 mean of about $62,000 compared with $39,000 in Jacksonville, $36,000 in Tampa and $37,500 in Miami – all close to the $37,000 for white median family income nationally). By comparison, Atlanta's predominantly black tracts (mean of $17,000) are much closer to the figure in the other cities (Jacksonville $20,000, Tampa $11,000, Miami $15,000) and nationally ($21,500). This suggests that the relatively high general prosperity of Atlanta has been to the particular advantage of the predominantly white parts of the metropolis, which helps to explain the greater racial disparities there. In Jacksonville the increased inequality among black tracts, their relatively high mean for median family income, and the failure of the gap between black and white tracts to widen, suggests that, at last, economic growth is generating significant benefits for blacks. The growing disparity between predominantly black and white tracts in Tampa, together with the low mean for black tracts, gives some credence to the possibility that here they have suffered in competition with Hispanics.

Trends in Miami are rather difficult to interpret. It has been argued that the peripheral location of black residential areas and the growing political and economic domination of the Cuban population has marginalized the African-American population (see, for example, Mohl, 1988; Vogel and Stowers, 1991; Warren, Corbett and Stack, 1990). While the mean value for median family income in Miami's predominantly black tracts is lower than in Atlanta and Jacksonville, and for blacks nationally, it is higher than in Tampa. And the increase in coefficient of variation for Miami's predominantly black tracts, from a very low figure in 1960, suggests some upward mobility within the black community. Thus, opportunities seem not to have been monopolized by the Cubans, although the movement of African-Americans to better neighbourhoods may well have consolidated the spatial marginalization of this population in the north-western segment of the metropolitan area.

These tentative interpretations suggest relationships between the relative status and internal differentiation of black urban populations, on the one hand, and such local considerations as level of prosperity and the extent of economic and political empowerment on the other. But it must be stressed that these local conditions act merely to modify, one way or another, the common trend towards disequalization, not to promote the reverse. For some further reflections on the origins of continuing and apparently deteriorating injustice for African-Americans, we will return to the broader national scene.

The enduring American dilemma

Half a century ago Gunner Myrdal wrote his classic *The American Dilemma* (1944). He explained how white prejudice and power to discriminate against those then termed negroes resulted in segregation and inter-racial economic disparities, which in turn reinforced the original prejudice. This is an example of the general process Myrdal referred to as cumulative causation. The abolition of slavery in 1863 had been followed by rigid and at times brutal exclusion of blacks from white American society. This included the (supposedly) democratic process; various devices such as all-white primary elections and violent intimidation were adopted, to prevent people other than whites from electoral participation. Blacks were, for the most part, treated as cheap labour, spatially segregated, and denied full rights of citizenship

– rather as in South Africa under apartheid. Old attitudes persisted: 'The system of slavery was augmented by philosophical and moral justifications of African-American racial inferiority and the "rightness" of their servitude' (Washington, 1992, p. 241).

Shortly after Myrdal wrote, a new mood of liberalism, along with increasingly insistent calls for civil rights, led the Supreme Court to judgements which effectively outlawed racial discrimination. The Civil Rights Act passed by Congress in 1964 was accompanied by various government programmes to combat the poverty which disproportionately afflicted the black population. Some of these were initiated by President John F. Kennedy, and subsequently brought together with other measures under President Lyndon Johnson's banner of 'The Great Society'. It was against the backdrop of civil-rights marches on the deep-South city of Selma, Alabama, in 1965 that Johnson made his own stand in words echoing the slogan of the movement: 'Their cause is our cause, too. Because it is not just Negroes, but really it is all of us, who must overcome the crippling legacy of bigotry and injustice. And we shall overcome' (quoted in Caro, 1990, p. xx).

As Weir (1993, p. 96) explains: 'The guiding notion was that of righting a wrong: the poor economic situation of blacks represented a national failure to apply the principles of justice equally to black Americans.' The moral climate created by the civil-rights movement facilitated the adoption of policies directed towards equal opportunities for economic advancement. This was accompanied by growing black political empowerment. Voter-registration drives, political mobilization and increased black participation overcame traditional constraints, and cities such as Cleveland, Detroit, Gary and, eventually, Atlanta, elected black mayors. Taking advantage of the end of legally enforced or overt racial discrimination, the small black middle class began to grow, assisted by improved educational opportunities and by a vigorous economy. Breaking out of the ghetto to which blacks had hitherto been confined irrespective of their status, the emergent bourgeoisie improved their housing and environments via suburbanization, to put geographical as well as socio-economic distance between them and the poor. There were hopes that the natural course of events, under an expanding economy with increasingly liberal institutions, would resolve the American dilemma. Indeed, the prescription some people advocated was, in the infamous words of sociologist (later Senator) Daniel Patrick Moynihan, one of 'benign neglect'.

But this optimistic scenario has proved to be fundamentally flawed. The War on Poverty and other Great Society measures provided some kind of safety-net for the inner-city and rural poor. But they failed to improve their position relative to the norms of a mass-consumption society in which material expectations were continually refuelled by the product innovation required for capital accumulation. And in some significant respects the position of the poor deteriorated. Problems assumed to be individual or racial, and addressed as such by equal opportunities legislation, were in fact structural: deeply embedded in the economic system. Those who did not gain advantage from the new programmes were increasingly viewed as a 'social problem', victims of their own inadequacies, and targets for white backlash against measures thought to favour blacks.

By the beginning of the 1970s a set of overlapping deprivations, of the kind identified earlier in this chapter, had taken hold of large inner-city communities on the verge of social disintegration if not outright revolt. And nothing seemed to be putting things right, despite substantial federal spending on welfare, housing improvement and neighbourhood renewal. The black poor began to slip from the political agenda. 'Removed from the public eye, however, black inner city communities were being devastated by an explosion of joblessness, decay of housing stock and neglect of the public infrastructure. High rates of crime, drug addiction, children born out of wedlock and welfare dependency marked these communities off from the rest of the nation' (Weir, 1993, p. 100).

The end of the 1970s saw an unhappy coincidence of economic, political and legislative developments which have had a profound effect on the lives of the poor in general and poor blacks in particular. Restructuring of what had become a stagnant economy, following the oil-crisis recession, severely eroded the 'blue-collar' manufacturing employment opportunities which had provided many blacks with a route to upward socio-economic mobility. The Ronald Reagan Presidency, and that of George Bush which followed, effectively abandoned the earlier liberal commitment to the poor, itself well short of a western European welfare state. And with this went the pursuit of racial equality. Whether he willed it or not, among the traditional American values invoked by Reagan's conservative popularism was racism. Reaganism sought to define the American people in terms which excluded poor blacks from membership, as 'others' who simply did not have the resources to conform and hence belong.

The mood of the new times, reflected for example in a more conservative Supreme Court, enabled some of the earlier gains with respect to equal opportunities, affirmative action and positive discrimination to be questioned and in some instances reversed. Such has been the impact that Washington (1992) suggests the possibility of reinstitution of the former caste-like system of African-American exclusion, which prevailed before the initiation of the class-inclusive process promoted by the commitment to equal rights in a growing economy. But it may also be a case of the blurring or fragmenting of old categories like race and class, as some interpretations informed by postmodernism suggest (e.g. Cross and Keith, 1993, p. 14; Winant, 1993). The divergence and separation of different groups, characterized by life-style as well as ethnicity and socio-economic attainment, is a definitive feature of what some see as the postmodern city.

The outcome in the United States metropolis has clearly been one of increasing inequality as well as diversity. Atlanta is a case in point. While 68 per cent of the black population nationally are not classified as poor by the government's official definition, and only 29 per cent of all the American poor are black, poverty remains a condition which afflicts African-Americans to a much greater extent than the white population. Much has been written about the consolidation of a so-called *underclass*, suffering not only poverty in the conventional sense of material deprivation but also beset by such conditions as high crime, homelessness and unmarried teenage pregnancies. In 1990, 35.5 per cent of black mothers had never been married, compared with 2.7 per cent for whites; 51.2 per cent of black children lived with only their mother, compared with 14.2 per cent for whites (Hacker, 1992, p. 231). Most serious of all is a drug culture and economy, the more dangerous the more potent and addictive each round of product innovation. This syndrome of affliction is asserted to be self-reproducing, subject to the not insignificant possibility of ultimate self-destruction.

This situation is sometimes conveyed as a culture of poverty in which the victims are blamed for their own inadequacy: a pejorative and oppressive appropriation of the notion of an underclass. The emphasis on such conditions as illegitimacy, violent crime and lack of conventional jobs assists an interpretation of those concerned in such terms as sexual profligacy, criminality and fecklessness. These are moral judgements of unworthy people, rather like those used to identify the 'undeserving poor' of the Victorian city (Cross and Keith, 1993, pp. 11–15). Such interpretations call into question whether the underclass deserve the meagre welfare benefits grudgingly conceded by the well-to-do majority.

However, it is not hard to see that those caught in the underclass locations can do little, if anything, to change things. They do not have the power, even if they still have the will. William J. Wilson (1987), the most influential non-conservative proponent of the underclass thesis, focuses on the pathologies of inner-city life but stresses, among other things, the historical burden of racism combined with the recent decline of manufacturing employment. As Cross and Keith (1993, p. 14) put it: 'black Americans in these zones have woken from the 'American dream', with its promise of a ladder out of poverty to the lunar landscape of deindustrialization.' City politics is also involved, African-Americans often having little bargaining power in the so-called transactional process which predominates in most cities, whereby deals are struck between groups on the basis of mutual advantage. Again, Atlanta illustrates the process. Wilson uses the south side of Chicago to exemplify the problems of the ghetto underclass: the land of Lafeyette Rivers (quoted at the beginning of this chapter), who hopes to live long enough to be a bus driver.

Geographical space is deeply implicated in the problem. Black residential areas are often far from the sources of new jobs in the suburbs, and the people themselves are unqualified for entry into the new, sophisticated service sector downtown. White flight to the suburbs, often beyond the city limits, has eroded the tax base on which inner-city improvement depends: the city of Atlanta now raises only 17.5 per cent of the tax revenues in the metropolitan area, compared with 45 per cent in 1966 (Fleischmann, 1991, p. 98). The suburbanization of the black middle class has deprived the inner city of role models as well as leadership and financial resources.

An elaboration of the underclass phenomenon is provided in figure 6.4. Galster (1992) follows Myrdal's cumulative causation perspective, identifying and linking elements in the process behind the perpetuation of localized poverty. The nub of the problem is the exclusion of people from certain parts of the labour market (elements 6 and 7), specifically the so-called primary-sector jobs with high wages, stability, security and so on, compared with low-wage work in the secondary sector characterized by poor working conditions, insecurity and little opportunity to advance. This in turn constrains access to better housing (element 5), neighbourhoods and what goes with them. Crucial to inferior labour-market position is low education and skills, and attitudes which may not be conducive to the conventional expectation of performance at work and which can also attract prejudice on the part of more fortunate and conforming people (element 3). The spatial separation of the underclass is implicated in constraints on labour-market opportunities and on the limitations of the public resource base available to sustain local services, and also in the formation of a subculture which may encourage alienation and isolation from mainstream societal values. The various feedback effects indicated in figure 6.4 help to explain the self-perpetuating nature of the urban underclass.

The outcome is summarized as follows by Galster and Hill (1992, pp. 1–2):

America's metropolitan areas appear to be more polarized along racial lines than at any time since the mid-1960s ... African-Americans, on average, are the poorest, most segregated, most disadvantaged urban racial (or ethnic) group, precisely because they are the most deeply entangled in the web of interrelationships connecting place, power, and polarization. Since these interrelationships form a comprehensive, interlocking set of social structures that oppress African-Americans, they can be judged racist at their core ... The racist structure of U.S. metropolitan areas creates obstacles that, although not insurmountable to all, prove to be so for many. In the U.S., societal claims of equal opportunity ring hollow because African-Americans face comprehensive barriers that render their success less likely than comparable European-Americans.

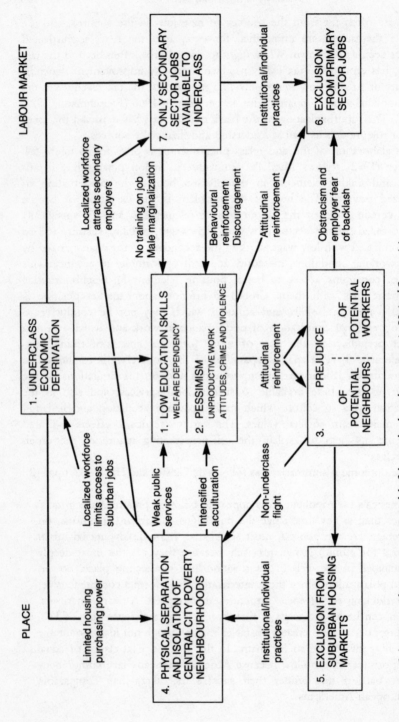

Figure 6.4 A cumulative causation model of the underclass phenomenon in United States cities.
(Source: Galster, 1992, p. 191, figure 11.1).

However, this polarization is not exclusively along racial lines: there are well-to-do blacks, and other ethnic groups experiencing localized poverty. Nor must racism be regarded as the sole source of African-American deprivation: the economy is deeply involved, especially the selective and exclusionary character of the dual labour market which has emerged in recent years. Coupled with slow (or no) economic growth, the restructuring of employment opportunities in the metropolis, including their location, has seriously truncated the process of upward and outward mobility of blacks which was the source of so much optimism two decades ago. And it should not be forgotten that the ethos of the political system remains grounded in laissez-faire attitudes to the economy; when the state intervenes, it is usually in the interests of large-scale capital. This helps to explain the country's continuing failure to provide the kind of social support developed under the welfare states of western Europe, and which soften the impact of socio-economic deprivation.

Before rounding off this discussion, a reminder that deprivation is not exclusively an urban or indeed racial or ethnic experience is in order. In his examination of the two sides to the Sunbelt, to which reference was made earlier in this chapter, Lyson (1989, p. 11) emphasizes that women and rural people as well as blacks are disproportionately concentrated in the underclass. In a critique of local economic development policies, he points out that the benefits to small-town and rural communities do not necessarily trickle down to those at the bottom of the ladder. In a rare reference to social justice within a literature far more concerned with the promotion of economic growth, Lyson (pp. 13–14) invokes John Rawls in asserting: 'Only when economic development policies enhance the opportunities and life chances of those at the bottom can they be considered just.'

This brings us, finally, to the social (in)justice of the American dilemma. The nature of the American version of capitalism, with its rampant material consumption, makes money a powerful dominant good. It buys other things of individual value, including political power as well as such sources of self-esteem as a nice home, new car, fancy clothes and the latest electronic refinements for personal amusement. It also buys neighbourhood quality, safety, security and a range of public services within which education is arguably the most important. These are closely linked spheres, to use Michael Walzer's term, in which one possibly unjust advantage or disadvantage compounds others, in a mutually reinforcing process captured by the concept of cumulative causation. An additional, ominous possibility is that, in the United States, race is still also effectively a dominant good, yet part of what should be the morally neutral natural endowment with which people are born, and which they cannot change.

American society is committed to capitalism or free enterprise, with a conviction approaching moral certainty. But within this structure, and its supporting ideology appealing to the highest ideals, the American dilemma can readily be portrayed as a problem of morality. As Keller (1992a, p. 159) puts it, 'Race is at root a moral issue, involving rectification of past injustices and implementation of equality.' Further (Keller, 1992b, p. 349): 'All Americans must have a "dream" about justice and equity and the institutional means for bringing these dreams to life.' Such a dream would fairly allocate the price of the more conventional American dream, and see it paid.

It is not the purpose of this treatment to prescribe a practical way out of the dilemma. Much of what is required is obvious enough: massive expenditure on housing and neighbourhood renewal, education, job training, family support services, and health care for those people and localities most in need, along with a serious crack-down on crime in general and the drug economy in particular. This, in turn, requires a Rawlsian commitment to society's poorest and weakest on the part of national government, far stronger and more sustained than under the transient Great Society. And it requires city governments committed to the transformation of disequalizing institutions and spatial structures, and to the opening up of exclusive regimes. Above all, it requires a commitment to economic and social well-being as part of the rights of citizenship. This is a point stressed by Wilson (1987, p. 121), who argues for universal programmes involving income redistribution rather than the race-specific measures which have politically alienated whites.

Self-evident though they may be, such proposals require fundamental change in a society's understanding of itself and its purpose: of what it means to be an American. Otherwise, any specific proposals will merely seem Utopian. And this change must be grounded in morality, in a practical commitment to social justice in keeping with the nation's grand ideals. Those who have been fortunate enough to realize their version of the American dream bear a heavy responsibility for its price, in localized and largely racialized deprivation. It is not simply a case of anonymous economic forces, like Adam Smith's hidden hand of the market. People have choices, in their personal lives, as electors, as elected representatives; they could chose to try to resolve the American dilemma. The facts are not hard to establish, and they point towards disequalization as the current tendency. Future claims to a just society must rest on evidence of a substantial and sustained movement towards equalization of life chances, in which race becomes irrelevant. Then, Americans will be in a better position to commend the morality of their way of life to others.

Epilogue[3]

In a southern city, volunteers arrive at the church at about 9.30 in the morning. Their main job is to make soup – lots of it, about forty gallons.

They mix canned vegetables, sent by the 'Food for USA' scheme, with whatever else public donations have provided. They also make up some salad. Last night's left-overs from the local branches of McDonalds and Mr Donut complete the meals. By about 11.30 the work is done, the food is loaded into a van and driven to the soup kitchen.

The soup kitchen opens at noon. The volunteers who prepared the food have now been joined by an assortment of students, 'lunch ladies' and people here in a less than voluntary capacity working a community service sentence. They feed up to 150 people a day, rising from about 70 at the beginning of the month to a peak at the end when times are hardest. About four-fifths of those served are black, the vast majority are men aged twenty-five to forty. There are a small number of drug addicts, but many are decently dressed, and some are at work in minimum-wage jobs. Many are regulars, recognized and greeted by the servers.

They stand in line, waiting their turn. A typical meal is a pint of soup, a burger or sandwich, a little salad, some desert (apple sauce or canned peaches), and a doughnut or two. Any Big Macs which have survived the cravings of McDonalds' paying customers are particularly popular, and may be requested by the more self-confident young men. It is hot, even in the shade, with stifling humidity. As time passes tempers flair. A well-built couple square up, ready to fight. An authoritative 'Chill, bro'!' from an even larger man cools them off, for a while. When finally served, they eat at picnic tables nearby. If stocks last, there may even be seconds.

Not everyone has to stand in line. Some elderly people, disabled and children have food taken home by relatives or friends. A few regulars are allowed to go straight to the serving place for their food. One is Eddie, a sixty-year-old white man who repairs ovens for a meagre living, and collects his lunch to take back to the one room with no electricity or water where he lives, not far away. If he fails to turn up, a volunteer may deliver his food for him. Another is Tillman, a black man over seventy who shares a house with others in the run-down ghetto on the other side of Main Street and the railroad tracks.

The soup kitchen has been running for about ten years. It is the only source in town for a free lunch, other than the Salvation Army and they cannot meet the demand. The organization that runs it also has accommodation for the homeless. They would like to develop a new facility to double their residential capacity and run the soup kitchen, all in the same location and more easily accessible to where the kind of people they help hang out. But there isn't the money.

---

[3] I am grateful to Tracey Smith for access to the experience on which these observations are based.

Service ends, the tired volunteers clear up and make for home. One walks past the University campus. A monumental new stand has been built for the already gigantic football stadium, and there is a fine enclosed basketball arena nearby. Some of the academic facilities are almost as impressive. She walks through a neighbourhood of expansive homes on wooded lots with neat lawns, central air, possibly a pool. She gets home, goes inside, turns on the fan. She opens a can to feed the cat and its kittens, waiting hungrily at the back door. They fight a little, but there is enough to go round. Chill, brothers and sisters.

7

Inequality in the East European City

From the point of view of promoting socialist relations, the central point
is strengthening the principle of social justice.

Tatyana Zaslavskaya, *Soviet Sociology in Conditions of Perestroika* (1990)

At the root of inequality in the American city is the capitalist mode
of production. While the United States demonstrates a particular and in
some ways extreme form of contemporary capitalism, different in important respects from western European welfare states, all capitalist societies
produce economic casualties. The largely black underclass concentrated in
certain parts of the American city is but one geographically and historically
specific version of the inequality generated by competition among people
whose differential resource endowment differentially influences the market
mechanisms and political processes which to a great extent determine life
chances.

It was in response to the blatant inequities of nineteenth-century laissez-
faire capitalism in Europe that socialism emerged as an alternative way of
organizing production and distributing its output. Considerable thought was
given by Marx, Engels and their associates (and successors) to how such
a society should actually be arranged, following the overthrow of the
capitalist and landowning classes. The Russian Revolution in 1917 provided
the opportunity to put theory into practice, the spatial scope extending as
the Union of Soviet Socialist Republics incorporated further territory. The
aftermath of the Second World War brought some European countries along
with China into what came to be known as the communist bloc.

Like capitalism, socialism as actually practised is subject to variations in
institutional form, and also in the degree of commitment to the egalitarianism
with which it is closely associated. What socialist societies have in common
is that the private ownership of the means of production, distribution and
exchange is replaced largely by state ownership and control. Outputs and
prices are centrally determined according to a plan under which economic
activity is co-ordinated. However, some private enterprise remains, especially
in agriculture, and private ownership of personal property may include

housing. This form of society was supposed to be transitional on the way to true communism, under which any residual class affiliation and bourgeois values would disappear, common ownership of property would be completed, and the increasingly redundant state apparatus would whither away.

It will be recalled, from the discussion of Marxism (chapter 4), that there are important differences in the concepts of social justice ideally associated with socialism and communism. Under the former, people contribute their labour according to their differential ability, and are rewarded according to the state's evaluation of the quantity and quality of work performed. This is 'a right of inequality', as Marx put it, with unequal contribution to society unequally rewarded. Under communism the famous dictum of 'to each according to need' would apply, with its strongly egalitarian expectations.

However, even under socialism there would be substantial progress towards equality. Equalization would be manifest in narrowing the inherited gaps between occupational groups, nationalities (as in the USSR), regions, and city and countryside. This would be accomplished by the planned restructuring of the economy and redistribution of its product, including central provision of a wide range of services on an equal basis. Furthermore, changes in personal attitudes, away from individualistic pursuit of private gain and towards collective action for the general good, would help to imbue an egalitarian spirit.

Not surprisingly, socialist society is prone to tension between an egalitarian ideology and the reality of unequal rewards. In effect, two conceptions of social justice are competing, one grounded in the idealism of perfect equality associated with equal rights as members of a collective, the other reflecting the pragmatism implicit in a state-approved conception of distribution according to labour contribution expressed as unequal desert. The resolution of this contradiction is one of the central motive forces in the way in which socialism actually operates.

The exploration of social justice under socialism in this chapter is concerned with both parts of this contradiction. There is some, limited, scope for the examination of our central principle of justice as equalization, in circumstances where the narrowing of gaps was an explicit aim of the state. We will also present evidence of the kind of inequality which emerged, with the implementation of unequal rewards. A further element in the analysis will concern the extent to which the process of distribution was open to other influences, distorting or subverting both equalization and differentiation according to some justifiable criterion of desert.

The spatial frame of reference is the city. This is not so much to enable comparison to be made with chapter 6, interesting though this may be, but again to get close to people's real lives. As in the case of the United States, this means by-passing an extensive literature on regional equalization. It also requires selectivity of material and circumspection with respect to the conclusions drawn, as information is less readily available and reliable than for the American city. The discussion relies mainly on secondary sources, supplemented by some field investigations and anecdotal evidence.

We begin with some introductory observations on the 'socialist city'. We then take the case of Moscow to examine conditions promoting both equalization and inequality. Evidence from a few other cities is added, to provide a broader basis for some conclusions as to the origins of inequality in the cities built or reconstructed under socialism. Finally, there are some speculations on social justice after socialism. Parts of what follow are revised versions of material originally presented in Smith (1989; see also Smith, 1992a, 1994a, 1994c), which contain further relevant background and case studies.[1]

The city under socialism

Certain features of socialism raise expectations of a distinctive kind of city. Urban living has a particular significance in the prevailing ideology, as a progressive force encouraging collective rather than individual identity, and city planning is an important means of achieving this purpose. Central planning along with state ownership of land means that urbanization can be subjected to much greater control than under capitalism. The internal structure of the city can be laid out to facilitate the delivery of social services, including public transport as a way of ensuring ready access to work, leisure and other sources of need-satisfaction. The public provision of housing is one of the most important means whereby the socialist state seeks to ensure satisfactory living standards for all.

An indication of how the ideal socialist city might be organized is provided by Demko and Regulska (1987, p. 290):

> The abolition of private property, removal of privileged classes, and application of equity principles espoused by Marxist/socialist leaders

---

[1] The research on which this chapter is based has been supported by grants from the British Academy and British Council, and by the co-operation of the Academies of Science and a number of universities in Poland and the (former) Soviet Union. Colleagues who have assisted in various ways include: B. Domański, B. Kortus and G. Prawełska-Skrzypek (Crakow); M. Kaczmarek and S. Liszewski (Łódź); M. Ciechocińska, M. Jerczińsky, P. Korcelli, A. Muziol-Węcławowicz, and G. Węcławowicz (Warsaw); M. Tajin (Alma Ata); S. Artobolevskiy, A. Beriozhkin, V. M. Gokhman and L. Smirnyagin, (Moscow); N. Barbash, P. Il'yin and Y. Medvedkov (formerly in Moscow); M. K. Bandman, A. Novoselov and T. Volyanskaya (Novosibirsk); O. Dmitrieva and N. Petukhova (St Petersburg); R. Gachechiladze and A. Rondeli (Tbilisi). Courtesy rather than the prudence of an earlier era requires the conventional disclaimer that all are absolved from any responsibility for my findings.

should radically alter urban patterns. In the housing arena, the expectation would be one of nondiscriminatory, nonspatially differentiated housing in general. No social or occupational group would have better or more favorably located residential sites so that one would find a randomly distributed housing pattern. Similarly, public services of all kinds, including transportation, should be of equal quality, availability and accessibility. Commuting to work . . . would be minimized and no group would be more dependent on or penalized by such travel than others. Such amenities as a high quality physical environment, including recreational environment, would be equally accessible to all. All such urban conditions would be similarly equitably arranged and available.

Of the various reasons why reality might depart from such an ideal, history is particularly important. Many of the cities originated in an earlier era, like Moscow, Prague and Warsaw which we will examine in this chapter, and there are differences in the extent to which socialist planning replaced the pre-existing urban fabric. New cities built entirely according to socialist principles were usually established for some specific function such as the exploitation of local resources. Another consideration is the time taken to construct the socialist city, or to impose it on the past, with changing planning styles and building standards.

A general model of the spatial structure of the East European 'socialist' city is illustrated in French and Hamilton (1979, p. 227). Its main features are as follows: the historic core; inner commercial, housing and industrial areas from the capitalist period; a zone of transition where modern construction has partially replaced inherited features; early socialist housing; and integrated neighbourhoods and residential districts of later construction. Broadly speaking, outward expansion of the city generated a concentric-zonal pattern, which tended to overlay a more sectoral or wedge-like distribution of functional zones often associated with major transport arteries. The inherited inner area is subject to more differentiation than the socialist outer urban areas with their planned uniformity.

This model indicates some similarity with those sometimes adopted to describe the advanced capitalist city, at least to the extent of finding sectors and wedges in the pattern of land use differentiation. We now turn to the question of how far such a form is accompanied by inequalities in living standards, in an attempt to elucidate something of both the patterns and the processes behind them.

Equalization and disequalization in Moscow

On the eve of the Revolution in 1917 Moscow was one of the largest cities in Europe, with a population of about 1.6 million. By 1939 it had reached 4.5 million. This has subsequently doubled, and if the built-up area beyond the official city limits is included the population now approaches 14 million. Present-day Moscow is very much a product of the socialist or Soviet period. The pre-Revolutionary city was of limited spatial extent, and much of what was inherited from Tsarist times has been rebuilt as what was supposed to be a show-place of a superior society. Soviet scholars were understandably reluctant to investigate intra-city inequalities in living standards and outsiders were not encouraged, so what follows is based on a limited and scattered literature (for earlier versions see Smith, 1979, 1987).

Following the Revolution in 1917, the first step towards a more equal society was the confiscation and re-allocation of large houses of wealthy families in inner parts of the city, which were reoccupied by poorer people particularly from the outer suburbs. The need for comprehensive urban planning was quickly recognized; land was nationalized and much of the economy and infrastructure was also taken over by the state or municipal authorities. However, industrialization had greater priority than housing, and it was not until the 1950s that a major programme of residential development was initiated under Khrushchev's leadership. The subsequent scale of construction transformed the city, as poor low-rise accommodation in the inner areas was demolished and the people rehoused in successively taller blocks of flats.

The basic building block of the Soviet city was the *microraion* (micro-region or district), adopted extensively during the 1950s and throughout the remainder of the socialist era. This comprised a neighbourhood unit in the form of blocks of flats, for a population of perhaps 5,000 to 15,000, along with such facilities as kindergartens, club rooms, libraries and sports fields as well as educational, health, retail and cultural services. The level of service provision was supposed to be on a per capita basis, involving specific 'norms' for square metres of shopping space and number of health personnel, for example. Thus people should all have a wide range of day-to-day needs satisfied within their immediate locality, often within a short walk from where they live.

At a broader spatial scale each *microraion* formed part of a nested hierarchy of service provision. Several micro-districts would be combined to form a larger residential complex of perhaps 30,000 to 50,000 people, for the provision of a wider range of more specialized services (French and Hamilton, 1979, pp. 60–1; Bater, 1989, pp. 113–16). These were aggregated up into urban districts of 100,000 to 300,000 inhabitants, which themselves formed part of urban zones with perhaps a million people in a major sector of the city.

In health care, for example, the polyclinic providing basic outpatient services might cater for the 20,000 to 50,000 population of three micro-districts, with general hospitals serving a wider area of perhaps 300,000 and major specialist hospitals in each of the larger zones.

While the individual *microraion* could reasonably be expected to deliver something like equal access to the elements of urban infrastructure built into it, this was not the case with respect to the broader hierarchy of service provision. A contradiction emerged between the need to locate certain facilities centrally in relation to large populations in the interests of efficiency, and the more even distribution (at the higher cost implicit in the loss of economies of scale) required to approach equal access. Thus the ideal of equality foundered on the reality of the necessarily uneven distribution of at least some services. Another source of inequality in the planned spatial distribution of services was the time lag between construction of the housing blocks and of the related services, as part of the general problem of under-provision of the norms which were supposed to ensure local parity of services. Quality of services could also vary among districts, and facilities provided locally for workers at a particular factory, for example, would not be open to other people living nearby.

It might therefore be expected that people in some parts of Moscow would have better access to services than others elsewhere. In particular, the inner parts of the city should be at an advantage, for it is here that the more specialized facilities will tend to be concentrated in any hierarchical structure, and from here that accessibility to other parts of the city will be best because of the focus of transportation lines. Evidence to this effect is provided by the work of (former) Soviet scholars (summarized in Smith, 1987, pp. 77–82). The central part of the city was found to be 'distinguished by the presence of theatres, a built-up area in keeping with Moscow's prominence as the nation's capital, a well-rounded urban environment and a high density of retail outlets selling manufactured goods' (Barbash and Gutnov, 1980, pp. 567–8), with outliers of such facilities in places where major transport nodes ensure good access.

Housing was a crucial element in the planned state provision which was supposed to ensure more egalitarian living standards under Soviet socialism. Space was allocated according to a per capita entitlement, the minimum having been set at 9 square metres in 1922. While this had been achieved as an average standard in Moscow by 1970, large numbers of families had much less while others enjoyed well above the average, so that 'within Moscow there are still very large differences in housing space on a per capita basis' (Bater, 1986, p. 96; see also Hamilton, 1993). In 1980 official figures for the thirty-one regions into which the city was divided varied from 18.8 square metres to 7.3, giving a ratio of just over 2.5:1 between the maximum and minimum.

Table 7.1 Indicators of social status of the population of Moscow by region, 1989

Indicator	Coefficient of variation	Correlation coefficient (r) with other indicators			
		1.	2.	3.	4.
1. People with higher education per 1000 population aged 15 and over	24.1		.80	−.76	−.75
2. Cars per 1000 population	14.8			−.66	−.68
3. Residents convicted of crime per 1000 population aged 15 and over	15.8				.60
4. Juveniles aged under 15 per 1000 population	10.6				

Source: Hamilton (1993, pp. 200, 201, tables 3 and 4).

Inequality in living space is exacerbated by variations in quality of accommodation. Housing quality in Moscow (and elsewhere in the former USSR and other East European countries) varies on the two main dimensions of type of tenure and period of construction. Housing tenure in the former USSR divides roughly into three-quarters 'socialized' and one-quarter privately owner-occupied. Private housing is often of timber construction and of poor quality by conventional (state) standards. It is confined largely to the fringes of cities, to small towns and to the countryside; very little survives in Moscow. The socialized housing sector was further subdivided into three parts: government, industrial or departmental, and co-operative. In 1989 almost three-quarters of Moscow housing was owned by the city government, and 16 per cent by industrial and other ministries which had built for their own workers. While enterprises may have had an incentive to provide good housing, and often services such as health care at the place of work, so as to recruit and maintain an effective labour force, period of construction seems more likely to be a source of differentiation in housing stock than the particular state institution responsible for it.

In general, the later the construction the better the quality of housing, but this is not always the case. For example, in the 1930s under Stalin a number of large apartment blocks were built in ornate style and to relatively high standards, for members of the Party and other privileged groups. However, those constructed during the early period of large-scale residential development initiated by Khrushchev were often badly built; they are now deteriorating and in need of replacement, and widely regarded as slums (French, 1987, p. 312). More recently constructed accommodation in micro-districts on the edge of the city is generally of a higher standard.

(a)

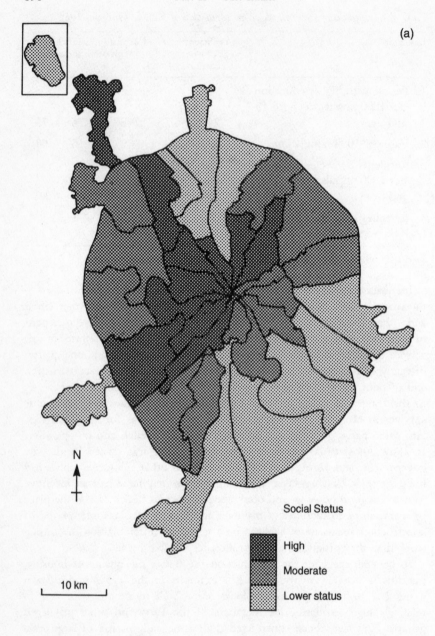

N

Social Status

High

Moderate

Lower status

10 km

(b)

N

10 km

Living Space
(sq. metres per person)

11.7–13.6

11.1–11.6

9.8–11.0

(c)

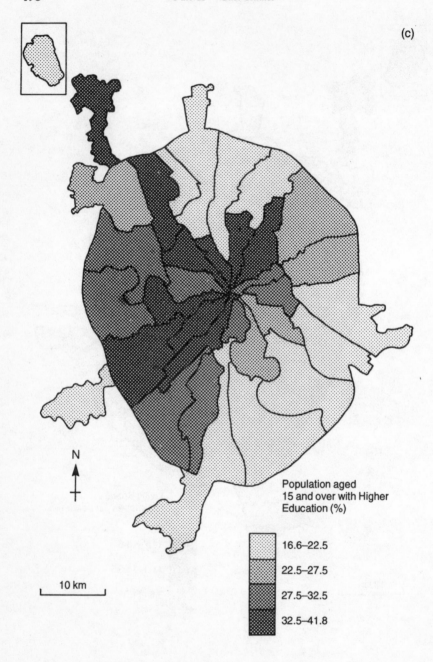

N

Population aged
15 and over with Higher
Education (%)

16.6–22.5

22.5–27.5

27.5–32.5

32.5–41.8

10 km

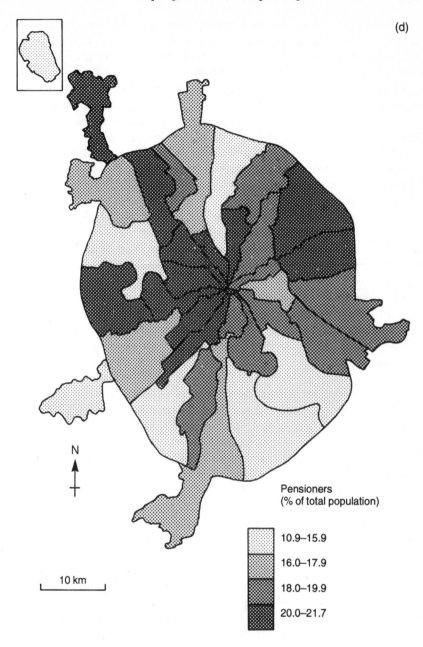

(d)

Pensioners
(% of total population)

10.9–15.9

16.0–17.9

18.0–19.9

20.0–21.7

N

10 km

Figure 7.1   Patterns of inequality in Moscow, 1989.
(Source: (a) and (b) from Hamilton, 1993, pp. 204, 212, figures 2 and 5; (c) and (d) courtesy
A. Beriozhkin, Moscow State University).

The third element of socialized housing, the co-operative, is an important source of qualitative differentiation. Co-operative housing was constructed on behalf of groups of individuals, usually based on the association of work-place (e.g. a particular enterprise or ministry), who thereby acquired collective ownership of their complex or block. Membership required an initial monetary deposit, and monthly payments higher than rent for a state apartment. Co-operative housing is concentrated in the largest cities; it accounts for about 10 per cent of all housing in Moscow. While not conspicuously different from the best state housing in external appearance, co-operative housing was usually built to higher standards.

The relationship between socio-economic status and housing at the end of the socialist era has been examined by Hamilton (1993), in a study undertaken at the scale of the thirty-three regions into which Moscow is divided. She measured social status by people with higher education, car ownership, residents convicted of crime, and proportion of juveniles in the population. The first two are fairly conventional affluence indicators often used in western research, while the other two would be expected to reveal relatively low family incomes. These four conditions were found to have similar degrees of inequality among Moscow regions, as measured by the coefficient of variation (table 7.1). They are also highly correlated one with another, suggesting the kind of spatial correspondence of socio-economic advantage which would be found in a capitalist city, though not nearly as marked.

A composite index derived from data on all four conditions reveals a distinct geographical pattern (figure 7.1a). When this is compared with per capita living space (figure 7.1b), the correspondence is clear; higher status population and more spacious accommodation is concentrated in the inner parts of the city and the western regions. The rank correlation between the two is .75. There is evidence that these patterns are closely reflected in people's perceptions of the relative prestige of residential areas (Siderov, 1992). Figure 7.1 also maps the rate of higher education, as the single indicator with the highest correlation with the others taken to measure social status. And for comparison, there is the proportion of pensioners in the population, indicative of relatively low incomes and perhaps the new poor of the post-socialist era, which reveals a different pattern with more of a concentration in eastern parts of the city.

Hamilton (1993) goes on to explore the role of the state housing allocation system in accounting for her observations. While housing has been considered a right of every citizen, with distribution according to need not ability to pay, it has also been treated as a privilege and reward for special categories of workers. This illustrates the contradiction in socialist justice highlighted at the beginning of the chapter. Hamilton (1993, p. 216) quotes Khrushchev in stressing the significance of contribution to society:

In construction and the distribution of housing we cannot think that just because someone is alive that we should give him a good apartment. It is necessary to consider what he does, what he gives to society. In our socialist society everyone should give something to the greater good of the people . . . only then will he receive the right to use the blessings of society, which are created by society.

Or, as Lenin put it in another sphere, 'He who does not work neither shall he eat' (quoted in Domański, 1991, p. 285).

The correspondence between high status population and most spacious housing suggests that those whose labour was most valued by the state enjoyed a double advantage. Low rents implied a state housing subsidy, the greater the more space people had. As high status would also be rewarded by relatively high incomes, those most able to pay for housing received the largest state subsidies. While this might be perfectly consistent with justice manifest in 'to each according to contribution', particular groups may have been able to ensure for themselves superior housing, along with other benefits, merely by virtue of their capacity to influence the allocation system.

The 'elite' in Soviet socialist society comprised the upper levels in political, administrative, managerial, military, academic and artistic life. As the capital city of a country with a high degree of central control, Moscow had a disproportionately large share of such people. As well as having relatively high salaries, they were rewarded by access to special facilities providing health care or goods not generally available, for example. An additional allocation of housing space may also have been provided, often in special buildings.

Evidence from a variety of sources suggests some spatial concentration of the elite. For example, Matthews (1979, pp. 107–8) points to the old aristocratic district of the Arbat in central Moscow being a favourite location for blocks of prestige flats belonging to the Central Committee of the Communist Party and the KGB, and villas built on the Lenin Hills near Moscow State University as well as new blocks in central locations. French (1987, pp. 313–14) reports a wedge of inner Moscow with a high proportion of apartment blocks inhabited by the elite. There are also indications of fine *dachas* or country homes outside the city. Andrusz (1984, pp. 277–8) suggests that, rather than the suburban living of their Anglo-American counterparts, the Soviet elite preferred to combine a flat near the city centre as permanent residence with a *dacha* often a considerable distance outside the city. Distinct *dacha* communities for the 'high and mighty' were identified in the 1970s by the American journalist Hedrick Smith (see Smith, 1979, p. 240).

Thus, despite a planning process driven by egalitarian ideals, inequality in living standards is evident in socialist Moscow. Some of this can be attributed to the hierarchical structure of service provision and to the process of physical development over time as well as space. But there is also evidence of some spatial sorting of the population by occupational group, including the creation of elite enclaves. The crucial question is the extent to which advantages with respect to housing and accompanying local environmental quality, adding to those of relatively high incomes and possibly other privileges, could really be justified as rewards earned for contribution to society. We will return to this point, after reviewing some more case material.

Some other cities

Rather than looking at other former Soviet cities, further case studies have been chosen from different countries, for their particular bearing on general issues relating to inequality and social justice under socialism. The cities concerned are Prague, Warsaw, and the Hungarian regional centres of Pécs and Szeged. Space available here permits inclusion of no more than the main findings; further details can be found in the original sources and in the summaries in Smith (1989).

Prague, the capital of what was formerly Czechoslovakia, has a population of about 1.2 million in the city, 1.6 million in the wider metropolis. The special interest of Prague is that it provides a case of the imposition of a new society onto an inherited urban spatial form. Unlike Moscow, there has not been an attempt to obliterate virtually all the old city. So instead of a simultaneous change of social structure and built form, Prague has seen the formation of socialist society largely on a pre-existing structure typical of the European city of industrial capitalism.

Prague was the first major East European city to be the subject of thorough investigation of internal differentiation after the advent of socialism (Musil, 1968). This has been followed up by a comparison of the structure of the city in 1930 and 1970 (Matějů, Večerník and Jeřábek, 1979). The pattern for 1930 revealed five types of areas, differentiated according to such conditions as proportion of working class in the economically active population, dwellings with a bathroom, and density of occupation. As Musil (1987, p. 29) describes it:

> Prague of the thirties had all the characteristics of other fast growing metropolises of western capitalist countries. In this period, the social-class differentiation of the society dominated Prague's social ecology and was manifest in the spatial separation of social classes, e.g. in the segregation of the working class and in a clear differentiation of the various social classes' housing and environmental conditions.

Matěju, Večerník and Jeřábek (1979, p. 190) saw an intensification of segregation during the inter-war period:

The once socially heterogeneous districts were gradually becoming homogeneous, due to their dependence upon the character of existing or constructed housing stock. The urban fringes were becoming proletarian, while wealthy strata tended to retreat from the centre of the city and from the industrial areas of the intermediate zone into newly built residential quarters. The city's centre was inhabited by the petty bourgeoisie, clerks and the working-class aristocracy.

It was onto this social geography that a new order was imposed. The early years of the socialist period, up to the latter part of the 1950s, were characterized largely by the redistribution of the existing housing stock according to new criteria of need. This favoured the working class, who were able to move into accommodation not previously available. There was thus an evening out of geographical differences, with the proportion of manual workers in the inner zones increasing to about 40 per cent in 1961 compared with little over a quarter in 1930 (Musil, 1987, p. 31).

The 1960s saw the beginning of a phase of accelerated housing construction, which continued through the 1970s. Large estates were built on the fringe of the city, to relieve congestion on the centre and facilitate reconstruction of the inner areas as well as to accommodate the growing work-force. The social ecology identified in 1970, reflecting the first part of this phase, revealed a pattern similar to that in 1930, but with significant changes in the character of various parts of the city. Differences among the zones had become smaller than in 1930, as reflected in decreases in the ratio of maximum to minimum values from 1.18 to 1.14 for proportion of population working-class, 3.39 to 1.69 for dwellings with bathroom, and 1.62 to 1.14 in the number of persons per room. Some equalization had taken place.

The socio-economic (or class) structure had become much less important in the spatial differentiation of Prague. More significant in 1970 was the material quality of the urban environment, with a distinction between the old, obsolescent parts of the city and the newly developed areas, along with family and age structure (Matěju, Večerník and Jeřábek, 1979, pp. 192–3; Musil, 1987, pp. 32–3). A process of homogenization of urban space had been set in motion, in the interest of social equality, but there was still spatial differentiation arising from the inherited built environment, its variability, and how it compared with new construction. And there was a social dimension to this differentiation: some areas still had a relatively high-status population, while old people were more likely to be in poor and overcrowded housing. The greatest social homogeneity was found in the new outer suburbs, where housing was allocated on the basis of need to families with similar characteristics.

The 1980s appear to have been characterized by a growing differentiation of both the old and new parts of Prague. The better-quality housing became dispersed, unlike that of the pre-socialist period. And in the new housing estates, state, enterprise and co-operative blocks of flats were mixed. Thus, Musil (1987, p. 35) saw 'an increase of heterogeneity in macrostructure', accompanied by 'a certain homogenization which contributes to the emergence of problem areas', occupied by old people and less qualified workers, in the inner districts and some older industrial parts of the city.

The inherited built form of the capitalist city clearly had an important bearing on the changing social geography of Prague during the socialist period. To quote Musil (1987, p. 32) again:

> [E]ven an extensive house building programme carried out in the sixties – and, it may be added, even in the seventies – combined with many other deep social changes, were not able to completely transform the inherited features of Prague's social ecology. The inner parts of the city did not essentially change and the traditional attraction of certain districts for certain social groups remained rather strong. Also the inherited location of industrial as well as non-industrial workplaces undoubtedly played an important role in shaping the ecological pattern of the city.

The socialist period expanded the city, creating new residential areas of relatively uniform quality, at least with respect to state housing. But districts of poor housing and low environmental quality remained. Access to housing of varied quality, along with the freedom of those with the means and ability to build or acquire private housing or join a co-operative, provided scope for people to become unequal, in terms of their accommodation and the local environment which went with it. However, it is not clear how far these advantages accrued to high-status occupational groups as an explicit and just reward for their contribution to society, as opposed to being fortuitous outcomes of differential access to a differentiated housing stock.

Warsaw, capital of Poland, has a special place in the creation of the socialist city. Its population had reached almost 1.3 million in 1939, but five years of war-time devastation left barely 162,000 people in 1945. The new society therefore had almost complete freedom to reconstruct a major city according to new ideals. Nowakowski (1979, p. 205) summarized the objectives of urban planning under socialism as follows:

> By stimulating industrialization and urbanization, the Polish authorities aimed to provide people with satisfactory dwelling conditions, thus

making their adaptation to new conditions and a new environment easier. Also, they aimed to form an egalitarian society, having equally well-equipped housing estates in the new towns where all social categories could share similar conditions.

Two important principles were: 'the right to adequate living conditions in cities – by the proper location of service centres for education, culture, etc.', and 'the principle of social equality – by applying uniform criteria with respect to every social group and area' (Regulska, 1987, p. 326).

In Warsaw the first priority after the war was to get the city working again. By 1949 sufficient progress had been made that idealism harnessed to practical necessity could be articulated as follows by President Bierut (quoted in Regulska, 1987, p. 327):

New Warsaw cannot be a reproduction of the old one, it cannot be only an improved repetition of pre-war concentration of private capitalist interests of the society, it cannot be a reflection of contradictions dividing this society, it cannot be a scene and base for exploitation of people and expansion of privileges of the owners' class ... New Warsaw should become the socialist capital. The fight for the ideological image of our city must be carried out with full consciousness and with all required energy directed towards this goal. New Warsaw through development of industry will become a centre of production, the city of workers.

Attending to the housing needs of the population would have been a daunting task even without war damage, for Warsaw was one of the most overcrowded cities in Europe in the inter-war period. Physical reconstruction and industrialization attracted large numbers of migrants, and the population had reached 1.0 million again by 1955. It is 1.7 million today. Shortage of housing has continued to be one of the most serious problems facing Warsaw, and is a major source of inequality in urban life.

In 1944 all existing housing was 'communalized' or taken into state control, except for small one-family dwellings. Most private housing remains on the outskirts of the city and is of relatively poor quality, though some inner enclaves of family villa-type homes of the pre-war middle class survive around the centre. The advent of socialism saw the state (or city of Warsaw) take the major role in housing, but pressure on resources led to the encouragement of large-scale co-operative development from the late 1950s, tapping people's savings in return for a shorter waiting time. The development of co-operatives was accompanied by a decline in city-financed construction, which was discontinued in 1973.

Relatively unconstrained by its pre-existing form, the overall structure of the city could develop according to the prevailing socialist planning practice, influenced by Soviet experience including the micro-region. However, there was uneven development of the service infrastructure, as in Moscow, with central areas tending to fare better. In the initial period co-operatives paid much more attention than municipal authorities to the appearance of housing estates and supply of services, but as co-operatives came to dominate the scene such concerns seem to have been less important (Ciechocińska, 1987, p. 11). Modern estates on the fringe of the city often lack good transport as well as services, though quality of accommodation may be some compensation. Thus urban environmental attributes as well as the dwellings themselves vary with location, date of construction and housing tenure.

We have been able to see something of the impact of the socialist period on Prague, which retained much of its pre-war urban fabric. A similar exercise is possible for Warsaw, but in quite different conditions associated with the almost total re-creation of the city under socialism (Węcławowicz, 1979). Data for enumeration districts on variables measuring population characteristics, occupation and housing in 1931 were used to derive an index of 'economic-class position'. There was a clear decline in socio-economic status, from the compact central zone, through a continuous transitional zone, and out into a peripheral zone. This reversal of the usual generalization concerning the capitalist city could be explained by the fact that the process of outward movement of wealthier people had begun in Warsaw only after 1918, generating few high-status areas on the periphery.

The population of Warsaw in 1970, at 1,315,000, was not much greater than in 1931. But the physical structure of the city had been very largely renewed. Węcławowicz (1979) chose variables which coincided as far as possible with those in 1931, to derive an index reflecting educational and occupational characteristics along with form of housing tenure. This captured what he termed 'socio-occupational position', rather than economic-class status as in 1931, because it was less concerned with the income differentials which predominate under capitalism than with the broader social evaluation of labour in particular occupations. In other words, the state rather than the market had become the means of assigning relative significance to different occupations. The highest index values tended to be in the central part of the city, reflecting the concentration of writers, journalists and artists along with others occupying crucial (and privileged) positions and working in nearby offices, educational institutions and so on. This was the outcome of a selective housing policy which enabled these groups to settle in central locations which had been rebuilt soon after the war. The lowest values denoted areas dominated by housing construction of the 1960s.

Węcławowicz (1979) concluded that there were great changes in spatial structure between 1931 and 1970. In the inter-war period Warsaw had an urban form strongly differentiated by class. The pattern in 1970 was more a reflection of socio-occupational position, a selective housing policy, and stages of settling the post-war city. The classic models of the capitalist city, with their wedges, concentric zones and multiple-nuclear patterns, are too simplistic to describe the reality of Warsaw's spatial structure in 1970, which was more of a mosaic differentiated in local detail. More recent research at the broader scale of the Warsaw urban region reveals a 'substantial increase of spatial disparities' between 1978 and 1988 (Węcławowicz, 1991, p. 29), reflecting the prevailing social and political transformation and in particular the increasing shortage of housing.

Another interpretation of socio-spatial disparities in Warsaw, at the end of the 1970s, is offered by Dangschat and Blasius (1987; see also Dangschat, 1987). They identified distinct clusters of districts, defined mainly on the basis of housing age and type. Education appears to be an important means whereby access to a differentiated housing stock is determined (pp. 188–9):

> Better educated people live in new, well-equipped co-operative dwellings; the poorly educated live either mainly in single-person households in very old houses, badly equipped in the inner city parts of Praga . . . or as bigger families in the rural outskirts in private small houses which are badly equipped. These concentrations are spatially adjacent. Their spatial position can best be described by a model of concentric circles, which are overlapped by sectoral patterns in the outer districts.

Thus differences in housing do not counteract other inequalities but tend to reinforce them. These authors claim that disparities in Warsaw are not fundamentally different from those of their western European counterparts.

An alternative position is advanced by Ciechocińska (1987, pp. 22–4), who is closer to Węcławowicz (1979) in asserting: 'The pattern of socio-spatial differences in Warsaw differs considerably from textbook examples of social inequalities which occur in many developed and third world countries.' She sees the basic source of inequality as the shortage of housing, which generates a distinctive process of differential access. The shortage could mean a wait of well over ten years in a housing co-operative, but especially valuable employees such as those in managerial or leadership positions in public organizations had a better chance of obtaining such flats. Only families with incomes well below average could obtain city-owned flats, and their concentration usually in older parts led to strong socio-spatial differentiation. Only the most affluent people could afford to buy their own flat or build a single-family house. Rigid regulations concerning the exchange of flats, along with the housing shortage, meant that most people were tied to their accommodation virtually for life. Such stability is conducive to a perpetuation of the existing differences in the socio-spatial structure, the justice of which is, at least, debatable.

Pécs and Szeged are regional centres in Hungary, both with population a little less than 200,000. They are the subject of one of the most thorough investigations of housing inequality under socialism. In 1968 George Konrad and Ivan Szelenyi carried out a survey involving 2300 families in the two cities, to find out whether a new pattern of urban inequality could be detected. In particular, they sought to reveal how the unequal distribution of social privileges and disadvantages arising from the differentiation of socialist society was related to the spatial distribution and mobility of the social groups concerned. The account here is based on Szelenyi (1983).

The allocation of occupational groups among different kinds of housing revealed a striking distinction between the relatively high proportions of bureaucrats, intellectuals, technicians and clerical workers in first-class state housing and the lower proportions of skilled, semi-skilled and unskilled workers. The same distinction was shown for those with their own bank-financed or co-operative apartment. However, in private family housing, of generally poor quality, the situation was the other way round. So in general, the higher status groups received the better housing, with the highest state subsidies.

Szelenyi (1983, pp. 58–9) identified the manner in which his Pécs and Szeged sample had acquired their housing. Those who had been awarded state housing included 37 per cent of the high bureaucrats and almost 40 per cent of intellectuals, compared with figures of around 21 to 25 per cent for skilled, semi-skilled and unskilled workers. The situation was reversed for those who had built or bought their own houses, however, with only 26 per cent of bureaucrats and 21 per cent of intellectuals in this category compared with about 35 per cent of skilled and semi-skilled workers and 44 per cent of the unskilled.

Szelenyi (1983, p. 63) summarized the trends as follows:

[T]he social groups with highest incomes move steadily towards the highest housing classes in the state and market sectors, and come close to monopolizing them. Below that, the highest class of housing available to most of those with lower incomes is the second market class, i.e. the range of family houses omitting the superior 'villa' category. The housing options and opportunities of these lower classes are limited more by the state policies which allocate state housing and credit than by the people's capacity to pay. Public policy thus provides that, on average, the richer classes get better housing for less money and effort, while the poorer classes get worse housing at the cost of more money or effort, or both.

So, whereas under socialism housing is supposed to have a special significance as an equalizing element of state provision, received as a right not as a reflection of income, it was found to be a source of inequality compounding other inequalities arising from occupational status.

Szelenyi went on to consider the spatial structure of the two cities, to see whether there was any correspondence between the physical and functional characteristics of areas, their housing, and their demographic and social composition. Relatively high proportions of intellectuals, other white-collar workers and skilled blue-collar workers lived in the new multi-storey housing estates (fitted with bathrooms, water, gas and electricity), and, to a lesser extent, in the city centre. Correspondingly lower proportions of the professionals lived in the more industrial areas and outer zones of private village-style dwellings. Unskilled workers made up more than half the households in these zones of poorer housing, with only 18 per cent in the new state housing areas.

Szelenyi (1983, p. 117) concluded as follows:

[T]he degree of segregation of our cities is measurable. It is also clear that all the measured social and spatial advantages tend to be superimposed on one another to increase the privilege of the privileged, while the corresponding disadvantages go together to worsen the situation of the disadvantaged. The higher social classes with the higher status and the better educational qualifications are situated in the better zones of the city; the lower social classes with lower status and less education tend to live in the poorer zones.

Furthermore, those with low incomes allocated poor housing in poor districts typically paid more for it than the richer people paid for better housing in better districts. State housing allocation favoured those of high status, the workers seeking new accommodation largely being forced out of the city to build for themselves. Thus, contrary to the expectations of socialist justice, the housing-allocation system was found to have a regressive redistributional impact.

Distribution under socialism

Among both indigenous and western students of the East European and former Soviet city, there is almost universal agreement that the degree of social segregation and inequality under socialism was less than under capitalism. However, there are differences in interpretation of both the spatial pattern of inequality and its extent. One school argues that urban inequalities were greatly reduced under socialism, and that what did exist could best be described as a mosaic, patchwork or in similar terms. This is essentially the conclusion arrived at by Węcławowicz (1979) in Poland, endorsed more generally by French and Hamilton (1979, pp. 16–17). This view has been challenged by Dangschat (1987), who found 'surprisingly high' segregation of social groups by education, age and household size in Warsaw, contradicting what he describes as the conventional wisdom of a low rate of segregation in the mosaic of the socialist city; he claims the existence of relatively large socially homogeneous areas. Szelenyi (1987, p. 6) adopts a similar position.

The most plausible resolution of these alternative views would appear to be that some broad spatial differentiation or inequality in occupational status, education, housing, certain demographic characteristics, and (less conspicuously) income was very likely to be found in medium-sized and large cities, but punctuated by smaller distinctive areas differentiated by the survival of pre-Revolutionary or pre-war housing, and by enclaves of superior or inferior state housing or co-operatives. Much depends on the history of the city in question, its pattern of (re)development, and the survival or otherwise of distinctive social areas, local communities or environments. There may also be population clusters based on ethnicity, depending on whether this source of communal identity survived socialist ideology, planned resettlement or the 'Holocaust' (in the case of the former large localized Jewish populations, one of which will be discussed in chapter 9).

The process whereby inequality arises in the socialist city is clearly different from what occurs under capitalism. However, residential segregation can be expected in any society if certain conditions are met: socio-economic disparities within urban society, variable housing stock, spatial concentrations of differing housing conditions, and competition for dwellings within the housing system. To these might be added differences in local levels of service provision and general environmental quality. All these conditions were in fact met in the East European socialist city, to a greater or lesser extent, and it is worth considering how they came about and contributed to inequality.

Socio-economic disparities arise to a large extent from the division of labour. Under capitalism the occupational structure is strongly reflected in income differentials, which are themselves the key to other sources of inequality in material consumption and services. Under socialism the social (i.e. state) evaluation of different occupations is less clearly defined by attributes that sharply differentiate people's living standards. And there may be a deliberate attempt to assign high status to manual labour and lower status to some professional occupations. Nevertheless, there are unequal rewards, as part of an incentive system designed to attract people into crucial roles, whether leadership positions or miners in some inhospitable location. Social stratification therefore does exist under socialism, though less pronounced and with some different characteristics when compared with capitalism.

Dissimilarities in housing stock arise in various ways. They are an inevitable outcome of the historical development of the socialist city, or part of the city, as standards of design, construction and fittings change. Special state accommodation may have been built for privileged groups. The co-operative is a further source of differentiation, though its scale, quality and quasi-private status differs from one country to another. There is also the pre-socialist housing stock, varying from the occasional palace and the detached villas of the bourgeoisie to the surviving slum tenements of old industrial quarters. Finally there is the private or market-sector stock of the socialist period itself, usually of poor standard by conventional criteria compared with state provision but including some fine homes in some countries where high incomes could be earned and spent on private housing.

The association of level of service provision with housing quality is close but not complete. Overall, the inner city has the largest concentration of specialized services and the best access to the city-wide service network. But some well-serviced inner areas may have poor housing and environment. The new estates may have good quality housing, but suffer from time-lags in service provision as well as being remote from central facilities. Some inequality is intrinsic to a spatial hierarchy of service provision, as we saw in Moscow.

That disparities in housing and associated local environmental conditions have a spatial expression in the socialist city is clear. This follows from the outward growth of the city, and from the planning practice of creating fairly large and homogeneous estates. It is also an outcome of the pre-socialist inheritance, not only because housing has survived from an earlier era but also because in other respects the pre-socialist form may have been preserved. For example, Regulska (1987, pp. 327, 333) points out that, in the initial post-war phase of reconstruction, limitations on resources directed urban policy towards those areas which required least investment, thus reproducing the pre-war urban network; old housing was also preserved to reduce the need for new apartments. Elements of the spatial form and differentiation of the pre-socialist city thus contributed to the opportunities for inequality.

Competition for housing and environment of differing quality arose from shortage, not only of housing in general but also of the kind people prefer. Some individuals were better placed than others to succeed in this competition. This may have been a matter of need, such as existing housing conditions or family size, qualifying people for state provision. But it could also reflect privileged access on the part of those in certain occupations. In the period immediately following the advent of socialism there was a strong ideological and practical commitment to rehousing the poor working class, demonstrated in the appropriation and redistribution of large houses of the bourgeoisie. With the passage of time priorities changed, better educated people in 'higher' occupational groups being advantaged in access to housing.

Once residential segregation has been established, the inequalities may be self-reinforcing. Szelenyi (1983, p. 105) sees the process as follows:

> If districts have different housing classes and social strata, they generate different needs under non-market conditions as well as under market conditions. They also generate different capacities to get what they want, by fighting or bargaining or any other means. People in middle-class districts have more contacts, they have more of the skills required in bureaucratic negotiations, they have better access to many sources of information. So a segregated middle-class district will often attract a department store before a working-class district does, and it will often get a larger share of the urban services and infrastructure that its residents want. Those advantages will be superimposed on the housing advantages such districts already possess. Meanwhile segregated working-class districts will suffer the corresponding disadvantages; their life-style and opportunities of mobility will suffer accordingly; so will their individual and collective capacities to do anything effective about the inequalities from which they suffer. In such districts the physical deterioration of the housing runs parallel to changes in the composition of the residents, leaving generally lower incomes, and declining standards in important local services and institutions, especially the schools.

If this process seems reminiscent of that in the capitalist city, it is important to recognize that what led to the initial pattern of segregation is significantly different, as is the way in which additional local advantages may be secured. It is tempting to see parallels with capitalism, and indeed to assert that East European socialism was not really very different. However, the vast majority of those who study the socialist city find a distinctive process of inequality at work. Even Dangschat (1987, p. 56), who sees close similarities in the pattern of inequality in Warsaw and the capitalist city, recognizes that 'residential segregation processes in Warsaw are different from those in west European cities'. And Szelenyi continues to assert that socialist cities are different from those under capitalism. He elaborates as follows (Szelenyi, 1987, pp. 4–5):

> [T]he state socialist society is producing and reproducing social inequalities, because its economic system is structured a certain way, because it is built on redistributive mechanisms, upon which the distribution of power and privilege is based in these societies. If one wants to alter in a significant way these inequalities one will have to modify the underlying economic structure.

The broad features of this structure are sketched out in figure 7.2, along with other elements contributing to inequality. On the right of the diagram is the differentiated housing stock, service infrastructure and local environmental quality, patterned by pre-socialist forms as well as by new urban development. To the left is a suggestion of the process whereby differential access arises, from the production and redistributive mechanisms and the role of individuals within them. While details may require modification in the light of how particular societies function nationally, this is general enough to capture the essence of East European socialism as an inegalitarian system.

We have tried to comprehend the central contradiction or paradox of socialism as actually practised: the continuing existence of inequality in a society built on egalitarian ideals. To quote Szelenyi (1987, p. 7) again: 'An ideologically egalitarian housing policy and urban planning produced an inegalitarian system of housing allocation, and produced, and keeps reproducing, the residential segregation of occupational groups.' It is not that those who run the societies concerned somehow deliberately subvert the system: 'They create inegalitarian cities not because they wish to do so, but because they operate as key agents in a new social structure, which is shaped by new types of class antagonisms.'

These observations may now be related more explicitly to social justice. Reviewing an extensive literature, Domański (1991, p. 294) concludes that 'there is very little evidence that distribution according to need was actually important', in such domains as housing, medical care, benefits in kind, income and social security. Furthermore, 'provision of some services free of charge does not ensure that access to them is equal for everyone or easier for the worst off'. While some notion of merit and performance may have been relevant in obtaining certain positions, there is even more evidence that they were not the most significant distributive principles. However, with respect to rewarding individuals or groups on the basis of the societal importance of their work, determined by its contribution to achieving strategic economic goals, he claims 'an overwhelming amount of evidence that this principle has played a crucial role in social practice' (p. 285).

The best paying branches of the economy were those seen as contributing most to material production. Social security benefits would be closely tied to employment, as the provision of child care, medical care and leisure facilities, for example, were allocated to a substantial extent through the work-place. Provision of housing on a ministry or enterprise basis enabled it to be treated as a reward to priority workers within a closed network. Thus, 'individuals, and social groups' value as manpower emerges as the fundamental criterion for the allocation of social goods under socialism' (Domański, 1991, p. 285). State evaluation of labour contribution could thus be regarded as a dominant good, in the sense elaborated by Michael Walzer (chapter 4): position in this sphere clearly generated inequalities in other spheres of life.

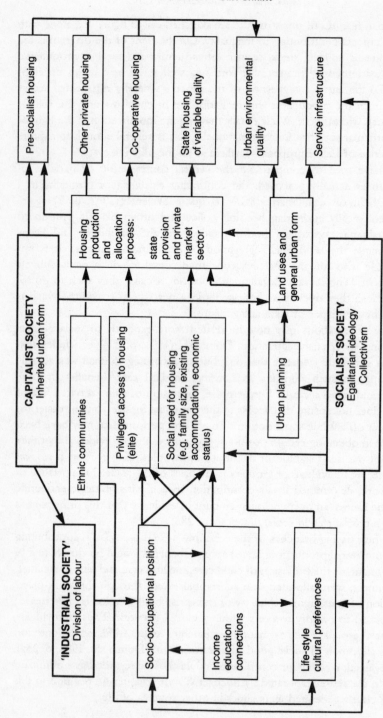

Figure 7.2 Elements of the process of inequality in the socialist city.
(Source: Smith, 1989, p. 72, figure 8.2).

One further principle may be identified, distinguished from need, merit or performance and labour contribution: 'allocation according to one's position in an elaborately stratified system, where rewards are granted on the basis of ideological conformity and political loyalty' (Domański, 1991, p. 285). A distinction could be made between the elite or policy-making group able to deal themselves special privileges, and the apparatus of implementation performing roles whereby goods, service privileges and information were assigned to some people and kept away from other members of the predominant class of 'claimants'. He concludes: 'Gatekeepers controlling access to various resources constitute a crucial element of specific socialist mechanisms generating and reproducing social inequalities' (p. 290). Kalinina (1992) adopts a similar concept of the 'distributor', meaning a place or mechanism whereby high-quality or low-cost goods or services in short supply are assigned. Position in such a system was another form of dominant good.

The significance of this interpretation for social justice is that socialism developed its own internal distributive criteria, which might be regarded as more of a functional necessity for the reproduction of the kind of society which actually emerged than an expression of moral principles. There is an obvious parallel with Marx's view of certain aspects of capitalism, most notably exploitation, which could be considered just within the framework of this particular mode of production (see chapter 4). But, unless we accept a relativist conception of social justice, the actual practices of socialism, like capitalism, must be related to some external standards. Distribution according to societal contribution might hold up, even to the extent of justifying some privileges for those in onerous positions of responsibility, especially if associated with a society satisfying Rawls's principle of making the worst-off as well-off as possible. But rewards arising simply from ideological conformity or opportunistic advantage certainly would not qualify as just, even if functional to the existing social order. As it happens, the functional argument also fails, with the collapse of this form of socialist society itself.

Social justice after socialism

The primary purpose of this chapter has been to explore social justice under socialism. However, the changes which have taken place in recent years in East Europe and the former Soviet Union invite some brief observations on distributional issues in post-socialist society (following in part Smith, 1994a).

With respect to inequality, the trend is fairly clear. While there are variations from country to country, many people, perhaps the vast majority, are markedly worse-off in a material sense than before. This is because of rapid inflation reducing the real value of both earnings and savings, the collapse of sectors of the economy causing unemployment on the one hand and shortages of goods on the other, and the erosion of state social security, on which people had come to rely. However, for a small minority the changing conditions have provided new economic opportunities, legal or otherwise, and the chance to become rich very quickly. The economic power gained by the so-called mafia in the former Soviet Union is legendary, and spreading to neighbouring countries.

The impact of increasing economic disparities is already evident within the city. With reference to Poland, former Czechoslovakia and Hungary, Węcławowicz (1992, p. 137) comments:

> A rapid increase in the numbers of poor, unemployed and homeless has been 'discovered' in the socio-spatial structure of the cities. It is accompanied by rapid wealth diversification followed by socio-spatial polarity. Another specific transition problem is the tremendous increase in different pathological phenomena [such as crime].

> The transformation of property rights through privatisation, in particular the withdrawal of subsidies in the housing economy, would generate a strong process of housing segregation according to criteria of wealth. Restructuring of this sort, given the massive shortage of housing units, will evidently cause social tensions and conflict.

These indications may point to permanent features of a new society formed as distorted market forces play themselves out on the wreckage of socialism. They raise profound questions of social justice, to which we will return in the final chapter of this book. However, for the remainder of this section we will examine some rather more specific issues involved in the process of transition itself.[2]

The privatization of state assets has become emblematic of economic reform, and even of democratization itself. Any privatization strategy will reflect considerations of social justice, explicit or otherwise, in the rules adopted. Thus, every citizen could be allocated an equal share, or some minimum quantity free of charge with the rest going to the highest bidder. Special entitlements could be recognized, for example shares set aside for those employed in the activities concerned. Each country has its own context in which the debate on privatization and its implementation unfolds.

---

[2] Most of the material here is derived from first-hand investigations, including discussions with local research workers and public officials, augmented by anecdotal evidence.

A few examples from the former Soviet Union provide illustrations of the kind of strategies adopted and issues involved. The Russian Republic has initiated an egalitarian strategy of issuing vouchers worth 10,000 roubles to every citizen, to buy whatever shares they wish; their value is roughly $10.00 (at the exchange rate prevailing in August 1993). By April 1993, 66,000 state companies had been privatized. However, few people are well informed about investment opportunities in a highly volatile economic climate, and the temptation to sell their vouchers (at less than face value) is concentrating ownership. And there are indications that factory managers and former bureaucrats of the communist era are finding ways of acquiring disproportionate shares of state assets.

Kazakhstan has begun to sell state housing, with each adult receiving a voucher worth 400 roubles for every year in work, and special allowances for invalids and children. The local authority fixes the price of all flats, and people can then purchase with their vouchers, possibly supplemented by savings. There have been practical problems, including a reluctance to acquire flats for private occupancy as opposed to sale, but the point is that the starting conditions, in the sense of the initial distribution of purchasing capacity, were related to specific criteria of desert linked to need.

Similar proposals with respect to the privatization of housing have been put forward in Moscow. For example, in 1990 it was suggested that every Muscovite would be allocated something like the average living space of 12 square metres free of charge. Those with more space would have to pay for it; those with less would receive paper securities in proportion to their deficit, which would act as an entitlement to new accommodation. Again, this represented an attempt to establish equitable starting conditions for a housing market. How the market actually functions when it gets going is another matter, of course; the prevailing shortage could push prices up to the point where few can afford to buy and the poor (especially the elderly on low pensions) are forced into inferior accommodation.

A further aspect of privatization concerns rights over mineral deposits and other natural resources hitherto owned by the state and (supposedly) exploited in the interests of the population at large. Are these to be distributed to individuals as part of the privatization of land, or returned to the families of former owners if they can be traced, or are the rights to the income such resources can generate to be attributed wholly or in part to some local or national authority? The answer to such questions has a crucial bearing on how widely or narrowly the benefits from variable local resource endowments are to be distributed. The same could be said for fixed capital in the form of major industrial plants and infrastructural investment, the location of which may have been determined by central state planning objectives such as more even regional development.

Property rights by no means exhaust the scope for the application of principles of social justice to spatial aspects of restructuring after socialism. Rights of citizenship, including democratic participation, depend crucially on the territorial jurisdictions adopted for electoral purposes. For example, ensuring that local concentrations of people of particular ethnic origin are neither dominant nor dominated in political life is important in the context of resurgent nationalism, as in the trans-Caucasian republics for example. Political (re)districting so as to ensure that the interests of all population groups are fairly represented is crucial to the success of political reform in the former Soviet Union (Kolosov, 1989).

A brief review of Polish experience helps to highlight further issues arising from privatization. The process has gone furthest in service trading, especially retailing, where the private sector accounted for 90.5 per cent of total employment in 1992 compared with 9.3 per cent in 1989 and only 3.6 per cent in 1980. This change has been as much a result of the setting up of new businesses as of the transfer of state enterprises to private hands. In construction, 71.8 per cent of employment was in the private sector in 1992 compared with 33.3 per cent in 1989 and 7.7 per cent in 1980. However, in manufacturing the 1992 figure was only 41.4 per cent, and in transportation only 23 per cent. It should be noted that there was a move towards privatization during the 1980s, before the collapse of the communist regime, associated with relaxation of restrictions on co-operative enterprises.

Privatization of industry has proceeded in two stages. The first involved a combination of transfer of state enterprises into commercial companies by the sale of shares (to domestic or foreign buyers, subject to some rights of purchase on the part of employees), and liquidation whereby the state disposed of assets of enterprises, usually the smaller ones, perhaps to the existing management and workers. By 1992, 460 of about 8000 state enterprises had been privatized by transfer and 1250 by liquidation. The second stage, referred to as 'mass privatization', is supposed to involve the entire population. About 600 enterprises were included in the programme initiated in 1993, with the population free to buy shares as they wish but with a proportion set aside for existing workers at a favourable price. A particular feature of this programme is the distribution of certificates of entitlement to buy shares to workers in the public sector (as compensation for low wages), pensioners and people on social security. The strategy has thus been influenced by some conceptions of equity, as well as by recognition that the legitimacy of privatization depends on wide public participation in a process which might otherwise be perceived as merely disposing of state assets to foreigners and those fortunate enough to have the money or to be able to obtain a private stake in their own enterprise.

Housing privatization is proving difficult in Poland, and major issues are still to be resolved. There is pressure on city authorities to sell their housing to sitting tenants at low prices, following the strategy adopted in Gdinia where a vigorous housing market has been created and other economic activity has thereby been stimulated. Housing acquired in this way can subsequently be sold at great advantage if in central locations or on land suitable for commercial redevelopment, which raises the issues of uneven access to this source of unearned windfall profits. The national government is concerned about cities disposing of valuable assets cheaply, however, and favours the realization of market prices – which only the rich could afford. Choice between these alternative strategies has important (re)distributive implications. In the co-operative housing sector the cost of taking on private ownership is beyond the financial means of most occupants.

Special problems arise in what is referred to as the 're-privatization' of property which remained in private ownership during the socialist period but with control of use and rentals in state hands. Restitution of full property rights to original owners or their descendants could lead to substantial increases in rents, particularly for inner-city property suitable for commercial use or even gentrification. A Ministry of Housing source estimates that 280,000 households could be affected, many of them poor, unable to pay higher rents, and with no other housing available. Such is the impact of market forces. It is hardly surprising to find Muziol-Węcławowicz (1992, p. 216) concluding, from a study of Warsaw, that 'the price levels in relation to salaries exclude the majority of society from utilizing the housing market as a means of solving their housing problems'.

We round off this discussion with a vignette of an East European city in transition. The city of Łódź grew up on textile manufacturing, as the Manchester of Poland. Massive red-brick mills dominate the inner districts, along with terrace rows and tenements for the workers, and nearby palaces built by the cotton kings who vied with the most successful in Europe in the late nineteenth and early twentieth century. The population had grown from 10,000 in 1840 to 320,000 by 1900, and to 680,000 by 1939, when Łódź accounted for 37 per cent of employment in the Polish textile industry. The city was the scene of some famous labour struggles, quelled with brutal inevitability by agents of a state bound to the interests of capital, and location of a large Jewish ghetto eliminated during the Holocaust (see chapter 9). Łódź is now the second largest city in Poland, with a population of about 840,000 and 1,130,000 in its wider metropolitan area.

Since the collapse of socialism changes have had a profound impact on Łódź. The formerly secure market for the city's textile products in the Soviet Union has disappeared (for background, see Paczka and Riley, 1992). Employment in manufacturing, which reached almost 230,000 in 1970, had dropped to 89,000 by the end of 1991. Huge old mills, along with some plants added during the socialist period, stand silent and empty. The city has set up an office to attract foreign investment, making what it can of its strategic location, tourist potential and the like. But new firms are providing only a small fraction of the jobs lost in plant closures or cut-backs. The city failed in negotiations with a major American manufacturer of jeans, which found a site elsewhere in Poland. Unemployment was estimated to be about 12 per cent in 1991, rising to 23 per cent in 1993. Much of the impact has fallen on the women who predominated in textiles, adding to high maternal health problems associated with harsh working conditions. People losing their job initially receive benefits equivalent to somewhat less than the prevailing minimum wage, but this is reduced after three months and ceases altogether after a year.

Privatization has proceeded rapidly in retailing and other services. By 1991, over 90 per cent of shops and 85 per cent of restaurants operated outside the public sector, the number of establishments having almost doubled in two years as opportunities for private trading were opened up. As at the national scale, much less has happened in industry: four-fifths of employment was still in state enterprises at the end of 1991. Taking over large, obsolete factories with no obvious market for their products is not an enticing prospect, despite experienced labour available; like the old mill buildings, much of the antiquated machinery is of more interest to the industrial archaeologist than to new investors. As to housing, opportunities for private ownership are unattractive or unaffordable for most people. Meanwhile, the emerging *nouveau riche* making fortunes in business build fine detached homes on the edge of the city or buy into the small enclaves of pre-war villas.

The families of some property owners from the pre-socialist period are trying to re-privatize what can be identified as theirs. Old mill-owning families have their representatives at work in the city. Uncertainties about ownership, especially on the part of former Jewish and German inhabitants, can be an impediment to privatization and new investment. The Geography Departments of the University of Łódź occupy (in 1993) a former girls' school built in 1903, and taken over by the state in 1944. The family of the original owner have now regained control and seek a substantial increase in rent, beyond the means of the University, so as to realize full market value. The building in question has an elegant façade and stands on a main street in a central location. It is ideal for renovation, and conversion into a bank. The geographers have to go.

Epilogue

In a Russian city the local mafia men assemble at the hotel soon after noon. Elsewhere they may be distinguished by jeans and leather jackets: here it is shell suits and an assortment of Adidas gear (authentic or otherwise). Looking more like Essex Man than conventional mafiosi, they hardly appear capable of more than Saturday night agro, far less the serious intimidation and killings for which they are credited. The most sinister-looking sports a bright red track suit that could almost be a relic of the Soviet era. The restaurant staff recognize a right to the table near the side door. Each new arrival greets the others effusively. Two men go outside to confer with more privacy. The one woman in the group, denim mini-skirt and fair hair further blonded, gets on with her salad, rissole and rice oblivious of the company.

Later, outside the hotel, someone takes a consignment of new tee-shirts from the boot of a car. The mafia men make their choice, unwrap the shirts and try them on: the one proclaiming 'Kick Ass' on its back attracts evident approval, though whether the full force of the message is understood isn't clear. Groups of kids nearby serve their apprenticeship hustling soft drinks and car washes, for money to be spent on cakes and cigarettes in the hotel buffet. A black Lada draws up and its driver distributes large wads of roubles to the shell suits.

The main source of mafia income here is reported to be extortion from the informal traders who set up stalls around the sparsely stocked shopping centre, and others tempted into private trading elsewhere. Participants in the informal sector sell anything from fruit and vegetables to second-hand clothing and single packets of cigarettes. The book shop near the supermarket joins in, with its own stall outside disposing of surplus volumes. A large truck disgorges eggs from a local farm to a growing queue. At night elderly ladies standing in the cold light of street lamps provide more choice of wine (including Russian champagne) than the hotel restaurant.

The mafia have divided the city into districts and sub-districts, control of which reflects the power of those involved. They have detailed knowledge of the local traders and of their earnings, a proportion of which is taken. In addition to the kiosks and stalls on the streets, the city's largest department store and some state shops are penetrated by private sections. The shadow economy is steadily augmenting the state sector, with control passing from the old managerial bureaucracy to the mafia (if indeed they are easy to separate). And the power of the mafia is not confined to the city: the high price of vegetables here is attributed to the money that has to be paid at various points on the road from the Asiatic former republics to the south.

The usual response to the obvious suggestion that the police and local authorities should take on the mafia is that bribery and collusion makes this unrealistic. The rise of the mafia is sometimes represented as an inevitable and perhaps necessary stage in the development of a capitalist economy. Familiarity with the seamy side of American history, derived largely from gangster films, gives some dubious credence to this interpretation. Thus there is a resigned, if at times angry, popular acceptance of growing mafia domination of important sectors of economic life. Knowledge that those in control today may owe their positions to earlier Communist Party affiliation underlines a sense that ordinary people are as powerless as ever.

Those who rule appear more concerned with getting western approval and financial aid by means of symbolic gestures towards a market economy, such as price reforms (i.e. increases) and privatization, than with the real economic consequences of the break-down of the old order. Among these is a growing concentration of power in the hands of those whose profits depend on the frustration of anything approaching truly free markets. For the population at large, the economic and social security of the communist period has been replaced by an unpredictable instability. Meanwhile, the mafia continue to give their own literal meaning to market forces.

8

South Africa after Apartheid

The National Party stands by its policy of separate residential areas, schools and institutions for different race groups.

F. W. de Klerk, as Minister of National Education (1986)

The aim is a totally new and just constitutional dispensation in which every inhabitant will enjoy equal rights, treatment and opportunity in every sphere of endeavour.

F. W. de Klerk, as State President (1990)

It was not our intention to deprive people of their rights and to cause misery.

F. W. de Klerk, as State President (1993)

In the middle of the 1980s South Africa's governing National Party still adhered to the policy of apartheid, or racial separation. But by the beginning of the 1990s those same rulers were proclaiming a new society characterized by equal rights and opportunities for all, accompanied by the occasional expressions of regret for the evils of the old order. The days of apartheid were clearly numbered, and the release of African National Congress leader Nelson Mandela in 1990 marked the beginning of a process of negotiation over a new non-racial constitution. The prospect of fundamental societal transformation has precipitated vigorous debates on the institutional arrangements required to promote redistribution, and reparation in the sense of making amends for historic injustice.

Chapter 7 was concerned with social justice under regimes which have largely given way to something else, with only brief reference to current issues. This chapter reverses the emphasis, giving slight attention to the obvious injustices of apartheid and concentrating on problems which have to be resolved if the new South Africa can make plausible claims to social justice. In the process, we will recognize that both the meaning and attainment of social justice in this particular situation are far from straightforward, and that the end of apartheid is only the beginning of a struggle to transcend the past.

We begin with some background on the apartheid system, explaining what it involved and something of its impact with respect to dispossession and racial inequality. Then, the bulk of the chapter addresses two specific issues. The first is the land question, taken as a context within which to explore the bases of entitlement to land and the reforms required to rectify past injustice. The second issue is that of redistribution more generally, examining the opportunities and constraints involved in the pursuit of racial equalization. The chapter is concluded with a brief review of the prospects for social justice after apartheid. More conventional geographical problems relating to urban and regional change are mentioned only in passing, having been addressed elsewhere (Smith, 1992b, 1992c, 1994b).

To keep the length of this chapter within bounds requires that material on apartheid and how the system operated be kept to a minimum consistent with adequately contextualizing the problem of social justice. Further general background can be found in Smith (1990b), and in numerous other volumes with varying perspectives on South Africa in transition – some of which are cited below. It must also be emphasized that the intention is neither to prescribe a just social order for South Africa after apartheid (although there will be some obvious pointers), nor to predict what is likely to happen (which could easily be overtaken by events). The aim is to use this particular case of a society in transition to examine some issues of broader significance to social justice.[1]

The apartheid legacy

The word 'apartheid' refers to separation in Afrikaans, the language of the descendants of the Dutch people who began to settle the southern tip of the African continent in the middle of the seventeenth century. The state policy and institutional system known as apartheid was introduced by the predominantly Afrikaner Nationalist Party, after coming to power in 1948.

[1] The research on which this chapter is based has been undertaken with the assistance of numerous South African colleagues. Particular gratitude is owed to Denis Fair, and to Keith Beavon and Ron Davies and their staff at the Universities of the Witwatersrand and Cape Town respectively. Roseanne Diab and Gerry Garrard helped to arrange visits to the University of Natal, and I have learned much from Dhiru Soni, Brij Maharaj and their colleagues at the University of Durban-Westville. All the other contributors to an edited collection (Smith, 1992b) have helped my understanding of particular issues. Financial assistance has been provided by the Central Research Fund and the Hayter Fund (University of London) and the Human Sciences Research Council (South Africa). Thanks also to the Venn family, via Linda Grant, for the opportunities to retreat to Salt Rock.

Previously the minority population of European descent had exercised control over those they described as 'natives' by means of a pragmatic form of domination and oppression typical of colonial regimes. However, the Nationalists sought to impose a more systematic ordering of the disparate groups of peoples who had come to occupy South Africa, strictly enforced by law, so as more effectively to ensure their own survival and prosperity against the 'winds of change' which British Prime Minister Harold Macmillan soon saw blowing through the continent. Central to the grand design was the distinctively spatial strategy of racial separation.

It is not necessary to explain the origins of apartheid in detail here. It is sufficient to point out that the architects of the system, Prime Minister H. F. Verwoerd and his immediate successors, saw separation as the answer to the conflicting material interests and cultures arising from a diverse population, which included substantial numbers from the Indian subcontinent as well as people of European descent, various indigenous African tribes, and the products of miscegenation traditionally referred to as coloureds. Full membership of South African society was to be confined to Europeans or 'Whites',[2] with provision made for the Africans (or 'Bantu', later 'Blacks') by the creation of so-called Homelands (or 'Bantustans') which would eventually become independent nation-states. The areas so designated were the tribal reserves, from which many Africans were drawn into the cities as migrant workers, a system which was used to restrict their permanent residence in the 'White' cities as well as facilitating their exploitation as cheap labour. The Homelands thus served the dual purpose of consolidating peripheral labour reservoirs and enabling African political rights to be externalized, in a literal geographical sense.

The legislation setting up the reserves which eventually became Homelands pre-dated the apartheid era. The Land Acts of 1913 and 1936 set aside 13 per cent of the total surface area of South Africa, for what is today about three-quarters of the total population. This disparity is all the more glaring when it is recognized that the areas subsequently allocated for the Homelands, as future Black nation-states, tended to be rather poor from an agricultural point of view, lacked mineral resources, and excluded major transport routes and towns regarded as 'White'. The fact that roughly half

---

[2] Capital letters are used to denote race groups as defined under the Population Registration Act, and also to refer to such apartheid institutions or myths as Homelands and White South Africa. The term 'black' with lower-case 'b' refers to all people who would not have been classified as White (i.e. Blacks or Africans, Coloureds and Indians). It must be recognized that, despite the repeal of the Act, racial categories remain relevant to life in South Africa as long as there are any race-based institutions or distributive criteria, established for such purposes as affirmative action or protection of 'minority' rights.

the Black population actually lived elsewhere, in what was supposed to be White South Africa, underlined the geographical inconsistency as well as the injustice of the land set aside for them.

Two other kinds of racial separation were involved in classical apartheid. One was the maintenance of separate facilities such as schools, hospitals, public transportation, parks, restaurants and other personal service outlets. This became known as 'petty apartheid', upheld by the Reservation of Separate Amenities Act of 1953. The other was the proclamation and implementation of separate residential areas for different race groups in every town and city, under the terms of the Group Areas Act of 1950, which sought to make existing patterns of incomplete segregation much more rigid.

Apartheid at all levels required people to be classified unambiguously with respect to race. The Population Registration Act of 1950 recognized the four groups of Whites, Blacks (originally Natives: people of negroid appearance), Coloureds and Indians (sometimes referred to as Asians). Assignment to one or other of these groups came to have enormous significance with respect to people's life chances, for such matters as the kind of work an individual could do, the level of remuneration, and the quality of social services provided varied according to race group, by custom and often by law.

For the Whites, the life-style was to be essentially western European, with the best of the farmland and residential areas. The Blacks (Africans) would have their own states, but would be permitted to live temporarily in the White state insofar as their labour ministered to the needs of the Whites, occupying hostels for single migrant workers and purpose-built townships for families. The Coloureds and Indians were in a peculiar position, having no designated lands within which to exercise full political rights, merely their own urban Group Areas with some limited local autonomy. However, in 1984 these two groups were found a place in a new constitution, which set up a 'tri-cameral' parliament with separate houses for the Coloured and Indian people along with one for the Whites (but none for the Black majority).

The apartheid system was sustained by means of the five forms of oppression highlighted by Iris Marion Young (see chapter 4). In addition to their exploitation, those not classified as White were marginalized in various ways (including geographically), rendered effectively powerless in economic and political life, subjected to the cultural imperialism associated with assertions of racial inferiority, and not infrequently treated with violent brutality.

The creation of racial separation at the national and urban scale required massive population movement. A study by the Surplus People Project (Platzky and Walker, 1985) arrived at a figure of 3.5 million people moved during the 1960s and 1970s when dispossession was at its height. Other estimates are even greater, for example a minimum of 4 million if unrecorded

Table 8.1 South African population affected by removal or relocation, c. 1960–80

Type of removal	Numbers
Eviction of black tenants, squatters and surplus labour from White farmland	1,129,000
Clearance of Black spots, and Homeland consolidation	647,000
Urban relocation and removal from White areas to Homeland townships	670,000
Removal from unauthorized (informal or spontaneous) urban settlements	112,000
Group Areas removals arising from racial re-zoning	834,000
Relocation due to development schemes and clearing sensitive areas	23,000
Political moves such as banishment and flight from oppression	50,000
Others (approx.)	35,000
Total (approx.)	3,500,000

Source: Platzky and Walker (1985); some figures rounded.

involuntary moves are included (for further details, see Unterhalter, 1987). African removals continued during the 1980s, to the extent of perhaps 250,000 since the Surplus People Project, before the reform of apartheid began to act as a constraint on further dispossession.

Table 8.1 shows the number of people (mostly Blacks/Africans) involved in various types of removals and relocations. The first category refers to changes in the way in which Africans could work on the land in White South Africa: under the Land Act of 1913, Africans hiring, leasing or owning land outside their scheduled reserves were said to be squatting illegally, and large numbers of these, along with labour tenants working part of the year for White farmers in return for land and grazing rights, were resettled. The term 'Black spots' describes parcels of land bought freehold by Africans before the 1913 Act; their elimination was an important feature of the territorial consolidation of the Homelands, and as the land had often been owned and farmed by the same families for generations, forced resettlement was a source of great hardship.

In the urban areas the demolition of old townships, 'shanty towns' and other 'unauthorized' settlements, along with the creation of Group Areas, resulted in the displacement of an estimated 1,600,000 or so people. Some were rehoused in new townships, others relocated in the Homelands, while many formed new spontaneous 'shack' settlements. The number of people

Table 8.2 Selected economic and social indicators by race group

Indicator	Black	White	Coloured	Indian	W:B
Average monthly household income (R) 1991	779	4679	1607	2476	6.01
Average monthly earnings in manufacturing (R) 1991	1056	3793	1187	1727	3.59
Monthly old age pensions (R) 1992	293	345	318	318	1.18
Infant deaths per 1000 live births 1990	52.8	7.3	28.0	13.5	7.23
Life expectation at birth (years) 1987	63	73	63	67	1.16
Tuberculosis (new cases per 100,000 population) 1987	216.7	14.8	579.8	53.2	14.64
Expenditure on school pupils per capita (R) 1991–92	1248	4448	2701	3500	3.56
Pass rate in matriculation examinations (per cent) 1991	41	96	83	95	2.34

Source: Cooper et al. (1993). The figures generally refer to the Republic of South Africa, without the 'independent' Homelands of Bophuthatswana, Ciskei, Transkei and Venda. R = Rand (R1.0 = approx £0.20 in mid-1993).

displaced by the creation of Group Areas was the equivalent of roughly one-third of the entire Indian population and one-sixth of the Coloureds. Something approaching one million people were moved up to the late 1980s, by which time enforced segregation was breaking down in parts of some cities to the extent of making the Group Areas Act inoperable. (Something of the experience of those displaced by the creation of urban apartheid is revealed in chapter 9).

That apartheid generated inequality between the race groups is unsurprising, for a primary purpose was to ensure Whites a privileged life-style. The highly unequal distribution of income in relation to population in 1987 was illustrated in an earlier chapter (figure 5.5). More recent data are as follows: 39.4 million Africans comprising almost 76 per cent of South Africa's population receiving 33 per cent of personal income, 5.1 million Whites (almost 13 per cent) with 54 per cent of income, 3.4 million Coloureds (8.6 per cent) with 9 per cent of income, 1.0 million Indians (2.5 per cent) with 4 per cent of income (1992 populations from Cooper et al., 1993, p. 254; 1990 income data from Cooper et al., 1992, p. 257).

Table 8.2 lists figures on a range of economic and social indicators by race group. The ratio of advantage of Whites over Blacks (W:B) varies from over 14 for the tuberculosis rate to only slightly greater than one for life expectation and for old age pensions (where equality has subsequently been achieved). Household incomes and infant mortality reveal similar disparities at about six or seven to one, as do earnings in manufacturing and expenditure on school pupils at around 3.5:1. The tuberculosis rate shows the Coloureds worse-off than the Blacks; otherwise the Coloureds and Asians occupy positions between the Blacks and Whites, the Asians generally having a marked advantage.

Such figures only begin to scratch the surface of inequalities in South Africa. Aggregate data at the national level hide inequalities within race groups, and also from one part of the country to another. For example, figures for the nine officially defined development regions show Gross Geographical Product (GGP) per capita in 1987 ranging from 1.89 times the national average in region H, covering the major economic heartland of Pretoria-Witwatersrand-Vereeniging, to only 0.32 times in region G with large Homeland areas. The Gini coefficient measuring regional inequality is a high 19.5 (see figure 8.1).

Aggregate numerical data also fail to capture the nature and extent of dire poverty affecting large numbers of the African population. Something of the challenge posed for the new South Africa is explained as follows by Professor Franklin Sonn (quoted in *Race Relations News*, February 1993): 'Social justice is not attainable in a society where some 60% of the population live below the breadline, 55% are illiterate, 40% are unemployed, 7–8 million live in urban shanties, where 25 people a day die of TB and 300 a day become HIV positive. This litany of misery could be much longer.'

And it is not merely a question of numbers: it is also what people experience, including an unquantifiable deprivation of economic and political empowerment. Pointing out that South Africa has the highest Gini coefficient of inequality among countries for which income data are available, Bundy (1992, p. 25) reminds us that statistics only present generalizations, tendencies and the 'shape' of poverty and inequality: 'They cannot reveal its texture: the dull ache of deprivation, the acute tension generated by violence and insecurity, the intricacies of survival and all its emotions – despair, hope, resentment, apathy, futility, and fury.'

In 1990 the Separate Amenities Act was repealed, after a decade during which many facilities in many parts of the country had effectively become open to all people irrespective of their racial classification. The Group Areas Act, the Land Acts, and the Population Registration Act followed in 1991. The elimination of these four legislative pillars of apartheid was accompanied by the ending of various other provisions, from the reservations of certain kinds of jobs for Whites to the proscription of sexual relations between

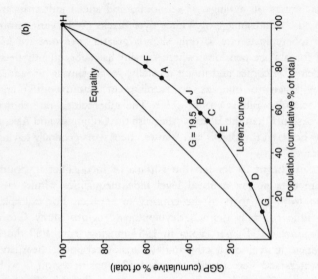

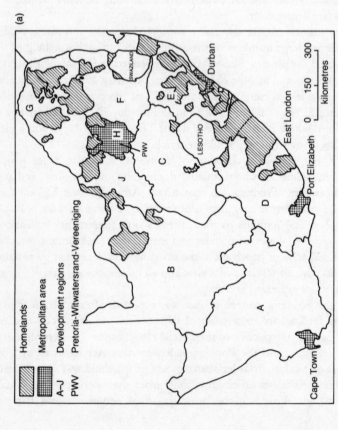

Figure 8.1   (a) South Africa's Homelands, metropolitan areas, development regions, and (b) a Lorenz curve of regional inequality in Gross Geographical Product.
(Source of data: Roux, 1992, p. 212, table 1).

members of different race groups. To some people this was virtually the end of apartheid, to be completed by the replacement of the tri-cameral parliament by a non-racial form of government. But it really represents only the start of the search for social justice, some of the complexity of which we will now explore.

The land question

> Of all the processes which have brought about the inequitable distribution of wealth and power that characterises present day South Africa, none has been more decisive and more immediately important to most black South Africans than the dispossession of land. To an agrarian community whose entire economic and social structure is based on the distribution of land, dispossession was an act akin to national destruction.

Thus said State President F. W. de Klerk in 1991 (quoted in Moore, 1992, p. 25), not long after his conversion from upholder to reformer of apartheid. The traditional African affiliation with the land had by this time been substantially reduced, by the urbanization of more than half the population. But the fate of a dispossessed agrarian people was something de Klerk could understand, at least in the abstract. His own Afrikaners had experienced something of this at the beginning of the century, at the hand of the British, and their determination never again to be subjugated in what they saw as their land was an important part of a national identity and destiny which they tried to resolve by apartheid.

It is hard to exaggerate the importance of the land question in South Africa, past, present and future.[3] All people need land, if not as an immediate source of material sustenance then at least as a place to live; it might even be considered a human right (see chapter 2). The land question impinges on the nature of the agrarian economy which provides food for South Africa's population, and also on the distribution of residence in both rural and urban areas. Land has been, and continues to be, an important source of power which some people can wield over others, from the traditional chiefly prerogative of allocating land, through the privatization of ownership introduced by the colonizers, to the racialized control of the apartheid era. And now, the question of land reform is high on the agenda as an issue of social justice to be resolved in the new South Africa.

The complexity of the land issue arises in part from the varying and

---

[3] Working with Tony Buckle helped to clarify aspects of the land question.

conflicting ways in which people make claims to land. In traditional African society land was valued as a source of communal well-being, allocated according to the imperatives of group survival and reproduction. All families were entitled to a share of their tribal land on which to grow crops or graze cattle, and this would be treated as theirs by usage. Membership was therefore crucial to the distribution of this collective asset: 'the relationship between man and land was not purely economic. The members of the society depended on land not only for subsistence but also for recognition as members of the social group' (Bundy, 1979, p. 21). Links with the past, manifest for example in the burial of the dead, were part of the close association between people and territory. Thus, 'Farming is more than just a productive activity, it is an act of culture, the centre of social existence and the place where personal identity is forged' (Sachs, 1990, p. 14).

As in other parts of the world subject to colonization, these traditional attitudes to land were an impediment to the process sometimes dignified as 'modernization'. The Europeans brought their own values, including the concept of private ownership by legal title necessary for the commodification of land and its exchange under market relations. In place of land as a communal asset to which people had a special personal responsibility as well as entitlement, ownership of land became one of the property rights associated with individual autonomy and liberty. Land thus came to be valued through the pecuniary calculus of the market. However, some of the people who colonized South Africa forged their own bonds with territory, a matter of particular significance to the descendants of those whose original acquisition had been the successful outcome of what they saw as an heroic struggle with the native population in which divine intervention played no small part. Such struggles were important to the forging of Afrikaner national identity, and its association with what they claimed as their land.

The conflict between African and European attitudes to land was resolved, usually in favour of the latter, by a combination of military and economic power. Racial identity was a crucial ingredient in a process which facilitated the dispossession and displacement of the African population when in the way of settler interests. Sachs (1990, pp. 3–4) summarizes the sequence of events as follows:

> The racialisation of land ownership began with the first wars of conquest and continued with appropriation through treaties and direct occupation. The dispossessed African population tried to retrieve their land through purchase; they were forbidden by law, as 'natives', from doing so. They then sought to retain access to the land as lease-holders; they were prevented by law, because they were black, from doing so. They entered into agreements as share-croppers; these agreements were invalidated on the grounds of race by law. They worked the

land as labour tenants; this was made illegal in terms of so-called native policy. Those who had managed to cling to legal title were forced to vacate their land because they were said to occupy black spots in white land.

The Land Acts of 1913 and 1936 were important instruments in this process, forcing many Africans into the reserves well before the removals of the apartheid era enumerated above in table 8.1. Individual Africans were free to own land in what became the Homelands, but for a long time the retention of communal tenure was encouraged. This was not so much a concession to African values as a way of preserving the traditional redistributive economy, in which all were entitled to sustenance by virtue of membership, even if working away much of the time, which was crucial to the reproduction of the migrant labour force on which the mines and other sectors of the 'White' economy had come to depend (Smith, 1990b, pp. 34–6). An additional dimension to the already complicated question of who has what kind of rights to which land is the displacement of urban population to create racial residential segregation under the terms of the Group Areas Act.

So, what should be done? How should the new South Africa resolve competing claims to land in a socially just manner? On the answer to this question depends not only the way in which land will change hands in the future, from some agreed starting position, but also the extent to which this will reflect reparation or the correction of past injustice. In addition, any proposals for land reform must have regard to the efficiency of the agrarian economy, for the cause of social justice would hardly be served by holdings of inappropriate size run by incompetent farmers, whatever their race.

What guidance might be found in theories of social justice, brought to bear on the distinctive circumstances of apartheid South Africa? The most obvious starting point is the entitlement theory of Robert Nozick (see chapter 3). This libertarian position should appeal to the ideology of free enterprise, market mechanisms and a reduced if not minimal role for the state, which finds favour in business and government circles in South Africa. It will be recalled that, under this theory, people are entitled to their holdings, and to do as they wish with them, providing that their original acquisition was by just means.

At first sight, this perspective would appear to invalidate the claims of large numbers of (White) landowners. While there are disputes among historians as to whether the early settlers actually got to some parts of southern Africa before the African tribes moving south, the land was, for the most part, subject to permanent or sedentary occupation by others when the Europeans arrived. Then, according to Sachs (1990, p. 10), 'The land was taken by force and deception. The structure of white domination which subsequently registered title deeds and created a market in land was itself illegitimate.' If we accept this, the illegitimacy of the original titles makes the subsequent transfer of land similarly illegitimate, even if accomplished by the legitimate means of market transfer, inheritance or gift. The prescription which follows from Nozick's principle of rectification is that of restitution: the land should be returned to those indigenous people who originally occupied it in circumstances that could be justified by their material needs, when plentiful supply meant that there was enough for everyone.

But there is an alternative interpretation. It could be argued that the acquisition of land by Europeans was actually legitimate, for the most part, by the standards, customs and laws of the times. African tribes fought with each other for land, and Europeans adopting the same practice were merely conforming to the prevailing rule of 'might is right'. However, such a relativist argument cannot easily withstand the response that brute force should not determine social justice in any society, any time anywhere. Rather more persuasive is the point that, whatever the circumstances of initial (dis)possession, those who subsequently acquired the land legally bear no responsibility for the original sin. As Moore (1992, p. 26) puts it: 'Many whites would argue that they personally never intended any wrong doings against blacks, but were unknowingly trapped into structures created by the Land Acts and other apartheid measures. Any new form of dispossession would unjustly deprive their present owners of what they have legally bought or inherited, and developed with their own sweat.' Indeed, they may have made more productive use of the land, for the benefit of society as a whole, than those from whom their ancestors took it would have done – an argument which would commend itself to utilitarians, if its truth could be demonstrated.

We are now faced with two conflicting propositions. One advocates 'turning the clock back', to the point in time of the initial injustice, and trying to restore the pre-existing state of affairs irrespective of what might have subsequently happened. The other says, in effect, 'let bygones be bygones', no matter what injustices were perpetrated in the past. Or as Sachs (1990, p. 1) put it, 'Either the original unjust dispossession of the land is condoned and recognised as a legal fact, or there is a new form of dispossession which, it is said, would unjustly deprive the present owners of what they have legally bought or inherited and developed with their money and their sweat.' Both positions have their problems. To restore the original distribution of land may be impossible, not least because of the practical difficulties of identifying those whose entitlement was actually founded on just acquisition, and who their descendants are, especially when communal tenure was involved. And to forget (and possibly forgive) may be impossible for those still suffering from past injustice, and should perhaps not even be suggested, far less expected.

Problems raised by reparation in circumstances of historic injustice have been explored by Waldron (1992). He argues against simply turning the clock back, on the grounds that circumstances change and that this has a bearing on property rights. For example, the exclusive access of groups of people to their own sources of water may be right in times of plenty, but wrong when the rains fail and all but one water hole dries up. Similarly, returning all land in South Africa to descendants of those who originally occupied it in circumstances of plenty, before European expropriation, could have disastrous consequences for those currently living on it in an era of scarcity. Historic injustice may to some extent be superseded, by events; what really matters is to distribute resources fairly to existing inhabitants. Waldron (1992, p. 27) concludes:

> It is a fact that many of the descendants of those who were defrauded and expropriated live demoralized in lives of relative poverty – relative, that is, to the descendants of those who defrauded them. If the relief of poverty and the more equal distribution of resources is the aim of a prospective theory of justice, it is likely that the effect of rectification of past wrongs will carry us some distance in this direction. All the same, it is worth stressing that it is the impulse to justice now that should lead the way in this process, not the reparation of something whose wrongness is understood primarily in relation to conditions that no longer obtain.

While offered as a general proposition, this suggests an approach to social justice in post-apartheid South Africa which is sensitive to both past and present. Let us consider some current proposals in this light.

De Klerk's Nationalist government made its position clear in its *White Paper on Land Reform*, published in 1991 (as quoted in Marcus, 1991, pp. 50–1):

> Provision is made for the continued use of land as a multi-purpose commodity and production asset, but without the racial restrictions. Private ownership is broadened and also extended to land in respect of which it was previously not available.

> The new policy has the definite objective of ensuring the existing security and existing patterns of community order will be maintained. The primary objective is to offer equal opportunities for the acquisition, use and enjoyment of land to all people within the social and economic realities of the country.

> Private ownership of land, including agricultural land, is the cornerstone of the Government's land policy. This is in keeping with the Government's opposition to any form of redistribution of agricultural land, whether by confiscation, nationalisation or expropriation . . . a

programme for the restoration of land to individuals and communities who were forced to give up their land on account of past policies or other historical reasons would not be feasible.

It has subsequently been reiterated that a system of private freehold ownership within the context of a market-orientated economy is central to the government's land policy. Any restitution of land from which people were removed by apartheid legislation would be restricted to land still in state hands and not developed or allocated for a specific purpose (Cooper et al., 1993, p. 383). Thus the distribution of land established under apartheid would be legitimated, for the most part; private ownership relations would be extended to replace other (e.g. communal) forms of tenure, and people of all race groups would be free to buy land provided they had the money to pay for it. The strategy was clearly designed to ensure security of White ownership, and to pre-empt redistribution under a future non-racial government.

It is hardly surprising that contrary views are held by the African National Congress (ANC), and by others who see a de-racialized market merely perpetuating injustices in the existing distribution of the wealth needed to purchase land, as well as in the distribution of land itself. In particular, it is pointed out that the security of ownership and freedom of market exchange, to which the government now attaches such importance, was denied Africans in the past by confiscating their title deeds and preventing them from purchasing land in 'White' South Africa. Some form of restitution, redistribution and perhaps reparation is required.

A discussion document issued by the African National Congress (1992a, p. 7) asserts: 'We need a new system of law which is based on land rights which go beyond current legal title. This should be based on values held by the majority of South Africans, including birthright, inheritance rights, and rights based on occupation and productive use of land.' The concerns of the ANC include security for those whose access to land is still through communal tenure and for labour tenants who fear expulsion by White owners, as well as reparation for people unfairly removed from their land and the acquisition of land for redistribution to those who need it to make a living. The ANC also challenges prevailing (White, capitalist) attitudes to land, by arguing that reform should rest on the underlying assumption among Africans that land has communal welfare functions as well as economic subsistence value (Cooper et al., 1993, p. 384).

Four groups have claims on land reserved for White ownership under apartheid (Sachs, 1990, p. 18). These are: (1) Black farmers of long-standing occupation who have never given up the insistence that they have rights to the land in question; (2) White owners who have the kind of rights recognized in both Afrikaner and African culture, by virtue of birthright, inheritance, occupation, investment and work; (3) owners from the wider economy who have bought land and invested in its productive potential; (4) those people from the wider economy whose ancestors were driven off the land by various forms or coercion – possibly the largest group. It is this diversity of claims which has somehow to be resolved if justice is to be done, and which the *White Paper* singularly failed to address.

A strategy more in keeping with the considerations suggested by Waldron (above) can be detected in proposals from non-government sources. This would begin with an estimated 1.25 million hectares of land in state hands, and which they have proposed to transfer to Homelands. This could be allocated to victims of removals, for example from so-called 'Black spots', without depriving anyone of their title. Indeed, removals may be of such recent origin that particular pieces of land could simply be restored to the people concerned. Sachs (1990, p. 32) stresses the symbolic significance of such a measure: 'Facilitating the return of victims of forced removals in the countryside and creating conditions where they can live and farm in dignity would both acknowledge past injustice and indicate the beginning of democratic solutions.'

However, the land in question comprises only about 1 per cent of the surface area of South Africa (including the Homelands). And although owned by the state, it is leased or otherwise occupied by people (mainly Africans) whose rights also have to be considered. Then there are perhaps millions of people with documentary proof of land ownership or other rights whose interests were expropriated. This leads to two further requirements for serious land reform: a means of resolving conflicting claims to the same land, and a means of acquiring more land for redistribution and possibly reparation.

A land claims court has been proposed by the ANC and others (e.g. Claassens, 1991), to deal with cases of conflict. This could decide who has which land, or what level of compensation if transfer of ownership is judged not to be the best solution. Such an institution would, of course, have to guard against the possibility, intrinsic to land reform in general, of favouring those with the resources to plead the most convincing case. This implies equal access to the necessary legal services.

Obtaining more land for redistribution gets to the heart of the practical problem of land reform in South Africa. It is here that the aspirations of social justice confront hard political reality. Blacks need more land, and have sustainable rights to it, but it can come only from Whites who have the advantage of legal title and, still, disproportionate power. There is vigorous and understandable opposition to the expropriation of land without full compensation, even though it could be argued that the means whereby many Whites or their ancestors acquired land and exploited African (Coloured or Indian) labour to farm it undermines their moral entitlement to market values. Yet the cost of full compensation would place strains on a state budget with many competing demands: for example, Moore (1992, p. 27) points out that to purchase one-tenth of White farms at market value would require R7 bn, which could build 200,000 new houses or 3000 primary schools. Nationalization of land is still advocated in some quarters, but this seems increasingly contrary to the new realism penetrating radical thinking (to which we return in the next section).

Land redistribution will be a crucial test of the dedication of some future government to social justice. One possible strategy has been put forward by Claassens (1991, p. 13), under the banner of 'regulated land ownership'. She suggests that acceptance of common societal values for the (re)distribution of land as a national asset, such as housing the population, maintaining and improving food production, and a sense of belonging to their land on the part of all South Africans, could generate particular ownership criteria. These include: ownership of land limited to areas occupied and in productive use; the amount owned by one person limited relative to regional productive capacity; prohibition of speculative land holding; ownership subject to proper care of the soil and acceptable treatment of people living on the land; and home ownership limited to one residence. Ownership rights within such constraints would be secure, while the state would be entitled to acquire land held in defiance of these criteria. This could then be redistributed.

Other proposals consistent with such a strategy would include state acquisition of farms heavily in debt or otherwise dependent on subsidy, and of land held by mining and agribusiness corporations well beyond their conceivable needs. A tax on land values has also been proposed, to subsidize land acquisition by blacks (Moore, 1992). Given the history of South African land policy, this is 'a particularly appropriate mechanism to assist in responding to the past' (Davis, 1992, p. 117). It would combine a solution to a practical problem with an element of collective reparation.

It is important, again, to stress that any comprehensive strategy of land reform must have regard to efficiency as well as to distributive justice. This requires an objective, technical appraisal of the efficiency of White farming on extensive holdings, the advantages of which are easily exaggerated by vested interests, compared with more intensive farming on the part of Africans for long denied the opportunity to exercise their full potential as food producers. The redistribution of some of the best White farmland, as well as more marginal areas, could well enhance efficiency, within what Weiner and Levin (1991, p. 112) refer to as 'socially appropriate land use'.

Further consideration of organizational aspects of agrarian reform is beyond the scope of this discussion. It is sufficient to recognize that the social relations of production which govern the distribution of benefits and burdens of working the land are at least as important as the considerations of technical efficiency which tend to dominate mainstream development thinking. As Brand et al. (1992, pp. 353–4) remind us, 'the most fundamental aspect of agrarian reform is ethical and not legal, material, or organizational'. This involves 'supplementing equal opportunity with the right to an equal start . . . fair access to resources, inputs, and product markets, and to the political market. This in turn requires entitlement (the legal ability to act) and empowerment (the wealth, income, and skills required to make action effective).' Putting substance on these aspirations is the essence of the positive action required for social justice in the South African countryside.

Some implications of urban land reform may be mentioned briefly. An exclusively agrarian focus is a repetitive feature of debates on the land question in South Africa, despite the claim by Moore (1992, p. 26) that, 'Most of those dispossessed by Group Areas legislation still cherish the prospect of regaining their ancestral land.' Perhaps the problem is, literally, too close to home for the (usually White) policy pundits in government and the academy, some of whom may own dwellings from which black people were evicted. Perhaps the repeal of the Group Areas Act, resolutely resisted by many Whites, is considered sufficient reform. But this is merely the urban equivalent of the *White Paper* position on rural land: de-racialize ownership and leave who has what to the market, without any regard for past injustice.

Group Areas removals affecting people classified as Asian and Coloured, and displacement of Africans under other legislation, had two major consequences. One was loss of homes, businesses and communities, and aspects of the lives that went with them. The other was the financial cost of moving and finding alternative accommodation, often in less convenient locations and congenial places than those from which people were evicted. Property of the dispossessed was often acquired at less than market value, as Hart (1988) shows in the case of Cape Town's Coloureds, for example. There is no doubt that large numbers of blacks suffered uncompensated financial cost, as well as deeper losses of the kind to be explored in chapter 9.

Group Areas evictions are fairly recent events and should be the subject of bureaucratic record, which would facilitate the establishment of claims to specific pieces of property. However, restitution of people's former homes and communities is often physically impossible. Group Areas evictions were frequently followed by the bulldozer, with the land subsequently redeveloped. Even if largely left empty, as in Cape Town's District Six (see chapter 9), to reclaim an empty lot is not a particularly attractive proposition except for the resale value. Dwellings that survived and were subsequently purchased by Whites may have been improved by their new owners, raising a similar problem to that of investment in farmland taken by Whites from Africans. It might be argued, similarly, that the White owners are not entitled to their ill-gotten gains.

These are the kind of issues that also arise in post-socialist societies, in the context of the restitution or re-privatization of property expropriated by the state (chapter 7), and it should be recognized that returning residential property to its original owners in South Africa involves a similar time frame and no greater practical problems than in Poland, for example.

There are, however, severe political constraints on residential restitution. It is almost inconceivable that any future government would adopt a policy of expropriating White homes and returning them to blacks, even with full compensation. Furthermore, residential property differs from agricultural land in that those dispossessed by Group Areas legislation found other places to live, inferior though they may have been, whereas many of those deprived of farmland lost not only their place but also the capacity to farm (the nearest urban equivalent is businesses which failed to survive Group Areas removals).

A different kind of resolution for Group Areas injustice is therefore suggested. Rather than attempt restitution of actual property, there should be a tax levied on White residential and commercial premises, the proceeds of which would be used to compensate those who can substantiate a claim to losses arising from deprivation of property values and the cost of relocation. While the scale involved would require careful consideration, the general principle of compensation of the one group who clearly lost by the other who clearly gained would be appropriate reparation.

As in the agrarian context, any resolution of the urban land issue must relate redistribution or compensation to broader issues of land use and planning. There is an enormous shortage of low-cost housing in South Africa, reflected in the emergence of vast informal or 'shack' settlements, estimated to accommodate over 7 million people or one in four of the African population and one in two in the major cities (Cooper et al., 1993, p. 215). Low-income (usually African) residential areas, formal or informal, tend to be on the fringe of the cities, adding high commuting costs and limited access to central services to the various other penalties of race under apartheid. Attention is now being given to the identification of closer land, and its development for affordable housing, in a process referred to as 'inward urbanization' as opposed to the dispersal of the apartheid city. As well as providing more convenient places for people to live, this strategy makes more efficient use of the urban infrastructure.

But land suitable for development is not necessarily in the right hands. The City of Johannesburg has disclosed plans to provide housing for 1 million people within 10 km of the central business district, but vacant land is owned by the mining houses (South African Institute of Race Relations, *Fast Facts* 6, June 1993, p. 3). This is but one example of a case for expropriation if the land cannot be acquired on reasonable terms. Such measures will be necessary, powerful opposition notwithstanding, if land use in the post-apartheid city is to reflect the interests of those most in need of somewhere to live.

Redistribution for equalization

We now turn from the land question to other aspects of redistribution, which raise somewhat different issues. No one would argue that land should be distributed equally among all South Africans: the issue is that of access to particular kinds of land for particular purposes. But if we consider other aspects of the resources at people's disposal – their wealth and incomes, the services received, and their levels of living or well-being – equalization becomes a more appropriate principle of social justice.

Given the morally arbitrary character of race, and the common understanding that race should be irrelevant to people's life chances, then in a just society there should be no racial inequalities in living standards. It follows from the scale of actual disparities by race group in South Africa that narrowing the gap between peoples in general and whites and blacks in particular must˜be an obligatory objective of post-apartheid society, to the extent that the only question is that of the pace at which equalization can be achieved. But there are practical impediments, as well as the reluctance of those currently advantaged to give anything up, which make redistribution a matter of some complexity and delicacy. This is the subject of extensive contemporary debate (e.g. Howe and le Roux, 1992; Moll, 1990; Moll, Nattrass and Loots, 1991; Schrire, 1992); all that can be done here is to highlight some of the main issues, revising an earlier publication (Smith, 1992c; see also Smith, 1994b).

A useful pointer to the pace of equalization required in post-apartheid society is provided by what has actually been taking place. Data used to illustrate the measurement of inequality earlier in this book (figure 5.5) suggested only a slight reduction of income inequality among the four race groups between 1936 and 1987 (see also Smith, 1990b, p. 7). Other figures for recent years show the share of personal incomes going to Africans at 29 per cent in 1985, 33 in 1990 and 37 in 1995 (estimated, assuming the optimistic annual growth rate of 2.5 per cent); the White share in these same years is 59, 54 and 49 per cent (Cooper et al., 1992, pp. 256–7, citing research by Charles Simkins). Changes of these magnitudes, if projected into the future, would take 40 to 50 years for race-group shares of income to approximate shares of national population.

Another indication is provided by figures for earnings in manufacturing over the 1970s and 1980s (table 8.3). The ratios of advantage of Whites over the other race groups indicate steady convergence. However, projecting the average rates of change over this period into the future, it would take about 20 years for African and White earning to reach parity and the same for Indians and Whites; for Coloureds and Whites it would be about 50 years, because of the relatively slow rate of improvement in Coloured earnings.

Three alternative but not mutually exclusive strategies may be adopted

Table 8.3 Average annual earnings in manufacturing (Rand) by race group, 1972–89

Year	White	Black	Coloured	Indian	W:B	W:C	W:I
1972	4,308	782	1,080	1,632	5.51	3.99	3.63
1975	6,132	1,272	1,620	1,812	4.82	3.79	3.88
1980	11,472	3,156	3,156	3,588	4.27	3.63	3.20
1985	22,188	5,628	6,372	7,980	3.94	3.48	2.78
1989	38,334	11,105	11,682	15,682	3.45	3.28	2.44

Source: Cooper et al. (1992, p. 259).

to accelerate equalization of living standards. The first is re-allocation of public expenditure, in a manner designed to enhance the capabilities of the poor to increase their earnings and general well-being for themselves, within the existing economic structure. The second is the redistribution of wealth, income and other assets, through the taxation system for example, so as directly to relieve economic hardship and increase the consumption possibilities of the poor. The third is structural change, for example in ownership or control of the means of production and in the distribution of economic power, so as to alter or eliminate the basic mechanisms generating inequality. We begin with the first of these strategies, which, as the least 'radical', is the one most extensively explored in the national debate on redistribution.

Once the end of apartheid has established formal equality of opportunities in all spheres of life, the next step is to ensure everyone the same capacity to take advantage of them. As Eckert (1991, p. 45) explains:

> The goal of equal opportunity raises a derivative concern in South Africa. Enormous differentials in capabilities exist today, as the result of apartheid, its precursor of social discrimination, widespread poverty and other social limitations. Simply ensuring an equal chance in the future is not enough when the capabilities of so many have been artificially lowered by past practice.

The sense of the term capabilities, as used here, is the same as adopted by Amartya Sen (see chapter 5), namely the capacity to function in ways that promote people's well-being.

Levels of service provision have a bearing on capabilities, and equal treatment is the least that might be expected. Indeed, there is a case for positive discrimination in favour of those whose greater need is manifest in lower living standards. Furthermore, in the production of sources of need-satisfaction or well-being (see chapter 5), the condition of diminishing returns means that more can be generated from the same resources at lower levels of attainment than at higher levels. Thus more educational or health benefits will be generated by spending a given sum on the ignorant and the sick than on the clever or the well. This is also consistent with the Rawlsian principle of maximizing benefits to the worst-off.

To improve social services for the Black population is an obvious priority. There is not only a moral case for racial equality of education, health care and so on, but also an expected productivity effect whereby Blacks will earn more from enhanced capabilities. But the task of actually achieving this is formidable. Van der Berg (1991, pp. 76–7; 1992, pp. 130–2) has shown that to equalize up to prevailing White levels of expenditure on primary and secondary education, health and social pensions would require an inconceivable three-fold increase in total spending. To equalize within the present budget constraint would require expenditure on Whites to be cut to about one-third of current levels, with that on Coloureds and Indians also reduced. To equalize educational expenditure alone at White levels in 1987 would have required expenditure to be trebled (Hofmeyr and McLennan, 1992, p. 184). Another calculation suggests that racial equalization of social spending, including housing, at White levels would increase this budget item from 9.5 per cent of GDP (a figure not out of line for a country with South Africa's GDP per capita) to 30.8 per cent (Moll, 1991, p. 125; van der Berg, 1992, p. 135). At the root of the problem highlighted by such figures is that, under apartheid, White standards were raised to levels unsustainable for the entire population in a normal country at South Africa's overall level of economic development.

Resources required for moves towards equalization can be found in three ways. The first is economic growth, always the most comfortable method because it can proceed by means of Pareto improvements whereby the poor gain but the rich do not lose. However, the past decade has seen South Africa's annual growth in GDP average less than 1.0 per cent, compared with population growth of about 2.5 per cent, and a reduction in GNP per capita from R3981 in 1980 to R3060 in 1993 (in constant prices; from *Financial Times*, 11 June 1993). The second possibility is transferring resources from Whites (and other groups) to make up the shortfall in expenditure on Africans, the necessary scale of which would greatly reduce White living standards. However compelling the moral justification for such redistribution may be, White vested interests tend to focus attention on a third strategy, that of re-allocation within the existing state budget.

Abandoning the formal apparatus of apartheid should facilitate some re-allocation of public expenditure. Van der Berg (1991, p. 80) estimates that the elimination of cumbersome institutions (for example, fourteen separate departments of education, covering South Africa's four official race groups and the ten Bantustans) could save about 1 per cent of GDP. Rather more could be found by reducing defence expenditure: if this item had not risen above its 1972 level of 2.2 per cent of GDP the subsequent saving could have built 1.9 million fully serviced houses, which is well over the estimated national shortage (van der Berg, 1991, p. 81). Moll (1991, pp. 122–5) suggests that a reduction in defence expenditure by 2 per cent of GDP, the abolition of apartheid institutions and the elimination of the industrial decentralization programme (designed to keep Africans in peripheral areas), along with a 'modest' increase in taxes and government borrowing on a 'prudent' scale, could yield the equivalent of 6.4 per cent of GDP. This compares with 21.3 per cent needed to equalize social spending at White levels. He concludes that racial equalization at current White levels is impossible at the present time, given South Africa's level of economic development, and that it will have to be achieved at substantially lower levels of expenditure per capita.

Re-allocation of priorities within particular services provides some further redistributive opportunities. In education, widely regarded as the key to black advancement in the labour market, the ratio of state spending on White children to African children was reduced from 18:1 to 3:1 between 1969 and 1991/2 (Cooper et al., 1993, p. 588), which indicates what could be done even under apartheid. The obvious priority now is African primary education, to break the back of massive under-achievement as well as to provide for large numbers of children not even in school. But past inequalities are reflected in fixed capital disparities and pupil/teacher ratios: it will take re-allocation of premises and personnel as well as current expenditure to implement effective redistribution. The location of existing services is also an impediment to redistribution in health care, where the obvious priority is to shift resources to basic primary care, especially in the informal settlements and rural areas, and away from high-cost intervention which favours well-to-do (mainly White) city dwellers.

More state expenditure is required in skills training and employment generation, in an economy where less than one-tenth of new labour market entrants now find work in the formal sector. Participation in the informal sector is difficult to measure, but an estimate for 1991 by the Development Bank for Southern Africa put the figure at 4 million or almost 30 per cent of the economically active population (Cooper et al., 1992, p. 173). Re-allocation of funds currently benefiting big business, to stimulate further the absorption capacity of informal activity, is an obvious strategy. The encouragement of small-scale 'appropriate technology' approaches to the production of 'affordable' housing could create jobs as well as much-needed shelter in the cities.

The severe constraints imposed on re-allocation of public expenditure leads to the possibility of more direct redistribution. Increasing personal taxation is constrained by the fact that South Africans are already relatively highly taxed by international standards. However, the burden is mainly on middle-income earners, and increasing taxes on high personal incomes, and also on businesses via capital gains and capital transfer taxes, are realistic possibilities (Davis, 1992), in addition to the reparation taxes on property proposed in the previous section. A general wealth tax should not be ruled out.

These kinds of redistributional proposals face strategic difficulties, as well as opposition from those likely to lose. Most Whites could sustain some losses without great discomfort; real incomes have already fallen in recent years, with increasing taxes and salaries in some sectors which have not kept up with inflation. But there are knock-on effects to consider. For example, tax increases on business may induce capital flight and the loss of valuable personnel, while tax increases on affluent individuals could put the livelihood of many of the hundreds of thousands of (Black) domestic servants at risk.

A recognition that measures which are supposed to promote positive redistribution can have perverse outcomes encourages caution, especially when coupled with White self-interest. The 'realism' prevailing in establishment circles needs to be leavened by more imaginative thinking. For example, distributing free shares to all gold-mining workers could be an effective way of allowing the market to redistribute the value of company assets from current shareholders to workers (though greater justice would be manifest if former workers' families could be similarly compensated for the exploitation of their labour). Redistribution of the existing housing stock may be inconceivable, but property taxes could encourage small (White) families in large homes to vacate them, making it easier for larger (Black) households to find accommodation suited to their needs. Black township housing could be given away to existing tenants, who may have already effectively paid for it in rent, though this would be accompanied by maintenance costs. Even a conservative voice has suggested that privatization of some state corporations could be accomplished by giving shares to all South Africans on an equal basis (Reekie, 1990, pp. 13–14), along the lines of some privatization strategies in East Europe (chapter 7).

The most radical approach to redistribution is fundamental structural change. Up to the time of Nelson Mandela's release in 1991, the widespread belief of the liberation movement was that some form of socialism would ensure rapid redistribution in a post-apartheid society. But the collapse of what passed for socialism in East Europe and the USSR has led to a growing recognition that South Africa is likely to remain capitalist, at least for the foreseeable future and possibly for ever. However, this is not to say that such measures as public ownership are now completely off the agenda. Nationalization was a central feature of the Freedom Charter around which progressive forces found common purpose, and the possibility of state appropriation of the giant Anglo-American Corporation, the mining houses and the banks continues to be raised. But this increasingly seems a rhetorical reminder of what could be, if big business is judged insensitive to the needs of a new society, rather than an indication of serious intent.

It is also questionable what nationalization would actually achieve, with respect to the redistribution of wealth. Moll (1990, pp. 78–9) has estimated that wholesale nationalization well beyond the 'commanding heights' mentioned in the Freedom Charter would enable the state to redistribute about R900 a year to the poorest 40 per cent of the population (compared with annual incomes of about R1400 for Black rural dwellers and R9200 for mining workers). Such a transfer from shareholders to the poor is far from trivial, and would be easy to justify from a moral point of view. But the process of disinvestment that nationalization would provoke, and the consequent negative impact on economic growth, could make this kind of redistribution merely a one-off bonus to the poor. The harsh truth is that, with the pace of redistribution dependent on stimulating the economy, international capital has the power to constrain a new South African government's freedom to change existing patterns of property ownership. Thus sustainable redistribution via large-scale public take-over of private business no longer seems to be a realistic possibility.

However, there is the possibility of structural adjustments to the economy short of revolutionary transformation. The slow rate of employment generation, which is a root cause of poverty, can be attributed in part to private investor preference in recent years for property speculation at the expense of the manufacturing sector. The re-allocation of investment in directions more consistent with basic human needs is a favoured strategy in progressive circles; the ANC stresses 'growth through redistribution', to stimulate development more responsive to the interests of the mass of the people. Some see the power already exercised by ordinary people to influence business behaviour, for example in disinvestment and boycott campaigns, as transferable to other arenas of struggle with the commanding heights of the economy (Bond, 1991). A new government could help to establish an environment in which greater social responsibility by business becomes part of the broader democratization of South African society.

Social justice after apartheid

What, then, of the prospects for social justice in post-apartheid society? As things currently stand, some of the indications are not encouraging. The constraints on redistribution are severe, and there is a danger, even in the more radical strategies, that transfers of resources from the relatively rich may not flow right down the socio-economic scale. For example, giving away shares to gold miners, or transferring assets of other corporations to their work-force, advantages those who are already relatively well paid by the standards of South African Blacks. The outcome could be merely to consolidate a labour aristocracy, leaving out the millions who currently have no prospect of any formal-sector employment.

This kind of redistribution could also be highly selective from a geographical point of view. It would benefit mainly the residents of formal urban areas in the major metropolitan regions centred on the Witwatersrand (including Johannesburg), Cape Town and Durban, without reaching far into either the peripheral shack settlements or the rural areas where the poorest people live. The outcome could be to exacerbate spatial polarization, adding to the marginalization of a growing majority of an African population increasingly divided by uneven access to the new opportunities opened up in a formally de-racialized society.

Even the most optimistic scenarios underline the limits to the redistributive capacity of any post-apartheid government, within a realistic set of economic and political constraints. If a socialist society is no longer on the agenda, then the major private economic interests which hitherto supported and profited from apartheid will still effectively control much of the new South Africa. Racial, and spatial, differences in life chances will remain marked for many years to come, and the franchise may not make much difference to the lives of substantial numbers of the poor African majority. If anything more than the universal franchise is expected, it is likely to fall well short of truly non-racial citizenship with equality of opportunity really open to all.

At present, the most likely scenario is that South Africa will steadily come more closely to resemble a normal capitalist society, its inherited racial inequalities interpenetrated and blurred by class cleavages. The United States may provide a pointer, and a warning. Aronson (1991, pp. 18–19) argues that a democratic non-racial government should avoid what he calls 'the American solution', where blacks achieve political rights without corresponding changes in social or economic power:

> Black rule in cities like Detroit allows a modicum of black power and pride, the building up of a black bureaucracy and political class, and creating the conditions for the rise of a small number of blacks in businesses affected by government contracts. But the real levers of power, corporate levers, national-political levers, remain firmly where they always were, outside the purview of any conceivable black (or indeed working-class) power. The majority of blacks, deprived of their traditional leadership – those one-time pillars of ghetto cohesion, inspiration and discipline – by new possibilities of social, economic, and

residential mobility, only sink deeper, and displace their despondency onto drugs, internalized violence, and crime.

I am talking about the built-in limits to 'equal opportunity' in a society systematically built on class privilege that has historically evolved intertwined with racial oppression ... it has been possible to talk about 'equal rights' and 'equal opportunity' in the abstract but not to talk about concrete right to adequate housing, health care, schooling or employment ...

The American lesson is a painful but simple one: because we have failed to make these universal rights available to everybody regardless of class, race or national origin, the heritage of racial domination continues to perpetuate itself ... Without vigorous political action on the national level, without social transformations stretching far beyond 'affirmative action' and 'equal opportunity', South Africa's black majority will follow in the pattern of America's black minority, reproducing itself 'spontaneously' in a hereditary poverty.

The figures illustrating the perpetuation of racial inequality in the United States, presented in chapter 6, indicate how much remains to be done, a quarter of a century after legislation established formal equality. As in the United States, the crucial issue in post-apartheid society is that of universal entitlements of citizenship, or what it means to be a new South African.

However, the scenario for change in South Africa prevailing in establishment circles (government and business) eschews radical social transformation, for redistribution accomplished under market forces by means of accelerated export-led economic growth. More Black workers would be drawn into an expanding labour force, their enhanced living standards being achieved (implicitly) without eroding those of the Whites. Research suggesting that higher economic growth increases the redistribution of income from Whites to Blacks (by Charles Simkins; see Cooper et al., 1992, pp. 256–7), helps to fuel the South African version of the familiar development strategy of 'redistribution through growth'.

A problem with this scenario is that, even if it can be achieved, faster economic growth by no means guarantees accelerated redistribution, through increased social welfare expenditures as well as personal incomes. Reflecting the resurgence of economic conservatism elsewhere, the policy discourse in establishment circles in South Africa links public spending with inflation and stresses the 'new right' panaceas of market mechanisms, privatization and deregulation rather than state responsibility for service provision. The economic power at the disposal of large private vested interests enables them greatly to influence the debate, by funding and publishing research supportive of market-led reform and opposed to measures involving a more proactive state.

In the face of formidable private-sector propaganda, added to the continued minority government's control of national broadcasting media, the voice of the former liberation movement has been muted. The ANC now embrace a 'mixed economy', in which national development planning will avoid 'commandist or bureaucratic methods' (African National Congress, 1992b, p. 11). But, while recognizing that market relations are an essential component of a mixed economy, the ANC 'does not believe that market forces alone will result in anything but the perpetuation of existing disparities in income and wealth' (African National Congress, 1992b, p. 11).

If post-apartheid South Africa is to make sustainable claims to social justice, then redistribution has to take place on a much larger scale, and at a much faster pace, and with much greater state intervention, than is currently envisaged in White political circles and in sections of the academy. Rapid equalization of living standards, by (former) race group, is the most obvious criterion by which a post-apartheid South Africa can be judged.

The only proviso to the principle of justice as equalization in the South African case is that equalization must not be at the cost of the general misery which would accompany continued reductions in per capita national product. This qualification opens up the possibility that the continuation and indeed protection of some White privilege may be justified to maintain the commitment of skills and enterprise necessary to sustain economic growth. For example, Schrire (1992, p. 7) asserts: 'it is a historical tragedy that the beneficiaries of apartheid are the only economic actors in South Africa with the economic resources and expertise necessary to get the country moving again. It is, alas, in the interests of the least advantaged in society that the most advantaged continue to prosper.' This implies a Rawlsian argument for continuing (racial) inequalities to be judged by their benefits to the least well-off. However, this can easily degenerate into an uncritical defence of the status quo, without serious consideration of the incentives actually required by the rich for the poor to gain as much as possible. It is also important to recognize that there is no racial monopoly on what is required 'to get the country moving': the informal sector is replete with African entrepreneurs.

Nevertheless, John Rawls's liberal egalitarianism provides a powerful framework within which to couch debates on redistribution in South Africa. For example, Hofmyr and McLennan (1992, following Simkins, 1986) consider its application to education. Rawls's principle of equal access to social primary goods entails impartiality in public spending on education. They invoke his difference principle as follows: 'extra compensatory monies should be invested in the education of historically deprived groups and affirmative action programmes should be allowed. The education system, like every other system, would therefore be so designed as to maximize the prospects of the least well-off members of society' (Hofmyr and McLennan, 1992, p. 181). They get to the heart of the matter in suggesting: 'South Africa will need to develop Rawls's mutual respect for a shared moral discourse' (p. 188).

The culture of racism which has for so long sustained the domination and oppression of people deemed 'non-white' by the ruling 'pigmentocracy' remains a formidable barrier to the development of a truly non-racial society based on recognized mutual interdependence. If South Africa is really to confront fundamental issues of social justice, the prevailing pragmatism and realism must be complemented by a more thoroughgoing concern for morality. It is rare to find explicit consideration of social justice in the voluminous literature on reform and redistribution, which tends to be dominated by conventional development economics. It is very much the exception to argue for a highly proactive policy of affirmative action, and that, given the magnitude of differences standing in the way of an egalitarian society, a policy 'designed to offset past injustices is a necessary and just expectation' (Eckert, 1991, p. 47).

Leaving the detail aside, social justice after apartheid requires the combination of two basic elements. One is the pursuit of equality based on the moral irrelevance of race, consistent with the principle of impartiality; the other is reparation reflecting past racial injustice, consistent with the recognition of morally relevant difference. An appropriate conclusion is provided by Waldron (1992, p. 6): 'Quite apart from any attempt genuinely to compensate victims or offset their losses, reparation may symbolize a society's undertaking not to forget or deny that a particular injustice took place, and to respect and help sustain a dignified sense of identity-in-memory for the people affected.' If those who gained from apartheid can come to understand that they owe something to others, and that to pay back is a moral obligation, there will be hope for social justice in a really new South Africa.

Epilogue

The last day in this South African city, and time for some final encounters with familiar scenes. First the refurbished sea front, with its stridently postmodern street furniture. Signs in Zulu as well as English and Afrikaans tell holiday-makers, 'We are getting there', as they trip over unfinished pavings, but the built environment is, literally, exclusively European. There are places assigned to the African souvenir sellers, with their gestures towards traditional dress and stocks of baskets, beads, pots and other symbols of native craft: exotic others positioned for the tourist gaze.

There are also places which the Africans have made their own, in the sense of dominant occupation. There are the water slides, and a section of beach reserved for Whites until 1990 and now full of more exuberant people shouting, leaping in the water, defying attempts of the life guard to keep them in the swimming zone and out of the way of the bronzed and blond-haired surf-board riders. A White family sits steadfastly in their row of deck chairs, kids playing in the sand with the African maid. Crowds of township school-children recently released on some outing converge on the beach. The sight and sound of Africa, and the story of a worker just 'retrenched' (South African for sacked) wanting money to take back to his family. Couples walk by, dressed in their week-end best: smart suits, crisp shirts, dresses or saris, and a few elderly White men still wearing safari suits – a little self-conscious in their recognition that the promenade is not what it used to be. But all is not lost: a few blocks away elderly ladies grace the bowling green, pumps and starched dresses, whiter than white.

Overlooking the scene is the Holiday Inn. A tall, white concrete slab set between smaller structures from a more elegant age, rather like a gigantic urinal as a disparaging friend once pointed out. I recall the last dinner there, before Margaret left for home: looking out from the restaurant through heavy tinted glass onto the other world of crammed 'combi' mini-bus taxis, radios full blast, filling up with smart fellows and girls in finery, shouting, drinking, preparing to leave the bright lights for twenty kilometres of hazardous drive to the townships or shack-lands on the city fringe. And the beggar always at the door. Half those in the restaurant were black, though none seemed tempted by the chef's special concession to African cuisine served in a miniature iron cauldron.

A last walk out along the break-water, for a panoramic view of the city. One of the universities is just visible on the ridge: reserved for Whites under apartheid, now admitting increasing numbers of Indian students, and with the first African lecturer in geography now appointed. The other university, originally built for Indians, is further inland where their Group Areas are: now 'democratizing' after years of domination by conservative Afrikaners, admitting lots of Africans, and electing a White student as Union president. It has been peaceful on the campus this visit: not even a whiff of the familiar tear gas.

Back to the block of holiday flats, to finish packing. The one nearby, which was home for a few months years ago, now has a sign indicating that the management has the right not to admit whoever it wishes: a discreet signal of what used simply to be understood: Whites only. Two street-wise lads try to chat up neatly-dressed teenage Asian sisters abandoned briefly by their parents; the girls handle the encounter with not quite dismissive courtesy, across a class divide now separating people of the same former racial classification.

My lift to the airport arrives. We drive through the city centre, along the freeway, past the docks and the Hindu temples of a once thriving Indian quarter (before it was broken up). On the hill-side opposite the airport loom the gigantic barracks built for migrant workers on the edge of a township. What will become of such structures? Family housing? Part of the awful legacy of bricks and mortar and of people made a commodity. A crowd gathers to watch the latest traffic accident cleared up: another speeding combi. I get out of the car, say goodbye, and make for the terminal's security check. Black men with guns, in place. My lift drives off, back to the city to which she chose to return after study abroad, to help build the new South Africa. I leave with mixed feelings. I no longer have to struggle with the ethics of breaking an academic boycott to do research in South Africa, but I still wonder about my responsibility, my morality, what I should be doing, where, and for whom.

9

Territory, Community and Home

> One place might be like another, but one community is never like
> another. A community is not just a place where you live. It is not just
> another locality . . . It is much more than that. It is alive. A community
> is our home.
>
> Richard Rive, *'Buckingham Palace', District Six* (1986)

Place is necessary for human existence. This goes beyond other basic needs,
such as for food and clothing, and indeed beyond the physical occupation
of space and of a structure thereon. Our place, and sense of geographical
space or territory, merges imperceptibly with a broader sense of identity, of
who we are, of position in the general scheme of things. Satisfaction with all
this is central to well-being. But place can also have repressive connotations.
The maxim of 'a place for everything, and everything in its place' implies
compulsion as well as accommodation; to know one's place can suggest
having been put in it, as well as a sense of security. The ghetto is a case in
point. Losing one's place can be much more traumatic than simply changing
location. But a new place may be liberating, perhaps providing the space
required for a new way of living, and even possibly forgiving past injustices
which may have deprived people of their original place.

For the most part, people come to life in an unchosen community, family
or home, and stay there unless they decide to move on. But some have a
more disturbing experience. There are obvious grounds on which people may
reasonably be evicted from their homes or have their communities broken
up, in the interests of what is held to be a wider social purpose. Few people
would dispute that houses in the path of road improvements necessitated by
public safety may legitimately be acquired by compulsion, with appropriate
compensation.

The days when the Duke of Devonshire could erase an entire village
because it spoilt the view from his new Chatsworth mansion have passed,
but neighbourhoods are still sometimes required to make way for urban
redevelopment and similar projects. However, the justice of such moves is
often far from self-evident. While they may be the outcome of a process

in which everyone involved is given the opportunity to express a view, fairly balanced with that of others, it could be that some sectional interests are powerful enough to influence matters in their favour while others are effectively impotent to save their homes and community or to insist on fair recompense. Such has been the case in the American city (as explained in chapter 6). And in socialist cities (chapter 7), the authorities showed no greater sympathy for people's attachment to old if not particularly salubrious neighbourhoods cleared to create modern micro-regions.

Chapter 8 opened up some cases of large-scale involuntary population movement. In South Africa, under apartheid, gestures towards a wider societal purpose hardly masked the power of a dominant minority to implement their self-serving plan for national or racial identity and its territorial expression. And as these words are written, a similar process is taking place in what was formerly Yugoslavia, the term 'ethnic cleansing' echoing the manner in which the removal of Jews was portrayed half a century ago in Nazi Germany. Europe is experiencing a frightening reminder of the depths of human wickedness in the nationalist struggle for place, just as the Holocaust fades from first-hand recollection.

This chapter is about the annihilation of place, or topocide as Porteous (1988) has termed it. Its central concern is the experience of place destruction and deprivation, which at the extreme may be accompanied by losing much of what else matters to people and even by their physical annihilation. To a greater extent than in the other case studies, we are concerned with people's experiences and how they express them, as representations of what it means to lose their place.

This material provides background against which to pose the question of the morality or justice of depriving people of their territory, community or homes. The wrong may seem perfectly straightforward, much more obvious than in conventional distributional issues concerning who gets what level of income, quality of housing, and so on. But perhaps not. In any event, it is part of the human struggle that should not be overlooked in pursuit of social justice in a geographical context. The cases presented have been deliberately selected to link back to some earlier discussions, as well as with one another; the tragedy is that there is so much from which to chose.

Community destruction in South Africa

The cold figures for population removals in South Africa (table 8.1), shocking though they are, fail to capture the experience of injustice manifest in community destruction. However, something of this can be recovered, for example from documentary evidence, oral history, fictional accounts, and talking to some of those affected. The account here concentrates on the

Coloured people of Cape Town, though similar material relating to Indian and African removals can also be found. While the emphasis is on people's experience, some contextual material is also provided, to help to provoke the underlying moral issue.

The creation of Group Areas in the Cape Town metropolis displaced large numbers of people classified as Coloured, mainly from inner residential areas along the base of Table Mountain to new estates on the sandy, wind-swept Cape Flats to the east (described in detail in Western, 1981). The intention was to impose ordered homogeneity on the complex racial geography of the pre-apartheid era which involved local intermingling of different peoples not greatly preoccupied with precise racial designations. The largest clearance project concerned the mainly Coloured community occupying the neighbourhood known as District Six, a case which came to symbolize the evil outcomes of the Group Areas Act.

The area in question is on the southern fringe of Cape Town's central business district. It began to be settled at the beginning of the nineteenth century, and was officially named District Six in 1867 when the municipality was divided into districts. Close proximity to the port attracted a wide variety of people, and the district developed a vibrant, cosmopolitan character with considerable racial, ethnic and socio-economic diversity. However, it was as the heart of the Cape Coloured community that District Six found its special identity.

As the home of predominantly poor people, District Six developed a reputation for violence, vice, crime, physical dilapidation and overcrowding. While understandable from the perspective of outsiders, such an image was subject to exaggeration on the part of city authorities, motivated by fear of threat to European health and safety (the so-called 'sanitation syndrome') which provoked slum clearance well before the Group Areas Act provided a more effective means of moving 'non-White' people. But there were two sides to places like District Six (Hart, 1988, pp. 610–11):

[A] paradox of warmth and variety, dirt and rubble, gaiety and sadness . . . of respectability and rascality; of poverty and decent comfort; of tenements shamefully neglected and homes well-cared-for and well-loved . . .

District Six hummed with the enterprise of its residents, boasting a bewildering assortment of stores that served the population far beyond its immediate boundaries. Mingled with the more commonplace small general stores, tailors, butchers, fruiterers, and fishmongers, were the spices and curry shops and dimly lit herbalists' stores, reflecting the diverse cultures of their owners and patrons.

Variety, community and vitality are words frequently used to evoke the essence of District Six.

In February 1966 most of District Six was proclaimed an area for White residence, under the terms of the Group Areas Act. Its officially enumerated population of 33,500 were given a year to prepare for removal to new Coloured areas. In addition to the apartheid fixation with residential segregation, this was seen as an opportunity to get rid of people not classified as White living close to the city centre (perceived as a threat to social order if not to sanitation), and to turn valuable land to more remunerative uses.

The material costs imposed on those forced to move could be considerable. Property owners did not necessarily receive compensation at full market value, and relocation to the periphery of the city entailed commuting costs as well as, for some, higher rentals in new accommodation than in the old run-down neighbourhood. Housing conditions may have been improved for many families, but in the Cape Flats human relations were more impersonal, social deprivation more evident and personal safety less secure than in the traditional Coloured parts of Cape Town (Western, 1981).

But, as Hart (1988, p. 616) points out, 'The inconvenience occasioned by the physical wrenching of people from long-time homes pales in the face of the more prolonged and damaging psychological distress.' Evidence from various accounts evokes fear, humiliation, bitterness, anger, and fragmentation of the identity and heritage of a particular community. Hart elaborates (p. 611):

> Particularly in the South African context, personal lives are in turn intimately moulded by places the people have known, lost, or been forced to know and by those they have been prevented from knowing. That District Six afforded its occupants a deep sense of place and belonging became increasingly clear as the pace of removals was accelerated, accompanied by an outburst of embittered literary and vocal response. Although its edifices have literally been crushed, an inimitable image and identity remain intact – in the words of an ex-resident, 'You can take the people out of District Six ... but you'll never take District Six out of the heart of the people.'

Perhaps the most telling expression of psychological damage was among so-called 'bulldozer kids': children who had witnessed the destruction of their community by great machines (Hart, 1988, p. 618).

One of the most powerful literary accounts of the impact of the demise of District Six is provided in a novel by Richard Rive (1986, pp. 126–8):

> Everyone in the District died a little when it was pulled down. Many died spiritually and emotionally. Some like my mother also

died physically although she was fortunate not to be alive to see the wholesale destruction. For her there would not be the painful memories we would experience. We buried her from 207 Caledon Street, which was still standing, and then the cortège moved to St Mark's Church, which is now still standing. It then went by rail to Woltemade, where she was laid to rest in a cemetery set aside for our so-called ethnic group. To part is to die a little. We all died a little when we parted from the District.

Many were forced to move to small matchbox houses in large matchbox townships which with brutal and tactless irony were given names by the authorities such as Hanover Park and Lavender Hill [from District Six] to remind us of the past they had taken away from us. There was one essential difference between the old places and the new ones. District Six had a soul. Its centre held together till it was torn apart. Stained and tarnished as it was, it had a soul that held together . . .

They had taken our past away and left the rubble. They had demolished our spirits and left broken bricks. They had destroyed our community and left dust and memories. And they had done all this for their own selfish and arrogant reasons. They had sought to regulate our present in order to control our future. And as I stood there I was overwhelmed by the enormity of it all. And I asked aloud, 'What men have the moral or political rights to take away a people's past? How will they answer on that day when they have to account for this? For the past will not be forgotten'.

No forgive and forget, as people continue to live the injustice.

The association with death is a repetitive feature of people's understanding of the destruction of Cape Town's Coloured communities. For example, one of the people displaced from the inner suburb of Mowbray, interviewed by Western (1978, p. 313), said:

A lot of people died after they left Mowbray. It was heart-breaking for the old people. My husband was poorly and he used to just sit and look out of the window. Then before he died he said, 'You must dress me and take me to Mowbray. My mum and dad are looking for me, and they can't find me in Mowbray.'

Continuity between the living and the dead represents one of the deepest human attachments to place. People mourn the loss of place and what happened there, as well as the people who are gone. Thus, Mowbray was 'much grieved for by its removees' (Western, 1978, p. 310), just as the annual 'coon carnival' was one of the local events in District Six 'mourned following the arrival of the bulldozers' (Hart, 1988, p. 611).

The resistance of residents, together with lack of enthusiasm on the part of the Cape Town city authorities for what central government required, prolonged the process of clearance. But District Six was gradually erased, physically if not from people's memory. This was not the end of the story, however. Rather than the redevelopment anticipated by proponents of apartheid, the land has remained largely vacant. A sense of tainted ground prevented wholesale reoccupation for many years. With a singular lack of sensitivity, the government designated District Six as one of the first 'free settlement areas' in 1989: part of a futile policy to legitimate some racially mixed (or 'grey') areas, hatched during the death throws of apartheid. But it needed the end of apartheid itself to overlay the emptiness so effectively preserved on the ground for more than two decades.

The district might well return to life now, even as a working-class residential area to which Coloured people would have access, if such noble sentiments can withstand the pressure of market forces for more profitable use. Perhaps the name of District Six will return to the map, replacing the official Zonnebloem – a local Afrikaans place name resurrected in the 1970s as part of the annihilation of former territorial identity.

Perhaps other names of places obliterated by apartheid will be restored, in the way some East European cities are trying to recover their pre-socialist identity in resurrecting former street names, for example. If so, then a prime candidate will be Sophiatown. Sophiatown was a largely African equivalent of District Six, not far from the city centre of Johannesburg. Hart and Pirie (1984) have eloquently contrasted its vitality and exuberance with the soul-less townships like Soweto to which its inhabitants were moved under 'slum clearance'. Sophiatown was replaced by a residential area for Whites, and renamed Triomf. Triomf is Afrikaans for triumph.

Erasing the Jewish ghetto

Approaching from the east, where the ghetto once stood, the Jewish cemetery in Łódź is at first sight hard to detect. It is only when scattered stones rising out of long grass become regular lines that their origin is clear. Row upon row, some simple, some ornate, many tilted or broken, receding into the woodland which has recolonized the site. In the centre, the awesome mausoleum of Izrael Poznański, one of the city's great textile magnates whose mills dominate the industrial quarter on the north side of the city centre and whose palaces grace main streets. This is reputed to be the largest Jewish cemetery in Europe. There are a few floral tributes, fading in the sun. An elderly man from Montreal, piece of paper with a plot number in his hand, is looking for his father. On the wall around the entrance are various memorial tablets. One reads: 'In loving memory of my dear sister Bluma . . . who was shot dead by a German murderer without any reason in the Ghetto Łódź Poland on 20 July 1940.' Outside, a small monument to the ghetto dead, and a scent of lily-of-the-valley in the early summer air.

Awful though the impact of Group Areas in South Africa was, it could have been worse. It could have been accompanied by the extermination of the population. Such was the case with Jewish ghettos which grew up in cities of central and eastern Europe, and into which Jews from elsewhere were concentrated by the Nazis during the Second World War.

Substantial numbers of Jews began to move into the emerging industrial city of Łódź in the 1820s. They were confined to the Old Town until 1862, when restrictions on where Jews could live in the city were lifted (Liszewski, 1991, pp. 29–30). Jews than made up about a quarter of the total population, a proportion more or less maintained thereafter with the city's rapid growth. The 1931 census, using the criterion of native language, enumerated 59 per cent of the city's population Poles, 31.7 per cent Jews, and 8.9 per cent Germans.

Łódź entered the Second World War with about a quarter of a million Jews, one of the largest such populations of any European city. Jews were prominent in the textile trade, most notably Izrael Poznański, and had a cultural life which produced the pianist Artur Rubinstein. As a chronicler of the ghetto remarked (Dobroszycki, 1984, p. xxx): 'If there were any place in Poland where Jews could consider themselves at home and safe, no city had more of a claim to this than Łódź.'

Most of the wealthy and many of the well-to-do Jews left before the war started, but more than 200,000 remained. When the Russian Army liberated the city at the beginning of 1945 there were 800 Jews left. Less than five years had seen the death of an estimated 240,000 (including those brought to Łódź from elsewhere), within the city, transported to concentration camps, or simply lost and absorbed into the Polish soil. Consistent with their customary practice, the Nazis had also erased virtually everything in the city associated with the identity of the Jewish people, especially places of worship (Liszewski, 1991).

When the Germans arrived in September 1939 they annexed Łódź into the Greater Reich. There followed a systematic Germanization of the city, aimed at excising its Polish identity, with death as well as deportation reducing the majority population group. But it was the Jews who posed the greatest threat to the ideology of national racial purity, requiring them to be removed or at least contained like some fatal infection. What happened to the Jews in Łódź, people and place, has been recorded in compilations of contemporary documentary accounts by Dobroszycki (1984) and Adelson and Lapides (1989). Some of the most eloquent are from the notebooks of

Oskar Rosenfeld, a writer and translator transported to Łódź from Prague in 1941; much of what follows is from this source.

The Germans soon began to concentrate the Jewish population in a ghetto. The need to create a strong German centre to the city required some parts to be 'cleansed of Jews', in the words of a German memorandum dated 10 December 1939 (Adelson and Lapides, 1989, p. 24). And the scattered population elsewhere had to be consolidated into working groups. Creation of the Litzmannstadt Ghetto, as it was referred to by the city's German name, involved combining two quite different districts. One was the Old Town, the oldest quarter of Łódź and site of the original early nineteenth-century ghetto, which had a high proportion of dilapidated wooden housing. The other was the adjoining district of Bałuty, renowned for its squalor, and described as follows (Adelson and Lapides, 1989, p. 35): 'Houses were built at whim, with no plan beyond their owners' desires, along crooked alleys, following no pattern and submitting to no fire, sanitation, or zoning regulations. Its isolation was evident by its having no gutters or street lighting. And it was a breeding ground for disease ... Its inhabitants were considered the city's outcasts.' Bałuty was now to accommodate a new group of people cast out of society and their existing homes. The ghetto's four square kilometres contained 31,721 apartments, mostly single rooms and only 725 with running water (Dobroszycki, 1984, p. xxxvii).

To those already living in Łódź were added Jews from other European cities. One fairly well-to-do group came from Prague. The manner of their eviction is described as follows (Oskar Rosenfeld's Notebooks, in Adelson and Lapides, 1989, pp. 169–70):

> Just before departure, everyone had to report in conveyor-belt fashion, with his money, papers, and house key. The next-to-last act of the show began. The order was: (1) Give up the house key. One's home was thus given over to the protectorate ... Take it, you who have taken our honor and possessions and existence and the meaning of our lives. The keys were given to German 'purchasers' on the same day, for the most part. (2) Give up all personal documents, certificates with photographs and other identification. (3) Give up all money and gold. (4) Sign a form the contents of which one was not allowed to read. With one's signature, one gave the Jewish authorities of Prague, i.e. the Gestapo, full power over all property left behind. (5) Accept a police statement with the stamp: 'Evacuated on ... '.

Thus was the dispossession and depersonalization completed.

In March 1940 there were reported to be 115,000 Jews in the Łódź ghetto, comprising the majority of those in the city. This was twice as many people as inhabited the area before the war. Some 65,000–85,000 Jews had already been moved elsewhere. On 1 May, when the ghetto was sealed off from the rest of the city, it held 164,000. A census on 12 July counted 156,402 people, living in about 48,000 rooms, with little more than 4 square metres of space per person (Adelson and Lapides, 1989, pp. 53, 58).

Something of the reaction to ghetto life is captured in the following vignettes (Oskar Rosenfeld's Notebooks, Adelson and Lapides, 1989, pp. 3, 212, 213):

> Grim clay huts – pathetic trees and bushes – lakes of mud, stink-ing garbage – countless creatures with backs bent over – next to them faces that had already gone beyond all pain, on which were written: We will hold out, we will outlive you, you cannot destroy us . . .

> We are lepers, outcasts, common thieves, people without music, without warmth, without beds, without a world. There is no other city like this in the world. Come here, people from the outside, from over there where there are normal days and holidays, where there are dreams and desire and resistance.

> Everyone and everything is without sense, like marionettes on a stage. And the more one observes this scene, the more senseless the whole thing seems. For whom? For what? How long? None of these questions can be answered.

It is of no consolation that the answer to the last question, for most people was – not long. The initial forced-labour function of the ghetto changed into that of entrepot, as quotas agreed by the ghetto administration with the Nazis were rounded up and sent away, to other places where what might be left of their labour could be squeezed out, or directly to the gas chambers. In September 1942, the population of the ghetto was down to 90,000, with 50,000 deported and 20,000 dead. Population continued to turn over; in May 1944 there were still 80,000. To Jews outside, including those in Warsaw, the Łódź ghetto appeared hermetically sealed: 'an island, totally cut off from the rest of the world' (Adelson and Lapides, 1989, p. 412).

It is the sense of dislocation in time as well as space, no longer being of the world, that comes most clearly through accounts from the ghetto. Deprived of home, community, belongings, often family, as well as so much else that was valued in life, most of those who remained lost life itself before the war ended. The rest of the story can remain unsaid, except for the following on the fear of not surviving (from Oskar Rosenfeld's Notebooks, Adelson and Lapides, 1989, p. 316): 'On our bones Palestine must be built, the only hope still left.'

Resettlement in Palestine

> We Palestinians are clearly struggling for our self-determination but for
> the fact that we have no place, no agreed-upon and available physical
> terrain on which to conduct our struggle. We are clearly anticolonialist
> and antiracist in our struggle but for the fact that our opponents are
> the greatest victims of racism in history, and perhaps our struggle
> is waged at an awkward postcolonial period in the modern world's
> history. We clearly struggle for a better future but for the fact that
> the state preventing us from having a future of our own has already
> provided a future for its own unhappy people.

This is how Edward Said (1992, p. 122) explains the distinctive situation of
the Palestinian Arabs, compared with other dispossessed people in history.
In order to make a place for themselves in what they regarded as their historic
homeland, the Jews displaced others, dealing them a similar experience of
exile and refuge to that which had been the fate of the Jews for so long.
The international legitimization of the return of Jews to Palestine, manifest
in the establishment of a Jewish nation-state, might be interpreted as a
gesture towards reparation for the centuries of suffering, culminating in
the Holocaust. But, 'Jewish claims for compensation generated through
persecution in *Europe* were transformed into claims fixed upon *Palestine*'
(Sayigh, 1979, pp. 56–78). In the process, the cost was transferred to a
people not implicated in the original injustice.

Jewish refugees from eastern Europe began to settle in Palestine from
the 1880s onwards. They established agricultural colonies, in a land that was
then under Ottoman rule and inhabited by an Arabic-speaking population.
Immigration built up, encouraged by a declaration by the then British Foreign
Minister Lord Balfour in 1918 favouring a national homeland in Palestine for
the Jewish people. By 1931 the Jewish population had reached about 175,000
out of a total of one million, and by 1946 it was 600,000 out of 1,900,000. The
establishment of the state of Israel in 1948 set the scene for one of the most
bitter and enduring struggles over land and settlement to afflict a turbulent
part of the world in a far-from-peaceful era.

The purpose of this section is neither to recount the history of contested
land and settlement, on which there is a voluminous geographical literature,
nor to provide a thorough review of the Arab-Israel conflict and its possible
resolution (see, for example, Newman, 1991b; Newman and Portugali, 1987;
Portugali, 1993). The intention is briefly to review the bases on which
conflicting claims to territory are made, and then to recount some of the
implications of resettlement. Jewish colonization and national consolidation
in Palestine displaced hundreds of thousands of Arabs, from existing towns
and from the villages where most of a predominantly agricultural population

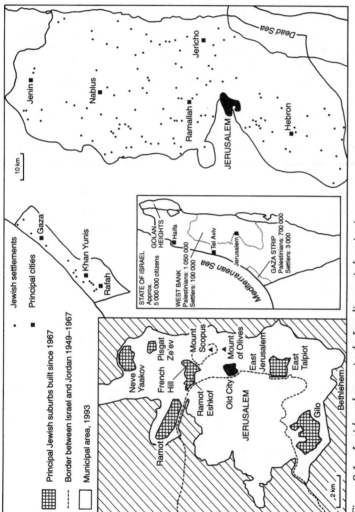

Figure 9.1 Jewish settlement in the Israeli occupied territories.
(Source: *The Real Map: a demographic and geographic analysis of the population of the West Bank and the Gaza Strip*, Peace Now Settlement Watch Committee, Report No. 5, 1992; Jerusalem based on *The Guardian*, 7 July 1993).

The following labels appear on the map:

- • Jewish settlements
- ■ Principal cities
- • Principal Jewish suburbs built since 1967
- ■ Border between Israel and Jordan 1949–1967
- □ Municipal area, 1993

10 km

Jenin
Nablus
Jericho
Ramallah
JERUSALEM
Hebron
Dead Sea
Gaza
Khan Yunis
Rafah

STATE OF ISRAEL
Approx.
5 000 000 citizens
GOLAN
HEIGHTS
Haifa
Tel Aviv
Jerusalem
WEST BANK
Palestinians: 1 050 000
Settlers: 100 000
GAZA STRIP
Palestinians: 700 000
Settlers: 3 000
Mediterranean Sea

Neve
Yaakov
Pisgat
Ze'ev
French
Hill
Mount
Scopus
Mount
of Olives
Ramot
Ramot
Eshkof
Old City
East
Jerusalem
East
Talpiot
JERUSALEM
Gilo
Bethlehem
2 km

lived. This case provides further depth to the earlier consideration of how claims on place are made (chapter 8), and what it means to lose.[1]

The state of Israel has a population of approaching 5 million, 17 per cent of whom are not Jews. This minority of 850,000 or so are Palestinian Arabs, citizens of Israel but deprived of some rights confined to people of Jewish nationality. There are also about one million Palestinian Arabs living in the West Bank, and a further 700,000 in the Gaza Strip (see figure 9.1). These, together with the less densely populated Golan Heights, are the 'occupied territories', taken by Israel after the Six Day War of 1967. There are also about 120,000 Jewish settlers in these territories. The city of Jerusalem has a population of about 550,000, 28 per cent of whom are non-Jews (compared with 40 per cent when the state of Israel was established). East Jerusalem now houses 160,000 Jews, slightly more than the Arab population; there were no Jews in this part of the city before it was annexed by Israel in 1967. In addition to the Palestinian Arabs in Israel or land occupied by Israel, there are well over 2 million living in such neighbouring states as Jordan and Lebanon.

The major dispersal of the Palestinian Arab population took place during the conflict which followed the establishment of the state of Israel in 1948, when an estimated 800,000 were displaced or left on their own accord. Many of them ended up in refugee camps which still hold large numbers today. Land has continued to be taken from Arabs for Jewish use, which since 1967 has involved numerous settlements in the West Bank and large suburban extensions of Jerusalem (figure 9.1).

The traditional basis of the claim made by Jews to Palestinian territory is biblical. Thus, 'the Lord appeared unto Abram, and said, Unto thy seed will I give this land' (Genesis, 12:7). As for the land itself, as described to the Children of Israel in preparation for their entry: 'the Lord thy God bringeth thee into a good land, a land of brooks of water, of fountains and depths that spring out of valleys and hills; A land of wheat, and barley, and vines, and fig trees, and pomegranates; a land of olive oil, and honey; A land wherein thou shalt eat bread without scarceness; thou shalt not lack anything in it' (Deuteronomy, 8:7–9). Jewish settlement in this region was seen as 'a religious imperative which no human law can negate' (Newman, 1984, p. 147). However, God's gift was not unconditional: religious practices

[1] Research for this section was assisted by invitations to visit the Ben-Gurion University of the Negev, the University of Haifa and the Hebrew University of Jerusalem. I am grateful to Yehuda Gradus and David Newman in Beer-Sheva, Yoram Bar-Gal and Stanley Waterman in Haifa, Amiram Gonen, Shlomo Hasson, Shalom Reichman and Arie Schahar in Jerusalem, David Grossman in Tel Aviv, Rafi Bar-El at the Development Study Centre in Rehovot, and others who helped in various ways. None bear any responsibility for my interpretations.

were required of the Jewish people, who were supposed to exercise a form of stewardship in the way the land was managed, all of which reinforced attachment to this particular territory (Houston, 1978; Shilhav, 1985). To the religious case is added the historical occupation, from about 1200 BC to 69 AD, by the Jewish kingdoms, the ancient centres of which were in Judea and Samaria in what is now the West Bank. When conquest by the Romans sent the Jews into almost two millennia of exile in the diaspora, their relationship with the promised land changed; not being in occupation prevented the performance of specific religious commandments which could only be carried out on the land itself (Shilhav, 1985, p. 113). Kimmerling (1983, pp. 8–9) explains the outcome as follows:

Zion or *Eretz Israel* (the Land of Israel) is a central pillar of the Jewish religion, and even though for many generations the Jews were entirely cut off from Zion, they continued observing rituals and customs which were directly connected to that country, such as festivals marking the changing of the seasons there, ceremonies relating to the specific plants which grow there, and most of all, in referring to specific places in the land as 'sanctified'. (In a sense, the entire country is considered to be sanctified or holy). During the course of time, the concept of Zion became increasingly metaphysical and abstract. Its boundaries were unclear and undefined, except for its center – Jerusalem.

The ambiguity of Old Testament descriptions of the borders still generates heated debate (see Berkowicz, 1991).

These Jewish claims are countered by similar claims on the part of Palestinian Arabs. Not only is there more than 1300 years of Arab occupation of the land, but also an association between the Islamic religion and territory which generates a Moslem assertion of sanctity comparable to that of the Jews. Jerusalem in particular highlights the conflict: the Western or 'Wailing' Wall, so revered by religious Jews, is barely a stone's throw from the Dome of the Rock and the Al-Aksa Mosque, which are of special significance to Moslems. To Palestinians, Jerusalem represents 'the heart of our identity' (Hanan Ashrawi, BBC radio, May 1992). The association between religion, territory and nationality has thus served a similar function for both sides in the conflict: Kimmerling (1983, pp. 215–16) notes that both see the entire expanse of Palestine as having moral or religious value, and use this as a means of legitimating their claim on the same territory.

Claims to territory grounded in its religious importance are powerful. Indeed, to Waldron (1992, p. 19–20), 'claims that land of religious significance should be returned to its original owners may have an edge over claims for the return of lands whose significance for them is mainly material or economic'. Religious rites may have to be performed in specific places, while the same kind of land elsewhere can serve the same purely material purpose. But in the case of Palestine there are two competing claims on the same grounds, and even if it could be shown that one was stronger than the other (e.g. that the Arab claim, like Palestinian nationalism itself, was of more recent origin than the Jewish claim), this is unlikely to convince those with the weaker case. Indeed, the very nature of a religious claim based on a god's will makes it utterly unconvincing to those who do not believe in that particular deity, and the more so if their own faith is in another almighty who has revealed a contrary will. It is also by no means obvious that a religious claim is always (or even ever) superior in a moral sense to all other kinds of claims. The mixing of labour, sweat and so on with the land (as invoked in South Africa, for example) could be even more persuasive, especially to those who recognize no divine authority.

The religious case has therefore come to be augmented by arguments of greater appeal in a largely secular world. Indeed, some ultra-orthodox Jewish claims concerning the absolute sanctity of the Land of Israel hardly lend support to the presence of a secular society and state (Glinert and Shilhav, 1991, p. 61). Hence the emphasis on historic occupation, or on the identity between people and territory without a deity to bind them together. Dissociated from the religious practices on which the sanctity of the land depends, the case becomes one of the fulfilment of national aspirations manifest in simply having certain territory: 'territorial fetishism' or 'paganism where territory is the god', as Shilhav (1985, p. 120) puts it, or an 'idolatry of the land' (Rowley, 1985, p. 125).

This kind of case is strengthened by working and improving the land, which is itself dependent on its occupation. Returning to the land as a source of livelihood was an important feature of Zionism, and once Jews began settling Palestine the struggle of the pioneers became enshrined in Zionist mythology. Kimmerling (1983, p. 227) elaborates:

> Overcoming the difficulties of conquering the land from nature, when nature included not only sand and swamp, but psychological, social, and political obstacles as well, gives the settler a deep emotional attachment to the land and a feeling of entitlement to it. Defining the struggle as primarily one against nature rather than against men or sociopolitical forces was necessary in order to give self-legitimacy to the Zionist activities.

The draining of the swamps in particular took on enormous symbolic significance. 'The swamps were not simply a hydrological phenomenon; they represented a series of dualisms: desolation versus rebirth; the ugly versus the beautiful; weakness and death versus heroism and life' (Bar-Gal, 1991, p. 20). Similar sentiments are attached to President David Ben-Gurion's vision of the greening of the Negev Desert. Insofar as the Palestinian Arab population entered the scene, they could be portrayed as not caring for the land, further justifying Jewish occupation. Presence and productive use of land, coupled with the money to purchase more, led to increasing Jewish ownership of the land, and ultimately to Jewish sovereignty, which in its turn gave further legitimacy to occupation.

Kimmerling (1983, p. 20) emphasizes the importance of being present on land, in terms of the law and customs of the Middle East: 'not living on it or working it – and even more, the presence of another on it – put one's title at risk.' Hence the importance of presence as a political means of controlling territory in Ottoman times. The Jews simply continued this practice, from early immigration to the contemporary strategy of settlement on the West Bank, referred to as 'establishing facts on the ground'. Strategic issues, including the protection of the state of Israel, especially its most vulnerable settlements, from demonstrably hostile neighbours, have played a part in Jewish occupation (and expropriation) of particular areas.

Former presence and the mixing of labour also constitutes a Palestinian Arab argument for regaining land now in Jewish hands. Presence may have been less individual and conspicuous than in the case of Jewish agriculture; for example where public rights of access existed as remnants of nomadic society, and letting land lie fallow for a few years to improve it (Kimmerling, 1983, pp. 38, 107). Such practices were a source of conflict with settlers unable or unwilling to understand Arab land use and associated rights. But it is hard to exaggerate the close attachment which Arabs developed with their land, forged through generations of hard toil. And the home settlement or village was central to people's sense of belonging, community and place.

Accounts of Palestinian Arab life emphasize village and clan solidarity, forming 'a warm, strong, stable environment for the individual, a sense of rootedness and belonging', typical of peasant society (Sayigh, 1979, p. 10). The strength of village identification is evident in the way it persisted in the refugee camps after people were evicted from their land or otherwise induced to leave. The impact of separation from home and property is captured in interviews conducted by Sayigh (1979, p. 101) as follows:

The village – with its special arrangement of houses and orchards, its open meeting places, its burial ground, its collective identity – was built into the personality of each individual villager to a degree that made separation like an obliteration of the self. In describing their first years as refugees, camp Palestinians use metaphors like 'death', 'paralysis', 'burial', 'non-existence', 'we lost our way', 'we didn't know where to go, what to do', 'we were like sheep in a field'. Thirty years after the Uprooting, the older generation still mourns, still weeps as it recalls the past.

Social and psychological effects included isolation, shame, loss of respect and family disruption, added to which was a sense of political oppression and the suppression of Palestinian identity (Sayigh, 1979, pp. 124–36).

Other accounts, reported by Rubinstein (1991, p. 29), evoke an almost physical love of the land: 'where blood ties are the backbone of the social structure, the repetition of motifs of erotic geography is readily understood.' There are references to 'stealing the past' as well as the village. 'For the first generation of Palestinian refugees, the meaning of "homeland" was very simple, concrete, direct: a field, an olive tree, a veranda, a well. Hence their loss was felt immediately, and deeply, as a great tragedy' (p. 13). He recounts a story of a beggar, apprehended by an Israeli officer in an incident in Gaza during the *intifada* (Palestinian uprising), and told to go home. When asked where his home was he replied that his house was in Majdal. Majdal is now the Israeli town of Ashkelon, and has not existed for forty years; but the man gave the answer common to most refugees of his generation: 'the name of a lost village. That is their identity' (p. 38).

The retention and even re-creation of the past is a prominent theme in the literature of Palestinian Arab experience of loss. Rubinstein (1991, p. 10) refers to the publication of a survey of places in Palestine that no longer exist: a guide for those he describes as 'the people of nowhere', just as they preserve the old place names in everyday usage. The Jews, for their part, create or re-create their own geography with new Hebrew names of ancient Biblical or Talmudic resonance or evoking nationalist/Zionist themes (Cohen and Kliot, 1992). Thus, past and present place are both contested.

An extension of the Palestinian refugee identity with home villages which no longer exist is the 'myth of return' (Kimmerling, 1983, p. 214). Such a deeply-held aspiration, which might be realized only after death (and reburial), is frustrated by irrevocable loss of place and the constraints imposed on Arab (re)settlement, and also by Israel's Law of Return whereby any Jew born anywhere is entitled to claim Israeli citizenship and residence (Said, 1992, pp. 48–9). The waves of immigrants from the former USSR in the early 1990s exemplify, to Arabs, the partiality of practices which grant to far distant others rights of membership they themselves, as Palestinians, cannot obtain in the land of their birth.

This brings us, finally, to the (im)morality or (in)justice of the situation. The circumstances in which Jewish immigration began, consolidated and ended up with a new nation-state in the old promised land were a triumph over the tragedy of past pogroms and attempted genocide. The Jews learned from awful experience to help themselves, and at a crucial stage in their history this meant, literally, to land which others held. Israel's far-flung responsibility to other Jews, reciprocated by support from international Jewry, is an unusually expansive if highly selective expression of the otherwise parochial ethic of care. In stark contrast is the unequal and at times brutal treatment of close and even spatially coincident others, who happen not to be Jews: an inversion of the customary spatiality of concern. Not to be a Jew is the difference which really matters.

Kimmerling (1983, p. 189) notes the tension between a particularist approach, focusing on the problems of the group, and a universalistic approach based on humanitarian values to which the Jewish religion became committed over the centuries. Pointing out that the sanctity of the land is conditional on the observation of the religious precepts and commandments given to the Jewish people, Shilhav (1985, p. 123) observes: 'Such precepts demand the leading of an exemplary individual and national life based on morality and brotherly love, not the worship of territory and extension of conflict.' A contradiction may also be noted between the socialist principles of the early Zionist movement, manifest most famously in the collectivism of the *kibbutz*, and the exclusion as well as unequal treatment of the Arabs. Egalitarianism was restricted by membership, and Israeli Arabs still struggle for full rights of citizenship.

As in South Africa, it is worth bearing in mind the argument of Waldron (1992) that, whatever the case for reparation in recognition of past injustice, it is justice for present people that really matters. Those present and relevant comprise four groups of people, in different geographical situations: Jewish Israelis, Israeli Arabs, Jews living in the occupied territories, and Palestinian Arabs in foreign countries. All have rights to assert, which need to be mutually understood and given due moral weight in finding a solution to the conflict over settlement of contested territory. A compromise in the contemporary spirit of *realpolitik*, between unequal contestants in a negotiating process brokered by some far from disinterested world power, is unlikely to generate either a just or a stable resolution. A better point of departure would be to try to decide what is right, guided by the biblical version of the universalist maxim: do to others what you would have them do to you.

The Jews have treated Palestinian Arabs in a manner they surely would not have wished upon themselves. Fervent Jewish nationalism may be an understandable reaction to a history of persecution, just as Palestinian nationalism has been forged out of the experience of dispossession and domination.

But history has also rendered impossible the coincidence of nation and territory here, without massive further population movements. So a choice has to be made, between full rights for all in a truly multi-national state, including an appropriate place, and national 'self-determination' which will involve some internal exclusion or expulsion. An apt finale is provided in a discussion of the relationship between territory and membership by Michael Walzer (1983, p. 43):

The state owes something to its inhabitants simply, without reference to their collective or national identity. And the first place to which the inhabitants are entitled is surely the place where they and their families have lived and made a life. The attachments and expectations they have formed argue against a forced transfer to another country. If they can't have this particular piece of land (or house or apartment), then some other must be found for them within the same general 'place'. . . New states and governments must make their peace with the old inhabitants of the land they rule.

Displacement by market forces

The displacement of people is not always a result of deliberate actions of others seeking their territory, motivated by such concerns as nationalism or racism. It can also be a consequence of the way the economy operates, selecting some places for prosperity and others for decline and possibly abandonment. Market forces are the 'hidden hand' which Adam Smith and his successors saw guiding a freely competitive economy, allocating resources and distributing returns according to the dictates of supply and demand, with anonymous impartiality. While some people find this concept morally appealing, to others it requires an act of faith akin to religious devotion. For those handed unemployment, the redundancy of their community, or insufficient money to pay the rent, the impact of market forces can be devastating.

It may even create pressure to move, to relinquish their place. To be a victim of market forces may be far more difficult to comprehend than being evicted by agents of apartheid, anti-Semitism or Zionism. The market's claims to moral purpose may seem more plausible, even to its victims, yet to be told that your loss helps to maximize society's aggregate utility is not much consolation.

A brief taste of the experience of the impact of market forces adds another dimension to the more conventional cases thus far considered. The sources available are similar to those used already in this chapter, including personal accounts, novels and newspapers as well as academic research. Two instances from the press provide illustrations.

The first concerns one of the communities affected by the pit closures which have greatly reduced the scale of Britain's coal-mining industry over the past decade. Johnston (1991b, pp. 108–12) has described something of the nature and strength of these communities, expressed so forcibly in the strike of 1984–5. The following is from a letter to *The Guardian* (from B. Richmond, 10 February 1992):

Long-term unemployment has a pernicious effect. It savages more than the larder. Confidence, pride, and above all dignity suffer, sometimes irreparably as people sink into a well of hopelessness. Despair such as this in any community is as serious as an outbreak of cholera and can ruin as many lives. Soon the realisation sinks in that there are no alternative forms of employment. You are forced to dismiss all thoughts of 'a new start' because you can't sell your house, therefore you can't move to a more prosperous region. The knock-on effect when a town's major employer closes heralds a creeping paralysis which descends on the town as support industries fold and high street shops close and remain empty.

This is the current picture of the town I live in: Golborne, west of Manchester. This small, friendly place lost its main industry last year when the colliery closed, throwing 1,000 men on the dole. I have seen the expressions on the faces of these men, some perhaps only 40 years old, who feel they will never work again. I have watched their wives shopping carefully in the local supermarket, intent on getting the best buy, harassed and shouting at their kids when they demand some unnecessary item like a packet of sweets. The For Sale signs are everywhere, but escape is impossible. It's the cruellest of ironies that the very industry responsible for shattering so many mining family lives in past disasters, has in its final death-throes inflicted this final cataclysm on a vulnerable community.

The physical analogies may be less persuasive than the account of economic impact, but it is the imagery of disease and death which most powerfully evokes the broken link between people and work-place.

Attachment to a mine or factory may be harder to understand than the more frequently idealized sentiments to the soil. But both involve hard labour, and, while it is easy to romanticize the means of production to which some people may be harnessed, almost literally, in brutal exploitation, industrial plants are, in a sense, the people who made them ('dead labour', as Marxists put it). Consider the following account of people's relationship with the Brymbo Steelworks in South Wales, closed in September 1990 with over 1100 redundancies (*Wrexham Evening Leader*, 2 October 1990):[2]

The steelworks has always been there. Our lives belonged to it and it belonged to us. It fed and clothed us, as it had our families for three generations. To children it was a scene of wonder – the emptying of the ladles enjoyed by day, became magical by night with molten liquid spilling gold as it bounced down the bank to empty and leave

---

[2] I am grateful to Thomas Law for this item.

a red glow which lit up the sky ... Generations of families were born, lived, worked and died in its shadow ... Its hooter awakened us in the morning and its humming and clanging put us to sleep at night ... If we couldn't see or hear the steelworks we got homesick.

The association suggested is with something far from inanimate, if not quite as physical as some of the relations with the land noted in the Palestine case.

So, people become attached to places which others may find forbidding, dark, even satanic. To suggest that the unemployed 'get on their bike' to find other work, as did British cabinet minister Norman Tebbit, is greatly to misunderstand deep human feelings about particular places as well as actual constraints on mobility, and to overlook the moral question of the degree of security of attachment to place to which people should be entitled. As Friedmann (1992, p. 40) puts it:

> We are interested in territoriality not because of some obscure spatial metaphysics but because people inhabit these spaces, and it is these flesh-and-blood people who suffer the booms and busts of the economy. People are not an abstract category of labor that moves mechanically at the right time and in just the right proportions to wherever economic opportunities arise. They are social, *connected* beings who live in families, households, and communities and who interact with neighbors, kinfolk, friends, and familiars. Over time, people inhabiting particular places evolve typical patterns of speech, ritual practices, and social practices with which they are comfortable and feel 'at home'.

Loss of community accompanying unemployment can mean loss of home in a literal sense. Homelessness is an issue of growing contemporary concern, even (or especially) in such generally affluent countries as Britain and the United States, where it has become a visually conspicuous feature of many cities. It is generating a large literature, including geographical treatments (e.g. Wolch, 1991). The word 'home' evokes some of the most elevated human claims: where the heart is, there is no place like it, even the Englishman's castle. More specifically: 'A home exists where sentiment and space converge to afford attachment, stability, and a secure sense of personal control. It is an abiding place and a web of trustworthy connections, an anchor of identity and social life, the seat of intimacy and trust from which we pursue our emotional and material needs' (Segal and Baumohl, 1988, p. 249). Somerville (1992, p. 533) identifies the following key signifiers of home and their connotations: 'shelter' – materiality, 'hearth' – warmth, 'heart' – love, 'privacy' – control, 'roots' – source of identity', 'abode' – place, and 'paradise'

– ideality. Homelessness involves the lack of some and perhaps all these desirable attributes.

The meaning of homelessness, like the concept of home itself, is by no means straightforward. Both seem to attract a predominantly technical definition and interpretation, yet have ideological and moral dimensions. Veness (1992, p. 445) points out that 'the figures, facts, and explanations used place the responsibility for homelessness at the feet of national and local governments, or at the feet of those communities and individuals most suffering from the situation'. It is therefore easy, and perhaps convenient, to overlook the underlying economics, and the fact that homelessness, in the general sense of people not having accommodation conforming to prevailing societal norms, tends to be a feature of societies in which housing has become a market commodity. Collectivist societies, from tribal to socialist, conceive of housing as a right, even if the average quantity and quality of provision may not match that of affluent capitalist countries.

The recent resurgence of homelessness in the advanced capitalist world seems to be associated with the end of the post-war era of relatively rapid economic growth, and of the accompanying erosion of state spending on housing and social welfare in general. Changing family structure has also played a role, with the growing number of female single parents particularly vulnerable. Homelessness is part of the process of socio-economic polarization, noted in chapter 6 in the case of the American city. And in Britain (Murie and Forrest, 1988, pp. 129, 131):

[H]omelessness is one symptom of multi-dimensional exclusion from the social consumption norms of the majority ... It is then this chronic and pervasive deprivation in the context of burgeoning affluence which gives rising homelessness a new and worrying dimension. It is a prospect of entrapment, containment and social and spatial immobility rather than temporary disruption which faces many households.

If money buys membership of modern affluent society, nothing more conspicuously symbolizes being black-balled than homelessness.

Table 9.1 shows something of the economic context in the United States. The increasing cost of new housing, in relation to what people earn, puts blacks in a particularly unfavourable position. At the end of the 1980s a typical 30-year-old American spent 45 per cent of income on housing compared with 21 per cent in 1974. The consequences have included a fall in home ownership rates, and a rise in the proportion of families in 'substandard' accommodation in need of repair or lacking some utilities. Homelessness is estimated at anything from 250,000 to 3 million people, depending on how it is defined. In Britain the number of mortgages in arrears and properties repossessed increased dramatically in the early 1990s.

Table 9.1 The receding vision of home ownership in the United States

	1970	1980	1990
Median family income ($) – whites	10,236	21,904	36,915
Median family income ($) – blacks	6,276	12,624	21,423
Median price of new single-family home ($)	23,400	64,200	122,900
as multiple of: white median family income	2.29	2.93	3.33
black median family income	3.73	5.09	5.74

Source: *Statistical Abstract of the United States*, 1992.

The number of people accepted as homeless by local authorities currently approaches 500,000. Meanwhile, one-sixth of London's office space stands empty. Such are the perverse outcomes of market forces.

Something of the experience of the American homeless is provided in a study by Culhane and Fried (1988). How people become homeless, what it feels like and the struggle to find a place to sleep, eat, wash and so on are described with poignant clarity in interviews with homeless people. Two extracts follow, the first from a female respondent, homeless for nearly two years, on beginning to realize what it meant (p. 175):

> I wasn't used at that time to walking around two or three days without a shower. I wasn't used to looking for a place to eat. I wasn't used to wearing the same clothes. These things, when I began to smell myself, these things told me something about society. These things told me that society says, 'You are now unprotected. You are now no good to us.'

And from a man who became homeless after losing his job, on sleeping in the subway (p. 178):

> I was awakened about 2:00 in the morning by four policemen and two German Shepherd dogs. And I just sat down there and said to myself, you know I did everything I was supposed to do. I went to school, I was mischievous as a child, but not a violent child. I went in the service. I came out of service. I worked. I took care of my children. Why? Why is this happening to me? And I started blaming myself for it.

As Culhane and Fried (p. 175) point out, to be homeless is 'to confront the overwhelming sense of being cast out and outcast, to be naked and deserted in the most profound social sense'. And as the respondents reveal, it is also to feel no good, to be to blame. The way the homeless are stigmatized in some conventional discourses is explained as follows (pp. 184–5):

> Much of this discussion virtually ignores the economic, social, and cultural contexts in which homelessness occurs and opts for an individualistic psychologism. The homeless and the conditions of homelessness are presented as caricatures, frozen in a space which silences them, makes them into outlandish images of tramps, bums, alcoholics and psychotics. Some meagre factors that may, indeed, provide a partial accounting of some small proportion of the homeless population, are generalized beyond all warrant. Even the sympathetic discussions often view the homeless as unfortunate failures without adequately evaluating the ways in which our society facilitates the process of skidding economically, socially, psychologically. Thus the discussion is wrapped around the homeless, to cloak them in a pseudo-explanatory otherness which ends up controlling them *and* our understanding of them.

There is no need to extend the discussion into the cities of poorer countries, or to those of the former socialist world in East Europe where homelessness is now emerging as an inevitable accompaniment of market forces. The central point should be clear. Just as there is something deeply wrong with various forms of 'ethnic cleansing', so there is with a process of allocating accommodation which leaves blameless victims not only suffering loss of place but also blaming themselves.

Loss of place

The purpose of this chapter has been to try to convey something of the meaning of having one's place in the world undermined, threatened, and perhaps destroyed. If we can grasp the accompanying sense of loss, we may more readily appreciate the enormity of the possible wrong done, the injustice perpetrated, in this most geographical of situations. The depths of attachment people form with territory and place have long been recognized in humanistic geography. For example, to Tuan (1974, p. 234): 'People demonstrate their sense of place when they apply their moral and aesthetic discernment to sites and locations.' And to Relph (1976, p. 49): 'To be inside a place is to belong to it, and the more profoundly inside you are the stronger is this identity with place.' But geographers have devoted much less attention to the loss of place.

Death is a repetitive theme in the accounts and interpretations we have drawn on in this chapter. A move can precipitate premature death, people may wish to be returned to their place of origin when they die, and the living may feel that they died a little when they left. But most profound is a sense of loss akin to losing a loved one. The analogy with bereavement and mourning has been explored in the context of slum clearance by Marris (1986, p. 57):

> Eviction from the neighbourhood in which one was at home can be almost as disruptive of the meaning of life as the loss of a crucial relationship. Dispossession threatens the whole structure of attachments through which purposes are embodied, because these attachments cannot readily be re-established in an alien setting. In this slum clearance represents the implications of any change where people are dispossessed of the familiar context of their lives, though the loss may be less sudden and the object of attachment less tangible. In all such situations, the ambivalence of grieving has to work itself out.

However, whereas societies have their own, often ritualized ways of mourning lost people, usually involving the completion of stages required to come to terms with death, this is not the case for loss of home and neighbourhood. This can make loss of place all the harder to bear. People can get stuck, perhaps at the stage of over-valuing what may not have been a particularly pleasant environment. This helps to explain what Cornwell (1984, p. 52) found in East London, for example, as people idealized a former community life which was actually one of poverty and violence: 'This is chronic grief, in which the bereaved person refuses to let go of the past, but holds on to it and mummifies and romanticizes it instead.'

A graphic account of the destruction, or annihilation, of place in the interests of greater profit has been provided by Porteous (1988). One of the people whose place was threatened by the expansion of an industrial plant is quoted as saying: 'I wonder to myself, how, if the positions were reversed, would they feel? . . . they have murdered our village' (p. 86). Perhaps it is not surprising, in more extreme circumstances, that the annihilation of place can also be accompanied by killing the people themselves. In some experiential sense the people and the place are one. Those who would take other people's place should have very good reason, and the moral principle of universalization, expressed in the question of how they would feel if the positions were reversed, is an appropriate test of whether the reason is good enough.

Epilogue

I am to spend the night in the West Bank. I am going to Tel Aviv tomorrow, and someone has invited me to stay at his home tonight so we can travel together next morning. I am a little apprehensive. I have driven and been driven in these territories before, but usually in daylight; now I have to go by bus, in the dark, to a place I do not know. The location is not even clear on my map, though I can actually see roughly where it is from my room on the Mount Scopus university campus in Jerusalem: among the pinpricks of light just visible at night on a far hill-side. I have asked people where it is. One replied, 'It is in the West Bank. I never go there.' The other described it as a suburb of Jerusalem. Such is the difference in perception of this kind of place, even by Israelis.

I get on the bus, and ask the driver to tell me when to get off. The bus cuts through the city, then out along the new road by-passing Arab settlements. It is very dark, and I feel nowhere. After half an hour we reach my stop, where my host is waiting as promised. We walk to his family home. What I can see certainly is suburban. But it is cold, wet and windy with a touch of snow in the air. Why would anyone want to live on such a bleak hill-top? This place it actually part of a block of Jewish settlements older than the state of Israel itself, destroyed in 1948 and resettled after the 1967 war. They separate and dominate Arab villages; part of the carefully contrived geography of survival. And the environment will be much nicer in summer, with fantastic views over the Judean desert to the Dead Sea.

My hosts describe themselves as religious, but not ultra-orthodox. They are descended from distinguished rabbinical families. They have ancient copies of the Talmud, among other religious memorabilia miraculously preserved and brought to Israel. Next morning he goes to the synagogue at six with one of his sons, for an hour of study before the working day. After breakfast we drive around, past neat, modern dwellings, shops, school and so on, serving some hundreds of people. Mist makes the neighbouring settlements barely visible, adding to a sense of enclosed isolation (rather like the re-creations of the European ghetto in orthodox districts of Jerusalem). Arabs are working on new structures: labour is probably the only link between the two different kinds of settlements, the two peoples. To its inhabitants, this place is home, part of the Land of Israel. If there is to be land for peace in some political negotiation, this is unlikely to be part of it.

We catch the bus back to Jerusalem. Daylight reveals huge refugee camps near Bethlehem, with high wire fences to protect passing vehicles from stones thrown by those within. We arrive at Jerusalem's bus station, and find a bomb alert. Everyone has to move back, as a team of soldiers remove a suspicious object. It is all over in half an hour, and we leave for Tel Aviv. We pass relics of war: old trucks left by the roadside as memorials to the dead. We pass Arab villages, and places where some others used to be.

Reflecting on the experience later, I have more of a sense of what the land means to Jews, and of some of the consequences. I saw Arabs, saw where they live and used to live. But I did not encounter any, hear their point of view. There have been other times and places, in villages and the Arab quarter of towns. But I can only imagine what it is really like, to be a people of nowhere. Perhaps I would understand better if I was a Jew, for they had nowhere for so long.

10

Conclusion: Returning to Social Justice

The real duty ... is not to explain our sorry reality, but to improve it.

August Lösch, *The Economics of Location* (1954)

The point of morality is not to mirror the world, but to change it.

Bernard Williams, *Morality: an introduction to ethics* (1972)

The previous four chapters have enabled us to explore social justice in some actual situations, from some of the theoretical perspectives introduced in Part I. While the intention has not been to demonstrate the power or superiority of any particular clearly-defined perspective, some have come to the surface more strongly than others, as anticipated in chapter 5. The purpose of this conclusion is to crystallize what might be thought of as a partial synthesis of theory and practice, bringing together those arguments which seem to have made most sense of the cases under review.

We begin with an extension of the discussion of the relationship between social justice and market forces in chapter 9. We then resurrect the egalitarian case, including John Rawls's formulation emphasizing benefits to the worst-off, and Michael Walzer's notion of spheres of justice. This leads on to the proposition that there may be defensible grounds for some universal principles of social justice. Finally, there is a brief reminder of the significance of social justice to geography.

Market (in)justice

It should be clear from some of the case material presented, if not already obvious, that social justice should not be left to market forces. Or, to put it another way, to commend observed market outcomes on the grounds that they are the results of a just process of distribution is not credible. However, the renewed faith in the market which has accompanied neo-conservative politics in countries like Britain and the United States, along with adoption of some semblance of a market economy in the former socialist countries of

East Europe and the USSR, requires a reminder of what can no longer be taken as understood by all but free market fanatics.

The basic problem with the conventional neoclassical formulation of the free market is its narrow conception of social justice. A perfectly competitive market working with the perfection prescribed in theory will distribute rewards to participants in the economy according to what purports to be society's appraisal of the value of the labour, capital and other resources which they contribute to production. In other words, people are paid according to the value other people place on their inputs, in a pecuniary calculus performed by the market. If the outcome of the perfect free market maximizes aggregate societal welfare, which by definition should be the case, then the attendant distribution of income and other benefits can also be justified on utilitarian grounds (see chapter 3). It is the coincidence of efficiency and equity which gives the market such appeal, along with its capacity to co-ordinate multitudinous individual decisions without conscious control. If left to its own devices, the system should establish a state of equilibrium conforming to the Pareto criterion, such that no one can be made better-off without someone else being made worse-off.

But such a system pays no regard to people's needs, except to the extent that they can back them with the purchasing power to influence market forces. And it is not that the market will respond to any capacity to purchase: once a particular structure of outputs has been generated, reflecting a generally preferred if not universally accepted or affordable way of life, it can in practice be universalized through the effective denial of alternatives. Thus, in the American and British city, for example, relatively poor people may be able to afford some modest expenditure on housing, for example, but producers find it more profitable to respond to the greater purchasing power of the well-to-do and ignore the ineffective demand of others. Hence the problem of what is referred to as 'affordable housing', and the necessity of state intervention even in the most affluent market economies, to provide that basic human need of a place in which to live.

At the extreme, the market does not even guarantee people a place *on* which to live. If all land is privately owned and available only at prices some people cannot afford, they are, literally, priced out of a place in the world. The same could even be true if the state owned some or all of the land, but allowed market forces to determine its use. Lest this scenario be regarded as rhetorical hyperbole, then, it must be recognized that numerous of the Third World poor, 'squatting' on land owned by others (e.g. in some of South Africa's shack settlements), are occupying illegally what may be the only place they can find on which to live. It is a bizarre system that can, in effect, deprive people of this basic necessity of life, along with others. Of course, governments step in to ameliorate such outcomes (for example, by legitimizing squatting in site-and-service developments), but not for everyone, everywhere. And even if it did, the basic point would still stand: if the right to life (once born) is to be respected, then a system that can logically deny some people the necessities for life is hard to defend from a moral point of view. It requires either some extreme form of libertarianism prioritizing individual freedom of action, or elevation of the maximization of aggregate welfare to the status of ultimate moral value (without regard for the egalitarian implications, the decreasing marginal utility of money), to justify the fate of those who lose, in the absence of a convincing demonstration that no one would be better-off under any alternative economic arrangements.

There are practical as well as moral problems in approving market outcomes. For markets to generate both efficiency in production and equity in distribution, as usually defined in the neoclassical framework, they must operate in a particular way. They require perfectly informed and rational profit/satisfaction-seeking behaviour on the part of producers/consumers, including instantaneous adjustment of prices, supply and demand to change, and a scale of units of production insufficient for individual participants to set prices rather than accept those generated in the market place, or otherwise to take advantage of size which at the extreme achieves monopoly power. The departure of these conditions from real life is obvious. Among other actual market imperfections, geographical space greatly constrains the mobility of people and resources in response to market signals, and creates the possibility of local producer monopoly as well as local lack of jobs.

But it is not even necessary to engage reality to reveal the fundamental practical difficulty posed in existing market economies with respect to social justice, within the restricted terms of the free-market model itself. This is the dependence of the distribution of life chances being generated on the pre-existing distribution of income, wealth and other resources. Those with most money will have the greatest power to influence what is produced, while those who happen to own (or otherwise control) land and its natural resources or have capital to invest can exert an influence denied those with only their labour to sell. Very simply, the claim to generate social justice depends on the justice of the distribution that already drives the system. That this crucial condition has been recognized for a long time is illustrated in the following passage from an early critique of neoclassical welfare economics (Graaff, 1957, p. 155):

> Much of orthodox welfare theory lacks realism precisely because it assumes that the desired distribution of wealth has already been attained (and is somehow maintained) and then proceeds to regard the price system as a highly specialized resource-allocation mechanism which exercises no influence whatever on the distribution of wealth. Such a view is not easy to defend.

That this point could not be ignored by mainstream economics is demonstrated in an old edition of a mass-circulation textbook (Samuelson, 1973, p. 458):

> If the dollar votes of different consumers represent an 'equitable' allocation, so that each person's dollar represented as ethically deserved 'pull' on the market as any other's, there would be no need to make the following qualification: Efficient production and pricing does not mean that the FOR WHOM problem of society is being properly solved; it only means that the WHAT and HOW problems are being solved consistent with the *existing distribution* of dollar-voting power and of sharing in natural wealth and GNP.

This vital qualification highlights the difficulty, if not impossibility, of describing as equitable or just the structure and distribution of outputs of an actual market economy, as well as the distribution of earnings, even without reference to market imperfections.

While the perpetuation of poverty, even in the most affluent capitalist countries, is the usual focus for the critique of market outcomes, in this book we have stressed the related issues of degree and trends in inequality (in chapters 6, 7 and 8) and deprivation of place (chapter 9). We return to (in)equality in the next section. A few more observations on the impact of market forces on people's homes and communities here may help to consolidate the point that markets create a kind of vulnerability that assails common-sense conceptions of what is right.

If people commit themselves to a particular life plan, realistically arrived at in the light of fairly reliable information about the world, and of their place within it, then it seems reasonable for them to have some security that it can be carried out. Not complete security, of course, as some uncertainty is part of human life, but enough security to make it worthwhile drawing up a plan rather than simply allowing things to happen. If, within their life plan, people commit themselves to a certain kind of work, perhaps involving time-consuming training, then they are surely entitled to a degree of security greater than, say, a month's notice and, if they are lucky, a little compensation. Similarly, if people put down roots in a place, merging their identity with it, they are surely entitled to more security of residence than the continuation of local market demands for their labour. Such entitlements arise from being human, and not an inanimate factor of production.

The moral issue at stake is one of responsibility and blame. When particular occupations become redundant, in the face of technological progress for example, and when particular communities become redundant with plant or pit closures, it is seldom the fault of the work-force, yet they are expected to bear much of the cost. They do not have the capacity to foretell the future, and while plant closure may be an outcome of ineluctable economic forces, to those affected it is surely akin to bad luck and should be morally irrelevant to their life chances. In this respect the profit surface over which capital moves in pursuit of maximum returns is analogous to the natural endowment of the land: something over which individuals have little if any control. The state may intervene, of course, with partial compensation for lost earnings, and schemes to attract new employment and train people for new kinds of work. But there is no guarantee, in a market economy, that people's original position (materially and geographically) can be maintained or restored.

The demise of an industrial community is a particularly vivid case of the kind of outcome which worries liberals who might otherwise be expected to laud the freedom of a market economy. For example, Walzer (1983, p. 301) sees this as something more than an economic problem: 'Surely to uproot a community, to require large-scale migration, to deprive people of homes they have lived in for many years; these are political acts, and acts of a rather extreme sort.' As he says elsewhere, while liberalism endorses mobility as an enactment of liberty, there is an underside to it: 'Moving may be a personal adventure in our standard cultural mythologies, but it is often a family trauma in real life' (Walzer, 1990, p. 12). He suggests that, at a certain point in the development of an enterprise, it must pass out of entrepreneurial control. With company towns in mind, he goes further: 'Men and women must collectively control the place where they live in order to be safe in their own homes' (1983, p. 300). This may afford people some protection from arbitrary plant closure, but not ultimately from the market forces to which any controllers have to respond. This is another way of recognizing that the market owes no one, anywhere, a living, or a place.

Arguing the alternative of a centrally planned or socialist economic system appears, at the moment, to be flying in the face of history. But this does not mean that there is no alternative at all to the kind of imperfect market capitalism which prevails in much of the world and promises (or threatens) to envelope much of the rest. Most people in advanced capitalist countries are undoubtedly better-off than they would have been under East European or Soviet-style socialism. This comparison would also pass a utilitarian test of aggregate maximization of some material index of well-being. But it is less obvious that capitalism satisfies the Pareto criterion of making everyone better-off, or no one worse-off, than under socialism, even by the criterion of material living standards. Indeed, post-socialist Russia seems bent on proving the reverse: most people are now worse-off than before.

It is therefore understandable as well as desirable that the possibility of some form of 'market socialism' will continue to be debated (e.g. Roemer, 1992). Combining the efficiency benefits of markets unimpeded by monopoly and similar imperfections, with sufficient state control to ensure production and (re)distribution in the interests of guaranteeing everyone basic material needs and the security of a place in the world, may not be unambiguously preferable to current capitalism. Some people would lose – the rich. But it will become increasingly necessary to argue for institutions which ensure the satisfaction of basic needs and social security, as universal welfare provision comes under mounting scrutiny even in the advanced capitalist world. After all, the logic of the system is for highly mobile capital to move to where most profit can be made, and this is often where the cost of labour, including social provision, is low. Relatively rapid economic growth along with favourable terms of trade has for a long time protected rich nations with high labour costs from competition from poorer ones; as the twentieth century comes to a close this may no longer be the case. Political struggles to uphold commitments to social security may provide some defence against the erosion of privileged people's living standards and security. But the convergence of returns to labour, which markets are supposed to promote, is uncomfortably consistent with the universal immiserization of the proletariat as capital competes to maintain profits: one of Marx's predictions which may yet be fulfilled.

Egalitarian social justice

The commitment to some form of egalitarianism as a foundation for social justice will have emerged fairly clearly from various parts of this book. In particular, it was proposed in chapter 5 that equalization, or moving closer to equality, provided a morally defensible pragmatic response to the degree of inequality manifest in the contemporary world. Very simply, the assertion was that inequality has become too great to be justified, so the gap(s) should be narrowed.

As was pointed out in chapter 3, egalitarianism is a difficult case to argue. On the one hand is the proposition that our common humanity gives us the same basic needs and capacity for pleasure and pain, as well as equal moral worth as individuals. Any advantages which some people are able to gain over others are a consequence of such attributes as genetic make-up, family background, or place of birth on the unevenly endowed earth or differentiated opportunity surface generated by economic forces, which are beyond people's control and therefore cannot underpin a moral case for desert or entitlement. On the other hand, not to reward people's effort or ambition may be wrong, even if their achievements arise from morally arbitrary attributes including luck, especially if some other people and possibly everyone else also benefits from them. Hence the power of John Rawls's compromise, which justifies inequality to the extent that it benefits all and especially the worst-off. Any egalitarian strategy must also face the technical problem of unscrambling the relationship between ultimate outcomes (people's well-being in the most comprehensive sense), the resources which people need to enhance their well-being (to an unequal extent, depending on their circumstances), and intervening considerations such as opportunities or Amartya Sen's capabilities (see chapter 5).

We will briefly reopen some issues raised in earlier chapters, which have a bearing on the egalitarian position. The first is the notion of justice as equalization, as developed in connection with Rawls's principle (in chapter 5), in the context of the cases of East Europe and South Africa explored in chapters 7 and 8. Take post-socialist society first, as exemplified by the former Soviet Union. Figure 10.1a is a version of a figure used earlier, in which the curve from O to R is a Rawlsian trajectory along which the least well-off do as well as possible by virtue of the benefits derived from others being better-off. To simplify matters, assume that society comprises the two groups of the mass (M) and the privileged elite or *nomenclatura* (N). Suppose that, under socialism, society was on the welfare frontier W_2. The actual distribution might have been at P on the Rawlsian track (however unlikely), at a point like Q which was too close to perfect equality (the line OE) to provide incentives for the most productive to produce more, or at a point like S at which elite privilege had gone too far. The implication of both Q and S is that future production possibilities (the attainment of a higher W) would be frustrated. What was hoped for, after the end of socialism, was to attain a higher level of production (like W_3), possibly at the Rawls maximin point R but in any event with the mass better-off even if the new entrepreneurs (N) driving economic growth did so well as to increase inequality. What has actually happened, in the early years of transition, is a move onto a lower production frontier (W_1), possibly to T, but far more plausibly to a point like U where the new elite are even better-off than the old *nomenclatura*, while the mass are worse-off than under socialism. What is required for life to improve for the vast majority is to establish the degree of inequality (incentives) necessary to stimulate economic growth, without entrenching the *nouveau riche* in such a position of privilege that the standard of living of the mass will not, soon, be made as advantageous as possible. To assert that the present depressed living standards of the mass are, in fact, as high as possible in the transition to a new economy requires enormous faith in the future capacity to restore a process of equalization. The great danger for social justice is that the newly advantaged group will be able to translate their economic power into the political power to reproduce the status quo, rather as under capitalism elsewhere.

There is also the question of who is in the new privileged position. There is no guarantee that former members of the *nomenclatura* or managers of state enterprises who have somehow come to control privatized assets are those best able to operate in a market economy. Furthermore, the harnessing of unbridled self-interest to some conception of the general good depends on the fulfilment of assumptions about how a market economy actually operates,

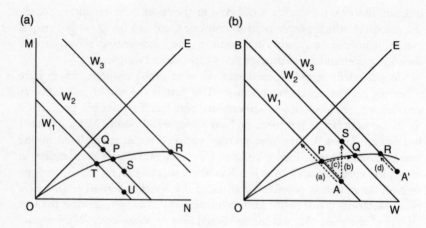

Figure 10.1   Interpretations of social justice in (a) Russia after socialism, and (b) South Africa after apartheid, within a Rawlsian framework.

outlined in the previous section, which are arguably even more inconsistent with the reality of the ruins of socialism than under mature capitalism. The absence of institutions such as a reliable system of credit, ignorance of investment opportunities, rampant inflation and general uncertainty heightening risk are among the more obvious examples.

If the efficiency benefits to be derived from market mechanisms are to be associated with distributive outcomes with some claim to equity, then the issue of social justice must be integral to the process of economic and political reform. This requires moral thinking, to begin to fill the vacuum left by the end of socialism. Expectations that the market will somehow perform magic are not enough. Indeed, it could be a prescription for the consolidation of a new privileged (and possibly oppressive) elite not much different from the old one, whose opportunities to accumulate wealth under the new conditions may have depended on neither enterprise nor honesty.

Figure 10.1b poses aspects of the post-apartheid South African situation in terms of Rawlsian egalitarianism. Under apartheid, the Whites (W) had a great advantage over the Blacks (B), as suggested by point A. Inequality was far greater than could be justified in the interests of the worst-off (Blacks). Point P on the Rawlsian track to the maximin position R would have been preferable. Three possible trajectories of redistribution are depicted. Path (a) involves redistribution of existing resources from Whites to Blacks, with the risk of overshooting P in pursuit of perfect equality (on the line OE). Track (b) represents the redistribution of growth (moving from W_1 to W_2), with the risk implicit in giving all the product of growth to the Blacks (at S) of taking equalisation too far, thus prejudicing the future position of the worst-off which would be better at Q. Track (c) is a version of growth through redistribution, where the extent of immediate redistribution (from A to P) is well judged and places society on a Rawlsian trajectory (P to Q) into the future. An alternative apartheid position to A might be A', leaving only the one option (d) of redistribution of existing resources (on W_3) from Whites to Blacks if society is to get onto a Rawlsian trajectory. The actual relationships are purely imaginary; the purpose is to show that the interdependence of the well-being of different groups provides some grounds for considering what kind of equalization strategy can best be justified.

The fundamental point of these two illustrations is that the general (universal) proposition that social justice is manifest in a process of equalization requires reference to the actual situation. Inequality among classes, race groups, genders or regions may so obviously require to be narrowed that this objective is pursued without regard to all the consequences. As we observed in chapter 5, and the South African case in chapter 8, a more equal society in which everyone is worse-off is not an enticing prospect. It must also be recognized that alternative strategies of reform and (re)distribution will be contested, within the specific (im)balance of forces prevailing in the situation in question, and that, once established (or re-established), economic–political–social structures have their own reproductive imperatives which may proceed independently of ideals of social justice. This stresses, again, the importance of getting the starting conditions right.

Another aspect of egalitarianism which we have found helpful, but which requires careful attention to actual situations, is the one explained by Michael Walzer in his concept of spheres of justice (see chapter 4). Walzer argued that different distributions could be justified in different spheres of life. The associated problem he identified, and which we have encountered under both capitalism and socialism, is that advantage in one sphere tends to generate advantage in other spheres: the role of the dominant good. Under capitalism the dominant good tends to be money, which buys a whole range of other advantages. Under socialism, it was state evaluation of labour contribution, and position in the controlling elite or the *nomenclatura*, which generated access to various goods, services and privileges.

These interlocking spheres compounding inequality are obviously a source of injustice. The starting point or dominant good could even be race, gender, or locality: once given (rather than chosen), unequal life chances in various spheres follow from what should be a morally irrelevant difference. Such interdependencies need to be blocked, if distribution in each sphere is to be on the basis of its own relevant criteria, manifest possibly but not necessarily in equality.

While it is not the intention here to provide a blue-print for a superior society, the following proposal might address this particular issue. People should not be able to begin life with, or subsequently acquire, great advantages over others in economic or political power, just as race, gender and so on should not constitute privileged starting positions. This would involve constraints on the inheritance of wealth, and on the amount which could be accumulated from a more or less equal start. The inheritance of position with some special status or potential political influence, like a seat in the British House of Lords, would not be allowed. Then, people would earn income according to the contribution of their labour (physical and mental), within a much narrower range than, for example, in Britain today (set by taxation if necessary), but wide enough to act as incentives to work to the best of their ability. Income could be spent on consumer goods, including a housing stock differentiated (as it already is) according to quality, local environment and attributes appealing to people with different life-styles and at different stages in the life cycle, with adequate provision for everyone by virtue of guaranteed minimum income or public housing provision. The interlocking of these limited spheres would not do much harm, providing that the range of goods available for purchase was not such as to leave many people feeling deprivation and envy.

Where the interlocking would stop would be in such spheres as education, health care and the law. Here any personal advantage can be turned to other advantages: a privileged education to occupational advantage, privileged health care to more effective and better remunerated work, and privileged access to legal services to all manner of advantages over possible adversaries. These are therefore spheres in which the principle of strict equality according to need should apply, so as to give people the same capabilities in society: education according to any need for remedial services, health care when ill, legal assistance when a case needs to be made. And no locational advantages, such as better schools or hospitals in places inhabited by richer people: the reverse would be more likely. Truly egalitarian services would be publicly provided, with no possibility for private practice. Once inequality in income or wealth is allowed to penetrate these crucial spheres, the rich can opt out into private provision of higher quality, and their personal vested interest in the quality of public provision is gone. If the question of privileged access for people in crucial leadership roles arises, the best test may well be, after Rawls, whether the worst-off in society would thereby benefit.

Another important aspect of egalitarianism, also raised by Walzer, is membership. Who is to count, in the distribution of things, equally or otherwise? This is where geographical jurisdictions become so important, extending or limiting those people who qualify for the benefits which membership of a local authority or nationality brings. There are some major moral issues involved in this question. We have already considered the implications of partial internal exclusion in the cases of apartheid in South Africa and Arabs in Palestine (chapter 9). Another topical case is the closure of western Europe (or the so-called European Community) to other peoples, especially those of the post-socialist countries to the east. Border controls are being strengthened, to keep out 'foreigners' and especially 'economic migrants'. And trade barriers are maintained: free movement of goods as well as people within the EC, but not between the EC and the rest. Thus, former socialist societies are exhorted to set up market economies, but denied equal access to the most lucrative markets close by. There is something deeply worrying about the exclusion of Polish steel, for example, from the western European markets needed to make up for those lost in the former USSR. But, if 'we' (in the EC) let in 'their' steel, or coal, textiles or other things for which they may have comparative advantage, it will be at the cost of 'our' jobs.

Thus, the rich and powerful countries entrench their privilege. At a more local scale, rich neighbourhoods add superior services to their fine homes, then erect barriers (sometimes literally) to keep others out. The moral problem is that, while some of this privilege may possibly have been earned, by people choosing to work hard while others elsewhere idled their time away, this is unlikely to justify the extent of national or local privilege arising from a geographical version of interlocking spheres. Much of this spatial inequality is likely to have arisen from the chance natural endowment of rich soil or bountiful mineral wealth, from the selective process of capital investment seeking profits, and from the local congregation of people in a position to benefit most and who may simply have been fortunate enough to be in the right place at the right time. None of this can readily be considered deserved. Any redistribution from rich to less well endowed neighbourhoods or regions takes place after the boundaries of membership have been set up, and at the discretion of the donors. As for more distant others, it is left to international development aid, at a trivial scale compared with the riches of the richest countries.

The possibility of universals

The emergence of what is usually referred to as postmodern thinking in recent years has discouraged the search for universals. This is true in social science, with the critique of grand, meta-theory which claims at least the possibility of bringing all social life within some overarching explanatory framework. It is also true in moral thinking, including that strand concerned with social justice. Something of the debate has been indicated in earlier chapters, in the discussion of relativism in moral philosophy (chapter 2) and in a geographical context (chapter 5), as well as in reviews of theoretical perspectives on social justice which challenge the mainstream from feminist and communitarian perspectives (chapter 4). In particular, the emphasis on human difference and practice of partiality confronts the human sameness on the basis of which equal and impartial treatment are held to be right. This is not the place for a full engagement with postmodern thinking;

the purpose of what follows is merely to sketch out a renewed case for the possibility of some universal propositions in the understanding and pursuit of social justice, bearing in mind aspects of the postmodern position.

The postmodern stance is relativist. Social justice has no universal meaning; it is specific to particular people, times and places, reflecting their 'situatedness' or 'positionality', i.e. the actual circumstances in which people find themselves. This is exemplified by Marx's proposition that a particular conception of justice is internal to capitalism (as discussed in chapter 4); the ruling class has the power to impose its own conception of justice. The postmodern perspective stresses what Harvey (1992b, p. 596) describes as, 'those power differentials which in turn produce different conceptions of justice and embed them in a struggle over the ideological hegemony between classes, races, ethnic and political groupings as well as across the gender divide'. Different interest groups try to promote their own conception of justice, emphasizing the goals of gender or racial equality, for example, or the right of people to realize whatever they can from their property or personal aptitudes. The conception of justice which prevails will reflect the relative power of interested parties to influence the process of competition between alternative discourses, as exemplified in the prominence of a government and business establishment perspective in South Africa (chapter 8). In short, might makes right, as Pratt (1993, p. 57) puts it: 'the view heard is of necessity the one whose supporters have the most clout.' And without an appeal to universals, who is to say might may be wrong?

Harvey (1993) has elaborated concern that the postmodern critique of universalism renders any application of the concept of justice problematic. It is the continuing and perhaps increasingly important need to identify and combat social injustice, as something which people actually experience and wish to challenge, which is turning attention back to the possibility of principles which can transcend local, group or cultural specificity, while still having regard to criticisms of universalizing theory which marginalizes 'others' by paying insufficient attention to human differences. Harvey commends the approaches of Michael Walzer and Iris Marion Young (see chapter 4), quoting with approval the following distinction between meanings of universality: 'Universality in the sense of the participation and inclusion of everyone in moral and social life does not imply universality in the sense of the adoption of a general point of view which leaves behind particular affiliations, feelings, commitments, and desires' (Young, 1990a, p. 105). To Young, it is not universality itself which is the problem, but the way the concept has been used 'to inhibit universal inclusion and participation'. There is much in the suspicion of Harvey (1992c, p. 321) that postmodern claims 'fetishizing situatedness' are 'sophisticated camouflage for claiming higher moral authority'.

Some aspects of similar concerns in contemporary moral philosophy may be considered briefly. A point of departure is provided by the discussion of responsibility to people in other parts of the world, introduced at the end of the previous section. The issue was also raised, in different contexts, in chapters 4 and 5; here we merely consolidate the case, in the context of universals. The argument from the perspective of impartiality would be that we owe distant others the same consideration that we give to those close to us; that is, we have no grounds for favouring 'our own' people over others, as all have equal moral worth. There are practical problems with this position, which at an individual level could require us all to share what we have in minute portions with all others, or at least to try to see things from the point of view of all others involved as well as from our own perhaps selfish perspective. But the most potent challenge in recent years has come from those who find it difficult to reconcile impartiality with close personal relationships intrinsic to which is partiality.

Friedman (1991, p. 818) begins a discussion of the practice of partiality with the following recognition: 'Hardly any moral philosopher, these days, would deny that we are each entitled to favour our loved ones. Some would say, even more strongly, that we ought to favour them, that it is not simply a moral option.' Partiality in this sense is closely related to the ethic of care deployed in some feminist critiques of conventional concepts of justice (see chapter 4). It is a natural human sentiment, a source of personal integrity and fulfilment, part of a mutuality which contributes to human well-being or the good life. However, partiality is by no means unproblematic. As Friedman explains, it is dependent on the nature of the relationships it helps to sustain. Caring for vulnerable members of the family, friends or neighbours has a different moral status from a woman putting up with domestic violence, for example, or people favouring fellow members of a chauvinistic national or racial group like the British National Party or the Ku Klux Klan.

But it is the uneven capacity to favour close people that raises most serious problems with partiality, especially when viewed geographically, as we hinted in chapter 5. Friedman (1991, pp. 828–9) explains as follows:

> The one who really needs moral attention is the person who lacks resources and who would not be adequately cared for even if all her friends and family were as partial toward her as they could be because they, too, lack resources. There are systematic social inequalities among different 'neighborhoods' in the distribution of resources for loving and caring . . .

[W]hether or not, and to what extent, someone benefits from certain partialist relationship conventions has a lot to do with her 'social location', the sort of luck she had in being born to, adopted by, or linked by marriage to, relations with adequate resources for caretaking, nurturing, and protecting.

Thus the benefit from partiality untempered by redistribution of wealth or resources is unevenly experienced: it could simply reflect and help to reproduce existing geographical patterns of material inequality. If partiality is everyone's moral prerogative, and responsibility, good both to receive and to give, then an argument for redistribution follows. Friedman (1991, p. 831) concludes: 'by viewing partiality as morally valuable because of what it ultimately contributes to integrity and human fulfilment, and by considering the reality of unequally distributed resources, we are led to a notion that sounds suspiciously like the requirement of moral impartiality.' And, she might have added, like the equalization of what is required to care for close people. This indicates a way of bridging the gap between local partiality and concern for distant others.

Another critique of the ethic of care has been offered by Mendus (1993), who recognizes that, because this is difficult to extend beyond the local and familiar, it is of limited use in addressing the political problems of the modern world. She sees insights from the ethics of care supplementing not replacing an ethics of justice (see the similar argument in chapter 4). But what is more important in the present context, she takes the case of gender inequality and argues that concentrating on what may be conveyed as women's natural role has not done much to improve their political position; rather, 'it is emphasis on common humanity *despite* difference which has served women far better since it has provided standards of impartiality which are necessary in the pursuit of equality' (p. 20). She also claims that the ethic of care may be vulnerable to the charge of nostalgia and lack of realism about the facts of the modern world: echoing earlier assertions, she notes that, 'unsupported by considerations of justice and equality, care may simply not extend reliably beyond one's own family, group, or clan, to the wider world of unknown others'.

Similar views can be found elsewhere. For example, in his introduction to Jürgen Habermas's attempt to ground a universal approach to morality in discourse ethics (see chapter 2), McCarthy (1990, p. xiii) asserts:

Postmodernist critiques of moral universalism too often simply ignore the fact that it is precisely notions of fairness, impartiality, respect for the integrity and dignity of the individual, and the like that undergird respectful tolerance of difference by placing limits on egocentrism. Typically, such notions are simply taken for granted in anti-universalist invocations of otherness and difference – which are, it evidently goes without saying, to be respected, not obliterated.

Habermas (1990, pp. 202–3) himself completes the circle by stating: 'The equal rights of individuals and the equal respect for the personal dignity of each depends on a network of interpersonal relations and a system of mutual recognitions.' We should not be surprised if these defensible universals, which underpin some form of egalitarian justice, are linked to the way people relate to one another in real geographical and historical settings.

Added to these indications of the universal significance of equality and impartiality are signs that geographers may be emerging from immersion in postmodern thinking, to recognize the need to address continuing problems. Susan Smith (1993, pp. 55, 72) points to 'persistencies, consistencies, and continuities in the social world ... inequalities and injustices that we have so far failed to address adequately', and asks: 'how and why do we, as reasonable people, tolerate enduring inequalities?' The answer has something to do with the extent to which recent preoccupations with human difference have tended to obscure the possibility, and desirability, of a universal perspective based on recognition of human similarity. Pratt (1993, p. 56) reminds us of Susan Bordo's caution that the affirmation of difference has become the new coercive orthodoxy, and warns of the danger of 'sliding into an uncritical celebration of plurality and uniqueness' (p. 61). Timely words indeed, if, to some, an echo from the past.

There was a debate in geography, years ago, about the uniqueness of place, which some saw as denying the possibility of generalization. The response was that places being different did not mean that they had nothing in common. The same is true of people, as individuals, as members of classes, races or genders, and as members of locality-based communities or nationalities. That they are different in respects significant to their members' sense of identity does not mean that this necessarily transcends or negates people's common humanity. It is time to reassert the importance of human similarity, and in certain respects their sameness, without going to the other extreme of denying the significance of any difference.

Thus, all human beings share what, for want of evidence to the contrary, we take to be the same capacity for pleasure and pain, to repeat a common starting point. They also share certain basic material needs, as well as others relating to security and the avoidance of harm (explained in chapter 5). And a place in the world, as we have repeatedly stressed. While we can argue about the details, about exactly what level of nutritional intake may be needed in particular environments, for example, about the most effective technical and organizational strategies for their provision, and about the particular attributes people require of place, basic needs remain universal, part of our human nature. They provide a possible, and desirable, basis for the recognition of universal rights (see chapter 2), which entail obligations on others.

The provision of what people require to satisfy basic needs constitutes a minimal case for the impartial treatment of everyone, whoever and wherever they may be. This implies equality, except insofar as particular circumstances may require differential resources, affirmative action or reparation, for example to make up for past deficiencies, discrimination, oppression or whatever may have generated disadvantage. But, at the risk of labouring the point, the universal commitment is to the equal realization at least of what is minimally required to be, and feel, human. Beyond this level, there are still powerful arguments for equality, or against inequality, at higher levels of living, explained earlier in this book. There are also grounds on which some degree of inequality may be justified. But the onus of proof should rest with those who argue against equality, as the natural starting position.

The principle of impartiality, and of universalizability, remain helpful tests of actual human practice. We should not be prepared to do to distant others what we would not do to ourselves and our own kind. For example, we should not be prepared to export noxious and personally or environmentally damaging industrial processes and products to poor countries, or those of the former socialist world, eager though they are for economic growth including some of its more dubious benefits. We should not be prepared to bomb Africans and Arabs into submission for mistreating others, while leaving Europeans in former Yugoslavia free to go about 'ethnic cleansing'. And we should not endorse and help to impose some American-proclaimed new world order on other people who had no say in its somewhat flexible definition.

This last point provides a reminder of the continuing danger, highlighted by the postmodern critique of universalism, that what is taken to be right is imposed by the rich and powerful on the poor and weak. Or by intellectuals with privileged access to existing knowledge and the power to disseminate, challenge or change it. Perhaps the satisfaction of everyone's basic needs or some such egalitarian case is merely an appeal to uninvolved abstraction, which most 'ordinary people' would reject – possibly in favour of rewards according to differential desert, with the weak as well as the idle going to the wall. If so, then this conception of social justice could be formulated in terms of universal principles of desert, for debate along with competing conceptions. What we cannot work with is the position that social justice is purely relative and contingent, with no possibility of critique external to the individual, group, locality or discourse concerned. Nor should we accept that those who devote their lives to the clarification of issues of morality and social justice have no grounds to challenge common-sense understandings.

We should not allow uncritical deference to other people's views and cultures to deny the possibility that some kinds of behaviour, ways of life and even moral codes are wrong. The best case to make against them is that they assail defensible universals. For example, punishment by physical mutilation assails the principle of integrity of the individual's body, denial of which opens the way to all manner of other bad practices – from torture to personality manipulation. Killing people for pleasure may have been part of the Imperial Roman way of life, but is universally condemned today and was surely not right two thousand years ago or even ever. Fox hunting and hare coursing may be part of country life to some people, as bull fighting may be part of a national culture, but they assail the principle that animals should not be killed for people's entertainment, which protects all manner of other creatures from the depravities of humankind. And so on.

To Harvey (1993), and some others, the task now is to reclaim the terrain of justice and rights for 'progressive' political purposes. This requires new ways of formulating and answering the old question, familiar in moral philosophy, of identifying relevant differences, or in more postmodern parlance, the difference between significant and non-significant others. Similar people, in similar geographical or structural positions, or suffering the same kind of oppression, may find common cause to challenge the prevailing conceptions of justice, and the ideological hegemony of which it forms part. As Harvey points out, and as we have already argued, the universalization of market-place justice is in urgent need of this kind of challenge. And what could be more potent, as a response, than a vision of the good life which replaces individual or parochial self-interest with a universal concern for others and in particular for those most in need, along with a commitment to create the institutions required to give practical force to such sentiments?

A well-known ethics text offers the following account of how people can contribute to the making of morals, or what it's subtitle describes as 'inventing right and wrong' (Mackie, 1977, p. 148, in the gender-specific language of that generation):

> What the individual can do is to remember that there are, in the different circles of relationships with which he is already concerned, various fragments of a moral system which already contribute very considerably to countering specific evils which he, like others, will see as evils; that he can at once take advantage of this system and contribute to its upkeep; but that he may be able, with others, to put pressure on some fragments of the system, so that they come gradually to be more favourable to what he sees as valuable or worthwhile.

The most important universal principle of social justice may be that, in such a process, all should have an equally effective voice, having due regard to the different circumstances, which may include past constraints on the expression of their views. The outcome should be what is most persuasive to those involved, and sustainable against the views of others elsewhere.

Social justice and geography

Little more needs to be said here of the link between geography and social justice. However, there is much contemporary work, and important debates, relevant to the central theme of this volume but which have been barely mentioned, if at all. Those immersed in the 'new cultural geography', locality and community studies, issues of race and gender, may wish to have found more specific connections with their concerns, implicitly if not always explicitly of a moral orientation. Similarly, those familiar with earlier forays into 'territorial social justice', in the tradition of geographical patterns of inequality, may have been surprised to see so little attention given to this theme. Economic geographers, ancient and modern, might have expected the resurrection of old expositions of the distributive impact of facility location, or of the disequalizing impact of industrial restructuring and uneven development. More could certainly have been made of environmental issues relevant to social justice. I have not tried to force the geography in; it emerged, some of it, in the context of social justice as a broad, trans-disciplinary concern of which space, location and distance are integral components.

Some aspects of special geographical interests have been explored. These include spatial variations in human life chances as a dimension of inequality, the constraints imposed on change by existing spatial structures including inherited patterns of inequality and built form of the environment, the importance of the land and how claims to it are made, and the role of place in people's lives. Some geographical issues are central to current debates in moral philosophy, though not necessarily recognized in that field as the partial province of another. Responsibility to distant others is a case in point, as is the spatial dimension of ethical relativism.

Some aspects of the literature on social justice reviewed here will have been of greater interest and relevance to current geographical concerns than others. It is not obvious that geographical research on the plight of poor or marginalized groups is greatly enriched by a grasp of utilitarianism or entitlement theory, for example, though we have found situations in which these perspectives have shed some light. More could have been brought in, for example from the mutual advantage approaches which Barry (1989) explores alongside the more familiar perspective of impartiality. Despite its abstraction, such work may yield important insights into how principles of social justice might emerge in the real world of interdependent self-interested people. But the line had to be drawn somewhere, and I suspect it was not at the expense of too little abstract theory and philosophy.

One of the main strengths of geographical practice, long revered, is the local case study. This approach has enjoyed a revival in recent years, after locality studies and regional geography became rather unfashionable in the era of geography as spatial science. The case studies developed in Part II, while far from comprehensive treatments of the places and issues concerned, should have been sufficient to stress the importance of the specifics of the situation, its temporal spatiality, in getting to grips with social justice in reality. This is where aspiring universals, such as the principle of justice as equalization, or need for place, must be refined in the experience of practice.

An implicit exhortation in the particular cases chosen is for geographers to engage the wider world of inequality and injustice. Some of those concerns which most captivate the discipline, not least during its current engagement with the postmodern turn, seem at times to be more those of a privileged and protected western intellectual elite than of people really in touch with those parts of the world where the most active struggles for new and (hopefully) more socially just institutions are taking place. The poor and oppressed of South Africa and the new poor (and possibly new oppressed) of East Europe attract less attention than those groups in North America or western Europe whose marginalized otherness, awful though it may be, is likely to be endured in comparative material comfort. Geography, and geographers, in richer parts of the world have their own moral conflict to resolve, between the parochial concerns of the relatively rich and responsibility to poorer distant others.

The main message of this book, then, is the importance of geography returning to social justice, in theory and in practice. Susan Smith (1993, p. 72) remarks: 'Without a better sense of the value of normative theory, without more willingness to enter the politics of prescription, geography is powerless to challenge the subtle ideologies that legitimize enduring social inequalities.' These are familiar sentiments to those old enough to have been engaged in geography's original excursion into issues of social relevance and justice, more than two decades ago. This seems to be the sort of time-span needed to recycle earlier ideas. But it is not simply a case of the discipline having come full circle. As with each of the dominant paradigms – spatial science, structuralism, humanism and perhaps postmodernism – geography's inclination to look outside itself and to embrace (albeit at times uncritically) the latest intellectual fashion leaves the discipline better equiped for the next round of new thinking or new times.

So, if geographers are now drawn back to social justice, as a more explicit part of their ever varied concerns, it will be with greater ability to address the issues than before. A re-engagement with social justice will, hopefully, also further strengthen the discipline of geography, giving it greater power to engage the world of moral problems. That geographers might themselves contribute to the further understanding of social justice and of morality in general is, now, a more realistic expectation than in the past, when the field was more isolated from social and moral theory. As for helping to create a better world, we will continue to make our contribution, but better able to judge better from worse.

Bibliography

Adelson, A. and Lapides, R. (eds) 1989: *Łódź Ghetto: inside a community under siege.* Harmondsworth: Penguin.

African National Congress 1992a: Discussing the Land Issue. London: Land Commission, ANC (mimeo).

—— 1992b: Discussion Document: economic policy. London: Department of Economic Policy, ANC (mimeo).

Andrusz, G. D. 1984: *Housing and Urban Development in the USSR.* London: Macmillan.

Ardrey, R. 1971: *The Territorial Imperative.* New York: Dell.

Arneson, R. 1989: Equality and equal opportunity for welfare. *Philosophical Studies,* 56, 77–93.

Aronson, R. 1991: Is socialism on the agenda? A letter to the South African left. *Transformation,* 14, 1–23.

Arthur, J. and Shaw, W. H. (eds) 1991: *Justice and Economic Distribution,* 2nd edn. Englewood Cliffs, N.J.: Prentice Hall.

Bair, A. C. 1987: The need for more than justice. *Canadian Journal of Philosophy,* supplementary vol. 13, 41–56.

Barbash, N. B. and Gutnov, A. E. 1980: Urban planning aspects of the spatial organization of Moscow. *Soviet Geography,* 12, 557–73.

Bar-Gal, Y. 1991: *The Good and the Bad: a hundred years of Zionist images in geography textbooks.* London: Department of Geography, Queen Mary and Westfield College, University of London, Research Paper 4.

Barry, B. 1989: *Theories of Justice.* London: Harvester-Wheatsheaf.

Bater, J. H. 1986: Some recent perspectives on the Soviet city. *Urban Geography,* 7, 93–102.

—— 1989: *The Soviet Scene: a geographical perspective.* London: Edward Arnold.

Bederman, S. H. 1974: The stratification of 'quality of life' in the black community of Atlanta, Georgia. *Southeastern Geographer,* 14, 26–37.

—— and Adams, J. 1974: Job accessibility and underemployment. *Annals of the Association of American Geographers,* 64, 378–86.

—— and Hartshorne, T. 1984: Quality of life in Georgia: the 1980 experience. *Southeastern Geographer,* 24, 78–98.

Berkowicz, S. M. 1991: Developing perspectives on the areal extent of Israel: a reply. *GeoJournal,* 23 (3), 187–96.

Bloom, A. 1975: John Rawls and the tradition of political economy. *Political Science Review,* 6, 648–62. As reprinted in J. Combee and E. Norton (eds) 1991, 251–60.

Bond, P. 1991: *Commanding Heights and Community Control: new economics for a new South Africa*. Johannesburg: Raven Press.

Boswell, T. D. (ed.) 1991: *South Florida: the winds of change*. Miami: Department of Geography, University of Miami.

Boyne, G. and Powell, M. 1991: Territorial justice: a review of theory and evidence. *Political Geography Quarterly*, 10, 263–81.

Brand, S., Christodoulou, N., van Rooyen, J. and Vink, N. 1992: Agriculture and redistribution: growth with equity. In R. Schrire (ed.) 1992, 353–75.

Brown, A. 1986: *Modern Political Philosophy: theories of the just society*. Harmondsworth: Penguin.

Browning, R. P., Marshall, D. R. and Tabb, D. H. (eds) 1990: *Racial Politics in American Cities*. New York and London: Longman.

Brunn, S. 1989: Ethics in word and deed. *Annals of the Association of American Geographers*, 79 (3), iii–iv.

Buchanan, A. E. 1982: *Marx and Justice: the radical critique of liberalism*. Totowa, N.Y.: Rowman and Littlefield.

Bundy, C. 1979: *The Rise and Fall of the South African Peasantry*. London: Heinemann.

—— 1992: Development and inequality in historical perspective. In R. Schrire (ed.) 1992, 245–48.

Burman, S. 1979: The illusion of progress: race and politics in Atlanta, Georgia. *Ethnic and Racial Studies*, 2, 441–54.

Buttimer, A. 1974: *Values in Geography*. Washington D.C.: Association of American Geographers, Commission on College Geography, Resource Paper 24.

Buzlyakov, N. 1973: *Welfare: the basic task*. Moscow: Progress Publishers.

Campbell, T. 1988: *Justice*. Basingstoke: Macmillan.

Caro, R. A. 1990: *The Years of Lyndon Johnson: means of ascent*. New York: Alfred A. Knopf.

Ciechocińska, M. 1987: Government intervention to balance housing supply and urban population growth: the case of Warsaw. *International Journal of Urban and Regional Research*, 11, 9–26.

Claassens, A. 1991: *Who Owns South Africa: can the repeal of the Land Acts de-racialise land ownership in South Africa?* Johannesburg: Centre for Applied Legal Studies, University of the Witwatersrand, Occasional Paper 11.

Clark, G. L. 1985: Making moral landscapes: John Rawls' original position. *Political Geography Quarterly*, 5 (4) supplement, 147–62.

Clark, S. E. 1987: More autonomous policy orientations: an analytical framework. In C. N. Stone and H. T. Sanders (eds) 1987, 105–24.

Clark, W. A. V. 1988: Racial transition in metropolitan suburbs: evidence from Atlanta. *Urban Geography*, 9, 269–82.

Cloke, P., Philo, C. and Sadler, D. 1991: *Approaching Human Geography: an introduction to contemporary theoretical debates*. London: Paul Chapman.

Cohen, G. A. 1986a: Self-ownership, world-ownership, and equality. In F. Lucash (ed.), *Justice and Equality Here and Now*. Cornell: Cornell University Press, 108–35.

—— 1986b: Self-ownership, world-ownership, and equality: Part II. *Social Philosophy and Policy*, 3 (2), 77–96.

—— 1991: Robert Nozick and Wilt Chamberlain: how patterns preserve liberty. In J. L. Arthur and W. H. Shaw (eds) 1991, 198–211.

Cohen, J. 1986. Review of *Spheres of Justice*. *Journal of Philosophy*, 83, 457–68.

Cohen, S. B. and Kliot, N. 1992: Place-names in Israel's ideological struggle over the administered territories. *Annals of the Association of American Geographers*, 82, 653–80.

Combee, J. and Norton, E. 1991 (eds): *Economic Justice in Perspective: a book of readings*. Englewood Cliffs, N.J.: Prentice Hall.

Cooper, C. et al. 1986: *Race Relations Survey 1985*. Johannesburg: South African Institute of Race Relations.

—— 1992: *Race Relations Survey 1991/92*. Johannesburg: South African Institute of Race Relations.

—— 1993: *Race Relations Survey 1992/93*. Johannesburg: South African Institute of Race Relations.

Cornwell, J. 1984: *Hard-Earned Lives: accounts of health and illness from East London*. London: Tavistock Publications.

Cross, M. and Keith, M. (eds) 1993: *Racism, the City and the State*. London: Routledge.

Culhane, D. and Fried, M. 1988: Paths in homelessness: a view from the street. In J. Friedrichs (ed.), *Affordable Housing and the Homeless*. Berlin and New York: Walter de Gruyter & Co., 175–87.

Curry, M. R. 1991: On the possibility of ethics in geography: writing, citing and the construction of intellectual property. *Progress in Human Geography*, 15, 125–47.

Dangschat, J. 1987: Sociospatial disparities in a 'socialist' city: the case of Warsaw at the end of the 1970s. *International Journal of Urban and Regional Research*, 11, 37–60.

—— and Blasius, J. 1987: Social and spatial disparities in Warsaw in 1978: an application of correspondence analysis to a 'socialist' city. *Urban Studies*, 24, 173–91.

Davis, D. 1992: Taxation in post-apartheid South Africa. In R. Schrire (ed.) 1992, 105–20.

Demko, G. J. and Regulska, J. 1987: Socialism and its impact on urban processes and the city. *Urban Geography*, 8, 289–92.

Dobroszycki, L. 1984: *The Chronicle of the Łódź Ghetto 1941–1944*. New Haven and London: Yale University Press.

Domański, B. 1991: Gatekeepers and administrative allocation of goods under socialism: an alternative perspective. *Environment and Planning C: Government and Policy*, 9, 281–93.

Doyal, L. and Gough, I. 1991: *A Theory of Human Need*. London: Macmillan.

Driver, F. 1988: Moral geographies: social science and the urban environment in mid-nineteenth century England. *Transactions of the Institute of British Geographers*, n.s. 13, 275–87.

Dworkin, R. 1981: What is equality? Part I: Equality of welfare; Part II: Equality of resources. *Philosophy and Public Affairs*, 10, 185–246, 283–345.

——1984: Rights as trumps. In J. Waldron (ed.) 1984, 153–67.

Eckert, J. 1991: National dialogue: towards an ethics charter. *Indicator South Africa*, 8 (2), 44–8.

Eisinger, P. K. 1980: *The Politics of Displacement: racial and ethnic transition in three American cities*. New York: Academic Press.

Elster, J. 1985: *Making Sense of Marx*. Cambridge: Cambridge University Press.

—— 1992: *Local Justice: how institutions allocate scarce goods and necessary burdens*. Cambridge: Cambridge University Press.

Engels, F. 1878: On morality [excerpt from *Anti-Duhring*]. In R. C. Tucker (ed.), *The Marx–Engels Reader*. New York: W. W. Norton, 1972, 666–8.

Etzioni, A. 1988: *The Moral Dimension: towards a new economics*. New York: Free Press.

Eyles, J. and Evans, M. 1987: Popular consciousness, moral ideology, and locality. *Environment and Planning D: Society and Space*, 5, 39–71.

—— and Smith, D. M. (eds) 1988: *Qualitative Methods in Human Geography*. Cambridge: Polity Press.

Fleischmann, A. 1991: Atlanta: urban coalitions in a suburban sea. In H. V. Savitch and J. C. Thomas (eds) 1991, 97–114.

French, R. A. 1987: Changing spatial patterns in Soviet cities – planning or pragmatism? *Urban Geography*, 8, 309–20.

—— and Hamilton, F. E. I. (eds) 1979: *The Socialist City: spatial structure and urban policy*. Chichester: John Wiley.

Fried, C. 1983: Distributive justice. *Social Philosophy and Policy*, 1, 45–59.

Friedman, Milton 1962: *Capitalism and Freedom*. Chicago: University of Chicago Press.

Friedman, Marilyn 1989: Feminism and modern friendship: dislocating the community. *Ethics*, 99. Reprinted in J. L. Arthur and R. W. Shaw (eds) 1991, 304–19.

—— 1991: The practice of partiality. *Ethics*, 101, 818–35.

Friedmann, J. 1992: *Empowerment: the politics of alternative development*. Oxford: Basil Blackwell.

Frye, M. 1983: Sexism. In *The Politics of Reality: essays in feminist theory*. Trumansburg: Crossing Press, 17–40.

Galster, G. C. 1992: A cumulative causation model of the underclass: implications for urban economic development policy. In G. C. Galster and E. W. Hill (eds) 1992, 190–215.

—— and Hill, E. W. (eds) 1992: *The Metropolis in Black and White: place, power and polarization*. New Brunswick, N.J.: Rutgers, the State University of New Jersey, Center for Urban Policy Research.

Gauthier, D. 1986: *Morals by Agreement*. Oxford: Oxford University Press.

Geras, N. 1985: The controversy about Marx and justice. *New Left Review*, 150, 47– 85.

—— 1992: Bringing Marx to justice: an addendum and rejoinder. *New Left Review*, 195, 37–69.

Gerwith, A. 1984: Are there any absolute rights? In J. Waldron (ed.) 1984, 91–109.

Giddens, A. 1984: *The Constitution of Society: outline of the theory of structuration*. Cambridge: Polity Press.

Gilligan, C. 1982: *In a Different Voice: psychological theory and women's development*. Cambridge, Mass.: Harvard University Press.

—— 1987: Moral orientation and moral development. In E. Kittay and D. Meyers (eds), *Women and Moral Theory*. Savage: Rowman and Littlefield, 19–33.

Ginsberg, M. 1965: *On Social Justice*. Harmondsworth: Penguin.

Glinert, L. and Shilhav, Y. 1991: Holy land, holy language: a study of an ultraorthodox Jewish ideology. *Language in Society*, 20, 59–86.

Graaff, J. de V. 1957: *Theoretical Welfare Economics*. Cambridge: Cambridge University Press.

Green, A. E. 1988: The north–south divide in Britain: an examination of the evidence. *Transactions of the Institute of British Geographers*, n.s. 13, 179–98.

Gregory, D. 1978: *Ideology, Science and Human Geography*. London: Hutchinson.

—— 1993: *Geographical Imaginations*. Oxford: Basil Blackwell.

Gregory, D. and Smith, D. M. (eds) 1993: *The Dictionary of Human Geography*, 3rd edn. Oxford: Basil Blackwell.

Griffin, J. 1986: *Well-being: its meaning, measurement and moral importance*. Oxford: Clarendon

Press.

Habermas, J. 1990: *Moral Consciousness and Communicative Action*. Cambridge: Polity Press.

Hacker, A. 1992: *Two Nations: black and white, separate, hostile, unequal*. New York: Macmillan.

Hamilton, E. 1993: Social areas under state socialism: the case of Moscow. In S. G. Solomon (ed.), *Beyond Sovietology: essays in politics and history*. New York: M. E. Sharp, 192–225.

Hanson, S. 1992: Geography and feminism: worlds in collision? *Annals of the Association of American Geographers*, 82, 569–86.

Haraszti, M. 1977: *A Worker in a Worker's State*. Harmondsworth: Penguin.

Hare, R. M. 1964: *The Language of Morals*. Oxford: Oxford University Press.

—— 1978: Justice and equality. In J. L. Arthur and W. H. Shaw (eds) 1991, 118–32.

Harrington, M. 1962: *The Other America: poverty in the United States*. New York: Macmillan.

Hart, D. M. 1988: Political manipulation of urban space: the razing of District Six, Cape Town. *Urban Geography*, 9, 603–28.

—— and Pirie, 1984: The sight and soul of Sophiatown. *Geographical Review*, 74, 38–47.

Hart, H. L. A. 1984: Are there any natural rights? In J. Waldron (ed.) 1984, 77–90.

Hartshorne, T. A., Bederman, S., David, S., Dever, G. E. A. and Pillsbury, R. 1976: *Metropolis in Georgia: Atlanta's rise as a major transactional center*. Cambridge, Mass.: Ballinger Publishing Company.

Harvey, D. 1972a: Social justice in spatial systems. In R. Peet (ed.), *Geographical Perspectives on American Poverty*. Worcester, Mass.: *Antipode* Monographs in Social Geography, 1, 87–106.

—— 1972b: Revolutionary and counter-revolutionary theory in geography and the problem of ghetto formation. *Antipode*, 4 (2), 1–18.

—— 1973: *Social Justice and the City*. London: Edward Arnold.

—— 1989: *The Condition of Postmodernity*. Oxford: Basil Blackwell.

——1992a: Classics in human geography revisited. Harvey, D. 1973: *Social Justice and the City*. London: Edward Arnold. *Progress in Human Geography*, 16, 71–4

—— 1992b: Social justice, postmodernism and the city. *International Journal of Urban and Regional Research*, 16, 588–601.

—— 1992c: Postmodern morality plays. *Antipode*, 24, 300–26.

—— 1993: Class relations, social justice, and the politics of difference. In M. Keith, and S. Pile (eds), *Place and the Politics of Identity*. London: Routledge, 41–66.

Hayek, F. 1944: *The Road to Serfdom*. London: Routledge & Kegan Paul.

Hofmeyr, J. and McLennan, A. 1992: The challenge of equalizing education. In R. Schrire (ed.) 1992, 174–92.

Hospers, J. 1967: *An Introduction to Philosophical Analysis*, 2nd edn. London: Routledge & Kegan Paul.

Houston, J. M. 1978: The concepts of 'place' and 'land' in the Judaeo-Christian tradition. In D. Ley and M. Samuels (eds), *Humanistic Geography: prospects and problems*. Chicago: Maaroufa, 224–37.

Howe, G. and le Roux, P. (eds) 1992: *Transforming the Economy: policy options for South Africa*. Indicator Project South Africa, University of Natal, and Institute for Social Development, University of the Western Cape.

Hume, D. 1739: *A Treatise of Human Nature*. L. A. Selby-Bigge (ed.) 1960. Oxford: Oxford University Press.

Hunter, F. 1953: *Community Power Structure: a study of decision makers.* Chapel Hill: University of North Carolina Press.

——— 1980: *Community Power Succession: Atlanta's policy makers revisited.* Chapel Hill: University of North Carolina Press.

IPPR 1993: *The Justice Gap.* London: Institute for Policy Research, for the Commission on Social Justice

Isard, W. et al. 1969: *General Theory: social, political, economic and regional.* Cambridge, Mass.: MIT Press.

Jackson, P. 1984: Social disorganisation and moral order in the city. *Transactions of the Institute of British Geographers*, n.s. 9, 168–80.

——— 1989: *Maps of Meaning: an introduction to cultural geography.* London: Unwin Hyman.

——— and Smith, S. J. 1984: *Exploring Social Geography.* London: Allen & Unwin.

Johansson, P-O. 1991: *An Introduction to Modern Welfare Economics.* Cambridge: Cambridge University Press.

Johnston, R. J. 1991a: *Geography and Geographers: Anglo-American human geography since 1945*, 4th edn. London: Edward Arnold.

——— 1991b: *A Question of Place: exploring the practice of human geography.* Oxford: Basil Blackwell.

Jordon, B. 1990: *Social Work in an Unjust Society.* London: Harvester-Wheatsheaf.

Kalinina, N. 1992: Housing and housing policy in the USSR. In B. Turner, J. Hegedus and I. Tosics (eds), *The Reform of Housing in Eastern Europe and the Soviet Union.* London: Routledge, 245–75.

Kearns, D. 1983: A theory of justice – and love. *Politics*, 18 (2), 36–42.

Keith, M. 1992: Angry writing: (re)presenting the unethical world of the ethnographer. *Environment and Planning D: Society and Space*, 10, 551–68.

Keller, L. F. 1992a: Leadership and race in the administrative city: building and maintaining directions for justice in complex urban networks. In G. C. Galster and E. W. Hill (eds) 1992, 143–65.

——— 1992b: Race and the American city: living the American dilemma. In G. C. Galster and E. W. Hill (eds) 1992, 336–55.

Kimmerling, B. 1983: *Zionism and Territory: the socio-territorial dimensions of Zionist politics.* Berkeley: Institute of International Studies, University of California.

Kirby, A. 1991: On ethics and power in higher education. *Journal of Geography in Higher Education*, 15, 75–7.

Knox, P. 1975: *Social Well-being: a spatial perspective.* Oxford: Oxford University Press.

Kolosov, V. A. 1989: Socialist federalism and spatial equity: review of a discussion. *Soviet Geography*, 30, 662–9.

Kotlowitz, A. 1991. *There Are No Children Here: the story of two boys growing up in the other America.* New York: Doubleday.

Kukathas, C and Pettit, P. 1990: *Rawls: A Theory of Justice and its critics.* Oxford: Polity Press.

Kuper, L. 1974: *Race, Class and Power: ideology and revolutionary change in plural societies.* London: Duckworth.

Kymlicka, W. 1990: *Contemporary Political Philosophy: an introduction.* Oxford: Clarendon Press.

——— (ed.) 1992: *Justice in Political Philosophy*, 2 volumes. Cheltenham: Edward Elgar.

Laws, G. (ed.) 1994: Special issue of *Urban Geography*, April/May.

Lee, R. (ed.) 1992: *Teaching Qualitative Geography: A Journal of Geography in Higher Education*

Symposium. London: Department of Geography, Queen Mary and Westfield College, University of London, Research Paper 6.

Le Grand, J. 1991: *Equity and Choice: an essay in economics and applied philosophy*. London: HarperCollins.

Lipshitz, G. 1992: Divergence versus convergence in regional development. *Journal of Planning Literature*, 7, 123–38

Liszewski, S. 1991: The role of the Jewish community in the organization of urban space in Łódź. *Polin*, 6, 27–36.

Lösch, A. 1954: *The Economics of Location*. New Haven: Yale University Press.

Louden, R. B. 1992: *Morality and Moral Theory: a reappraisal and reaffirmation*. Oxford: Oxford University Press.

Lukes, S. 1985: *Marxism and Morality*. Oxford: Clarendon Press.

Lyon, D. 1984: Utility and rights. In J. Waldron (ed.) 1984, 110–36.

Lyson, T. A. 1989: *Two Sides to the Sunbelt: the growing divergence between the rural and urban South*. New York: Praeger.

MacDonald, M. 1984: Natural rights. In J. Waldron (ed.) 1984, 21–40.

Mackie, J. L. 1977: *Ethics: inventing right and wrong*. Harmondsworth: Penguin.

MacKinnon, C. A. 1987: *Feminism Unmodified: discourses on life and law*. Cambridge, Mass.: Harvard University Press.

McCarney, J. 1992: Marx and justice again. *New Left Review*, 195, 29–36.

McCarthy, T. 1990: Introduction. In J. Habermas (1990), vii–xiii.

Marcus, T. 1991: Palace coup on land reform. *Indicator South Africa*, 8 (4), 49–54.

Marks, S. 1986: *The Ambiguities of Development in South Africa: class, nationalism and the state in twentieth-century Natal*. Johannesburg: Raven Press.

Marris, P. 1986: *Loss and Change*, revised edition. London: Routledge & Kegan Paul.

Marx, K. 1875: Critique of the Gotha Program. In R. C. Tucker (ed.), *The Marx–Engels Reader*. New York: W. W. Norton, 1972, 382–98.

Matějů, P., Večerník, J. and Jeřábek, H. 1979: Social structure, spatial structure and problems of urban research: the example of Prague. *International Journal of Urban and Regional Research*, 3, 181–200.

Matthews, M. 1979: Social dimensions in Soviet urban housing. In R. A. French and F. E. I. Hamilton (eds) 1979, 105–18.

Mendus, S. 1993: Different voices, still lives: problems in the ethics of care. *Journal of Applied Philosophy*, 10, 17–27.

Mellor, J. R. 1977: *Urban Sociology in an Urbanized World*. London: Routledge & Kegan Paul.

Mill, J. S. 1863: *Utilitarianism*. In M. Warnock (ed.), *Utilitarianism, On Liberty, Essay on Bentham*. London: Collins, 1962.

Miller, D. 1991: Recent theories of social justice. *British Journal of Political Science*, 21, 331–91.

—— 1992: Distributive justice: what the people think. *Ethics*, 102, 555–93.

Minnesota Geography Readings Group 1992: Collective response: social justice, difference, and the city. *Environment and Planning D: Society and Space*, 10, 589–95.

Mitchell, B. and Draper, D. 1982: *Relevance and Ethics in Geography*. London: Longman.

Mohl, R. A. 1988: Ethnic politics in Miami, 1960–1986. In R. M. Miller and G. E. Pozzetta (eds), *Shades of the Sunbelt: essays on ethnicity, race, and the urban South*. Westport: Greenwood Press, 143–60.

Moll, P. 1990: *The Great Economic Debate*. Braamfontein: Skokaville Publishers.

—— 1991: Conclusion: what redistributes and what doesn't. In P. Moll, N. Nattrass and L. Loots (eds) 1991, 118–34.

Moll, P., Nattrass, N. and Loots, L. (eds) 1991: *Redistribution: how can it work in South Africa?* Cape Town: David Philip.

Moore, B. 1992: The case for a land tax: from entitlement to restitution. *Indicator South Africa*, 9 (2), 25–9.

Morris, M. D. 1979: *Measuring the Condition of the World's Poor: the physical quality of life index.* Oxford: Pergamon Press.

Murie, A. and Forrest, R. 1988: The new homeless in Britain. In J. Friedrichs (ed.), *Affordable Housing and the Homeless.* Berlin and New York: Walter de Gruyter & Co., 129–45.

Musil, J. 1968: The development of Prague's ecological structure. In R. E. Pahl (ed.), *Readings in Urban Sociology.* Oxford: Pergamon Press, 232–59.

—— 1987: Housing policy and the sociospatial structure of cities in a socialist country: the example of Prague. *International Journal of Urban and Regional Research*, 11, 27–37.

Muziol-Węcławowicz, A. 1992: The housing market in Warsaw according to the mediators of the estate agencies. In B. Turner, J. Hegedus and I. Tosics (eds) 1992, 207–17.

Myrdal, G. 1944: *The American Dilemma: the negro problem and modern democracy.* New York: Harper & Row.

Naser, S. 1992: Why international statistical comparisons don't work. *The New York Times*, 8 March.

Newman, D. 1984: Ideological and political influences on Israeli urban colonization: the West Bank and Galilee Mountains. *Canadian Geographer*, 28 (2), 142–55.

—— 1991a: On writing involved political geography. *Political Geography Quarterly*, 10, 195–9.

—— 1991b: *Population, Settlement and Conflict: Israel and the West Bank.* Cambridge: Cambridge University Press (*Update* series).

—— and Portugali, J. 1987: Israeli–Palestinian relations as reflected in the scientific literature. *Progress in Human Geography*, 11, 315–32.

Nielson, K. 1984: *Equality and Liberty: a defence of radical egalitarianism.* Totowa, N.J.: Rowman & Allanheld.

—— 1988: *Marxism and the Moral Point of View.* Boulder, Col.: Westfield Press.

—— 1991: Does a Marxian critical theory of society need a moral *theory?* *Radical Philosophy*, 59, Autumn, 21–6.

Nowakowski, S. 1979: Some aspects of postwar urban sociology. *International Journal of Urban and Regional Research*, 3, 203–8.

Nozick, R. 1974: *Anarchy, State, and Utopia.* New York: Basic Books.

Oakley, A. 1974: *Housewife.* Harmondsworth: Penguin.

Okin, S. M. 1989a: *Justice, Gender, and the Family.* New York: Basic Books.

—— 1989b: Reason and feeling in thinking about justice. *Ethics*, 99, 229–49.

Paczka, S. and Riley, R. 1992: Łódź textiles in the new Polish economic order. *Geography*, 11, 361–3.

Peet, R. (ed.) 1978: *Radical Geography.* London: Methuen.

Peffer, R. G. 1990: *Marxism, Morality, and Social Justice.* Princeton, N.J.: Princeton University Press.

Philo, C. 1989: Enough to drive one mad: the organization of space in the 19th-century lunatic asylum. In J. Wolch and M. Dear (eds), *The Power of Place: how territory shapes social life.* London: Unwin Hyman, 258–90.

Pigou, A. C. 1920: *The Economics of Welfare*, 4th edn (1932). London: Macmillan.

Pirie, G. H. 1983: On spatial justice. *Environment and Planning A*, 15, 465–73.

Platzky, L. and Walker, C. 1985: *The Surplus People Project*. Johannesburg: Raven Press.

Porteous, J. D. 1988: Topocide: the annihilation of place. In J. Eyles and D. M. Smith (eds) 1988, 75–93.

Portugali, J. 1993: *Implicate Relations: Society and space in the Israeli–Palestine conflict*. Dordrecht: Kluwer Academic Publishers.

Pratt, G. 1993: Reflections on poststructuralism and feminist empirics, theory and practice. *Antipode*, 25, 51–63.

Rakowski, E. 1991: *Equal Justice*. Oxford: Clarendon Press.

Rawls, J. 1971: *A Theory of Justice*. Cambridge, Mass.: Harvard University Press.

—— 1985: Justice as fairness: political not metaphysical. *Philosophy and Public Affairs*, 14, 223–52; reprinted in J. Arthur and W. H. Shaw (eds) 1991, 320–39.

—— 1993: *Political Liberalism*. New York: Columbia University Press.

Reed, A. 1987: A critique of neo-progressivism in theorizing about local development policy: a case from Atlanta. In C. N. Stone and H. T. Sanders (eds) 1987, 199–215.

Reekie, W. D. 1990: Privatisation and the distribution of income. In F. Vorhies (ed.), *Privatisation and Economic Justice*. Cape Town: Juta & Co., 4–15.

Regulska, J. 1987: Urban development under socialism: the Polish experience. *Urban Geography*, 8, 321–39.

Relph, E. 1976: *Place and Placelessness*. London: Pion.

Rive, R. 1986: *'Buckingham Palace', District Six*. Cape Town: David Philip.

Rivlin, A. 1971: *Systematic Thinking for Social Action*. Washington, D.C.: The Brookings Institution.

Roemer, J. E. 1992: The morality and efficiency of market socialism. *Ethics*, 102, 448–64.

Rose, G. 1993: *Feminism and Geography: the limits of geographical knowledge*. Cambridge: Polity Press.

Roux, A. 1992: Regional options for equity and efficiency. In G. Howe and P. le Roux (eds) 1992, 211–28.

Rowley, G. 1985: The Land of Israel: a reconstructionist approach. In D. Newman (ed.), *The Impact of Gush Emunim: politics and settlement in the West Bank*. New York: St. Martin's Press, 125–36.

Rubinstein, D. 1991: *The People of Nowhere*. New York: Random House.

Sachs, A. 1990: *Rights to Land: a fresh look at the property question*. London: Institute of Commonwealth Studies.

Said, E. W. 1992: *The Question of Palestine*, 2nd edn. London: Vintage.

Samuelson, P. A. 1973: *Economics*, 9th edn. New York: McGraw-Hill.

Sandel, M. 1982: *Liberalism and the Limits of Justice*. Cambridge: Cambridge University Press.

Savitch, H. V. and Thomas, J. C. (eds) 1991: *Big City Politics in Transition*. Newbury Park, Calif.: Sage (Urban Affairs Annual Reviews, 38).

Sayigh, R. 1979: *Palestinians: from peasants to revolutionaries*. London: Zed Books.

Schrire, R. (ed.) 1992: *Wealth or Poverty: critical choices for South Africa*. Cape Town: Oxford University Press.

Segal, S. P. and Baumohl, J. 1988: No place like home: reflections on sheltering a diverse population. In C. J. Smith and J. A. Giggs (eds), *Location and Stigma: contemporary perspectives on mental health and mental health care*. London: Unwin Hyman, 250–63.

Selby, D. 1987: *Human Rights*. Cambridge: Cambridge University Press.

Sen, A. 1973: *On Economic Inequality*. Oxford: Clarendon Press.

—— 1987: *On Ethics and Economics*. Oxford: Basil Blackwell.

—— 1992: *Inequality Reexamined*. Oxford: Clarendon Press.

Shilhav, Y. 1985: Interpretation and misinterpretation of Jewish territorialism. In D. Newman (ed.), *The Impact of Gush Emunim: politics and settlement in the West Bank*. New York: St. Martin's Press, 111–24.

Sibley, D. 1988: Purification of space. *Environment and Planning D: Society and Space*, 6, 409–21.

Siderov, D. A. 1992: Variations in the perceived level of prestige of residential areas in the former USSR. *Urban Geography*, 13, 355–73.

Sillince, J. A. A. (ed.) 1990: *Housing Policies in Eastern Europe and the Soviet Union*. London: Routledge.

Simkins, C. 1986: *Reconstructing South African Liberalism*. Johannesburg: South Africa Institute of Race Relations.

Singer, P. 1991: Rights and the market. In J. Arthur and W. H. Shaw (eds) 1991, 184–97.

Smart, J. J. C. 1978: Distributive justice and utilitarianism. In J. Arthur and W. H. Shaw (eds) 1991, 106–17.

Smith, D. M. 1973a: *The Geography of Social Well-being in the United States: an introduction to territorial social indicators*. New York: McGraw-Hill.

—— 1973b: *An Introduction to Welfare Geography*. Johannesburg: Department of Geography and Environmental Studies, University of the Witwatersrand, Occasional Paper 11.

—— 1974: Who gets what *where*, and how: a welfare focus for human geography. *Geography*, 59, 289–97.

—— 1977: *Human Geography: a welfare approach*. London: Edward Arnold.

—— 1979: *Where the Grass is Greener: living in an unequal world*. Harmondsworth: Penguin.

—— 1981a: *Industrial Location: an economic geographical analysis*, 2nd edn. New York: John Wiley.

—— 1981b: *Inequality in an American City: Atlanta, Georgia, 1960–1970*. London: Department of Geography, Queen Mary College, University of London, Occasional Paper 17.

—— 1984: Recollections of a random variable. In M. Billinge, D. Gregory and R. Martin (eds), *Recollections of a Revolution: geography as spatial science*. London: Macmillan, 117–33.

—— 1985a: *Inequality in Atlanta, Georgia, 1960–1980*. London: Department of Geography and Earth Science, Queen Mary College, University of London, Occasional Paper 25.

—— 1985b: Social aspects of urban problems: inequality in the American city – Atlanta, Georgia, 1960–1980. *Geographica Polonica*, 51, 65–86.

—— 1987: *Geography, Inequality and Society*. Cambridge: Cambridge University Press.

—— 1988: A welfare approach to human geography. In J. Eyles (ed.), *Research in Human Geography: problem, tactics and opportunities*. Oxford: Basil Blackwell, 39–54.

—— 1989: *Urban Inequality under Socialism: case studies from Eastern Europe and the Soviet Union*. Cambridge: Cambridge University Press (*UpDate* series).

—— 1990a: Introduction: the sharing and dividing of geographical space. In M. Chisholm and D. M. Smith (eds), *Shared Space: Divided Space: essays on conflict and territorial organization*. London: Unwin Hyman, 1–21.

—— 1990b: *Apartheid in South Africa*, 3rd edn. Cambridge: Cambridge Univesity Press (*UpDate* series).

—— 1991: Market forces, uneven development and social justice. In R. Shniper and A. Novoselov (eds), *Economic Diagnostics and Forecasting of Regional Development.* Novosibirsk: Soviet Academy of Sciences.

—— 1992a: Geography and social justice: some reflections on social change in Eastern Europe. *Geography Research Forum*, 12, 128–42.

—— (ed.) 1992b: *The Apartheid City and Beyond: urbanization and social change in South Africa.* London: Routledge.

—— 1992c: Redistribution after apartheid: who gets what where in the new South Africa. *Area*, 24, 350–8.

—— 1994a: Social justice and the post-socialist city. *Urban Geography* (in press).

—— 1994b: Redistribution and social justice after apartheid. In A. Lemon (ed.), *The Geography of Change in South Africa.* London: Belhaven Press (in press).

—— 1994c: The socialist city. In G. Andrusz, M. Harloe and I. Szelenyi (eds), *Post-Socialist Cities.* Oxford: Basil Blackwell (in press).

—— and Pile, S. 1993: Inequality in the American city: some evidence from the South. *Geographica Polonica* (in press).

Smith, S. 1989: Society, space and citizenship: a human geography for the 'new times'? *Transactions of the Institute of British Geographers*, n.s. 14, 144–56.

—— 1993: Social landscape: continuity and change. In R. J. Johnston (ed.), *A Changing World: a changing discipline.* Oxford: Basil Blackwell, 564–75.

Social and Cultural Geography Study Group Committee 1991: De-limiting human geography: new social and cultural perspectives. In C. Philo (compiler): *New Words, New Worlds: reconceptualising social and cultural geography.* Lampeter: Department of Geography, St David's College.

Soja, E. 1989: *Postmodern Geographies.* New York: Verso.

Solomon, R. C. and Murphey, M. C. (eds) 1990: *What is Justice?: classical and contemporary readings.* Oxford: Oxford University Press.

Somerville, P. 1992: Homelessness and the meaning of home: rooflessness or rootlessness? *International Journal of Urban and Regional Research*, 16, 529–39.

Sterba, J. P. 1986: Recent work on alternative conceptions of justice. *American Philosophical Quarterly*, 23, 1–22.

Stone, C. N. 1976: *Economic Growth and Neighborhood Discontent: system bias in the urban renewal program of Atlanta.* Chapel Hill: University of North Carolina Press.

—— 1989: *Regime Politics: governing Atlanta 1946–1988.* Chapel Hill: University of North Carolina Press.

—— 1990: Race and regime in Atlanta. In R. P Browning, D. R. Marshall and D. F. H. Tabb (eds) 1990, 125–39.

—— and Sanders, H. T. (eds) 1987: *The Politics of Urban Development.* Lawrence, Kansas: University Press of Kansas.

Szelenyi, I. 1983: *Urban Inequalities under Socialism.* Oxford: Oxford University Press.

—— 1987: Housing inequalities and occupational segregation in state socialist cities: commentary on the special issue of IJURR on East European cities. *International Journal of Urban and Regional Research*, 11, 1–8.

Taylor, P. J. 1992: Understanding global inequalities: a world system approach. *Geography*, 77, 10–21.

Taylor, S. M. 1989: Community exclusion of the mentally ill. In J. Wolch and M. Dear (eds), *The Power of Geography: how territory shapes social life*. Boston: Unwin Hyman, 316–30.

Taylor-Gooby, P. 1991: Welfare state regimes and welfare citizenship. *Journal of European Social Policy*, 1, 93–105.

Tronto, J. C. 1987: Beyond gender differences in a theory of care. *Signs*, 12, 644–63.

Tuan, Y-F. 1974: Space and place: humanistic perspectives. *Progress in Human Geography*, 8, 211–52.

Turner, B., Hegedus, J. and Tosics, I. (eds) 1992: *The Reform of Housing in Eastern Europe and the Soviet Union*. London: Routledge.

UNDP 1990: *Human Development Report 1990*. Oxford: Oxford University Press.

——— 1992: *Human Development Report 1992*. Oxford: Oxford University Press.

Unterhalter, E. 1987: *Forced Removal: the division, segregation and control of the South African people*. London: International Defence and Aid Fund for South Africa.

US Department of Health, Education and Welfare 1969: *Toward a Social Report*. Washington, D.C.: U.S. Government Printing Office.

van der Berg, S. 1991: Redirecting government expenditure. In P. Moll, N. Nattrass and L. Loots (eds) 1991, 74–85.

——— 1992: Social reform and reallocation of social expenditure. In R. Schrire (ed.) 1992, 121–42.

Veness, A. R. 1992: Home and homelessness in the United States: changing ideals and realities. *Environment and Planning D: Society and Space*, 10, 445–68.

Vlastos, G. 1984: Justice and equality. In J. Waldron (ed.) 1984, 41–76.

Vogel, R. K. and Stowers, G. N. L. 1991: Miami: minority empowerment and regime change. In H. V. Savitch and J. C. Thomas (eds) 1991, 115–31.

Waldron, J. (ed.) 1984: *Theories of Rights*. Oxford: Oxford University Press.

——— 1992: Superseding historic injustice. *Ethics*, 103, 4–28.

Walzer, M. 1983: *Spheres of Justice: a defence of pluralism and equality*. Oxford: Basil Blackwell.

——— 1990: The communitarian critique of liberalism. *Political Theory*, 18, 6–23.

Warren, C. L., Corbett, J. G. and Stack, J. F. 1990: Hispanic ascendancy and tripartite politics in Miami. In R. P Browning, D. R. Marshall and D. F. H. Tabb (eds) 1990, 155–78.

Washington, C. 1992: From caste to class to caste: the changing nature of race relations in America. In G. C. Galster and E. W. Hill (eds) 1992, 236–57.

Western, J. 1978: Knowing one's place: 'the Coloured people' and the Group Areas Act in Cape Town. In D. Ley and M. Samuels (ed.), *Humanistic Geography: prospects and problems*. Chicago: Maaroufa Press, 297–318.

——— 1981: *Outcast Cape Town*. London: Allen & Unwin.

Węcławowicz, G. 1979: The structure of socio-economic space in Warsaw in 1931 and 1970: a study in factorial ecology. In R. A. French and F. E. I. Hamilton (eds) 1979, 387–424.

——— 1991: *The Socio-spatial Differentiation in Urban Region of Warsaw*. Warsaw: Institute of Geography and Spatial Organization, Polish Academy of Sciences.

——— 1992: The socio-spatial structure of the socialist cities of east-central Europe. In F. Lando (ed.), *Urban and Rural Geography*. Venice: Cafoscarina, 129–40.

Weiner, D. and Levin, R. 1991: Land and agrarian transition in South Africa. In J. Pickles and D. Weiner (eds), *Rural and Regional Restructuring in South Africa*. Special issue of *Antipode*, 23, 92–120.

Wier, M. 1993: From equal opportunity to 'the new social contract': race and the politics of the American 'underclass'. In M. Cross and M. Keith (eds) 1993, 93–107.

Williams, B. 1972: *Morality: an introduction to ethics*. Cambridge: Cambridge University Press.

—— 1985: *Ethics and the Limits of Philosophy*. London: Fontana Press/Collins.

Wilson, W. J. 1987: *The Truly Disadvantaged: the inner city, the underclass, and public policy*. Chicago: University of Chicago Press.

Winant, H. 1993: Difference and inequality: postmodern racial politics in the United States. In M. Cross and M. Keith (eds) 1993, 108–27.

Wolch, J. 1989: The shadow state: transformations in the voluntary sector. In J. Wolch and M. Dear (eds), *The Power of Geography: how territory shapes social life*. Boston: Unwin Hyman, 197–221.

—— (ed.) 1991: *Homelessness*. Special issue of *Urban Geography*, 12 (2).

Wolff, J. 1991: *Robert Nozick: property, justice and the minimal state*. Oxford: Polity Press.

Young, I. M. 1990a: *Justice and the Politics of Difference*. Princeton, N.J.: Princeton University Press.

—— 1990b. The ideal of community and the politics of difference. In L. J. Nicholson (ed.), *Feminism/Postmodernism*. London: Routledge, 300–23.

Zaslavskaya, T. 1990: Perestroika and socialism. In *Soviet Sociology in Conditions of Perestroika*. Moscow: Nauka, 7–33.

Further Reading

Citations in the text have been selected and placed so as to assist readers in following up the subject matter. For those seeking more specific guidance on further reading, these notes highlight particular works likely to be most helpful. Full publication details will be found in the Bibliography.

For a taste of geography's earlier encounter with social justice, mentioned in chapter 1, see David Harvey's *Social Justice and the City* (1973, chapter 3), and my *Human Geography: a welfare approach* (Smith, 1977, chapter 6). Contemporary geographical concerns with a moral dimension are conveyed in *New Words, New Worlds*, a compilation by Chris Philo for the Institute of British Geographers' Social and Cultural Geography Study Group Committee (1991). Geography's new engagement with social justice is reflected in a special issue of *Urban Geography* (March/April, 1994), edited by Glenda Laws.

The varied subject matter of chapter 2 does not lend itself to the selection of key works, its purpose being to provide sufficient background for the subsequent discussion of theories of social justice in chapters 3 and 4. To take this further, the best single book is Will Kymlicka's *Contemporary Political Philosophy* (1990), which further elaborates the various alternative perspectives. Kymlicka has also compiled a valuable (if expensive) two-volume collection of carefully selected readings, as *Justice in Political Philosophy* (1992). Alan Brown's *Modern Political Philosophy* (1986) provides a somewhat narrower version of the material covered by Kymlicka, but with some interesting extensions. Tom Campbell's *Justice* (1988) offers an overview from a rather different perspective. Arthur and Shaw's *Justice and Economic Distribution* (1991) is the most useful book-length set of readings. Of the major works examined in chapters 3 and 4, Michael Walzer's *Spheres of Justice* (1983) is recommended for its breadth of scope and cases, while Iris Marion Young's *Justice and the Politics of Difference* (1990) provides a challenging critique of much conventional wisdom from feminist and postmodern perspectives.

The more applied focus in chapter 5 highlights three books in particular which have a bearing on the central problem of universality versus relativism in distributive issues. Len Doyal and Ian Gough's *A Theory of Human Need* (1991) spans both theoretical and empirical issues, and should be read by any geographer interested in human well-being. John Friedmann's *Empowerment: the politics of alternative development* (1992) provides a link with contemporary development issues. Amartya Sen's *Inequality Reexamined* (1992) is the latest exposition of his influential approach based on human capabilities.

The case studies in Part II of the book are best followed up by reading more of the background material on which their specific challenges to thinking about social justice rest. My *Geography, Inequality and Society* (Smith, 1987) introduces the cases of the United States, the former Soviet Union and South Africa, along with a general discussion of inequality as a geographical issue. Also highly relevant are three volumes in the Cambridge University Press *UpDate* series: *Urban Inequality under Socialism* (Smith, 1989), *Apartheid in South Africa* (Smith, 1990), and David Newman's *Population, Settlement and Conflict: Israel and the West Bank* (1991).

On the contemporary American city, Galster and Hill's edited collection *The Metropolis in Black and White* (1992) directly addresses racial inequality and polarization, though a rounded grasp of the issues requires more reference to the perspectives of political economy and postmodernism. Some contributions in Cross and Keith's *Racism, the City and the State* (1993) fill the gap. The best background work for the Atlanta case is Clarence Stone's *Regime Politics: governing Atlanta 1946–1988* (1989). The latest major works on the East European city, looking back and forward respectively, are Tony French's *Plans, Pragmatism and People: the failure of Soviet city planning* (University College London Press, 1994) and the collection *Post-Socialist Cities*, edited by Andrusz, Harloe and Szelenyi (Basil Blackwell, 1994).

As with the American and East European urban scenes, there are a number of works on change in South Africa which could be consulted. Robert Schrire's edited collection *Wealth or Poverty: critical choices for South Africa* (1992) is the most bulky of the recent general volumes. More geographical focus will be found in Tony Lemon's *The Geography of Change in South Africa* (Belhaven Press, 1994). The papers in my *The Apartheid City and Beyond* (Smith, 1992) take a backward and forward look at urban issues. These are further explored in M. Swilling, R. Humphries and K. Shubane's edited collection *Apartheid City in Transition* (Oxford University Press, 1991). *The Atlas of Apartheid* by A. J. Christopher (Routledge, 1994) is a valuable new source.

Some of the case material exemplifying loss of place in chapter 9 rests on the more general background to apartheid in South Africa and conflict over land in Palestine (see above). But to get closer, John Western's *Outcast Cape Town* (1981), on the displacement of the city's coloured people, remains a classic. Baruch Kimmerling's *Zionism and Territory* (1983) opens up a number of important general geographical issues arising from the Israel/Palestine case. Homelessness may be explored further in the special issue of *Urban Geography* (1991) edited by Jenifer Wolch.

If social justice is indeed returning to the geographical agenda as firmly as is proposed in this book, then by the time of its publication, or soon after, there will be other volumes and references of direct interest. And, of course, in moral and political philosophy and related fields, the abiding concern with distributive justice continues. The publication of John Rawls's *Political Liberalism* (Columbia University Press, 1993), available too late to be adequately reflected in the present book, is indicative of the problem faced by any author committed to completing a book in a changing field, just as the substantive content can be affected by the changing world. Indeed, it is very much to be hoped that, by the time this book is published, some further progress will have been made in the promotion of social justice in South Africa and reconciling conflicting claims to parts of Palestine, for example. The final responsibility is therefore left to the reader, to try to keep up with a subject in which aspirations towards some universal theoretical perspective must continually have regard to the here and now of people struggling to make a living, and trying to make moral sense of the world and their place in it.

Index

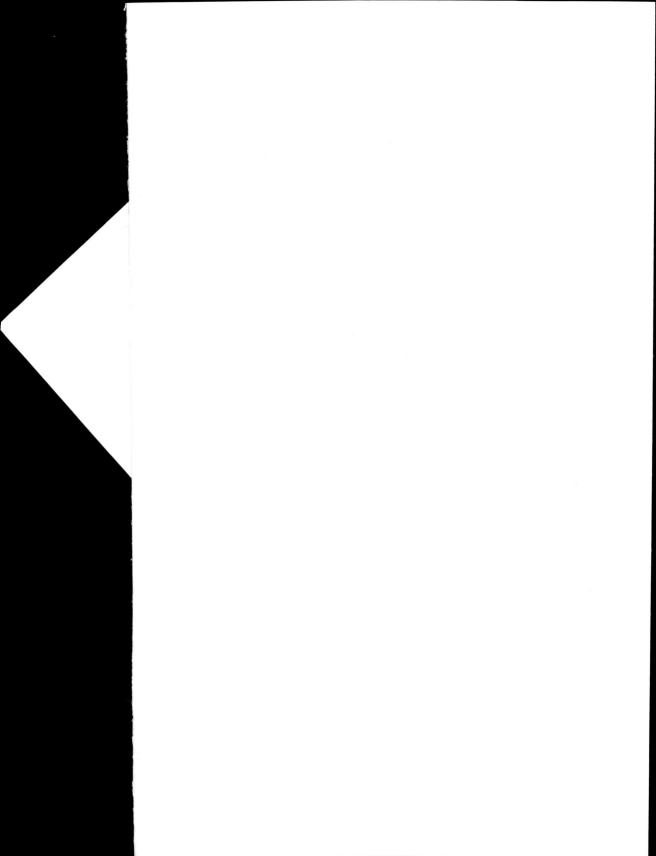

Date Due

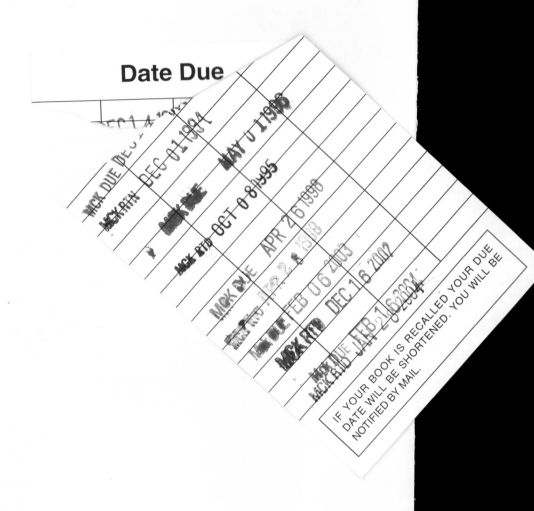

DEC 01 1994

MCK DUE DEC 01 1994

MCK RTN

MAY 0 1 1995

MCK RTD OCT 0 8 1995

MCK DUE APR 2 6 1998

MCK RTD FEB 2 6 1998

MCK DUE FEB 0 6 2003

MCK RTD DEC 1 6 2002

MCK DUE JAN 1 6 2004

MCK RTD JAN 2 0 2004